CAPITAL STOCK GROWTH:
A MICRO-ECONOMETRIC APPROACH

CONTRIBUTIONS
TO
ECONOMIC ANALYSIS

XXXI

Honorary Editor

J. TINBERGEN

Editors

J. JOHNSTON

D. W. JORGENSON

J. WAELBROECK

NORTH-HOLLAND PUBLISHING COMPANY

AMSTERDAM · LONDON

CAPITAL STOCK GROWTH:
A MICRO-ECONOMETRIC
APPROACH

by

EDWIN KUH

Massachusetts Institute of Technology

Second edition

1971

NORTH-HOLLAND PUBLISHING COMPANY

AMSTERDAM · LONDON

ISBN North-Holland   0 7204 3118 2

PUBLISHERS:

NORTH-HOLLAND PUBLISHING COMPANY – AMSTERDAM
NORTH-HOLLAND PUBLISHING COMPANY,LTD.– LONDON

PRINTED IN THE NETHERLANDS

INTRODUCTION TO THE SERIES

This series consists of a number of hitherto unpublished studies, which are introduced by the editors in the belief that they represent fresh contributions to economic science.

The term *economic analysis* as used in the title of the series has been adopted because it covers both the activities of the theoretical economist and the research worker.

Although the analytical methods used by the various contributors are not the same, they are nevertheless conditioned by the common origin of their studies, namely theoretical problems encountered in practical research. Since for this reason, business cycle research and national accounting, research work on behalf of economic policy, and problems of planning are the main sources of the subjects dealt with, they necessarily determine the manner of approach adopted by the authors. Their methods tend to be 'practical' in the sense of not being too far remote from application to actual economic conditions. In addition they are quantitative rather than qualitative.

It is the hope of the editors that the publications of these studies will help to stimulate the exchange of scientific information and to reinforce international cooperation in the field of economics.

THE EDITORS

PREFACE

This study is a sequel to an earlier study on investment behavior by John R. Meyer and myself, *The Investment Decision*. As with any research, the termination of one phase opens up many more questions than were answered in the study itself. This non-convergent aspect of research is as operative today as it was six years ago when the present investigation began.

For instance, this study has finished at a time when new techniques to estimate parameters of a dynamic system are being developed. Parametric forms of lag distribution as developed and applied to investment studies by Robert M. Solow and Dale Jorgenson represent a worthwhile advance. Further, developments by James Durbin and William Phillips of powerful estimation techniques using modern methods of time series analysis are just now in an exploratory stage and the outlook appears most promising. In this study standard linear regression analysis and some variants have provided the main analytical tools. New estimation methods and further adaptations of the existing techniques should yield relevant insights into the investment process.

As a second observation, I think that the question of 'proper research strategy' still remains, as it must by its very nature, an open question. After all, the ready availability of a cut and dried formula for success would leave few problems yet unsolved. It is to be hoped that the present efforts portray an approach to research which will prove applicable in other circumstances.

Last of all, aggregation is clearly one of the most important and as yet inadequately analyzed topics. The pathmaking efforts of Theil notwithstanding, the fact remains that we know little about the costs and benefits of different sorts of disaggregation for the purposes of creating policy models. However, the testing of hypotheses can be carried out most efficiently with disaggregated information when only short time series are available.

Massive assistance from several sources was needed to carry out this study. Perhaps I am most conscious of all of the assistance rendered by the computer programmers who have done such worthwhile work. The original program for this study was written by Malcolm Jones who entered the armed forces when the program was nearing completion. The programming work was concluded through the efforts of Steve Goldfeld. The basic computer program was lengthy and complicated, using much of the capability of the I.B.M. 704 (later I.B.M. 709) computer installed at M.I.T. The assistance rendered by the M.I.T. Computation Center, especially by Richard Steinberg is most gratefully acknowledged. The program for example, took in the time series for 60 firms and calculated a large number of estimated coefficients and test statistics for each of several regressions associated with each firm. Error sums of squares were accumulated and the analysis of covariance performed. Residuals were calculated for each of 180 regressions from which the Durbin-Watson test statistics were calculated. A great many of the estimated parameters and test statistics were then rank ordered. These operations were repeated on many sets of data. It would be unilluminating to estimate how long it would take one to have done all these calculations by hand – no one would have considered doing it prior to the development of millisecond or microsecond computation speeds. Suffice it to say that computer programming is intricate work requiring a high order of skill and patience.

The energies and intelligence of a stalwart crew of research assistants also made an essential contribution. Present and former students of the M.I.T. School of Industrial Management who have helped so very much include Charles Pimlott, Robert Larsen, William White, and Alan Wofford. The original data were painstakingly collected by Mrs. Joan Steckler from *Moody's Industrials* as well as other sources. Secretarial assistance of the highest order was provided by Mrs. Audrey Olmstead and Mrs. Virginia Olszewski; Mrs Kathleen Wolf and Miss Beatrice Rogers were indispensable to proof-reading and index construction. Miss Janet Holland of the London School of Economics obligingly carried out the final revisions.

Intellectual obligations are also recorded with gratitude. Chapter 2 benefited from searching criticism by John Bossons, Svend Laursen and Morris Mendelson. Discussions with Carl Christ on the theoretical sections of Chapter 5 clarified a number of ideas. John Lintner made helpful comments on Chapter 10. Gregory Chow's suggestions on statistical techniques were most beneficial although he should not be held accountable for my abuses. Robert M. Solow helped me over several troublesome mathematical hurdles.

The Sloan Research Fund provided the financial wherewithall for research assistants and computation as well as a moderate teaching load which enabled time to be devoted to research. I owe the M.I.T. School of Industrial Management much more than a perfunctory thanks for support. Its active encouragement of research has been a real factor in enabling this work to be carried out.

E.K.

CONTENTS

LIST OF TABLES

LIST OF CHARTS OR FIGURES

INTRODUCTION TO THE 2ND EDITION

This volume was nearly complete by 1960. A second printing by North-Holland thus presents a convenient opportunity to relate my results to other work published during the intervening decade. The impressive number of empirical studies and new theoretical elaborations cannot be comprehensively reviewed here. Instead, I will restrict these observations to a survey of important additional evidence or principal innovations that have appeared during this period. There have been noteworthy efforts on the following topics:

(1) Several major studies have turned up further evidence on the relation between profits and investment.
(2) Investment behavior has been more closely integrated with production theory, capital theory and the theory of the firm.
(3) Additional research on the time-series, cross-section problem has led to improved statistical theory.
(4) Better data and more efficient estimation procedures has shed additional light on the nature of investment dynamics.

A. Profits and Accelerator Determinants of Investment Demand

The main conclusion that emerges from an examination of studies concurrently testing propositions about acceleration and profits is this: capacity-accelerator motivation is more important than profits or internal funds in explaining the time path of investment, although profits too play a significant role. That role could arise through the internal funds, cost approach which has been advanced in the main body of this book or from more conventional neo-classical origins for expectational reasons according to Lester Thurow (1969). However, when profits are viewed mainly as an expectational variable, expected output with which profits are correlated, (and to which they are systematically related as well) is probably the dominant motivation.

One of the most comprehensive analyses of profit and accelerator determinants of investment is that of Robert Eisner (1960). Some two-hundred rather heterogeneous firms were divided into three groups, according to whether recent profits were relatively high, moderate, or low. Within each of the three profit-experience categories, cross-section 1955 firm gross investment outlays were regressed against three preceding year sales changes, three preceding year profit rates and two other variables. The squared multiple correlation coefficient was nearly twice as great for the high profit group as it was for the other two profit groups, while the regression coefficients were roughly of the same magnitude. This strong interaction between the effectiveness of the accelerator and recent profit experience is similar to that observed earlier by John Meyer and myself (Meyer and Kuh, 1957).

In a later study, Robert Eisner (1967) concludes that new light is cast on the role of profits in distributed lag investment functions including numerous lagged sales changes. While coefficients of the profit variables are uniformly low in cross sections, they are relatively high in most of the time series. Firms appear to be more inclined to make capital expenditures in the period immediately following higher profits even though firms earning higher profits do not make markedly greater capital expenditures than firms earning lower profits. This evidence is consistent with the hypothesis that past profits play some significant role in the timing of capital expenditures but need not affect its long-run average, as the Meyer and Kuh volume had also suggested.

A distributed lag investment relation of Robert M. Solow, E. Cary Brown, Albert A. Ando, and John Kareken (Brown et al., 1963) leads them to conclude: "we do not wish to choose once and for all between a profits theory on one side and an acceleration theory on the other—nor do we believe the two to be necessarily mutually exclusive … We seem to get stabler empirical results when we include corporate profits as an independent variable and exclude a rough measure of 'capacity' (meant as a surrogate for the stock of capital itself)." They estimated the dependence of quarterly orders for producer durable equipment orders on the following variables: output measured by the Federal Reserve Board Index of Industrial Production, a private long-term interest rate, and corporate profits.*

John R. Meyer and Robert Glauber (Meyer and Glauber, 1963) have estimated time series investment functions for about fifteen two-digit manufacturing industries and the manufacturing aggregate, using a capacity-accelerator formulation along with internal funds and several other variables, with postwar quarterly data. The capacity-accelerator variable for total manufacturing has a short-run impact elasticity of 0.68 in contrast to 0.28 for gross internal funds.* Meyer and Glauber (1963) and Frank de Leeuw (1962) report that capacity requirements coefficient estimates are statistically more reliable than those for internal funds. Using annual time series for sixty individual capital-producing firms over the period 1935 to 1955 (though excluding war years), I have also found that the capacity-accelerator influence to be substantially greater than that of internal funds. The typical elasticity of investment with respect to sales is about unity, which substantially exceeds the 0.10 to 0.15 for the internal fund flows.

Earlier, John R. Meyer and I (Meyer and Kuh, 1957), using cross-section data for 1946–50, reported that the capacity accelerator mainly determined investment in two different circumstances; first, in the "long run," where long-run data were represented by five-year data averages (which substantially reduce short-run transient influences), and second, based on annual data when capacity pressures were extremely high. During periods of less intense capacity pressures, profits and depreciation, interpreted primarily as measures of internal liquidity flows, proved relatively more influential. In these circumstances, the statistical explanatory power of profits was not great, although more pervasive than accelerator influences. The last conclusion was dependent on year-to-year comparisons of changes in the degree of cross-section multiple correlation, in order to extract as much time series content from the cross sections as seemed feasible.

---

* High elasticities of investment orders with respect to gross profits appeared, the smallest impact elasticity being 0.50 with a corresponding long-run elasticity of 1.20. Corresponding output elasticities are 0.27 and 0.67. Even when two lagged dependent variables were included, profits continued to be a major statistical explanatory variable.

* From related quarterly postwar data for manufacturing, Frank de Leeuw came to similar conclusions for the best fitting "inverted V" lag structure, one of several that he explored in some detail.

Others have since corroborated this finding using data extending five years beyond that of our original sample period, the years 1946 to 1950 (Brown and Roseman, 1957).

B. Investment and the Theory of the Firm

In recent years, attention has shifted from the question of profits or the level of output as determinants of investment, to more precise measurement of the cost of capital within the context of neo-classical capital theory. Dale Jorgenson plus co-authors (Jorgenson, 1963; Jorgenson, in J. S. Duesenberry et al., 1965; Jorgenson and Stephenson, 1967; Jorgenson and Siebert, 1968) have made a valuable contribution by redirecting the economic profession's attention toward the relationship between production functions and present value maximization in the context of a distributed lag formulation. Empirical measurement of investment behavior has thus been integrated with capital theory. Capital theory provides a static equilibrium target to which the firm adjusts through a series of investments. Thus investment itself is conceived of as a complex series of dynamic adjustments, and quite properly so. Two genuine benefits stem from this treatment. First, it brings investment theory into much closer juxtaposition with conventional economic theory, potentially enriching the theoretical and empirical basis of both. Second, we should be in a better position to evaluate government policy actions relating taxes to income, final sales and depreciation provisions because of explicit parameterization required by properly formulated theory.

Production functions have appeared in investment studies in three different ways. First, Jorgenson, in his original contribution, derived an investment function by maximization of the firm's present value subject to a Cobb–Douglas production function. In this formulation, Jorgenson (1963) restricts the capital costs variable to have the identical effect on investment as output changes and so does not test the relative importance of output changes and capital cost changes. Second, and in a related theoretical vein, Charles Bischoff (1966) performed the same formal operations but for a more complicated and, in my opinion, more realistic fixed-coefficient vintage model. Robert Eisner and Mohammed Nadiri (1968) developed reasonable empirical tests which raise serious doubts about the empirical relevance of capital costs by relaxing the Jorgenson–Bischoff restriction that forced output and capital costs together, so that in effect the primary influence of output change carries along the statistically much weaker capital cost variable. While Bischoff later showed that some technical statistical operations may increase the independent weight accorded cost of capital, the statistical evidence remains very much against the role of capital costs, at least as a short-run determinant of investment. Third, Nadiri and Sherman Rosen (1969) have generalized factor demand theory and measurement by treating demand for capital and demand for labor symmetrically. As so often happens, increased realism in one dimension is obtained at the cost of less relevance elsewhere, since they employ a concept of capacity utilization which implicitly assumes fixed coefficients despite their explicit reliance on a Cobb–Douglas production function.*

The influence of static competitive neo-classical theory on investment by now has been clarified. Yet in a world of imperfect competition and pervasive uncertainty, the matter is so complex that presently we are unable to accept any one theory of investment strictly derived from standard neo-classical considerations on the basis of empirical evidence. The crux of the matter appears to lie in an operational definition of "cost of capital". While some clarification of that concept can be found in the work of Franco Modigliani and Merton Miller (1958), the core difficulty of how to characterize uncertainty remains unsolved and is perhaps insoluble. The problem is compounded by the fact that cost of capital calculations involve expectations about what individual firms expect to pay or earn on new capital. We note that this dim view of the matter puts investment theory on the exact same level with most economic theory confronted by the need to treat uncertainty explicitly.

Jorgenson's (Jorgenson, 1963; Jorgenson, in J. S. Duesenberry et al., 1965) various articles together with criticisms and modifications proposed by Eisner and Nadiri, Bischoff and Thurow, have advanced our empirical understanding while revealing the severe limitations of economic theory in its applications to the complicated domain of investment behavior. The empirical evidence strongly favors the role of the rate of change of output over that of the cost of capital.

---

* They are aware of these shortcomings: "... much work remains to be done. There are two major requirements that will have to be met ... One is the production of more conceptually adequate data particularly on capital utilization rates. The other is a comprehensive treatment of the market and the role of expectations."

Lester Thurow (1969) has approached the problem of capital cost based upon neo-classical theory in the context of imperfectly competitive markets and disequilibrium in the stock of a firm's capital, in contrast to the perfectly competitive equilibrium plus certainty assumptions of Jorgenson and his collaborators. From this he shows that a profit model is most appropriate. The initial rather casual empiricism of profit models can be properly incorporated into profit maximization models so that the "either accelerator or profits" view of investment behavior has been further attenuated. At the same time, however, the question of what investment function is unequivocally best remains unanswered. Thurow reaches the pessimistic though, in my opinion, well-founded conclusion that "there is very little chance that the real world will ever generate data which are orthogonal enough to estimate the partial effects of the different factors which influence investment without making assumptions about the character of the economy's production function and the cost of capital ... Both the disequilibrium investment function in this paper and the Jorgenson investment function are based on neoclassical investment theory. Both would seem to be compatible with it, but they yield very different results" (p. 435).

On balance, areas of ignorance have been narrowed over the past decade. Valiant efforts to blend the theory of the firm with investment equations have not been overwhelmingly successful. Economists are left in the uncomfortable position of "knowing" that neoclassical optimization models of firm behavior "must" contain important elements of truth while the data fail to reveal the influence of this central neo-classical ingredient unless aided by severe *a priori* restrictions. I believe this to be true for three reasons. First, uncertainty has not yet been incorporated into economic theory in a way that permits effective measurement. New theory is needed, since present theory is inadequate. Second, data do not exist in satisfactory form to permit estimation and testing of the most promising theoretical formulation based on vintage, fixed-coefficient production functions. Hence, in my view, serious specification errors are committed by those using, e.g., Cobb–Douglas production functions or by the application of simplifying assumptions (such as those of Bischoff) to a more correct model thus enabling it to be used with available data. Third, standard econometric methods are best applied to routine investment outlays where technical change is unimportant; however, where innovations are important, standard simplifications distort reality too much. And in a dynamic, growing economy, this component constitutes an important part of total investment outlays.

I am, therefore, pessimistic about clearcut validation of the neoclassical approach applied to investment, not because the fundamental insight is incorrect, but because it is too hard to implement with existing data and theoretical models. The empirical substance of investment equations will remain what it has been for quite some time, the acceleration principle, augmented by more effective ways of estimating distributed lags than existed ten years ago.

C. Contrasts Between Time Series and Cross-Sections

Another major strand in this volume was an examination of the sort of inferences that can be made between cross-sections and time series. Pietro Balestra and Marc Nerlove (1966) have developed the statistical theory required to cope with several cross-sections at once, by using a variant of generalized least squares based on the intraclass correlation coefficient. Robert Eisner (1967) has also made useful contributions to the empirical side of this problem:

> "Among the variety of estimates of parameters of investment functions which have been presented, it has been noted, particularly, that estimates derived from cross sections of data have differed from those obtained from time series. (See, for example, Kuh (Kuh, 1959).) Estimates have also differed when derived from time series aggregates, time series of industry data, or time series of data of individual firms. Production function estimates have varied as well, when derived from cross sections of individual firms, "two-digit" or "three-digit" industries, states, or nations. A common element, I submit, in all of these differences is that in each case the observed variables are in a different relation to the unobserved variables from which we start in our economic theory. In particular, with regard to the investment function, the variance in past sales changes or profits or other variables may be related to expected demand or the expected profitability of investment in quite varied ways among different types of cross sections and time series. It will be one purpose of this paper to use the extensive and multidimensional body of data at our disposal to explore these differences as they relate to certain plausible hypotheses about economic behavior."

Some of his major conclusions based on his consistent body of data are these:

> 1. The role of past sales changes, presumably as a proxy for expected long-run pressure of demand on capacity, appears greatest in the case of industry cross

sections, and large in cross sections of firms across industries, particularly in cross sections of firm means.

2. The coefficients of past sales changes are correspondingly lower in the within-industry cross sections.

3. The variance of past sales changes about the mean of sales changes for each individual firm (firm time series) has significantly less to do with the variance in capital expenditures than the corresponding variances in the firm cross sections. This is consistent with the view that firms would look upon the short-run variance in their own sales as mostly transitory.

4. Coefficients of sales changes are generally higher in industry time series than in firm time series. This is consistent with the hypothesis of a greater permanent component in industry sales change variance over time.

Eisner's analysis has helped to clear up some of the basic statistical properties of cross-sections and time series. Yet it seems to me that ultimately most reliance has to be placed upon time series. The heart of the investment problem is in the correct characterization of the adjustment process. The adjustment process, in turn, is essentially a dynamic process. Since no effective way has yet been found to estimate dynamic processes other than with time series, spurious estimates will tend to dominate wherever cross sections are used for this purpose. That view has also been advocated in this book. Most recent investment literature has veered away from heavy reliance on cross sections, a trend which I consider to be altogether healthy.* Thus, while better statistical methods proposed by Nerlove and Balestra for combining cross sections will prove useful in other more static econometric applications, investment studies are less likely to yield superior insights from these technical improvements.

D. Distributed Lags

The importance of using a finer time grid for improving understanding of the investment process should not be underestimated. Recent papers by Robert Engle and Ta-Chung Liu (1969) and Christopher Sims (1968) show that substantial biases are likely when aggregates over time are used. In this book, one of the most suspect findings was the exceedingly low value of the reaction coefficient on sales in the standard Chenery–Koyck model which was typically 0.10, implying an average ten-year delay. Even though the firms included here are

---

* Reliance on cross-section data in earlier studies properly and significantly extended the range of measurable considerations that influence firm investment decisions usually neglected by time series hypotheses.

low growth, capital producing firms, this figure nevertheless implies a remarkably slow response. It may be significant that the monthly models of Brown et al. (1963) and Liu (1969) attribute substantially more weight to profit or cash flow than do quarterly or annual models. There appears to be some interaction between profit and acceleration motivation and the interval of observation. For instance, T. C. Liu found that, besides long-term interest rates and trend, corporate profits after taxes were important but that "neither the rate of change of output nor the stock of capital shows up significantly in these functions."* This may occur, as Eisner has proposed, because profits affect timing or perhaps the investment decision itself is also influenced.

Jorgenson (1966) has done much to provide the statistical basis for estimating and interpreting rational distributed lags in the investment context and, more generally, estimating. A technique for finite lag structures which permits the imposition of *a priori* restrictions on some of lag parameters was devised by Shirley Almon (1965), also for the study of investment behavior. While the techniques and data necessary to the accurate study of short-run investment behavior have been substantially improved over the last decade, the actual lag is extremely sensitive to model specification. Thurow (1969) has found a lag of one year using a profit model while Jorgenson and Stephenson (1967), perhaps because of some arbitrary elements in the lag specification itself, find a lag that was twice as long.

Quarterly and monthly data increase degrees of freedom and reduce biases that arise from too coarse a time grid. Primary reliance on these data and less dependence on annual data represent a significant gain in the precision with which investment dynamics can be estimated. These gains, however, are restricted by pervasive multicollinearity. Since the statistical importance of different investment determinants has shown sensitivity to the time interval, improved specification of investment behavior calls for more intensive work with these data than has yet been undertaken.

* He qualifies this finding by observing that "the crudeness of my monthly data, however, does not justify the rejection of the accelerator hypothesis on the basis of this very tentative model, as the accelerator approach is apparently successful in many well-known quarterly and annual models" (Liu, 1969) p 9–10.

REFERENCES

ALMON, SHIRLEY, "The Distributed Lag Between Capital Appropriations and Expenditures", *Econometrica*, **33** (1965) pp. 178–196.

BALESTRA, PIETRO and MARC NERLOVE, "Pooling Cross Section and Time Series Data in the Estimation of a Dynamic Model: The Demand for Natural Gas", *Econometrica*, 34, No. 3 (July 1966) pp. 585–612.

BISCHOFF, CHARLES W., "Elasticities of Substitution, Capital Malleability, and Distributed Lag Investment Functions", presented to the San Francisco Meetings of the Econometric Society (December 28, 1966).

BROWN, E. CARY and ROBERT M. SOLOW et al., "Lags in Fiscal and Monetary Policy", *Commission on Money and Credit* (1963).

BROWN, MURRAY and HERMAN ROSEMAN, "A Cross-Section Analysis of Manufacturing Investment During 1951–1955", *Proceedings of the Business and Economics Section of the American Statistical Association* (1957) pp. 344–351.

DE LEEUW, FRANK, "The Demand for Capital Goods by Manufacturers: A Study of Quarterly Time Series", *Econometrica* (July 1962) pp. 407–423.

EISNER, ROBERT, "A Distributed Lag Investment Function", *Econometrica*, 28, No. 1 (January 1960) pp. 1–29.

EISNER, ROBERT, "A Permanent Income Theory for Investment", *The American Economic Review*, LVII, No. 3 (June 1967) pp. 363–390.

EISNER, ROBERT and MOHAMMED I. NADIRI, "On Investment Behavior and Neoclassical Theory", *Review of Economics and Statistics* 50 (August 1968) pp. 369–382.

ENGLE, ROBERT F. and TA-CHUNG LIU, "Effects of Aggregation over Time on Dynamic Characteristics of an Econometric Model", *NBER*, Conference on Research in Income and Wealth (November 1969).

JORGENSON, DALE W., "Capital Theory and Investment Behavior", *The American Economic Review*, 53 (May 1963) pp. 247–259.

JORGENSON, DALE W., "Anticipations and Investment Behavior", in: J. S. Duesenberry, E. Kuh, G. Fromm, and L. R. Klein (eds.) *The Brookings Quarterly Econometric Model of the United States* (1965).

JORGENSON, DALE W., "Rational Distributed Lag Functions", *Econometrica*, 32, No. 1 (January 1966).

JORGENSON, DALE W. and JAMES A. STEPHENSON, "The Time Structure of Investment Behavior in U. S. Manufacturing, 1947–60", *The Review of Economics and Statistics*, 49 (February 1967) pp. 16–27.

JORGENSON, DALE W. and CALVIN D. SIEBERT, "A Comparison of Alternative Theories of Corporate Investment Behavior", *The American Economic Review* XVIII (Sept. 1968). "Optimal Capital Accumulation and Corporate Investment Behavior", *The Journal of Political Economy*, LXXVI (Nov./Dec. 1968) pp. 1123–1151.

KUH, EDWIN, "The Validity of Cross-Sectionally Estimated Behavior Equations in Time Series Applications", *Econometrica*, 27 (1959).

KUH, EDWIN and JOHN R. MEYER, "Investment, Liquidity and Monetary Policy", *Commission on Money and Credit* (1963).

LIU, TA-CHUNG, "A Monthly Recursive Econometric Model of United States: A Test of Feasibility", *The Review of Economics and Statistics*, LI, No. 1 (February 1969) pp. 1–13.

MEYER, JOHN R. and EDWIN KUH, *The Investment Decision* (1957).

MEYER, JOHN R. and ROBERT GLAUBER, Investment Decisions, *Economic Forecasting, and Business Policy* (1963).

MODIGLIANI, FRANCO and MERTON H. MILLER, "The Cost of Capital, Corporation Finance and the Theory of Investment", *The American Economic Review*, XLVIII, No. 3 (June 1958).

NADIRI, MOHAMMED I. and SHERMAN ROSEN, "Interrelated Factor Demand Functions", *The American Economic Review*, LIX, No. 4, Part 1 (Sept. 1969) pp. 457–471.

SIMS, CHRISTOPHER A., "Discrete Approximations to Continuous Time Distributed Lags in Econometrics", Discussion Paper Number 43, Harvard Institute of Economic Research, Harvard University, Cambridge, Massachusetts. (September 1968).

THURROW, LESTER, "A Disequilibrium Neoclassical Investment Function", *Review of Economics and Statistics* (November 1969).

E. K.

CHAPTER 1

INTRODUCTION

This study has four objectives. First, to suggest certain modifications in existing theories of investment behavior, particularly dynamic specification and explicit recognition of financial influences on capital outlay decisions. Second, to provide tests of the hypotheses generated from theoretical propositions, as well as to obtain estimates of the coefficients of principal interest. Third, to utilize in a systematic fashion existing statistical techniques and suggest some alternative procedures in a few instances in order to improve the estimation and hypothesis testing that will be attempted. Fourth, to improve predictive capability, which depends ultimately on the successful attainment of the first three aims, and to set out relevant standards of predictive performance.

A fundamental statistical problem facing every econometrician is "The Specification Problem". By specification problem, we mean the selection of variables to be included in a behavior relationship, as well as the manner in which the variables are related. As Herman Wold and P. Faxer have shown precisely, specification error in least squares regression coefficients will be small if either of two conditions hold: the disturbance or error term is small, or the disturbance is nearly uncorrelated with the explanatory variables.[1] Granting the validity of this statement of the problem (with which no quarrel need be taken), the basic unsolved task remains of how to ensure that explanatory variables are uncorrelated with the error term and the disturbance term is small enough. A brief illustration from an investment study by John R. Meyer and myself exemplifies an important class of specifi-

---

[1] See HERMAN WOLD and P. FAXER, "On Specification Error in Regression Analysis,' *The Annals of Mathematical Statistics*, Vol. 28, No. 1, March, 1957, pp. 265–7; HERMAN WOLD and LARS JUREEN, *Demand Analysis*, New York, 1953, p. 37 and 189; and extensions by FRANKLIN M. FISHER, "On the Cost of Approximate Specification in Simultaneous Equation Estimation," *Econometrica*, April, 1961.

cation problems.[2] We found that in some years one set of variables was dominant, while in other years different variables were central. If we had limited our examination to only one set of years, we would have specified, confidently but erroneously, that only one set of variables was important in explaining investment. In short, our ultimate goal is the attainment of stable unbiased relationships which hold under a variety of different conditions. When we have found such stable and unbiased relationships, we have a reasonably well-specified system. An overriding goal, then, will be to establish tests and methods of evaluation of the data which will minimize, or at least help to reveal, specification error.

By the time this study has been completed, the alternative hypotheses will have been subjected to the scrutiny of numerous standard statistical tools. Concentration upon one, or a few, tests, which has occurred in much previous econometric work, will usually fail to uncover many important aspects of specification, since one, or only a few, tests can ordinarily reveal but limited amounts of information. Hence, while the primary objective has been to advance understanding about investment behavior in particular, it is hoped that the approach adopted here and some techniques devised in this study will have more extensive application.

In order to meet the specification problem for investment behavior most directly, we have resorted to individual firm data rather than economic aggregates. This particular emphasis is in line with a recent strong trend in the attitude of econometricians about data. Second thoughts about the quality and nature of much aggregative economic data have led to increased exploitation of micro data either from cross-sections or individual time series, as excitement over newly discovered econometric methods gradually receded from the post-war intellectual limelight. The inclination to place greater reliance on disaggregated information was motivated by two considerations. The first was a reaction to estimation difficulties that are encountered when the independent variables are highly correlated, an effect called collinearity. Numerous investigators came to favor cross-sections where this problem did not appear so weighty. The second major impetus was the desire to construct and test more complicated behavior models which required many degrees of freedom that were often to be found

[2] JOHN R. MEYER and EDWIN KUH, *The Investment Decision: An Empirical Study* 1957.

in cross-sections but not ordinarily in time series. Furthermore, cross-section and micro-economic data generally were an appealing source of information, particularly since most aggregative economic hypotheses are simple analogues of micro-economic behavior. Hence, observations on micro-economic data improved estimation accuracy through reduction in collinearity, enhanced possibilities of hypothesis testing by using samples that potentially have many more degrees of freedom and also correspond more closely to the sort of hypotheses that most economists formulate in terms of individual behavior.

Recently, increasing doubts have been voiced about the comparability of estimates from different kinds of data, micro or aggregated, cross-section and time series. For example, the question has been raised repeatedly about the comparability of parameters estimated on cross-sections and those estimated on time series. In many actual cases the estimates turn out to be strongly divergent. While estimates of the same theoretical coefficients from different information sources might be averaged, the suspicion is bound to arise that different universes generated the observations, should the alternative estimates disagree violently or consistently.[3] To probe further, are there any systematic ways to reconcile the different estimates, or at least understand the nature and extent of persistent divergences? Thus, the laudable search for more powerful data has opened up a field of inquiry about relations among types of data.

The fourth major objective that cuts across the first three goals is one common to most quantitative econometric endeavors: improved predictive power. With the micro-economic information in our possession, we can investigate how increased knowledge of the micro structure can assist in making aggregate predictions. Most often, our interest is in how the aggregates behave; yet it is increasingly realized that aggregate predictions can often be improved by better understanding the structure which generated the micro observations. Hence, one concern will be with the general problem of efficiently handling micro-economic information, when the objective is prediction of an aggregate and the estimation of structural coefficients in a behavior equation.

Increased availability of sample survey and other micro-economic

[3] See E. KUH and J. R. MEYER, "How Extraneous are Extraneous Estimates?" *Review of Economics and Statistics*, Vol. 39, No. 4, November, 1957, pp. 380–393; and ARNOLD C. HARBERGER, Review of *The Measurement of Consumers' Expenditure and Behavior in the United Kingdom 1920–1938: Volume I* by RICHARD STONE, in *Econometrica*, 23, 217–218 (April, 1955).

data has added relevance to the problem of predicting aggregates from micro-economic information. More important, however, econometric models are now being designed to exploit the rapidly progressing potentialities of the modern large-scale digital computer. It is now computationally possible to take advantage of micro-economic data generated by a large number of complex and realistic equations describing sub-sector economic behavior. Guy H. Orcutt has proposed that such an approach currently holds the greatest promise for predictions and the evaluation of policy actions on the part of government or business: "Predictions about aggregates will still be needed but will be obtained by aggregating behavior of elemental units rather than by attempting to aggregate behavioral relationships of these elemental units."[4] In short, the behavior coefficients for large, complex models call for estimates based on micro-economic information, even when the ultimate purpose of the model is to predict the aggregates.

Testing hypotheses, estimation, and improved prediction call for a more exhaustive treatment of cross-actions than has previously been undertaken. To analyze cross-section behavior most completely, many cross-sections for adjacent years were assembled, so that both cross-sections and comparable time series for the included cross-section observations might be obtained. The basic data are investment and several explanatory variables for 60 firms, running from 1935 to 1955 in all cases and for some firms to 1956. The war years, 1942 to 1945, were excluded. These data constitute one of the longest available consecutive sets of micro-economic time series and, by implication, cross-sections which contain the same individuals. The Meyer-Kuh study used five post-war years, 1946 to 1950, for several hundred firms; Lawrence Klein used three different periods in his cross-section study of railroad investment behavior; Martin Taitel used numerous adjacent cross-sections to study investment behavior, but the approach was suggestive and not as rigorous as might prove useful.[5] The availability of these numerous cross-sections will be exploited in order to evaluate how time series predictions might be facilitated from the

[4] GUY H. ORCUTT, "A New Type of Socio-Economic System," *The Review of Economics and Statistics*, Vol. 39, No. 2, May, 1957, p. 116.

[5] JOHN R. MEYER and EDWIN KUH, *The Investment Decision: An Empirical Study*, Cambridge, 1957; LAWRENCE R. KLEIN, "A Study of Investment," *Conference on Business Cycles*, New York, 1951; MARTIN TAITEL, *Profits, Productive Activities, and New Investment*, Temporary National Economic Committee Monograph No. 12, Washington, D.C., 1941.

cross-section studies. While cross-sections are sometimes of interest in themselves, ordinarily it is their contribution to understanding time series behavior which leads us to study them in the first place, particularly in the case of investment behavior where the dynamic aspects dominate variations in behavior most effectively portrayed by cross-sections. At the same time, of course, both micro and macro time series estimates of behavior will be obtained. These are required as a main ingredient of the study and also as a standard for cross-section estimate comparisons.

One of the main economic purposes of this study has been to disentangle further the relative importance of profits compared to sales, or acceleration hypotheses. To do so, I have chosen cash flow definition of profits so that it is statistically as well as theoretically easier to separate the individual influence of profits from that of the level of sales or output. Furthermore, the effect of lags, although treated in obvious fashion, has been more systematically estimated than in much previous work. Not surprisingly, the lag structure has a crucial bearing on which variables appear most important in the investment decision.

The concluding chapter summarizes the main results from this study. Since so much of the subsequent empirical material is highly detailed, an aerial view of that jungle is strongly recommended at some point prior to sampling the factual underbrush comprising the bulk of this monograph.

CHAPTER 2

SOME MODELS OF INVESTMENT BEHAVIOR

2.1 Introduction

Some central elements of modern investment theory provide a basis for the statistical models.[1] Initially and briefly we will describe profit theories of investment. Next, we examine recent innovations in investment theory devised by Goodwin, Chenery, and Koyck, the capacity-acceleration models. At this point consideration will be given to some factors which influence the timing of investment, including gestation lags and irreversibility conditions which should be imposed on investment equations. The third part of the chapter presents a formal relationship between internal funds and investment behavior, in a construction intended to bridge a gap in investment literature, the absence of explicit functions relating internal financing to investment. The fourth section of the chapter broadens the range of entrepreneurial choice to encompass external financing by certain modifications of a Domar growth model. The fifth part considers some macro-economic implications of the investment model. In the sixth part, recent investment theories, particularly that of Duesenberry, and also those of Modigliani and Chenery, are discussed in connection with the theories advanced in the central portions of this chapter. The chapter concludes with a brief section on the relation of expectations and autonomous investment to the induced investment models which have appeared there in. It should be remembered that throughout we deal exclusively with induced investment, reserving comment on autonomous investment to the last section.

[1] This will not be a doctrinal roundup since several are already available. See JOHN R. MEYER and EDWIN KUH, *The Investment Decision: An Empirical Study*, 1957, Chapter 2 and A D. Knox, "The Acceleration Principle and the Theory of Investment," *Economica*, N.S., Vol. 19, August, 1952. The excellent methodological study of T. HAAVELMO, *A Study in the Theory of Investment*, 1960, provides a valuable additional reference.

2.2 Profit Theories

Profit theorists contend that, since the entrepreneur should maximize the present value of expected future profits through investment activity, he will invest according to present profits because these closely reflect future profits. Investment expectations geared to the present correctly reflect the unimportance of the distant future if nearby future profits are not expected to diverge greatly from present profits and most revenues from an investment are "paid back" rapidly, as often happens in manufacturing concerns. Others look to cost-revenue relations to provide a rationale. When total revenue and cost functions are linear, total profits will be a linear function of output. According to this view, profit theories are actually a subsidiary hypothesis under the capacity utilization theories. A third view of profits' influence on the rate of investment stresses supply effects, as well as institutional barriers and entrepreneurial caution. Because of limited availability of funds either from capital market imperfections or self imposed restrictions on the business firm designed to avoid external financing, the actual investment rate will be restricted predominantly to gross profit levels. Major contributors to one or the other of these three views are Tinbergen, Kalecki, and Klein.[2]

2.3 Capacity Utilization Theories

In the original J. M. Clark formulation, the acceleration principle asserted that the change in capital stock is strictly proportional (according to the value of "the" capital coefficient) to the positive rate of change in output, although Clark himself was more aware of numerous essential qualifications than some later proponents.[3] This proposition has been fundamentally modified in two related directions. The first modification is toward a level of output, rather than the rate of change

[2] JAN TINBERGEN, *Statistical Testing of Business Cycle Theories*, Geneva, 1938; MICHAEL KALECKI, "A New Approach to the Problem of Business Cycles," *Review of Economic Studies*, Vol. 16, 1949–50, pp. 57–64; LAWRENCE KLEIN, "Studies in Investment Behavior." in *Conference on Business Cycles*, National Bureau of Economic Research, New York, 1951. Tinbergen and Klein's work reflects the first and third views listed, while Kalecki has put most emphasis on the third viewpoint. TSIANG (see footnote 5) has emphasized the second point. Also see MEYER and KUH, *op. cit.*

[3] J. M. CLARK, "Business Acceleration and the Law of Demand: A Technical Factor in Economic Cycles," *Readings in Business Cycle Theory*, American Economic Association, 1944.

of output orientation, and the second is the introduction of distributed lags.

Provided a simple expectational relationship between current and expected output exists, namely, that the two are equal, the capacity-oriented branch of acceleration investment theory has in large measure come full circle to acceptance of one neo-classical view on capital accumulation, stressing as it does the effect of the absolute level of sales in combination with the firm's capital stock. Given the rate of interest (and/or "normal" rate of profit) and labor inputs, the marginal value productivity of capital is a declining function of the capital stock for a given output but subject to shifts as output changes, in one neo-classical version.[4] Some writers favoring capacity-accelerator theories of investment have also emphasized the fact that profits are closely related to both output and capital stock.[5]

The most straightforward version of a capacity model is shown in equation (2.1):

$$I_t = a_1 X_t - a_2 K_{t-1}. \qquad (2.1)$$

Hollis Chenery, in a theory very similar to one proposed several years earlier by Richard M. Goodwin, suggests how to rationalize the coefficients a_1 and a_2 in terms of pure acceleration reasoning plus a reaction coefficient that indicates how rapidly the capital stock will adjust to a disequilibrium relation between output and capital stock.[6] In Chenery's case the equation is:

$$I_t = b(\beta X_t - K_{t-1}), \qquad (2.2)$$

I_t = Investment,

X_t = Output,

K_t = Capital stock,

b = Reaction coefficient, $0 < b \leqslant 1$,

β = K_t^p/X_t^p, the desired capital coefficient, i.e., the desired capital-output relation.

[4] This has been most effectively presented by RICHARD S. ECKAUS, "The Acceleration Principle Reconsidered," *Quarterly Journal of Economics*, Vol. 67, May, 1953, pp. 209–30. The reader should not confuse marginal physical productivity, which is a production function concept, with marginal value productivity, which is a (related) capital theory concept showing the *ceteris paribus* change in profit for a change in the total quantity of capital. Marginal revenue value productivity in the production function sense is also irrelevant in this context.

[5] See especially S. C. TSIANG, "Accelerator, Theory of the Firm and the Business Cycle," *Quarterly Journal of Economics*, Vol. 65, August, 1951, pp. 325–341.

[6] HOLLIS CHENERY, "Overcapacity and the Acceleration Principle," *Econometrica*, Vol. 20, January, 1952, pp. 1–28. and RICHARD M. GOODWIN, *Income, Employment*

We can thus identify the coefficient a_1 in equation (2.1) with the $b\beta$ and the coefficient a_2 with b of Chenery's relationship. According to the Chenery equation, investment is proportional to the difference between the optimal capital stock (represented by the term βX_t) and the actual capital stock at the beginning of the period, where the desired capital stock is predicted on the assumption that the current levels of sales will continue into the future.

A fraction of the difference between desired capital stock and that in place at the beginning of the period is acquired during the current period. Since b is assumed to be a positive fraction, the partial adjustment can in part be viewed as indication of doubt that "truly," current sales are expected to continue indefinitely. Gestation lags and decision-making delays will also cause the reaction coefficient, b, to be fractional. When stated in this manner, the theory is almost a truism, merely stating that investment is proportional to the difference between the actual and desired capital stock. Once the identification of current sales with expected sales is made, the theory acquires operational content.

Equation (2.1) can be written as a difference equation (2.3);

$$K_t = a_1 X_t + (1 - a_2) K_{t-1},\qquad(2.3)$$

with its solution shown in (2.4);

$$K_t = (1 - a_2)^t K_0 + a_1 \sum_{T=1}^{t} (1 - a_2)^{t-T} X_T,\qquad(2.4)$$

or, using notation from the Chenery model:

$$K_t = (1 - b)^t K_0 + b\beta \sum_{T=1}^{T=t} (1 - b)^{t-T} X_T.\qquad(2.5)$$

On the assumption that b in (2.5) is a positive fraction, the first term in equation (2.3) will gradually damp out. The dominant part of the expression is contained in the second term, the sum of an exponentially declining set of weights applied to previous period outputs. Thus, we can view the current capital stock according to the capacity principle formulation as primarily a weighted average of previous and

and Public Policy, Essays in Honor of Alvin H. Hansen, by LLOYD A. METZLER and others, 1st ed., New York: W. W. Norton and Co., 1948. The discrete Chenery version will be presented for discussion instead of the continuous model developed by Goodwin since later analytical propositions are most conveniently treated in discrete terms.

current output in which prior outputs are given steadily decreasing weight the more remote they are in time. Since $0 < b \leqslant 1$, the discrepancy between desired and actual capital stock is never totally eliminated, so that past outputs continually influence current investment.

Recent literature, particularly *Investment Analysis and Distributed Lags* by Koyck, provides worthwhile insights into some of the more explicitly dynamic aspects of investment theory.[7] Koyck makes two main theoretical points. First, the adjustment of the capital stock in response to a change in output will not be instantaneous so that there will be distributed lag effects.[8] Second, if one assumes that the distributed lag declines exponentially in time after a certain point, an estimated coefficient in a regression model involving the capital stock, output, and investment can be interpreted to reflect the parameters of the distributed lag.

Here is a simplified representation of Koyck's model, in which it has been assumed that the exponential decline occurs immediately after the current period:

$$K_t = \alpha_0 \sum_{i=0}^{\infty} \lambda^i X_{t-i}, \; 0 \leqslant \lambda < 1. \tag{2.6}$$

Equation (2.6) represents the capital stock as an exponentially weighted sum of previous outputs. From this relation, Koyck shows that investment, defined as the rate of change in capital stock can be represented as:

$$I_t = \Delta K_t = \alpha_0 X_{t+1} = -\lambda K_t. \tag{2.7}$$

This is immediately recognizable as being virtually identical to the capacity model presented in (2.2). In (2.7), λ is a speed of adjustment coefficient. Upon looking back at the Chenery model (2.2), it is clear that $\lambda = 1 - b$. For values of λ near zero, investment will adjust

[7] LEENDERT M. KOYCK, *Distributed Lags and Investment Analysis*, Amsterdam, 1954. Also see R. G. D. ALLEN, *Mathematical Economics*, London, 1956, 240–262, in an excellent discussion of Goodwin and Kalecki's models which in essence are similar to the Chenery and Koyck models.

[8] To this extent, Koyck's model is equivalent to Hicks' distributed lag acceleration investment relation in which:

$$I_t = a_0 \Delta X_t + a_1 \Delta X_{t-1} + \ldots + a_n \Delta X_{t-n} \text{ and } \sum_{i=t-n}^{t} a_i = \beta,$$

the capital coefficient. Hicks did not restrict the values of the a_i coefficients nor does he seriously consider the micro-economic aspects of investment decisions except for their macro-economic business cycle implications. See J. R. HICKS, *A Contribution to the Theory of the Trade Cycle*, Oxford, 1950.

rapidly to the capital stock so that the capital stock will always be approximately proportional to output, according to α_0, which can now be identified as "the" capital coefficient. This result corresponds to the instantaneous, or strict rate of change accelerator. Conversely, when λ is near unity, the capital stock adjusts extremely slowly to changes in output.

An examination of Koyck's estimates of λ reveals some intriguing facts. Most of the λ's that Koyck has estimated for various industries, including railway freight, electric light and power industry, cement, steel and petroleum are distinctly large, ranging from 0.7 at the lowest to 0.90 and above. This implies for a fairly typical λ of 0.9, that slightly less than *half* of the "required" change in capital stock will remain unfulfilled after about *seven* years have gone by,[9] for a given initial change in output. These λ values imply a sluggishness of response that requires fuller explanation.

Observed time relationships will be influenced by the following considerations, among others. First, once a decision variable—sales, for instance—has changed, there will be a delay in reaching a decision to alter existing plans. After the decision lag, arises the lag between capital goods production and the time when these new assets are in place and operations can begin, called the gestation lag. Gestation lags will prove unimportant in some situations, particularly when they are short relative to the period of observation, which ordinarily is a year. In a detailed study of World War II and the Korean War investment data, Thomas Mayer and Sidney Sonenblum found a modal lag of three quarters of a year for construction and two quarters for equipment where "...lead times given here relate only to the construction of new plants and those additions to existing plant which are assumed large enough to be capable of independent operation. The numerous additions of individual machines or similar facilities to already existing plants are therefore excluded, though it is recognized that such "partial" additions may well dominate a normal expansion."[10] Taking

---

[9] See Koyck's chart on p. 24. Koyck ordinarily estimated the first two lagged year reaction coefficients separately, using the third lagged year's regression coefficient to estimate the distributed lag. Therefore, the λ values imply the rate of response of all years prior to the third year. Since in general the first two years' coefficients are small, the proposition in the text sentence is approximately correct, but a slight overstatement of the inertia in capital stock adjustment.

[10] "Lead Times for Fixed Investment," *Review of Economics and Statistics*, Vol. 37, August, 1955, No. 3, p. 30.

"partial" additions into account, we may hazard the guess that average equipment lead time might be as low as a quarter and the over-all average lag not in excess of a half year. Of course, circumstances vary immensely from industry to industry as well as through time as supply elasticities in the capital goods producing industries systematically change over the business cycle. At the other extreme, some items take two or three years to produce: freighters, power plant installations or a complete oil refinery, for instance. Financial constraints can also affect observed lags. If financial constraints curb actual outlays, we will not observe in the firm's behavior some investment outlays which would have been made had the firm followed more generous external financing policies. This point will be elaborated soon.

A limitation common to all the linear capacity models is the assumption of exponential weights. A "more realistic" description of reaction patterns might be a declining rate of reaction for say two or three periods, with no effect of any other previous periods (although small reaction coefficients on lagged values have a roughly equivalent effect). Similarly, the firm that has a delayed reaction to an increase in output two years ago may find that output has decreased in the interim so that it will not in fact place the order that it would have according to rigid decision lag behavior. Thus, the origin of the delay—expectation, decision or gestation—can lead to quite different sorts of dynamic responses.[11] While it is not empirically possible to separate the replacement from the expansion component in gross investment outlays, the possibility should be recognized of variable lags depending upon which motivations dominate.[12]

The capacity models that have been described require several elaborations and qualifications although I believe that the simple models as they now stand suggest worthwhile analytical insights, particularly concerning relations between internal financing and investment behavior to be explained in the next section. More complex distributed lags and certain irreversibilities will be discussed here.

---

[11] In numerous instances replacement investments require rapid reactions to take advantage of cost reducing potential of the new machines in the face of increased demand, so that short time periods might be the most appropriate for a particular firm or industry in these circumstances.

[12] In this connection, it should be noted that Koyck has proposed that during periods of increasing sales the reaction coefficient for net investment will be larger than during periods of decreasing sales. He has empirically tested the proposition with results that support his contention, a different hypothesis from that suggested above.

One apparent limitation of equation (2.2) is that second and higher order lag structures are not treated. In particular, gestation lags have been slighted. We could modify the expression to read as follows:

$$\Delta K_t = b_1(\beta X_t - K_{t-1}) + b_2(\beta X_{t-1} - K_{t-2}). \tag{2.8}$$

The first part of the current period's investment is currently induced while the second part is "gestated" investment induced by capacity needs of the previous period. The roots of the corresponding homogeneous second order difference equation can never lead to explosive results provided both reaction coefficients are less than unity. Damped oscillations are a theoretical possibility, although when the gestation lag coefficient (b_2) is small relative to the current lag (b_1) reaction coefficient, even this outcome is unlikely.[13]

While it is true that for many purposes "greater realism" can be imputed to a dynamic model by the introduction of high order lags, a closer scrutiny of entrepreneurial behavior can (as will be indicated shortly) lead to some alternative formulations which strongly suggest that rational behavior will eliminate a large number of lagged effects which, as part of a difference equation, would otherwise lead to substantial fluctuations. In the present context, let us assume that there are a number of delays, for instance such as those indicated in equation (2.8) where we consider the lagged investment to be put into place this period as largely beyond control of the firm, whereas the first component to be invested will be at the discretion of the firm for the current period. If we were slightly to rewrite equation (2.2) in the following manner,

$$\Delta K_t = b(K_t^* - K_{t-1}), \tag{2.9}$$

we can readily redefine the desired change in the capital stock to depend upon the difference between the desired end-of-period capital stock (which we still take to be a function of the level of sales for the present discussion) and the beginning period capital stock which however should be redefined to include equipment and plant on order during the current period which will be put into place during the cur-

---

[13] Further pursuit of this point is unprofitable. If w_1 and w_2 are the roots of the auxiliary equation for (28), then:

$$w_1 = [(1 - b_1) + \sqrt{(1 - b_1)^2 - 4b_2}] \div 2,$$

$$w_2 = [(1 - b_1) - \sqrt{(1 - b_1)^2 - 4b_2}] \div 2, \qquad 0 < b_1, b_2 < 1.$$

Elementary calculations lead directly to the proposition stated in the text.

rent period. Define all previously ordered equipment to be delivered during the current period with a hat ($\frown$) where the orders have been given over the previous periods as in equation (2.10). Therefore, the only disequilibrium to be considered during the present period is the beginning of period capital stock plus $\hat{I}_t$ as shown in equation (2.11).

$$\hat{I}_t = f(X_{t-1}, X_{t-2}, , X_{t-\tau}) \qquad (2.10)$$

$$\Delta K_t = b[K_t^* - (K_{t-1} + \hat{I}_t)] \qquad (2.11)$$

Alternatively, we write the current period's investment as the current "voluntary" (i.e., ungestated) additions with a ($\sim$) which means rewriting equation (2.11) as (2.12) below. This equivalent way of writing equation (2.11) shows that the "voluntary," current additions to capital stock are less by the amount $1 + b$ of $\hat{I}_t$.

$$\Delta K_t = \hat{I}_t + \tilde{I}_t, \text{ where } \tilde{I}_t = b(K_t^* - K_{t-1}) - (1 + b)\hat{I}_t, \qquad (2.12)$$

the capital stock expected to come into place as a result of previous period decisions.

While the algebra is decidedly unimportant, the implication for behavior may not be trivial. It indicates that the businessman who takes account of available information about the fruition of previous plans will not in fact be governed by previous history in the same way implied by a mechanistic system subject to high order delays. In control engineering terms, the phenomena described above are called negative feedback loops. In short, it is probable that the entrepreneur will actually damp out some, and possibly most of the destabilizing fluctuations inherent in mechanical high order distributed lag accelerators.

Whereas this redefined dynamic problem has a decided advantage in explaining what I believe to be the case, namely that violently destabilizing plant and equipment outlays arising from long delays do not typically take place, it leaves us with a purely statistical problem which properly belongs in Chapter 4 but should also be mentioned here. Specifically, the definition of previous period capital stock is now truly a variable subject to error since it more appropriately should include gestation investment to be put in place during the current period.

A standard problem with all investment models is that of how irreversible the investment function should be. A general (but not universal) empirical proposition is that gross plant and equipment investment cannot be negative. Exceptions can arise when one firm sells assets to another or, if dealing with the total economy, when physical assets are exported, While both operations occur in practice, the latter is likely to be insignificant, the former more frequent. Let us set up the distributed lag model as shown by equation (2.8) wherein today's investment consists of some fraction of the current desired capital stock plus some parts left over from the previous period. We can make the notation more compact by substituting equation (2.13) for the more complete indication of the desired capacity increment. We can then rewrite equation (2.8) as (2.14):

$$C_t^* = \beta X_t - K_{t-1}, \text{ the desired capacity increment,} \qquad (2.13)$$

$$\Delta K_t = b_1 C_t^* + b_2 C_{t-1}^*. \qquad (2.14)$$

In the simplest possible case, b_2 will be zero and since according to the usual irreversibility rule ΔK_t must always be non-negative, it follows from the theory that C_t^* must be non-negative. More generally, however, when the capital being installed this period is dependent upon several previous periods, the irreversibility criteria are the considerably weaker ones shown by equation (2.15).

$$b_1 C_t^* + b_2 C_{t-1}^* \geqslant 0. \qquad (2.15)$$

(2.15) is satisfied when:

or

(a) $C_t^*, C_{t-1}^* \geqslant 0$,

or

(b) $C_t^* < 0$, $\dfrac{b_2}{b_1} C_{t-1}^* > |C_t^*| > 0$,

(c) $C_{t-1}^* < 0$ $\dfrac{b_1}{b_2} C_t^* > |C_{t-1}^*| > 0$.

These conditions allow for somewhat greater realism than that permitted by the simpler kinds of "off-on" accelerators. When C_t^* is negative, a certain amount of investment which would have been made on the basis of previous period experience will be cut back. Retrenchment can occur in two ways. First, if the previous period experience results in current investment, it might have been due to the expectational effects of previous output so that the current "bad" experience causes the previously planned capacity increment to be scaled down.

Second, some investment, which because of gestation lag is only being installed during the current period, will not be completely cancelled but the rate of installation will be retarded. It often happens, for instance, that a plant begun in boom times will not be completely abandoned when a slump occurs but its construction will be stretched out. These particular conditions could easily be generalized to more lags provided we treat C^*_{t-1} as representing all previous lags and C^*_t as representing the current period desire for additional capacity.

2.4 Financial Restrictions

Quite clearly, the financial policies of industrial enterprises should be meshed with their investment behavior, but exactly how remains an open question. An apparent widespread preference for internal financing on the part of manufacturing firms constitutes an important dimension of business activity which ought to be incorporated into a systematic theory of investment. Some interesting clues to the nature of corporate financing behavior can be found in two studies on dividend behavior by Dobrovolsky and Lintner.[14] Lintner found that "on the basis of our work so far, at least, the essential explanation seems to be simply that investment outlays have over long periods been quite consistently and highly correlated with current profits, sales volume and internal fund flows, and that allowance for these relationships in past experience has been built into the dividend policies of corporations in such a way that corporations can pay the dividends implied by these policies with considerable consistency over long periods of time, and do so (in the light of their planning) with considerable comfort and success."[15] Lintner's approach which will be described in greater detail soon, differs from Dobrovolsky's. Dobrovolsky treats entrepreneurial retained earnings decisions as primarily caused by the rate of return on investment (average efficiency of investment). Lintner on the other hand concentrates on the dynamics of the dividend decision making process, by setting up an adjustment mechanism in which the dividend change is related to profits and the previous dividend rate.

It turns out that the two ingredients, rate of return on capital and

[14] See SERGEI DOBROVOLSKY, *Corporate Income Retention, 1915–1943*, National Bureau of Economic Research, 1951; and JOHN K. LINTNER, "Distribution of Incomes of Corporations Among Dividends, Retained Earnings and Taxes", *Proceedings of the American Economic Review*, Vol. 46, No. 2, May, 1956, pp. 97–113.

[15] LINTNER, *op. cit.*, pp. 112–113.

dynamics of dividend decision-making as described by Lintner, have a role in a complete theory of internally-financed investment. The most promising line of attack, in my opinion, will be to consider Lintner's dividend hypothesis which yields some interesting results when appropriately related to certain investment models.[16]

Space cannot be expended here to indicate the great care and empirical sophistication Lintner employed to validate his propositions, which stand among the more thoroughly founded behavioral hypotheses in the area of business behavior. Lintner, through interviews and regression estimates, has concluded that the behavior of individual firm policy to change dividends can best be described according to the following equation:

$$\Delta D_t = c(D_t^* - D_{t-1}) + a. \tag{2.16}$$

D_t^* represents the *desired* dividend and c is a reaction coefficient, assumed to be a positive fraction that reflects rapidity of adjustment. D^* in turn is determined by the firm's desire to pay out a constant fraction of profits so that:

$$D_t^* = rP_t. \tag{2.17}$$

We can rewrite (2.16) as:

$$\Delta D_t = c(rP_t - D_{t-1}) + a. \tag{2.18}$$

Then,

$$D_t = crP_t + (1 - c)D_{t-1} + a. \tag{2.19}$$

This difference equation, it should be noted, is similar in form to (2.3) with solution:

$$D_t = (1 - c)^t D_0 + cr \sum_{T=1}^{t} (1 - c)^{t-T} P_T - \frac{a}{c}[(1 - c)^t - 1]. \tag{2.20}$$

Because the constant or intercept term in equation (2.16) conflicts with the main elements of Lintner's theory, it will be suppressed for the time being.[17]

[16] MEYER and KUH, *op. cit.*, pp. 200–204 present a verbal argument similar to the algebraic formulations to be developed shortly.

[17] In (2.16) assume $D_t^* = D_{t-1}$ but $a \neq 0$. Then the dividend will change ($\Delta D_t = a$), an occurrence at odds with the assumption of constant long-run desired payout. If $a \neq 0$, the observed inconsistency can be rationalized in a trivial and unsatisfactory way by defining $D_t^* = rP_t + a/c$ according to which the long-run desired dividend payout is an essentially arbitrary variable. Hence, when $D_t^* = D_t$, $D_t/P_t = r + a/cP_t$, which is a function of P_t that need not be a positive fraction and in which r no longer has much behavioral content.

If we choose $D_0 = 0$ as an initial condition or alternatively suppose $D_0 > 0$ but take t relatively large so that $(1 - c)^t$ is small, the sole or major explanatory component of dividends is a geometrically declining weighted average of previous profits. While equation (2.20) at first glance might appear to encompass only a narrow range of behavior, such is not actually the case. For instance, if the reaction coefficient c were equal to zero, the firm would pay a constant dividend, namely D_0. At the other extreme, a firm with highly stable profits might choose a reaction coefficient of unity so that it would always be paying its desired long-run dividend. While it would be foolish to suppose that this equation exactly governs dividend behavior in all circumstances, it does seem plausible to suppose that for a number of years appreciable stability of the relation could exist, and indeed has existed for manufacturing aggregates at least according to Lintner's results. Actual behavior will be influenced by extreme business cycle fluctuations. How the business cycle should be fitted into the complete picture will be deferred until we have demonstrated the relation of this particular equation to investment in plant and equipment.

The major hypothesis that will be advanced is this: firms that adjust dividend outlays according to the Lintner hypothesis and their capital stock consonant with the Chenery hypothesis can select reaction coefficients and long-run desired dividend payout that are compatible with financing net investment from retained earnings on a continuing basis.[18] Subject to a number of qualifications, especially those relating to the role played by external finance, there seems to be enough interview and statistical information to warrant further investigation of the proposition.[19]

Before implications of the suggested combined dividend and investment behavior can be assessed, it will prove convenient to translate profits into sales, if empirically valid approximations of this relationship are available. Common support to the three profit-sales relations that will be suggested below [see equations (2.21)–(2.23)] rests upon two empirical propositions. First, most manufacturing firms operate along approximately linear short-run total cost functions. Statistical investigations of short-run cost functions by Joel Dean and Jack Johnston,

---

[18] Net investment is defined here as the excess of gross investment over depreciation expense. The role of depreciation is better explained later in the context of a growth model.

[19] A review of some literature bearing on this subject can be found in MEYER and KUH, *op. cit.*, Chapter 2 and appendix.

among others, offer substantial empirical support to this proposition.[20]

After a specified output level has been attained, marginal costs increase rapidly as inefficient equipment comes into use and over-time pay mounts in importance. Finally, an absolute limitation on output will be reached when plant is being fully utilized, implying infinite short-run marginal cost. While the extent of this hypothesized behavior can only be conjectured, statistical estimation and widespread reliance on multiple machine operations within plant, as well as multi-plant operations, combine to lend credence to the proposition.

The second empirical ingredient called upon to buttress the selected profit-sales functions is that prices appear to be relatively cost responsive although comparatively unresponsive to demand changes, a type of behavior that is consistent with widely used variable cost plus a stable per cent markup pricing policy. Empirical work by Richard Ruggles and Joseph Yance bolsters this proposition considerably although clearly much more remains to be discovered about industrial price policy.[21] Sticky product prices, and/or a fairly stable per cent markup price policy in combination with constant variable cost (for given factor prices) will lead to approximately linear profit functions. Furthermore, widespread use of linear break-even charts in business budgeting procedures suggests that much planning is based on the assumption of linear profit functions.

In an aggregative study on the behavior of corporate profits, certain results bearing on these propositions have been found. Part of this study deals with corporate profit markups, defined as the ratio of net receipts to wage bill costs where national income definitions have been used in all cases.[22] It is true that the markup shows systematic cyclical variability. The variability however is not extreme. The Korean War

---

[20] JOEL DEAN, *Statistical Determination of Costs with Special Reference to Marginal Cost*, University of Chicago, Studies in Business Administration, Vol. 7, No. 1, Chicago, 1936; JACK JOHNSTON, *Statistical Cost Analysis*, 1960. See MEYER and KUH, *op. cit.*, footnote 1, p. 192 for additional references.

[21] RICHARD RUGGLES, "The Nature of Price Flexibility and the Determinants of Relative Price Changes in the Economy," in *Business Concentration and Price Policy*, Princeton, 1955; and JOSEPH V. YANCE, "A Model of Price Flexibility," *American Economic Review*, Vol. 50, No. 3, June, 1960, pp. 401–18.

[22] E. KUH, *Profits, Profit Markups and Productivity: A Study of Corporate Behavior Since 1947*, Study Paper No. 15 of Joint Economic Committee, Study of Employment, Growth and Price Levels, Government Printing Office, Washington, D.C., January, 1960.

peak reached 1.38. The extreme low for this business cycle was reached in the fourth quarter of 1953, when the markup equalled 1.23. The subsequent peak in the markup, achieved in the fourth quarter of 1955, was only 1.30 while the trough of the same cycle was reached in the first quarter of 1958 when the markup equalled 1.19. The maximum peak to trough variability is thus about 8 per cent. While far from constant, the markup is subject to relatively much less variation than corporate profits.

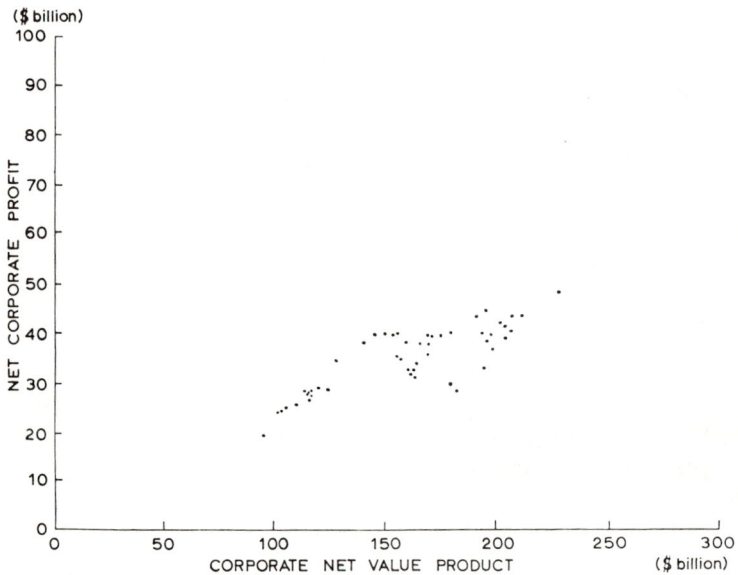

Chart 2.1

Second, we can further support the results by looking at the following charts based on the same study. The simple scatter diagram of profits against corporate net output is shown in Chart 2.1, while the scatter diagram of corporate profits against corporate gross value product appears in Chart 2.2. While neither diagram shows a perfect fit, to a first approximation a linear equation obviously explains most of the variation in corporate profits, especially for the gross magnitudes.

While this study covers only the post-war period, it represents somewhat over half the sample period with which we are concerned. Furthermore, the fact that the data are quarterly magnifies the observable variation compared to annual data. The variability of the net markup, characterized by moderate cyclical variability, in addition to a small trend, is best summarized in the following relations. Over the post-war period we have observed a steady increase in wages relative to prices. Hence, the simple markup (as defined) has been declining steadily. However, a sharp increase in output per man-hour has been offsetting the increase in wages relative to prices, so that the simple markup, adjusted for increases in productivity per manhour, has been subject

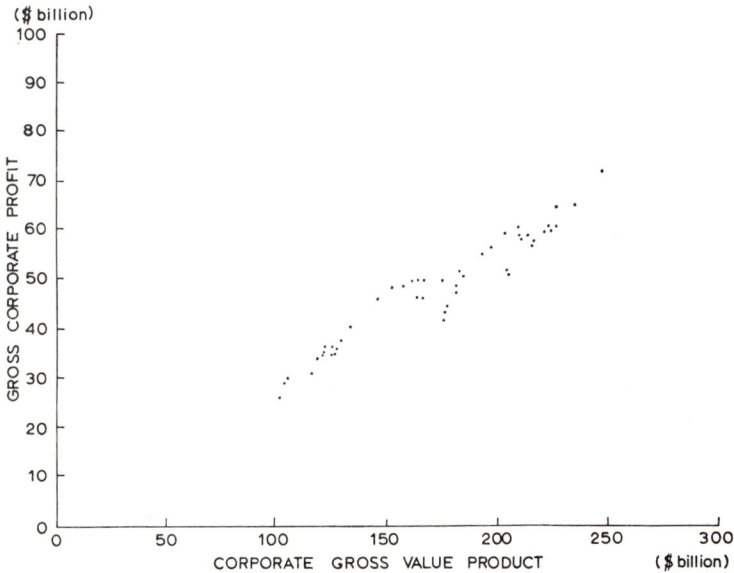

Chart 2.2

to much slighter variation than either of its principal constituent elements, the ratio of final prices to wages and output per manhour. In sum, the short-run static model assuming given technology and factor combinations ought to be modified by taking into account productivity per manhour which includes effects of increasing capital per worker, changes in technology, and returns to scale. Quite clearly, possible compositional changes in output limit the validity of these findings and, furthermore, how much this analysis applies to individual enterprises has yet to be determined. The tentative results are included here as being further evidence of a suggestive nature useful in evaluating the hypotheses about profits and sales of concern in the remaining portions of this chapter.[23] Therefore, because costs are relatively sticky, and because demand function shifts are relatively volatile, the postulated relationships could hold over wide ranges in behavior. To this extent, we can expect that direct profit-sales functions can provide quite acceptable approximations.

Three possibilities that come to mind are:

$$P_t = \alpha X_t, \tag{2.21}$$
$$P_t = \alpha' X_t - \gamma', \tag{2.22}$$
$$P_t = \alpha'' X_t - \gamma'' K_{t-1}. \tag{2.23}$$

Relation (2.21), the simplest proposition, asserts that firms have a constant profit margin.[24] While palpably incorrect in the short run, this statement conveys greater plausibility if one considers a long-run average profit margin. If the desired capital-output ratio, β, is relatively fixed *and* "fixed" costs are approximately proportional to capital stock as indicated in (2.23), then;

$$P_t = (\alpha'' - \gamma'' \beta) X_t. \tag{2.24}$$

This homogeneous relation adjusts the profit margin of (2.21) by netting out a fixed cost element. The assumption of constancy for the profit margin is not so implausible for dividend and investment decisions based upon long-run considerations. However, in the short run when capital stock is relatively fixed, and similarly for overhead costs, most firms will have variable profit margins, according to the intercept term appearing in either equation (2.22) or (2.23). Both non-homogeneous profit relations have something to recommend them. Equation (2.23), for instance, implies that as the firm's capital stock increases, so do its fixed costs. Since the profit figure is measured net of depreciation, on this account alone the non-homogeneous component of the profit function should and would be inversely related to the size of the

[23] In the same corporate profit study, an equation explaining price in terms of wage rates, output per manhour and an index of demand, the ratio of current to trend-adjusted peak previous output, showed that the net effects of demand were less discernible than the cost factors. While indicative of greater cost responsiveness, the results are too provisional to lend strong support to the constructions we have developed here.

[24] For periods over which investment decisions are made, almost certainly a year or more, the highly relevant short-run distinction between sales and output is of less importance. Strictly speaking, investment decisions depend on capital-output relations while profits depend upon current production costs and sales. Only when inventory change is large relative to sales change will the two values diverge substantially.

firm as measured directly by its capital stock. Offsetting this effect somewhat is the fact that certain types of fixed labor costs will be replaced by fixed capital costs so that the net effect might be a negligible change in fixed costs as a function of increased capital stock. Thus, no unambiguous *a priori* grounds can be adduced in favor of (2.22) or (2.23) so that the matter must remain open until empirical investigations provide enlightenment.

A firm that decides to pay dividends according to Lintner's hypothesis and add to their capital stock according to the Goodwin-Chenery relation must choose a unique, compatible combination of reaction coefficients for both relations and a long-run dividend payout if it is to adhere consistently to an internal financing policy. The mathematical counterpart of this proposition requires the transformation of the dividend relation into a retained earnings equation and the equating of coefficients of the retained earnings equation with the coefficients of the investment equation. To do this, express (2.20) as a retained earnings equation;

$$R_t \equiv P_t - D_t = (1 - cr)P_t - rc \sum_{T=1}^{t-1} (1 - c)^{t-T} P_T - D_0(1 - c)^t. \quad (2.25)$$

In the above, R_t is defined as retained earnings. We will set $D_0 = 0$ as an initial condition so that only the first two terms on the right of the equality sign will be used subsequently. Substituting profits for sales in (2.24) according, first, to the homogeneous profit relation (2.21) yields:

$$R_t = (1 - cr)\, \alpha X_t - \alpha rc \sum_{T=1}^{t-1} (1 - c)^{t-T} X_T. \quad (2.26)$$

The solution to the Chenery-Goodwin investment equation shown in (2.5) is reproduced here for convenience.

$$K_t = (1 - b)^t K_0 + b\beta \sum_{T=1}^{T=t} (1 - b)^{t-T} X_T. \quad (2.27)$$

By substituting (2.27) into (2.2) and setting $K_0 = 0$, an investment equation can be readily described:

$$\Delta K_t = b\beta X_t - b^2\beta \sum_{T=1}^{t-1} (1 - b)^{t-T} X_T. \quad (2.28)$$

All that remains is to equate coefficients term by term since the equation forms are identical, in order to analyze how firms whose actions are simultaneously governed by (2.26) and (2.28) will behave.

$$b\beta = (1 - cr)\alpha \qquad\qquad (2.29)$$

$$b^2\beta(1 - b) = \alpha rc\ (1 - c) \qquad\qquad (2.30)$$

$$(1 - b) = (1 - c) \qquad\qquad (2.31)$$

These three equations in the three unknowns b, c, and r can be readily solved, given the parameters α and β. Clearly, the same reaction coefficient must be used in both equations, since $b = c$ from (2.31). Once b (or c) has been eliminated from (2.29) and (2.30), these two equations can be solved for c (or b) and r with a quadratic expression which always appears to have one economically inadmissible root.

One rough example of how this model operates with actual data will be presented for aggregate manufacturing data. Sales statistics from the FTC-SEC *Quarterly Financial Report* Fourth Quarter 1956 and First Quarter 1957, have been adjusted to a value added basis.[25] Capital coefficients were computed from the same data. Table 2.1 below shows

TABLE 2.1

Simultaneous Estimates Based on Equations (2.29)–(2.31)

Coefficients	Gross Capital Coefficient	Net Capital Coefficient	Lintner Estimate
$b = c$	0.09	0.20	0.21
r	0.92	0.83	0.69

estimated coefficients for which net and gross capital coefficients have been used in equations (2.29)–(2.31), along with results from a regression equation estimated by Lintner for the years 1918–1941. These profit data have not been adjusted for inventory valuation changes, so that his coefficients are based on accounting data similar to my own. The valuation problems inherent in using original cost or book value render these calculations suggestive at best.

Since firms by hypothesis pick their reaction coefficients and long-run dividend payout for given capital-output ratios and profit margins,

[25] The gross capital coefficient (Gross Fixed Assets ÷ Value Added) is 1.33 at an annual rate, and the net profit margin (profit after tax ÷ value added) equals 0.147. The net capital coefficient is 0.725.

it remains to show how the variables of choice are related to each other. From equations (2.29)–(2.31), it can be seen that:

$$r = \frac{1}{1 + b}.$$
(2.32)

This implies that the long-run desired dividend payout can never be less than one-half since b can never exceed one. When the reaction coefficient is very small, the long-run dividend payout is almost unity.

A further matter of considerable economic interest can be derived from a simple rearrangement of equation (2.30). It can be rewritten as

$$\frac{b}{r} = \frac{\alpha}{\beta}.$$
(2.33)

We know that $\alpha/\beta = P_t/K_t^p$ is net profit divided by (desired) stock of capital. As a rule, this, ratio will not exceed 0.20. Since the long-run desired dividend payout, r, cannot exceed unity and will usually be less, it immediately follows that the reaction coefficient will not exceed 0.20 except when profit margins are extremely high relative to capital requirements. Otherwise, given the dominant role of the dividend relation, the firm must seek outside financing (or reject the Lintner payout formula) in order to react more rapidly. At this juncture, however, we wish to emphasize that the hypothesized relations provide an upper limit (to be sure, a provisional one) for the reaction coefficient which might go far toward explaining the extremely low coefficients estimated by Koyck. Firms restricting themselves to internal financing and Lintner-type dividend policy are obliged to react slowly to variations in capital requirements. While this is not at all surprising, the theory advanced here, together with some plausible magnitudes provides reasonable limits on important behavior parameters.

Introduction of the non-homogeneous linear profit function (2.22) into (2.20) does not materially alter the algebra although interpretation must be made with care. Once this step has been taken, the solution (2.26) has added to it the last term shown below:

$$R_t = (1 - cr)\, \alpha X_t - \alpha cr \sum_{T=1}^{t-1} (1 - c)^{t-T} X_T - r\gamma[(1 - c)^t - 1].$$
(2.34)

While we excluded the intercept term in Lintner's equation (2.19) on *a priori* grounds (see footnote 17), it has crept into the solution in a more reasonable fashion via the intercept of the profit function. Because the term in square brackets $[(1 - c)^t - 1]$ is negative and is preceded by a negative sign, the result will be a steady increase in retained earnings.

The additional intercept term introduced into the dividend equation has a logical counterpart in the investment equation, a constant increment to the firm's capital stock often designated as "autonomous" investment. There are two main possibilities. If desired autonomous investment exceeds the amount of autonomous internal finance, (i.e., retained earnings independent of profits) firms will nevertheless restrict such outlays to internally available funds. Then, letting d equal autonomous investment in equation (2.4), we would have the additional equation (2.35) to determine simultaneously coefficients compatible with internal financing.

$$\frac{d}{b} = r\gamma. \tag{2.35}$$

Alternatively, if desired autonomous investment were less, the equations would be inconsistent, and the firm could accumulate current assets equal to the excess of "autonomous" internal fund flows over autonomous investment demand. It is unreasonable to suppose that (2.35) would hold exactly in the real world except by accident or initially as an inequality, as suggested above.[26]

2.5 External Financing and Long-Run Growth

To this point a simplified theory of internally financed investment has been elaborated and a few complications arising from distributed lags and irreversibilities considered. Many actual firms do not have long-term debt and do not issue new long-term equity so that the basic

---

[26] Equating coefficients of a first order retained earnings equation and a second or higher order investment equation is not possible. It is not feasible to equate coefficients between a first order system retained earnings equation and the second (or higher order) distributed lag investment equation, since the resulting equations are inconsistent. In short, a firm cannot exactly gear its dividend policy to investment when gestation or other delays are substantial and the firm simultaneously follows a Lintner-type dividend policy. This is not particularly surprising, and if a "realistic" speculation is not too far out of place here, one can often observe that firms completing large investment projects will resort (temporarily) to external financing, in order to maintain their dividend policy and at the same time pay for capital assets whose demand was generated several periods back.

internal financing stipulation has numerous real world counterparts.[27]

Nevertheless, a crucially important segment of the industrial sector has been neglected, the firm whose investment is partly externally financed, sometimes to a significant extent. Two different though not mutually exclusive hypotheses could be advanced. The first, which must be given short shrift, is that individual firms plan to obtain outside financing in the form of new debt, new equity or both, since they are either indifferent to the nature of the fund source or see positive advantages to external funds. For instance, firms may wish to maintain a stable proportion of debt in their long-term capital structure to enable "trading on the equity", thus increasing the per share earnings of the existing stockholders. The standard advice of corporation finance books on the benefits of leverage to the common stockholder need not be repeated here. However, most manufacturing firms appear strongly averse to debt, and therefore, with few exceptions, other reasons why firms go into debt must be sought. Most firms, in addition, are reluctant to issue new common stock because of the risks of diluting the equity earnings accruing to the existing stockholders, or because of other risks associated with loss or dilution of control.[28]

Hence, we must reject the proposition (straw man, if you will) that firms are indifferent to outside sources, or prefer them. To put the matter more affirmatively then, what incentives are required in order to overcome the widespread managerial distaste for external financing?

In its simplest form, the answer is that the internal investment policies of the firm permit a limited rate of growth which can only be exceeded by resort to external funds. In short, when the profits foregone become so large "that it hurts," businessmen will overcome their reluctance to borrow or acquire additional common stock.

Verification of this proposition requires scanning the businessman's psyche for profit rates and other circumstances that would overcome distaste for external financing. As an alternative to direct evaluation of subjective profit rates, a model relating external funds and internal financing to the firm's rate of growth will be developed to achieve the objective more directly: a demand function for external funds will be

---

[27] True, many firms of this genre often have resorted to temporary short-term borrowing for purposes of inventory accumulation or other shortrun needs.

[28] A bibliography and discussion more extensive than will be gone into here can be found in MEYER and KUH, op. cit., pp. 16–20.

generated as a function of the demand for real assets and the supply of internally generated funds.

The relation of the more "direct" growth hypothesis to the subjective profit rate hypothesis depends upon two separate considerations. First, the relation between future profits and future growth is likely to be very close indeed. While profits foregone may be the ultimate incentive to the acquisition of external funds, the firm's present and expected rate of growth can often be regarded as functionally related to expected profits. Second, market structure considerations provide significant additional reason for focusing on output growth rates. The rate of growth itself can often be of prime importance, particularly when, as with many oligopolistic industries, maintenance of market shares is important in its own right. If total demand for industry output is growing, failure to grow along with other firms could mean an over-all deterioration of the firm's long-run profit position, despite the fact that the added assets are not directly profitable at the margin. In such instances it is the opportunity costs of not growing which provide the relevant profit measure, so that growth itself becomes the central variable.[29]

The growth model to be investigated is derived from that of Evsey D. Domar in an article, "The Case for Accelerated Depreciation".[33] More elaborate or different models might prove more cogent, although it is hoped that the relevant components have been assembled. The most basic assumptions of the model are:

1. Gross investment grows at a constant relative rate per annum.
2. Capital assets have a constant average life span.
3. Straight line depreciation methods are used.

A few general remarks, but no detailed defense of these assumptions will be provided here. The first assumption about constant relative rate of growth per annum in investment does not accord with actual firm behavior. In the present context this concept is thought to be a relevant approximation for long-term planning purposes. We can think of the growth pattern as providing a trend around which the

[29] Cf. JAMES DUESENBERRY, *Business Cycles and Economic Growth*, New York, 1958, pp. 120–24.

[30] EVSEY D. DOMAR, *The Quarterly Journal of Economics*, Vol. 67, November, 1953, pp. 493–519. This has been reprinted as Essay 8 in *Essays in the Theory of Economic Growth*, New York, 1957, pp. 195–222, see especially pp. 200–201. Also, ROBERT EISNER, "Depreciation Allowances Replacement Requirements and Growth," *American Economic Review*, Vol. 42, No. 5, December, 1952, pp. 820–31.

short-run variations in investment occur, perhaps according to the capacity acceleration models described earlier. The second assumption is sufficiently convenient and relevant to merit its tentative acceptance. It of course embodies the famous "one horse shay" assumption, namely that the productive capacity of the assets is maintained on the average until the end of life. The fact that we are talking about average length of life lends somewhat more credence to the proposition than would apply to an individual piece of equipment. Through maintenance policies the firm can often maintain a stable average productive life and where technological change is not violent, the often ridiculed one horse shay assumption need not turn out to be grossly inaccurate. The third assumption about straight line depreciation corresponds to actual behavior during the sample period. While it would be somewhat more complicated, the model could be modified to take account of current methods of rapid write-off permitted under the 1954 Internal Revenue Code, it is a problem which does not presently concern us.

A list of symbols, including some that have been previously used, will prove convenient here.

$K =$ Gross capital stock

$I =$ Gross investment

$P =$ Net profit after taxes

$D =$ Dividends

$E =$ External funds

$F =$ Depreciation expense

$R =$ Retained earnings

$g =$ Rate of growth of all flow magnitudes

$m =$ Average life of capital assets

$p =$ Net profit rate $(P_t \div K_t)$

$r' = P_t/D_t =$ Actual dividend payout rate

$v =$ Present value of an annuity[31] $= \dfrac{1 - (1 + g)^{-m}}{g}$

On the assumption of a constant growth rate of investment,

$$K_t = I_t \sum_{n=1}^{m} (1 + g)^{-n} = I_t \left[\frac{1 - (1 + g)^{-m}}{g} \right] = I_t\, v. \qquad (2.36)$$

Straight line depreciation is a constant fraction of the gross capital

[31] The annuity value enters into the series sum of equation (2.36) and has no significance other than serving as a convenient computational device.

stock, namely the reciprocal of asset life and therefore can be expressed as:

$$F_t = \frac{K_t}{m} = \frac{I_t v}{m} . \qquad (2.37)$$

Once again we will adopt the assumption of a constant profit margin, which we argued earlier is especially plausible in a long-run planning context:

$$P_t = pK_t = pI_t v. \qquad (2.38)$$

The concept of a constant long-run payout is also used here although in the present steady growth situation (assumed for long-run planning purposes) actually attained, not desired magnitudes are involved.

$$D_t = r'P_t. \qquad (2.39)$$
$$R_t = (1 - r')P_t. \qquad (2.40)$$

Combining (2.38) and (2.40), we find:

$$R_t = (1 - r')\, pK_t = (1 - r')\, pI_t v , \qquad (2.41)$$

where $(1 - r')p$ is the rate of retained profit on gross capital stock.

All that remains is the definition of total financing, which is simply:

$$I_t = R_t + F_t + E_t. \qquad (2.42)$$

Substituting relations (2.37) and (2.41) into (2.42) for F_t and R_t, we have:

$$I_t = (1 - r')pI_t v + \frac{I_t v}{m} + E_t. \qquad (2.43)$$

Dividing (2.43) through by I_t yields (2.44):

$$1 = v \left[(1 - r')p + \frac{1}{m} \right] + \frac{E_t}{I_t} . \qquad (2.44)$$

Finally, if the assumption is adopted that external funds too are obtained *on the average* at an exponential rate, the fraction E_t/I_t will be a constant also. Hence, equation (2.44) provides an expression for the proportion of funds originating respectively from retained earnings, depreciation and external funds.[32]

The next immediate objective is to synchronize the short-run invest-

[32] If total, not just fixed, assets are also growing at the same rate, then a further proportionality constant will be required.

ment-retained earnings model with the long-run external finance growth model. Before plunging into details, however, it would be well to state baldly the central proposition that joins these two quite different theories. This link could be fallacious, (a hypothesis which can be tested) while either one or both of the two models could be correct, yet lead lives quite independent of each other. The basic hypothesis is this: For given profit margins and desired capital-output ratio, firms will first choose a long-run dividend payout target and reaction coefficients that are compatible with exclusive internal financing. These coefficients in turn will determine the availability of internal funds and, in the context of geometric growth, will also imply a growth rate that could be obtained if no external fund were obtained. When the profit incentive (or pure growth incentive) to use additional funds becomes too great to resist, firms whose funds are thus supplemented will then be able to grow more rapidly. Accordingly, we can generate a demand function for the fraction of funds demanded from external sources as a function of the firm's rate of growth in excess of that which can be financed from internal sources.

It will be convenient at this point to relate growth rates to cost-of-capital considerations in an explicitly optimizing framework, by way of a digression. Growth rates will be used here to provide observable substance for marginal efficiency and capital cost models, involving both internal and external fund sources. At this point, it should be made clear that we are dealing with four growth rates. The first growth rate, usually the lowest, is that implied by the Domar model (equation (2.44)) when its parameters are derived using the short-run internal finance restraint. The second growth rate, usually the highest, is that obtainable when market suppliers' cost of capital is accepted by the firm. The third is a subjective, hypothetical growth rate which must be exceeded if the firm is to grow faster by any resort to external funds. This rate measures the opportunity costs (i.e., growth and profits foregone) which must be covered if the firm is to seek outside funds. Fourth, there is the actual growth rate, which is the rate at which the firm will actually grow and from which the demand function for external funds is derived. The greater the reluctance of the firm to seek external funds, i.e., the larger is the third growth rate, the greater will be the difference between the second "market" growth and the fourth i.e. actual growth rates.

Since the actual rate of growth will be influenced by capital market conditions as well as the subjective elements, relations among growth rates will be explained by assuming away the third rate at first and therefore explain relations among the internal rate, the market rate and the actual rate, directly by reference to Chart 2.3 in a cost-of-capital framework.

Two demand schedules for investment and two supply or cost-of-capital functions are drawn, one pair of each for two periods, e.g., two years. By construction, the shifts in the two curves are related. It is

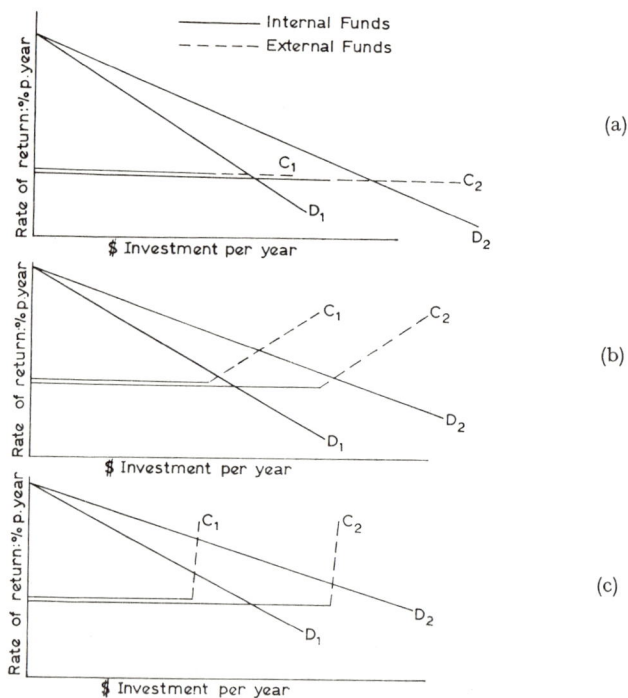

Chart 2.3

assumed that sales increased in the second period so that retained earnings, as a function of increased profits, and depreciation expense, as a function of the larger capital stock, have increased, both elements causing the internally generated supply of funds to grow. Also, the demand for fixed assets increased to accommodate the higher level of demand. In the general constant growth case, both curves would continuously be shifting outward by the same relative amount per period. C_1 and C_2 represent capital cost functions in year one and year two, while D_1 and D_2 are the corresponding investment demand curves.

Chart 2.3a portrays an implausibly extreme situation in which our hypothetical firms have access to large quantities of external funds at the internal opportunity cost of capital. In 2.3b the firm has internally generated funds at a comparatively low cost while external funds can be acquired at gradually increasing capital costs. This firm has, relatively speaking, easy access to external funds. In Chart 2.3c our hypothetical firm has an extremely sharply rising external funds capital

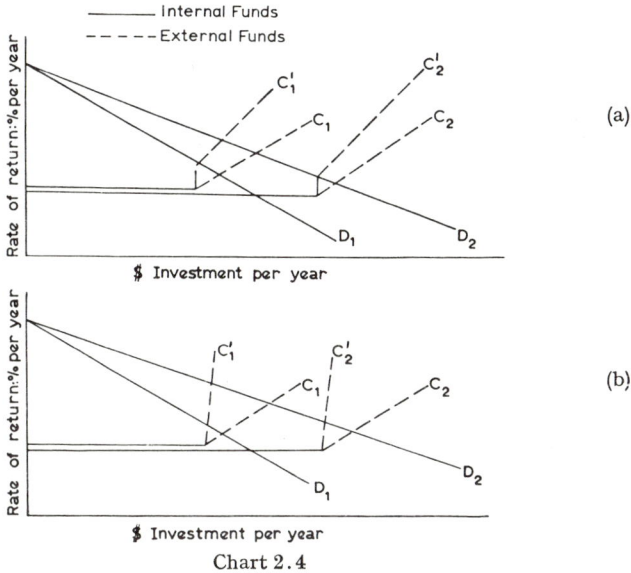

Chart 2.4

cost so that the amount of external funds actually obtained would be relatively slight because of their high cost.[33]

In Chart 2.4, two among many conceivable situations have been illustrated that involve the additional fact of subjective reluctance, or self-rationing on the part of the business firm with respect to external funds. Hence, the third, subjective growth rate which must be exceeded before firms will be induced to use external funds now appears on stage. In Chart 2.4a, as before, C_1 represents the terms at which the market will supply funds to the firm while the new ingredient, C'_1, shows the higher cost function as the firm views it, to reflect aversion to external funds. The vertical distance between C'_1 and C_1 measures

[33] When turning to the discussion of Duesenberry's model later in this chapter, a closer link will be made to capital cost functions of the sort described here.

the additional opportunity cost of external financing to the firm. In both Charts 2.4a and 2.4b a discontinuity, represented by the vertical segment of C_1 and C_2, indicate that a barrier must first be surmounted before outside funds will be sought in any event. To avoid needless complications, discontinuities in outside fund sources will not be discussed further. In addition, C' diverges from C indicating the increasing burden of outside funds as viewed by the firm. This last construction need not hold generally since C'_1 and C_1 could just as well be parallel or indeed might even converge. In general, the vertical distance between C'_1 and C_1 (or any other such pair) represents the added subjective cost of borrowing. Chart 2.4b illustrates a situation of almost complete self-rationing. Even though the firm has identical access to external funds as in the 2.4a case, (i.e., C_1 and C_2 are the same for both) the nearly vertical C' line implies that outside funds will not be acquired no matter how great the opportunities foregone, as measured by the vertical distance $C'_1 - C$.

The discontinuity between C'_1 and C_1 represents bias against external financing. The fastest the firm could profitably grow would be by investing at the rate corresponding to the C, D intersection which represents the price the firm will pay when it acquires external funds. The discrepancy between the C' and C curves shows the additional premium required by the firm to obtain outside financing.[34] Although growth rates are not shown explicitly, it is the rate of growth in investment implied by the intersection of D_1 and C'_1 which determines investment in each period and therefore, as the demand and supply curves shift, it is these intersections which will determine the actual rate of growth of the firm. The question might arise as to why the cost curve includes these subjective costs rather than the demand curve. The answer to this reasonable query is that ordinarily the marginal efficiency schedule is understood to reflect engineering and sales estimates of future revenues and costs suitably discounted for operating risk, as well as the present cost of capital equipment.

The relation of capital markets to the cost of capital functions that

---

[34] Discontinuities in the firm supply-of-funds schedule are emphasized by EDGAR M. HOOVER, "Some Institutional Factors in Business Investment Decisions," *American Economic Review*, May, 1954, although the explanation of such discontinuities is not complete. Another reason for discontinuities in the imputed capital cost schedule arise from retained earnings, when allowances are made for retained earnings not being taxed at personal marginal tax rates. Cf. EZRA SOLOMON, "Measuring a Company's Cost of Capital," *The Journal of Business*, Vol. 28, No. 4, October, 1955, 245–246.

were developed here differs from the conventional relationship predicated on the assumption of one type of financing, debt, whose price is "the" rate of interest. Instead, there are the less tangible opportunity costs imputed by businessmen in arriving at capital expenditure decisions. Thus, we are denied access to observable market prices in order to predict how different capital market situations might affect financing decisions. Nevertheless, some suggestions about the influence of capital market conditions on individual firm cost-of-capital relations can be made.

In the first place, the level of the "low cost," internally generated component of funds in the supply schedule in the main will be influenced by two factors, one of which is not too closely related to capital market conditions. The unrelated cause is the influence of retention rates on the market price of the firm's outstanding equity. Should a firm retain an amount of profit considered "excessive" by the stock market relative to firms whose securities are close substitutes, the market valuation of the shares will be reduced. Hence the percentage reduction in the price per share on this account can be construed to be an additive component of opportunity capital costs. This effect is likely to be strongly dependent upon the conventional behavior of other similarly situated firms and hence insensitive to capital market circumstances. A second circumstance affecting the flat portion of the curve is directly related to the capital market. While the relevant opportunity costs by which capital costs are measured for this segment of the funds is not altogether clear, one may conceive of the firm's alternative to investing in real assets as investing in monetary assets as one obvious possibility, for instance government bonds or high-grade corporate securities.[35]

However, the greatest impact of capital market conditions on the firm's cost-of-capital schedule will occur in its rising portion, particularly on the acquisition of long-term debt. When credit rationing prevails, there will be a more steeply inclined segment of the C curve than otherwise. And, of course, credit rationing will be greater the more stringent are capital market conditions and will be less the greater the supply of funds relative to demand at a given yield. Similar remarks can be made about the behavior of funds ordinarily associated with the flotation of new equity securities.

---

[35] Still another alternative must be mentioned, the next best opportunity available to stockholders.

In what has been set out above, capital markets thus play a crucial role as the supplier of marginal funds to the rapidly growing firms in the economy. Furthermore, the circumstances surrounding capital markets and valuation of monetary assets directly influence individual firm cost-of-capital functions. However, the primary effect is observed when the rapidly growing firms seek outside funds. Having taken a long excursion into capital market relations to individual firm growth decisions, the most efficient procedure will be to derive the relation between the short-run model, which assumes that the firm uses only internal funds, and the long-run growth model that permits the acquisition of external funds as well.[36]

To illustrate how the short- and long-run models are formally related, it will be assumed that in the short-run model output grows at a constant relative rate, instead of treating it as an arbitrary function of time. Recall [from equation (2.27)] the time path for capital stock when output is an arbitrary function of time:

$$K_t = K_0(1 - b)^t + b\beta \sum_{T=1}^{t} (1 - b)^{t-T} X_T. \qquad (2.45)$$

Then assume that $X_T = X_0 (1 + g)^T$ and (2.45) becomes:

$$K_t = K_0 (1 - b)^t + b\beta X_0 \sum_{T=1}^{t} (1 - b)^{t-T} (1 + g)^T. \qquad (2.46)$$

After simplification[37] the series sum (2.46) reduces to:

---

[36] I have deliberately ignored the question of optimum debt-equity structure, a matter dealt with theoretically in "Capital Theory and Capital Budgeting," *Metroeconomica*, December, 1960. This matter will often be relevant to individual decisions, but in most cases, I believe the internal-external dichotomy is much more important than the proportions of debt and equity finance that should be obtained.

[37] The principal intervening algebraic steps between (2.46) and (2.47) are:

$$K_t = K_0(1 - b)^t + b\beta X_0[(1 + g)^t + (1 - b) (1 + g)^{t-1} + (1 - b)^2(1 + g)^{t-2} + \cdots$$
$$\cdots + (1 - b)^{t-1}(1 + g) + (1 - b)^t]. \qquad (2.46a)$$

$$K_t = K_0(1 - b)^t + b\beta X_0(1 + g)^t \left[1 + \frac{1 - b}{1 + g} + \left(\frac{1 - b}{1 + g}\right)^2 + \cdots + \left(\frac{1 - b}{1 + g}\right)^t\right]. \qquad (2.46b)$$

$$K_t = K_0(1 - b)^t + b\beta X_0(1 + g)^t \left[\frac{\left(\frac{1 - b}{1 + g}\right)^t - 1}{\frac{1 - b}{1 + g} - 1}\right]. \qquad (2.46c)$$

$$K_t = \left[K_0 - \frac{\beta X_0 b(1 + g)}{b + g} \right] (1 - b)^t + \left[\frac{b(1 + g)}{b + g} \right] \beta X_t. \quad (2.47)$$

Behavior of the particular solution (2.47) will be governed by the coefficient $[b(1 + g)/(b + g)]$ in the long run. Assuming that the growth rate g is a positive fraction, this term will be always a positive fraction. Further, as the reaction coefficient b tends to unity, $b(1 + g)/(b + g)$ also tends to unity for any given growth rate. Thus, for the moment ignoring the first term of the expression which damps out as time progresses, the capital stock will be proportional to output when the reaction coefficient is unity and will be less, the smaller the reaction coefficient. A second point worth noting is that the partial derivative of this term with respect to the growth rate is negative, i.e., for a given reaction coefficient and level of output, the capital stock will be smaller the larger the rate of growth in output.

A third point of some interest is the behavior of the expression within brackets in the first term, which is the coefficient of the damped term $(1 - b)^t$. Where the initial conditions governing the time path of K_t are subject to change from time to time, as occurs for instance when irreversibility conditions have taken over, expressions such as this can become quantitatively significant even though tending to zero with time, for given initial conditions. This happens either when a new investment policy is introduced or when a firm emerges from a long period of excess capacity and begins once again to accumulate capital. If the assumption is made that desired output equals actual output and desired capital stock equals actual capital stock when initial conditions are established, the expression in big square brackets reduces to (2.48)[38]:

$$K_0 \left[1 - \frac{b(1 + g)}{b + g} \right]. \quad (2.48)$$

It can be readily seen that the effect of the term in brackets becomes large for small reaction coefficients, approaching unity as the reaction coefficient approaches zero. Conversely, the faster the reaction, the less important is this "transient" effect which can be important when t is near the initial time period. Similarly, the expression in brackets becomes larger the greater the rate of growth for a given reaction coeffi-

[38] While a variety of other initial conditions might be discussed, not much of value would emerge if we were to discuss them in more detail than has been allocated to the present paragraph.

cient. As might have been expected, low reaction coefficients and high rates of growth can lead to a pronounced influence of the first term which reflects transient effects that are often paramount.

The behavior of dividends in a steady growth context contains several noteworthy aspects. Equation (2.49) shows the particular solution.

$$D_t = \left[D_0 - P_0 \frac{cr(1+g)}{c+g} \right] (1-c)^t + \left[\frac{cr(1+g)}{c+g} \right] P_t. \qquad (2.49)$$

Given the reaction coefficient and profit level, the dividend will be relatively less the greater the rate of growth. This qualitative result corresponds to the frequently observed quantitative fact that rapidly growing firms often retain an exceptionally large fraction of internal funds. This behavior is also consistent with a spurt in the level of output (and hence profits) exactly as with the capital stock model, when new initial conditions are established upon the re-emergence of a profitable condition after an interval when dividends had been suspended according to the coefficient of $(1-c)^t$. By now, it should be clear that the first bracketed expression bears a close relation to the short-run model. It supplies a link between the two types of relationship, long and short-run, which becomes weaker as steady growth takes over, and the initial conditions recede into the background as the term $(1-b)^t$ diminishes.

Another link between the long-run growth model and the short-run investment-internal funds model is supplied by effects of availability of external funds on the speed of reaction. The enterprise resorting to external funds can react more rapidly to a given discrepancy between actual and desired capital stock than the firm which deliberately restricts itself to internal funds alone, to the extent that financial inhibitions rather than technical delays or uncertainty explain the observed reaction coefficients. The relation between the new additional speed of reaction and the rate of growth of external funds is explained by the following three equations, in which it is assumed that the actual rate of investment is growing exponentially, in line with previous assumptions.

Define σ = fraction of investment externally financed = E_t/I_t

$(1-\sigma)$ = fraction of investment internally financed = $(R_t + F_t)/I_t$

ϱ = coefficient of *additional* reaction made possible by resort to external funds

Then:

$$(1 - \sigma) I_t = b(\beta X_t - K_{t-1}). \tag{2.50}$$

$$\sigma I_t = \varrho(1 - b) (\beta X_t - K_{t-1}). \tag{2.51}$$

$$\varrho = \left(\frac{b}{1-b}\right) \left(\frac{\sigma}{1-\sigma}\right). \tag{2.52}$$

Equation (2.52), the solution of (2.50) and (2.51) for ϱ in terms of b and σ, shows the value of the additional coefficient implicit in external financing. Other things equal, the greater is σ, i.e., the greater the fraction of external funds and hence the greater the actual rate of growth, the faster can the firm react to a given capital stock deficiency. The restriction $0 < \varrho + b - \varrho b \leqslant 1$, must obviously be respected. When, for instance, the internal financing reaction coefficient $b = 0.5$, and the fraction of external finance, σ, is equal to 0.33, $\varrho = 0.5$. But this is an implausibly high upper limit to the value of the internal financing reaction coefficient. For a more plausible upper value, setting $b = 0.25$, Table 2.2 traces out values of ϱ for different fractions of external finance. Also in Table 2.2 are shown values of ϱ for $b = 0.10$, a fairly typical value of the internal financing reaction coefficient.

TABLE 2.2

Values of ϱ for Alternative Values of b and σ

If $\sigma =$	When $b = 0.25$, $\varrho =$	When $b = 0,10$, $\varrho =$
0.20	0.094	0.031
0.30	0.143	0.045
0.40	0.221	0.073
0.50	0.333	0.111
0.60	0.500	0.167

This table indicates that for plausible values of the internal finance reaction coefficient b, it is highly improbable that the sum of this coefficient and the external finance reaction coefficient ϱ will exceed unity. Even in the case where external finance is 60 per cent of total finance and the internal reaction coefficient is 0.25, ϱ is equal to only one-half. For what we consider to be a more plausible value of the reaction coefficient, 0.10, the external reaction coefficient slightly exceeds the internal financing reaction coefficient for $\sigma = 0.60$.

Some differences in the structures of the long- and short-run model call for additional comment. First, funds from depreciation expense are treated quite differently in the two instances. Depreciation in the short-run model has been ignored. There are two ways that depreciation expense can be recognized explicitly in the short-run internal finance model. One way would be to ignore depreciation as a separate item and develop a capacity investment model in which the dependent variable is gross investment and the independent variables are output and the gross capital stock. However, if we also wish to explain dividend behavior whose explanation must originate in a net profit concept, this alternative must be foresworn. As a sensible alternative, we may assume that funds from depreciation are reinvested and hence subtract depreciation expense from gross investment to arrive at the relevant quantity of investment to be financed from net retained profit. In the Domar growth model, it has already been made clear that depreciation expense plays an essential role in determining the firm's attainable rate of growth.

A second feature distinguishing the two models is that the short-run model is theoretically compatible with any constant rate of growth according to equation (2.47). In principle, output could grow at any rate whatever, yet the demand for additional capital could be "just" financed out of retained earnings. In the growth model, attainable rates are determined by depreciation up to the point where external funds must be sought for given actual dividend payouts and profit margins. This divergence represents a different aspect of the first point noted, namely that depreciation is not explicitly included in the short-run model. Depreciation exerts a major influence on the firm's attainable rate of growth in the long-run model. Short-run variations in the demand for capital, however, are most influenced by variations in retained earnings, dependent on short-run demand variations, while variations in depreciation have only a marginal effect. Hence, the growth model would have small explanatory value for firms or industries whose output was subject to wide cyclical or seasonal swings and small rates of growth while the short-run model would be of small explanatory value in explaining long-run movements.

Finally, the relation between actual and desired dividend payout can be established for the long-run model. To find the "short-run" dividend payout, divide equation (2.49) through by P_t. Neglecting the first expression which becomes insignificant in a continued steady growth situation, equation (2.53) shows the actual dividend payout under conditions of steady growth.

$$\frac{D_t}{P_t} = \frac{cr(1 + g)}{c + g}.$$

(2.53)

Then divide (2.53) by the long-run dividend payout r to obtain the ratio of the current growth "dividend payout" to the long-run desired payout.

$$\frac{D_t/P_t}{r} = \frac{c(1 + g)}{c + g}.$$

(2.54)

This expression will nearly always be less than unity for positive growth rates and as indicated previously in discussion of the investment-model's analogous coefficient, becomes smaller the greater the rate of growth. Also, the larger the reaction coefficient, the more the actual dividend payout indicated by the growth model approaches the long-run desired payout. In the limiting case of a reaction coefficient of unity, the model implies that the actual and long-run payout will be the same. The qualitative behavior of the model is certainly appropriate in this respect.

The antecedent investment theory includes short-run reactions and long-run growth considerations. It is fundamentally a two-part model where the point of separation depends on comparative reluctance to seek external financial resources and real asset requirements. The two parts consist of the basic demand for additional capacity on the one hand and a set of reaction coefficients on the other, both embedded in the fundamental investment and dividend models. The reaction function which multiplies the additional capacity requirement is inherently non-linear.[39]

The final investment equation can thus be written in the following form:

$$I_t = [b + \varrho(g) (1 - b)] [\beta X_t - K_{t-1}],$$

(2.55)

$\varrho = 0$ for $g < g^*$.

[39] Starting from quite a different set of hypotheses about aggregate industry behavior (but which is also based on the Goodwin-Chenery investment model), ALBERT K. ANDO in "Over-and-Under Capacity of Firms and the Industry Acceleration Principle," an unpublished paper presented at the Econometric Society Meetings, September, 1957, has derived interesting theorems about non-linear relations between investment and demand, although in his case it was the desired capacity component which displayed the non-linearity. The matter of which component of the theory-reaction coefficient or the desired capacity addition — (or perhaps both) should be made to respond in non-linear fashion ultimately should be resolved through statistical testing. Irrespec-

TABLE 2.3

Growth Rates and Sources of Funds

Attainable Growth Rate	10% Profit Rate $\sigma =$ External Funds $\div$ Total Funds for Alternative Dividend Payouts			5% Profit Rate $\sigma =$ External Funds $\div$ Total Funds for Alternative Dividend Payouts		
	$r' = 0.80$	$r' = 0.50$	$r' = 0.30$	$r' = 0.80$	$r' = 0.50$	$r' = 0.30$
20-year asset life:						
1%	0.00	0.00	0.00	0.00	0.00	0.00
3%	0.00	0.00	0.00	0.11	0.00	0.00
5%	0.13	0.00	0.00	0.25	0.07	0.00
7%	0.26	0.00	0.00	0.36	0.21	0.10
9%	0.36	0.09	0.00	0.45	0.31	0.22
$10\frac{1}{2}$%	0.42	0.18	0.02	0.51	0.38	0.30
25-year asset life:						
1%	0.00	0.00	0.00	0.00	0.00	0.00
3%	0.00	0.00	0.00	0.13	0.00	0.00
5%	0.16	0.00	0.00	0.30	0.08	0.00
7%	0.30	0.00	0.00	0.42	0.24	0.13
9%	0.41	0.12	0.00	0.51	0.36	0.26
$10\frac{1}{2}$%	0.48	0.21	0.04	0.56	0.44	0.34
35-year asset life:						
1%	0.00	0.00	0.00	0.00	0.00	0.00
3%	0.00	0.00	0.00	0.17	0.00	0.00
5%	0.20	0.00	0.00	0.37	0.12	0.00
7%	0.37	0.00	0.00	0.50	0.30	0.18
9%	0.49	0.17	0.00	0.59	0.43	0.33
$10\frac{1}{2}$%	0.55	0.28	0.08	0.64	0.50	0.43

Note: Based on Equation (2.44), p. 30.

The nonlinearities in the reaction function are basically of two sorts. First, there is the presumption that the firm can grow at a positive rate on the basis of internal financing so that ϱ is equal to zero for a rate of growth less than the critical rate of growth g^*, necessitating resort to external funds. Second, ϱ is a linear function of σ (for a given internal financing reaction coefficient b), but this is a non-linear function of the firm's actual rate of growth. Table 2.3 illustrates several hypothetical growth rates and corresponding σ's (fraction of funds obtained externally) for a variety of different growth rates, profit rates, dividend payouts and depreciation rates.[40]

---

tive of this outcome, however, it is to be supposed for a variety of reasons that the relation between excess capacity and the observed investment response will be non-linear.

[40] Whereas the original conception underlying this table can be found in E. D. DOMAR,

While it would be pointless to discuss at great length what the table silently reveals by itself, a few observations are in order concerning the values likely to be encountered when investigating actual data for manufacturing industry. Let us pick the twenty-five year asset life as representative, although if a great deal of plant construction is involved, the thirty-five year life is better; whereas the twenty-year life should be selected for capital stock heavily weighted with equipment. Again, picking a typical dividend payout of 50 per cent, we notice that firms earning a 10 per cent profit can grow slightly in excess of 7 per cent without any external financing. Many industries can reach or exceed the 10 per cent net profit rate in boom years, but as a long-run average, 5 per cent is a more reasonable figure when it is recalled that the relevant profit rate is net income after tax divided by *gross* fixed assets.[41] However, the 10 per cent and 5 per cent rates constitute a useful bracket. With the 5 per cent profit rate, again for a 50 per cent payout, firms can grow at about a 4 per cent rate in the absence of external funds. To attain 9 per cent growth, which is a very fast rate indeed, outside funds must be sought at a 35 per cent ratio to the total of funds generated from all sources. Even with the extremely low dividend payout rate of 30 per cent, a quarter of total funds necessary to finance a 9 per cent rate of growth would have to come from external funds. By reference to this or similar tables one can visualize the demand schedule for funds as a function of the firm's rate of growth.

The internal investment model and the long-run external funds growth model are intended to be theoretical descriptions of actual behavior which can shed light on both the demand for real assets and the demand for financial resources. The relevance of these propositions, at least as working hypotheses, is limited largely to periods ranging

op. cit., the variables selected are slightly different. Domar uses as a profit rate net income after tax and depreciation divided by net fixed assets while I use the same profit numerator but gross fixed assets in the denominator. This construction is more practical for explaining gross asset growth, since the symmetrical treatment of net profit and depreciation lead to the ratio of gross retentions from net income and depreciation divided by gross fixed assets, a profit rate uninfluenced by arbitrary changes in the denominator resulting from changes in depreciation accounting methods.

[41] For all manufacturing, fourth quarter profit rates at an annual rate for the years 1954–1957 were respectively, 10%, 13%, 12%, 9%. These rates are net profit divided by book value of gross fixed assets from various copies of the SEC-FTC publication, *Quarterly Financial Report for Manufacturing Corporations*. If these had instead been gross fixed assets at replacement cost, all the rates would have been less than 10 per cent, although some high profit industries' earning rates are substantially in excess of those cited here.

from moderate decline to rapid growth. Should the economy undergo a period of large-scale, protracted decline, the relationships suggested would almost certainly be superseded by different behavior rules. Severe contractions, such as the depression of the 1930's take place most infrequently. However, in such situation, or even for 1937–38 type depressions, the consequent decline in sales and revenues can be very great, so that possibly for several years the firm is faced with large negative net profits. In such circumstances, of course, the gross demand for additions to physical capital will be small but will usually not drop to zero. How do firms react when faced with a continued reduction in their net assets because of negative profits? In particular, would the sort of dividend policy postulated by Lintner be maintained consistently?

Up to a point, the dividend relationship suggested can indeed be maintained. Because of extremely rapid liquid asset accumulation arising from reductions in accounts receivable and inventories, firms can continue to pay dividends, as occurred during the 1930's. However, the dividend relation cannot withstand such extraordinary pressures for long. Dividends will stop before the only alternative is bankruptcy. This latter possibility is the ultimate restriction on the dividend equation. It need not be effective for quite a long time because of current asset liquidation which accompanies a severe general contraction.

2.6 Macro-Economic Implications

The main intention of the present study has been to evaluate individual firm investment behavior from both an empirical and theoretical point of view. Nevertheless, the temptation to show some macroeconomic implications has been strong. To this end, one possible view of how investment and retained earnings behavior plus a few other relations affect the time path of aggregate output will be sketched out. The investment model described has properties of stability in the sense that, for any particular firm, a displacement from equilibrium will, through the simplest feedback mechanism, lead to a restoration of an equilibrium capital stock level. The behavior portrayed is essentially simple, namely that of a first order difference equation, and stands in contrast to a scheme of unstable oscillations that arise when the same objective—namely a restoration of an equilibrium capital stock—is sought through a distributed lag accelerator such as that developed by

Paul A. Samuelson and later by J. R. Hicks.[42] According to Hicks un-damped cycles would occur for a capital coefficient greater than unity (for plausible values of the marginal propensity to consume) except for restraints imposed by ceilings and floors. The difference, which can be stated in a purely formal way as being that between a stable first order or a higher order explosive system, is one of substance. The substantial question is whether or not the economy is fundamentally stable but subject to occasional and sometimes prolonged departures from equilibrium or whether it is inherently unstable.

The fact remains that substantial oscillations can be generated by a quite stable system. It may well be that authors whose constructions reflect the belief that the economy is fundamentally unstable have been led to this belief through viewing fluctuations in actual economic time series from too pessimistic a viewpoint. In the 1930's Frisch put forward the view that a stable system subject to shocks would display oscillations. More recently, the view of a stable system whose oscillations are generated by shocks of one sort or another has been advocated most persuasively by James Duesenberry,[43] whose work will be discussed in greater detail below. Suffice it to say that the exposition which follows is in accord with the Frisch, Duesenberry position. It is also similar in a number of respects to a business cycle model developed by Albert K. Ando and Franco Modigliani.[44]

In order to close out the macro economic system, it is necessary to select a consumption function. Of the eligible candidate consumption functions, among which those of Duesenberry, Modigliani and Brumberg and T. M. Brown deserve attention, the Brown equation has been selected mainly because it conforms most closely to the other equations that have been considered up to this point.[45] The equation is expressed as follows:

$$C_t = \alpha Y_t + \lambda C_{t-1}. \qquad (2.56)$$

[42] PAUL A. SAMUELSON "Interaction Between the Accelerator and Multiplier" in *Readings in Business Cycle Theory*, American Economic Association, 1944; and JOHN R. HICKS, *A Contribution to the Theory of the Trade Cycle*, Oxford, 1950.

[43] JAMES S. DUESENBERRY, *Business Cycles and Economic Growth*, 1958.

[44] A report of this can be found in "Growth, Fluctuations, and Stability," Papers and Proceedings, *American Economic Review*, Vol. XLIX, May, 1959, No. 2, pp. 501–524.

[45] J. S. DUESENBERRY, *Income, Saving and the Theory of Consumer Behavior*, 1949, T. M. Brown, "Habit Persistence and Lags in Consumer Behavior," *Econometrica*, Vol. XX (July, 1952), pp. 355–71; RICHARD BRUMBERG, in *Post Keynsian Economics* edited by K. KURIHARA, Rutgers University Press, 1954. Milton Friedman, more re-

This equation asserts that persistence in consumption patterns leads to continuation of last period's consumption plus some change dependent upon current income. Lawrence Klein has obtained statistically consistent estimates of these coefficients, with the following coefficients[46]:

$$C_t = 0.145\ Y_t + 0.849\ C_{t-1}. \tag{2.57}$$

In short, consumption is sluggish in response to current income but depends heavily upon previous consumption. The Duesenberry-Modigliani ratchet yields qualitatively similar results in most instances. Duesenberry has recently indicated that previous consumption might be preferable to peak previous income as in the earlier formulation.[47] The same interpretation can be put on this particular consumption function as upon the investment and dividend equations for corporations.

$$C_t^* = \gamma\ Y_t. \tag{2.58}$$

Specifically, if it is assumed, as in (2.58), that desired consumption is equal to some fraction of current income and that the change in consumption is some fraction d of the difference between desired and previous consumption, an exactly parallel result is obtained, according to equation (2.59).

$$\Delta C_t = d(C_t^* - C_{t-1}). \tag{2.59}$$

Using parameters from equation (2.57), γ equals about 0.90 which corresponds closely to the long-run average propensity to consume found by Kuznets and others. Equation (2.60) indicates the exact analogue between equation (2.56) and the adjustments form of consumer behavior portrayed by equation (2.59).

$$C_t = d\gamma Y_t + (1 - d)C_{t-1}. \tag{2.60}$$

With a consumption function in hand, it is a simple matter to pro-

---

cently, has also advocated this particular function. See MILTON FRIEDMAN, *A Theory of the Consumption Function*, Princeton, N.J., 1957. A detailed review of interesting implications of this consumption function which we cannot go into here will be found in LAWRENCE R. KLEIN, "The Friedman-Becker Illusion," *The Journal of Political Economy*, Vol. 66, No. 6, December, 1958, pp. 539–545.

[46] LAWRENCE R. KLEIN, *op cit.*, Equation 12, p. 542.

[47] JAMES S. DUESENBERRY, *Business Cycles and Economic Growth*, New York, 1958, pp. 177–178.

duce the three basic equations which determine a simplified macro system. Among other simplifications, government outlays and taxes have been excluded. Equations (2.61), (2.62), and (2.63) portray savings, retained earnings and net investment. The last two equations have been derived previously while the first was obtained by identical operations. The equilibrium condition of equation (2.64) is the standard one that *ex ante* saving must equal *ex ante* investment.

$$S_t = (1 - d\gamma)(Y_t - R_t) - d\gamma \sum_{T=1}^{t-1} (1 - d)^{t-T}(Y_T - R_T) \qquad (2.61)$$

$$R_t = (1 - cr)\alpha Y_t - cr \alpha \sum_{T=1}^{t-1} (1 - c)^{t-T} Y_T \qquad (2.62)$$

$$\Delta K_t = b'\beta Y_t - b'^2\beta \sum_{T=1}^{t-1} (1 - b')^{t-T} Y_T \qquad (2.63)$$

$$S_t + R_t = \Delta K_t. \qquad (2.64)$$

This portrayal of endogenous response cannot, of course, pretend to be a complete explanation of behavior since no exogenous variables have been included. Shortly, two types of exogenous forces will be considered that might be imposed on this system, autonomous growth and random shocks. Until then, (2.61)–(2.63) should be taken to represent deviations from an equilibrium level determined by the autonomous functions. While these equations were derived on the assumption that Y_t is exogenous, the solutions obtained in this manner can be viewed as intermediate solutions when the three behavioral equations are related through the equilibrium condition of equation (2.64), leading to a final homogeneous equation. Then the true exogenous factors, population or exogenous shocks, for instance, must be introduced to obtain a complete particular solution.

When R_t and R_T are inserted into (2.61), the saving function, after some algebra, can be rewritten as:

$$S_t = (1 - d\gamma) cr\alpha Y_t + \sum_{T=1}^{t-1} \left\{ \left[(1 - d\gamma)cr\alpha - \frac{(1 - d)d\gamma}{c - d} \right] (1 - c)^{t-T} + \right.$$
$$\left. + \left[\frac{d\gamma(1 - c)}{c - d} \right] (1 - d)^{t-T} \right\} Y_T. \qquad (2.61a)$$

Thus, the equilibrium conditions (now expressed wholly in terms of Y_t)

can be determined by equating coefficients of current and lagged income variables, much as for equations (2.29)–(2.31). Note that no solution exists if the two saving function reaction coefficients are equal.

$$(1 - d\gamma)\, cr\alpha = b'\beta \qquad (2.65)$$

$$\left[(1 - d\gamma)\, cr\alpha - \frac{(1 - d)d\gamma}{c - d}\right](1 - c) +$$
$$+ \left[\frac{d\gamma(1 - c)}{c - d}\right](1 - d) = b'^2\beta\,(1 - b'.) \qquad (2.66)$$

These two equations, with parameters α, β and γ are insufficient to determine the four unknowns—b', c, d and r. Even if the reaction coefficient for consumers were treated as independently determined, one too few equations is available to establish the equilibrium values among the business sector parameters. However, if the long-run dividend payout too was determined outside the immediate framework of analysis, (2.65) and (2.66) could then be solved for the dividend reaction coefficient and the investment reaction coefficient. From this cursory examination, it can be seen that there is a substantial possibility of inequality between *ex ante* savings and investment in this type of model.

The simplest case of all arises when retained earnings are zero and the equilibrium condition is personal saving (= total saving) equals investment. Then equating coefficients as before leads to:

$$1 - d\gamma = b'\beta \qquad (2.67)$$
$$d\gamma = b'^2\beta \qquad (2.68)$$
$$1 - b' = 1 - d \qquad (2.69)$$

The relation of corporate saving to the attainable rate of growth can be indicated by means of equation (2.44), here reproduced as equation (2.70). As before, to use equation (2.70), the average profit rate and the average actual dividend payout will be treated as known parameters.

$$1 = v\left[(1 - r')p + \frac{1}{m}\right] + \sigma \qquad (2.70)$$

Equation (2.70) is an implicit equation in the actually obtainable rate of growth. The fraction of external funds used for all purposes in the corporate sector for the period 1946–57 was 0.32. For the entire economy, Fabricant estimated the longevity of equipment to be about 35 years.[48] Referring back to Table 2.3 for the 35 year asset life category and assuming a dividend payout of 50 per cent, the implied rate of growth with 30 per cent external funds corresponds to 7 per cent. The average annual geometric rate of increase in corporate product for this period is about 8 per cent. There is thus fairly close correspondence so far as the *ex-post* figures are concerned.[49]

This section has brought together certain formal relations that were developed primarily for the micro model, in order to see how the parameters of these micro equations, when treated as macro equations, should be related in order to generate a stable level of income or a steady rate of income growth. Since the equations are first order, it is not possible to generate oscillations internally. However, when the equilibrium conditions are not satisfied in the sense that *ex ante* saving is unequal to *ex ante* investment or, to put the matter more precisely, when the coefficients are not compatible with this condition, the differences between savings and investment can generate oscillations in income. To insist on this point is not to assert that lags and delays in higher order difference terms are irrelevant or unimportant, but it is to emphasize that differences in speeds of adjustment by themselves are sufficient to cause fluctuations in the level of output. If some or all of the three equations are subject to random disturbances the actual discrepancies can generate cycles in exactly the manner that a damped first order system subject to random perturbations will generate fluctuating time series with quasi-cyclical characteristics. The stochastic implications of the Klein-Goldberger model investigated by Irma Adelman further strengthen support for this position.[50]

---

[48] SOLOMON FABRICANT, *Capital Consumption and Adjustment*, New York, 1938, p. 34. The figures derived from the grand total for 1934 using gross capital assets, i.e., it is the reciprocal of depreciation and depletion as a per cent of gross fixed assets in 1934.

[49] Corporate product is to be found in U.S. Department of Commerce, Office of Business Economics, *U.S. Income and Output*, a supplement to the *Survey of Current Business*, Washington, D.C., 1958, Table I–14, pp. 136–37. The growth rates were taken from the first quarter of 1946 and the third quarter of 1957 for "Income Originating in Corporate Business." The average fraction of external funds was obtained from Table V-10, p. 195 by averaging the ratio of external funds to total sources for the years 1946–57. Of course, the figures showed year-to-year variation and a somewhat different figure would have been obtained if we had instead taken the ratio of total external funds for the period total sources. The ratio would have been slightly larger than that actually used.

[50] IRMA ADELMAN, "Business Cycles—Endogenous or Stochastic?", *Economic Journal*, Vol. 70, No. 280, December, 1960.

Among the many oversimplifications, the assumption of a single investment function requires further comment. At a minimum, there should be different rates of reaction for inventories, equipment, structures, and housing. In general, reaction coefficients for inventories will exceed plant and equipment reactions. In one of the most complete studies of inventory behavior in manufacturing, Michael Lovell found an overall estimated reaction coefficient to be 0.46.[51] Highly durable goods such as housing probably have lower reaction coefficients than those relating to plant and equipment. One can thus conceive of a weighted average aggregate reaction coefficient in which the weights are the fraction of national income produced by the particular income producing sector. A sensible business cycle model which used this particular approach would have to supply an equation for each of these sectors leading to simultaneous first order difference equations in capital stock, or if an aggregate model were to be used, the reaction coefficient would vary over the cycle.

While possibly some analytical insights can be gained in ways suggested above, and I believe a few such can be found, major advances in business cycle research are more likely to come from detailed sector analyses that are more complex than this relatively simplified structure.

2.7. Recent Investment Theories

A. Duesenberry

A recent book on business cycles by Duesenberry advances an investment theory similar in numerous respects to Sections 2 and 3 of this chapter. A useful way to approach Duesenberry's theory will be to rely on some of his more fundamental behavioral propositions as support for certain plausible propositions which were presented without probing motivation to the same extent. As with my hypothesis, Duesenberry believes that "The primary determinant of the level of the marginal efficiency schedule (for investment in existing product lines) is the ratio of capital stock to a measure of demand."[52]

---

[51] MICHAEL LOVELL, "Manufacturers Inventories, Sales Expectations, and the Acceleration Principle," *Econometrica*, pp. 293–314, July, 1961. Our own results for fixed plant and equipment suggest that for manufacturing the total reaction coefficient is roughly equal to 0.15 (this is obtained by using the internal reaction coefficient of 0.09 and the external financing reaction coefficient from (2.52) where we have taken $\sigma = 0.32$).

[52] JAMES S. DUESENBERRY, *Business Cycles and Economic Growth*, New York,

Duesenberry departs fairly sharply from the formal mode of presentation of my argument by developing a more elaborate picture of the individual firm's cost-of-capital schedule. One conclusion of his argument is that the imputed capital costs for depreciation and retained earnings sources are relatively low and, as in our case, he too accepts the Lintner hypothesis as correctly describing the availability of retained earnings. Further increments in capital supply to the firm are acquired only at increasing rates. Duesenberry visualizes the initial segment of the firm's cost-of-capital schedule as fairly flat for the portion generated by depreciation and retained earnings. Next, the cost curve corresponding to debt financing rises slowly at first and then steeply later on. The terminal financial source, new external equity, is approached by a steep rise (since equity funds are typically more expensive than debt) and then equity costs tend to level off. Because of the relatively sharply rising segment of the cost-of-capital schedule associated with debt, Duesenberry asserts that "in periods of high prosperity many firms will be operating in the inelastic range of their supply-of-funds schedule. As long as they do so, limited variations in the marginal-efficiency-of-investment schedule, whether due to expectations or other factors, will have little influence on the rate of investment."[53]

Hence, even if the marginal-efficiency-of-capital schedule is highly returns-elastic (which Duesenberry argues to be the case), variations in the cost of funds will have small effect on the firm's rate of investment because, the marginal efficiency schedule is "trapped" in the steeply rising range of the firm's cost-of-capital schedule. This provides a rationalization for paying slight attention to capital costs, which Duesenberry quite rightly shows to be very different from market rates of interest.

Duesenberry suggests that certain imputed costs affect the costs of capital funds to firms beyond observable bond yields. These further opportunity costs are related to the increased variability of earnings

1958, p. 110. He also adds that "it will also be influenced by expectational factors, some of which are themselves influenced by the pattern of past movements of income. Prices of capital goods, and other outputs, and rates of technical change will also be influential."

[53] DUESENBERRY, *ibid.*, p. 111. To view different types of external funds as having different costs is questionable, since it is clearly within the capability of the firm to "mix" external funds to achieve the cheapest combination. However, prior remarks indicate agreement with the discontinuity or "trap" proposition at the individual firm level.

per share on common equity when the firms's financial structure is heavily debt laden, and default risk which increases as the ratio of debt to equity (and to earnings) increases. Also, a good measure of equity cost of capital is the relation between (expected) earnings and market price. These concepts are compatible with my formulation, although the principal emphasis here is on the extent to which the demand curve shifts relative to the supply curve, rather than the cost of funds. Firms will invest internally, which will be done at a rate which depends upon profit margins and capital requirements for demand curves shifting rightward. But for rapid rates of growth, external funds must be used. The cost of these funds will vary, of course.[54]

Looking at a growing firm, one can conceive of the demand schedule shifting rightward at a given per cent per annum rate while at the same time the supply schedule will be shifting rightward, to the extent that additional depreciation and retained earnings become available as a result of increased demand and the growing capital stock. Hence, the more inelastic the supply schedule of funds, the less will be the actual rate of growth. What is most important, however, is that *the relation between demand growth and investment will be relatively invariant if the demand and supply curve shift rightward at the same rate.* This Duesenberry believes will often be the case. "During a period of income growth the whole supply schedule slowly shifts to the right. At the same time a firm which increases its real assets in proportion to demand will have a marginal efficiency schedule which stays at about the same level for zero investment and slowly shifts rightward (or flattens out) as the scale of the firm grows. In this case, the firm will continue to operate within a segment of the cost-of-capital curve having the same elasticity."[55]

A second point at which, qualitatively at least, my theory agrees with Duesenberry's concerns what he describes as "backlogging." "If income rises very rapidly (with business savings fixed), investment will be held back by the rising cost of obtaining funds. The size of the resulting backlog will vary with the rate of increase of income.[56] But this is exactly what happens in the capacity models employed here, up to the point that the firm resorts to substantial outside funds in order to keep the backlog from becoming excessive. That is, the larger the

[54] A capital cost function embodying debt-equity considerations in an optimizing model will be found in my article, "Capital Theory and Capital Budgeting," *Metroeconomica*, December, 1960.

[55] DUESENBERRY, *op. cit.*, p. 97.

[56] *Ibid.*, p. 45–46.

increase in demand, the larger will be both investment and backlog. Thus the *total* effect will be a larger backlog as Duesenberry puts it, and simultaneously, larger investment. It is precisely at the stage where this backlog becomes "too great" that firms resort to external funds. There should be and, according to my hypothesis, is a limit beyond which the backlog will not be permitted to go because of the implied profits foregone by not investing.

A third point at which the two hypotheses overlap is in postulated behavior of profits over the business cycle. While I have hypothesized either a constant profit margin on sales or a linear profit function (as a function of sales), Duesenberry suggests that "we usually expect the ratio of both net and gross profits to invested capital will decline as capacity utilization declines."[57] This will happen to firms whose profits behave in a manner consistent with that postulated in section 2.3. Even with a constant margin on sales, the ratio of profits to capital will decline, if the level of sales falls relative to the capital stock (exactly the same thing as a decline in capacity utilization). Thus, "We can assume that whenever the firms in an industry increase capacity at a rate faster than the rate of growth of demand, the rate of return on capital will fall, and conversely."[58]

Finally, Duesenberry's examination of entrepreneurial motives lends additional support to some of the propositions advanced earlier in this chapter. The influence of market share rivalry on investment behavior has been extensively treated by Duesenberry as well as in the Meyer-Kuh book. He demonstrates that firms have every incentive to maintain market shares because of the following asymmetry: it is much easier for a firm to hold onto a given market share than it is to regain a share, once lost. During periods of rapid expansion, therefore, individual firms in an oligopolistic industry will tend to respond rapidly to capacity pressures in order both to maintain their prices (which they could not do profitably if their marginal costs were rising extremely rapidly in the period of full or overfull utilization) through the expansion of capacity.

B. Chenery

A principal objective of Chenery's model, deliberately overlooked to this point in order to show the common basis of Chenery's model

---

[57] DUESENBERRY, *op. cit.*, p. 102.
[58] *Ibid.*, p. 102.

with other capacity models, is to relate scale economy effects to the investment process. On certain quite plausible assumptions, which will not detain us here, Chenery shows that the greater scale economies that there are, the further ahead does it pay firms to invest. Thus firms will ordinarily carry excess capacity in amounts which will be larger the greater are the potential scale economies. To allow for the usual rate of excess capacity because of as yet unexploited scale economies, Chenery modifies the basic investment equation by inserting the factor λ, which he terms the "capacity factor," before the beginning of period capital stock.

$$I_t = b(\beta X_t - \lambda K_{t-1}). \tag{2.71}$$

As Chenery puts it, "If demand increases at a constant relative rate (instead of the constant absolute rate used for simplicity before), the optimum degree of overcapacity will be a constant proportion $(1 - \lambda)$ of total capacity."[59] Elsewhere in the article Chenery indicates that excess capacity will also be maintained in order to meet cyclical peak demand loads.

C. Modigliani

Recent work by Franco Modigliani on investment behavior has provided certain elaborations and amplifications on the basic model which deserve some comment. One of Modigliani's most pertinent findings or aggregative business cycle models is that, in contrast to acceleration models of the Hicks variety, the units of time measurement have been eliminated from their important analytical position. To quote Modigliani, "Now, in the models based on the acceleration principle, the value of the acceleration coefficient typically turns out to play a critical role in determining whether the time path of aggregate output will be damped or explosive. It would appear therefore that the stability implications of a given model can be changed by the purely formal trick of changing the choice of the time unit. Once we introduce our "speed of adjustment" coefficient, this disturbing possibility tends to disappear in that the stability of the system will generally depend on the product of this coefficient and the conventional acceleration coefficient and this product is *independent* of the choice of time unit (since the speed of adjustment has dimension 1/time)."[60]

[59] CHENERY, *op. cit.*, p. 15.
[60] FRANCO MODIGLIANI, Comment on "Capacity Utilization, and the Acceleration

2.8 Statistical Tests of Capacity and Profit Models

Several empirical tests of capacity principle formulations have been attempted. The earliest explicit test of the capacity principle, by Alan Manne, showed that a relative capacity utilization hypothesis explained the demand for railway freight cars much better than the naive form of the acceleration principle.[61] In 1952 Hollis Chenery found that the capacity formulation proved superior to the naive accelerator in four out of six industries tested. These tests were conducted on annual physical capacity data during the inter-war period for electric power, steel, portland cement, zinc, petroleum refining and paper and paperboard. More recently, and in the theoretical framework described earlier, Koyck applied his hypothesis to many of the same industries as Chenery. In most cases the fit was good and the empirically estimated coefficients had plausible magnitudes. A summary of the Chenery and Manne tests is in the appendix to Chapter II of Meyer and Kuh.

One recent, extensive empirical testing is that of Kisselgoff and Modigliani.[62] Kisselgoff and Modigliani are among the first to evaluate the influence of financial considerations with primary interest in the capacity principle. They did so by including profits and interest rates in their estimating equations. While their findings were not unambiguous, it appeared that financial considerations were relevant although possibly of secondary importance. As the authors suggest, the particular nature of the electric power industry would lead one to believe that capacity considerations would be paramount since the utilities are virtually guaranteed a minimum profit rate. This study was among the most complete and at the same time made further empirical refinements by explicitly taking into account both the irreversibility

Principle" by BERT G. HICKMAN, in *Problems of Capital Formation, Studies in Income and Wealth*, Vol. 19, by the Conference in Research and Wealth, Princeton, 1957, p. 457. Illustration of the influence of time units on stability are contained in HANS BREMS, "How Induced is Induced Investment?," *The Review of Economics and Statistics*, Vol. 37, No. 3, August, 1955, pp. 267–278.

[61] ALAN, S. MANNE, "Some Notes on the Acceleration Principle," *The Review of Economics and Statistics*, Vol. 27, pp. 93–99, May, 1945.

[62] AVRAM KISSELGOFF and FRANCO MODIGLIANI, "Private Investment in the Electric Power Industry and the Acceleration Principle," *The Review of Economics and Statistics* Vol. 39, No. 4, November, 1957, pp. 363–379. ROBERT EISNER, "A Distributed Lag Investment Function," *Econometrica*, Vol. 28, No. 1, January, 1960, pp. 1–29 estimates cross-section accelerator functions along with profits and finds profits are "knocked out" by the lagged (deflated) change in sales variables. The value of this result is low because of questionable industry aggregation procedure.

factor and the influence of gestation lags on decision making, the latter being of particular importance in electric power generation.

Finally, the Meyer-Kuh study considered both profit effects and capacity influences. The principal findings were these: during the years of extremely rapid growth in demand, 1946 and 1947, the relative capacity utilization (or capital requirements) variable dominated investment rates, whereas in the years of decline or moderate growth, 1949 and 1950, liquidity flow variables, like profits and sales, were much more closely correlated with the rate of investment. In the intervening years, or years of transition, usually 1948 (but 1947 and 1949 for some industries), the transition from capacity dominated investment to a profit orientation was largely brought about by changes in the profit rate. In the long run, or average data models of investment behavior, it was found that the capacity and sales variables were of the greatest importance. From this it was concluded that although short-run behavior might reflect either predominantly profit or capacity influences depending upon the rate of growth and levels of liquidity flows, in the long run it was a capacity oriented model which most accurately reflected entrepreneurial action. It should be observed that the Meyer-Kuh study used cross-section evidence for a large number of firms in fifteen different industries whereas all the other studies mentioned used industry aggregates and time series, so these results are based on disparate data types.

2.9 Expectations and Autonomous Investment

Summarization of the two main theories described in this chapter, the first relating cyclical investment to internal finance, the second long term growth to external finance, leaves a number of matters unexplored. First of all, what about autonomous outlays, such as those associated with innovations in the broad sense (most closely associated with Professor Schumpeter's writings), or arising from secular growth elements such as population growth or, last, the Hicks concept of an investment that "is only expected to pay for itself over a long period."[63] The relevance of such investment is undoubtedly great for explanation of secular developments, but for shorter periods further questions must be asked. As a preliminary point, it seems reasonable to suppose that long-range investments will be little affected by small changes in

[63] HICKS, *Trade Cycle*, p. 59.

recent data in output or other key variables such as profits or sales. For large changes the situation is likely to be very different. That is, current investment plans are likely to be invariant with respect to current changes in the determining variables within discrete intervals. In general, for each investment, there are certain ranges within which current variables may fluctuate without disturbing plans to undertake the investment, because fluctuations are expected and therefore already allowed for in the initial set of calculations. Once the variable goes outside these bounds on the downward side, the project will be halted. Those for which the normal range is small will, strictly speaking, be induced investment. At the other extreme, those that are based on a very broad permissible range of fluctuation can rightly be called autonomous, if we are to avoid the meaningless semantic quibble that on the view presented here, all investments are induced.

The tentative description of behavior could formally be approximated by either non-linear forms or a distributed lag. The more important are current relative to prior values of sales, the more concentrated is the lag and *vice versa*. Alternatively, changes in sales will have a proportionally greater effect for larger changes in sales in the non-linear case according to the behavior hypothesis suggested.

Buried just below the surface of most investment theories is that analytically intractable and highly important fact of life, technical change. The measurement of technical change is, for obvious reasons, a most difficult chore.[64] Its treatment is therefore ordinarily relegated to a subsidiary role. Does the omission of explicit treatment of technical change destroy the usefulness of the investment theories that are considered? The answer to this question depends in large measure on the purpose to which the theory is to be put. For an industry in the process of large-scale technical change, predictions based upon the standard, more easily measured variables will clearly be wrong by wide margins. The expectations upon which entrepreneur's actions are based are quite independent of the current or readily extrapolated position of the firm with respect to either profits or capacity utilization rates. At any one time, few firms face this situation. In general, we can conceive of the profitability from innovation at a point of time as possessing a highly skewed frequency distribution. Thus, the technical opportunities facing a firm in a given year will ordinarily consist of a large num-

[64] The problem has been exhaustively treated in EVSEY D. DOMAR, "On the Measurement of Technological Change." *Economic Journal*, Dec., 1961, Vol. 71, pp. 209–29.

ber of technical changes with a small net marginal profitability and comparatively few advantageous possibilities with large yields. In most industries, then, the intra-marginal potential innovation will yield a return not far different from the marginal technologically originating investment opportunity. For much of macro economics, innovation is critically important. As Schumpeter so aptly described certain aspects of the process, the innovation which of itself might be unsubstantial can have widespread repercussions throughout the rest of the economy. The effect, however, will be transmitted through the response mechanism of induced investment theories of the sort described above. Hence, when we leave technical change out of consideration, its importance for the economy or in many cases for the individual firm is not to be denied. We are recognizing the difficulty of treating it simultaneously with the other variables and at the same time believe that its exclusion need not seriously interfere with the theoretical usefulness or empirical applicability of induced investment models.

Subsequent statistical results will be interpreted in light of the two theories described. Can the short run profit, capacity theories and long run capacity, growth theory, or combinations of them, successfully capture the essentials of business behavior? Any casual student of business cycles or everyday managerial deeds cannot help being impressed by an overabundance of forces and intricate motivations, far more than we have begun to consider here. Some of these excluded categories are, however, largely irrelevant, either because they are quantitatively unimportant or only important in other contexts. A favorite variable, liquid assets, appears to be quantitatively unimportant, not because liquidity is unimportant but because liquidity stocks are usually quickly adjusted when they start to depart sharply from desired levels, by the acquisition of other assets or other disbursements, such as dividends. Hence the major source of liquidity stock change, profits, is correlated with investment (a stock change) not the stock itself. In any event, empirical results of Lawrence Klein and Meyer and Kuh show liquidity having remarkably little effect on investment. Second, a number of significant factors of a primarily cross-section (time invariant) nature like firm size, industry, etc., played an important role in the Meyer-Kuh investigation. These are deliberately ignored in the present study whose aim is to specify time series behavior and to investigate cross-sections only for the purpose of illuminating time series behavior.

While some of these qualifications can be legitimately shoved aside, it would be both immodest and wrong to claim that these theories are above reproach. Indeed, much of the remainder of this study will be a stream of reproaches.

CHAPTER 3

SAMPLE ORIGINS AND REGRESSION MODELS

3.1 Introduction

This chapter deals with four closely related quantitative elements. The first describes how individual firms were selected. Second, construction of the basic variable and price corrections will be explained. Third, the combination of these variables in different functional forms, according to the dictates of both economic and statistical reasoning, will be presented. The concluding section sketches out the main aspects of the economic environment in which manufacturing firms operated from 1935 to 1956.

3.2 Selection of Sample Firms

Since much policy interest focuses on the capital goods producing industries, at the very beginning of this study the arbitrary decision was taken to restrict attention to this group. While expansion of industrial coverage would be desirable to permit inter-industrial comparisons, even the costs of this single sample were considerable. Furthermore, a major methodological interest is in inter-firm comparisons.

Stringent requirements were placed on the information contained in firm balance sheets and income statements, so stringent in fact, that of several hundred firms that were considered for inclusion in the sample on the basis of industry alone, only 60 ultimately could meet all the conditions. First and most important of all, the key variables for each firm had to possess a continuous record from the beginning year, 1935, until the last sample year, 1955. Second, because firms do not typically present the accounting information about capital gains and losses and expensing of capital items that would be essential to obtain a reasonably accurate gross investment figure from published accounting records, the sample was restricted to firms registered with the Securities and Exchange Commission, which began to collect such information in 1934. Since many firms did not file a report with the Securities and Exchange Commission in its first year of operation, the initial sample year was advanced to 1935. Much of the remaining supporting data came from balance sheets and income statements shown in *Moody's Industrials*, although individual entries for many firms were missing which required delving into the Securities and Exchange Commission records for publicly undisclosed information.

The third requirement, that firms in the sample could not be parties to mergers destructive of their identity, caused the loss of many firms that were otherwise eligible. Firms that bought out or merged others into themselves were left in the sample however. Hardly a firm exists of any appreciable size that was not involved in some merger. Fourth, about a dozen firms were eliminated from the sample because of their extreme size. All firms with gross fixed assets in excess of 120 million dollars in 1953 were removed from the sample, which meant that General Electric, Westinghouse and most of the large steel producers were excluded.

Even though the largest firms do not appear, the possibility remains that some of the firms retained would cause biased estimates of variance ratios, or inefficient estimates of regression coefficients when their inclusion caused unequal error variances in regression equations, an effect termed heteroscedasticity. Of the remaining sixty-five firms considered for inclusion in the study, five were eliminated after a test statistic indicated error variance heterogeneity.[1]

What sort of sample remains? According to Table 3.1 the final sixty firms, all capital goods producers, are small and middle sized, two-thirds having 1955 gross fixed assets worth less than $30 million, measured in 1953 prices. Within the S.E.C. list these firms are a selected group too. They are likely to be the more stable firms and because big mergers were excluded, the least dynamic. The complete list of firms appears in the appendix to this chapter.

This selection process excludes very small firms, the very active firms engaged in aggrandizement through merger, as well as the largest firms. While for many purposes these limitations would badly distort analysis of industrial firm behavior (for instance in an analysis of oligopolistic behavior or any study of long-run market adjustment), no

---

[1] The test statistic devised by H. A. David is described in Section 3, Chapter 4.

major damage has been done to our present restricted list of objectives. The sample restrictions are independent of one major purpose, the measurement of various parameters of firm behavior, and the implications of such measurement for certain prediction problems. A final point on the constitution of the sample should be noted: no absolutely or relatively large isolated sample values were made the basis for rejecting a firm.

TABLE 3.1

Relative Frequency Distribution of Gross Fixed Assets For 60 Sample Firms

Gross Fixed Assets	Relative Frequencies		
in $ millions[1]	1935	1947	1955
0–5	23%	12%	7%
5–10	32	25	18
10–15	13	15	12
15–20	10	10	15
20–25	2	13	8
25–30	5	3	10
30–35	2	3	3
35–40	2	3	3
40–45	3	5	2
45–50	2	3	3
50–55	2	3	3
55–60	3	0	3
60–105	2	3	12
Total[2]	101	98	99

[1] In 1953 constant dollars.
[2] Totals do not add to 100% because of rounding errors.

3.3 Variables and Price Deflation

A. *Variables: Definitions and Content*

Only' five basic variables will be used subsequently. However, these will appear in different combinations, in different functional forms, and with several transformations of variables so that the actual number of estimated regression equations far exceeds the plausible number of relations implied by five basic variables.

The dependent variable will be dollars of gross investment in plant and equipment corrected for price changes. As mentioned above, the investment figures are obtained from Form 10K reports of companies registered with the Securities and Exchange Commission. The accounting and definitional difficulties of this variable are well known. Normal tax procedures require that these assets must have an expected life of more than a year to be capitalized and hence to be considered as gross investment. Durable assets which are consumed more quickly are often charged directly through expense accounts and never capitalized. Hence, it is economic life expectancy rather than physical characteristics which determines whether or not a durable good is considered an investment outlay. This definition corresponds fairly closely to the economists' definition of gross investment and also to the firm's capital budgeting procedures in many instances.

Price corrected sales is one of the key independent variables. A question which naturally arises in this connection is whether output rather than sales would be the more appropriate explanatory variable. The difference between the two by definition is the changes in finished goods inventory. Over short periods the difference between production and sales can be large. On the other hand, for periods of a year or longer the change in finished goods inventory will typically be small relative to sales level. For many purposes nevertheless, output ought to have been selected as the appropriate index of the relation of production decisions to capacity. On the other hand, the desire to find an empirically valid functional relation between sales and profits leads us in the reverse direction; sales would be the theoretically preferred variable since profits are measured at time of sale, not production. Short of adjusting the sales figure for inventory change when data on change in finished goods inventory data were available, a process fraught with error, the most accurate available information, sales, has been used in this study.

The second important independent variable is a measure of gross retained earnings, also corrected for price level changes. This variable is equal to net income after taxes plus the current year charge to depreciation minus cash dividends. To get an accurate appraisal of increase in funds, other non-cash charges such as capital losses or capital gains should be taken into account. Because of erratic differences in accounting procedures among firms, this particular adjustment to the estimated cash flow was not made. However, there are two aspects of the sample which tend to minimize the impact of neglecting these practices. First, since the initial sample year is 1935, most major readjustments in the firms' capital accounts, which would often appear as a capital loss when the entry was made through the income statement, were completed. Most large scale revisions occurred in the years of greatest economic desperation, 1930–1934. The business cycle trough was in 1933 so

that by 1935 relatively few firms were inclined to undertake such drastic accounting action as occurred during the crisis years. A second
procedure that guards against adverse effects neglecting "capital loss"
is the close inspection of the firm's property accounts. When changes in
a property account could not reasonably be accounted for by merger,
gross investment outlays, and retirements, firms were excluded from
the sample. If firms indulged in dubious capital accounting practices,
it was assumed that their records were sufficiently unreliable to counsel
total elimination. This gross retention or gross internal profit variable
measures additional funds available to the firm as a result of the year's
operations, less dividend payments. Liquidity flow hypotheses of investment behavior have received support in previous empirical tests,
particularly those by Klein, and Meyer and myself. The decision was
made to evaluate this hypothesis most directly, in the manner portrayed by this particular variable.

The firms's gross capital stock, also corrected for price level changes,
is the third key independent variable. In estimating a firm's capital
stock, the choice must be made between gross or net property account.
Since depreciation represents the "using up" of capital on one widely
accepted definition, it can be argued that the depreciated capital stock
most correctly represents the firm's current stock of assets. Theoretical
considerations as well as practical accounting difficulties weigh the
scales heavily against this proposition, reasonable as it may first appear.
First, our concern is with capacity in place rather than the unexhausted
economic value of the firm's fixed assets. Intensive maintenance policies
on the part of the firm ordinarily make it possible to maintain productive capacity of a given gross capital stock whose net value appropriately measured by a given depreciation method might be negligible.[2]
Second, the inadequacy of existing accounting techniques further
reinforces the conceptual reason just noted. In particular, the choice of
the accounting methods is often arbitrary. Granting that the estimated
economic lifetime of an asset is correct, the manner in which the depreciation ought to be spread over the asset life remains in dispute at
both theoretical and applied levels. Inter-firm comparisons can be
severely distorted if differences in capital size or changes in capital

---

[2] T. HAAVELMO, *A Study in the Theory of Investment*, 1960, has a perceptive and
interesting discussion on appropriate definitions that go far beyond these casual
observations. Also see Z. GRILICHES, "The Demand for Farm Tractors," in ARNOLD
C. HARBERGER, Editor, *The Demand for Durable Goods*, 1960, for a good discussion of
some points raised here.

stock were attributable to alternative depreciation policies. Gross capital stock was therefore selected to avoid such erratic bookkeeping effects from damaging subsequent estimates.

A similar decision was made in computing capital coefficients for the Leontief Dynamic Model at the Harvard Economic Research Project. Professor Leontief summarizes the position with these remarks:

> "Recent information indicates that the undepreciated coefficients correspond much more closely to the incremental coefficients than do the depreciated ones. Use of the depreciated coefficients implies that capital stocks decrease in efficiency in exact relation to the depreciation charge. Most available evidence indicates that this is not a reliable assumption. Use of the undepreciated coefficients implies that capital stocks have a constant efficiency from the time of purchase until the time they are fully written off, when their usefulness is assumed to be zero. Both methods are dependent upon accounting procedures, both fail to take account of technological change, and both present an index number problem for the reduction of stock of capital accumulated over time."[3]

The capacity-acceleration models described in the previous chapter implicitly assume that marginal and average capital coefficients are similar, while Leontief quite rightly makes the more general assumption that marginal and average coefficients are likely to differ because of technological change and/or scale effects. It is therefore a useful finding for our purposes that the average undepreciated capital coefficient most closely approximates the incremental capital coefficient.[4]

The firm's capital stock plays an important part both in profit and acceleration investment theories. In profit theories, the capital stock influences the firm's profit rate, as can be most easily seen when profits per annum are divided by the firm's capital stock. It could also be considered as a shift variable in the investment demand function so that as the firm's capital stock increases, less would be invested for a given cash flow because of the diminishing marginal efficiency of capital. This particular interpretation is not a strong one in the context of liquidity flow theories which stress rationing effects, imposed either by the loan market or by firms restricting themselves to internal funds. When there is an unexhausted supply of profitable investment opportunities due to either type of rationing mentioned, the declining mar-

---

[3] Harvard Economic Research Project, *Estimates of the Capital Stock of American Industries*, 1947, Cambridge, June, 1953, pp. 21–22.

[4] The incremental capital coefficients referred to are based upon technological information contained in war-time certificates of necessity reported by ROBERT GROSSE in the article, "The Structure of Capital" which appeared in *Studies in the Structure of the American Economy*, by W. W. LEONTIEF and others, New York, 1953, pp. 185–242.

ginal efficiency influence would be negligible. The capital stock enters into the capacity-acceleration models in ways that were extensively explored in the previous chapter. A full description of complex price correction process for the capital stock will be deferred until a subsequent section of this chapter on price indices.

The last independent variable appears only in the cross-section regression equations, as a measure of inter-firm differences in capital intensity. The ratios of sales to capital stock, both variables price corrected, were averaged for years of peak or high level activity as measured by aggregative indexes, in particular the years 1937, 1940, 1941, 1948, 1951 and 1952. This variable, which is an approximation to a reciprocal capital coefficient, i.e., a measure of desired output or sales and capital stock relations, will clearly be subject to errors of observation. By relying on aggregate measured years of high activity, the potentially serious upward bias arising from the selection of individual peak years, firm by firm, was avoided. It proved necessary to average a large number of years since firms reach their peak "economic" capacity utilization rates at different times. For example, even though 1948 was a peak year for a great many firms, many others were operating below capacity because of either materials shortages or a temporary adverse occurrence. By averaging a large number of peak years including some pre-war when there was undoubtedly some excess capacity, and post-war years when there was deficient capacity in some years, it is hoped that an accurate economic full utilization rate will have been measured. Years of extraordinary activity such as 1947 and 1950, both of which were strongly war-influenced have been excluded so that uneconomic peacetime utilization of capacity would not bias the measure. For some firms the final measure might be as low as unity (e.g., a steel producer), a typical value for the more capital intensive firms, while for other firms (e.g., a metal fabricator) using relatively much less capital, the measure of sales to fixed assets might be as high as five or six. Of course, the degree of integration will affect the range of values that we observe for an estimate such as this. Quite clearly though, if two firms are utilizing their facilities fully, the firm with a capital intensity measure of 6 or 7 is less capital intensive than the one with a value of unity.

B. *Price Indexes: General Purpose Price Deflator*

Except for the capital stock which required special deflating procedures, the basic variables, investment, sales, gross retained profits, (and also the capital intensity measure numerator) were converted into constant 1953 dollars by the Department of Commerce National Income implicit price deflators for producers durable equipment and non-residential construction.[5]

The basic indexes were prepared by the Department of Commerce for comparatively fine sub-divisions of the categories "equipment" and "other non-residential construction". The Department of Commerce used fixed value-added weights based upon the 1939 census to combine the sub-sector indices for the years 1939 and all previous years. Fixed value weights were also used from 1947 onward, derived from the 1947 and 1948 Census of Manufactures. In the intervening years (1940–1946), weights were interpolated linearly between the two benchmark dates. The two implicit price indexes, which were extracted from the aggregate categories, have been combined by using current value weights for the corresponding categories for purposes of this study. The index was shifted to a 1953 base. Final results appear in Table 3.2.[6]

This price deflator was used to correct for variations in the absolute price level, not to measure relative price changes. Since these firms produce capital goods, it seemed both feasible and desirable to use a single deflator for all the series (except the capital stock) so that later on, particular empirical results could not be ascribed to the use of different deflators for the different series. Deflation of investment, sales and gross retained profit by a single (capital goods) price index is appropriate provided intra-sectoral price movements were not too great.

C. *Price Indexes: Retirement Cost Index and Capital Stock Price Correction*

Constructing a time series for one firm's capital stock presents extraordinarily formidable problems. Most vexatious of all is that the value productivity of older capital stock declines through time. Only on the "one horse shay" hypothesis would it be correct to assume constant value productivity. Indeed, this assumption would only be

[5] *1954 National Income Supplement to the Survey of Current Business*, U.S. Department of Commerce, Office of Business Economics, p. 216.

[6] *National Income Supplement*, *ibid.*, pp. 154–6, explains the index construction in detail. These data were obtained for the years 1935 through 1953 and the subsequent two years were derived from corresponding data presented in the *Economic Report of the President*, 1956, Tables D1–D3, pp. 165–8.

strictly valid if there were no technical progress, among other restrictive assumptions. Although obviously the latter assumption is never fulfilled, the industries and firms selected happen to represent relatively stagnant technology.

A second sticky problem relates to the treatment of retirements out of the capital asset account. Since retired assets were originally entered on the books in dollars of different purchasing power, special pains must be taken to value their removal in a manner that recognizes this fact. The procedure finally adopted for a typical firm is this. Gross

TABLE 3.2

Weighted Price Index of Capital Goods for the United States Corporate Sector 1934–1955
1953 = 1000

Year	Index	Year	Index
1934	419	1947	770
1935	427	1948	840
1936	427	1949	869
1937	461	1950	886
1938	468	1951	963
1939	461	1952	978
1940	474	1953	1000
1941	504	1954	1020
1942	556	1955	1050
1943	584	1956	1100
1944	598	1957	1156
1945	606	1958	1180
1946	661		

Source: *1954 Supplement to the Survey of Current Business*, U.S. Department of Commerce, Office of Business Economics, p. 216, and *Economic Report of the President*, with adjustments that are explained in the text.

fixed assets recorded at the end of 1934 were re-valued in terms of 1929 dollars, on the assumption that both retirements and additions were comparatively minor in the years intervening between 1929 and year-end 1934, in line with the drastic overall investment decline during this period. In any event, had any retirements taken place, most would have been valued in 1929 dollars since the capital goods price level from 1922 onward was comparatively stable. Price indexes for "Industrial Machinery" and "Electrical Equipment" categories showed changes of no more than five percent from 1923 to 1929.[7]

[7] See RAYMOND GOLDSMITH, *A Study of Saving in the United States*, Table P–10, Part 2, Vol. 1, pp. 884–887. Goldsmith's underlying data were compiled by W. H. SHAW, *Value of Commodity Output Since 1869*, 1947.

Next the change in the value of gross fixed assets between two years was split into two components. The first part is additions at cost, i.e., gross investment, a figure available in published records or from the Securities and Exchange Commission. The retirements (and/or fixed assets sales figure) estimate was then obtained by subtracting the change in gross fixed assets over the year from investment of the same period. Provided write-ups, write-downs, capital losses and capital gains were small relative to the original dollar value of retirements, this accounting procedure will yield a close estimate of the correct retirements (and/or sales) figure. By and large, the frantic write-downs and other revaluations of property accounts that occurred in the 1930's were concentrated in the first three to four years of the period so that with the possible exception of 1934 the re-valuations were typically minor for the remaining years considered in this study. However, some large errors could still occur.

Second, current gross investment was converted into constant dollars by deflating the additions at cost figure by the price index outlined in Part B of this section. The thorny problem remains: how to make price corrections for retirements from the property account since these retirements are recorded in original dollars representing many different price levels? The approach adopted was to construct a "retirement cost" price index for which an estimate of durable assets' age distribution was used to weight price indexes for the year of original purchase. This weighted index was used as a deflator for the original dollar value of estimated retirements from the property account. This describes in broad outline an operation that must now be stated in more detail.

The basic set of weights was extracted from a table of Solomon Fabricant, who evolved a frequency distribution of estimated economic lifetimes of producers' plant and equipment for the year 1929 after the most precise and careful research.[8] Examination of Fabricant's figures reveals "lumping" took place at lifetime estimates of five and particularly ten, fifteen, and twenty years, apparently because of a preference for reporting lifetimes in round five year intervals. To overcome what seems to be a human proclivity rather than the inherent characteristics of machinery and equipment, the unadjusted frequency figures were averaged for five years and the mid-points of the averages were joined to form a smooth curve that gradually rose from zero to a

---

[8] SOLOMON FABRICANT, *Capital Consumption and Adjustment*, National Bureau of Economic Research, New York, 1938, p. 181.

modal value at about 13 years. The outcome of this operation has been recorded in Table 3.3. The curve might very well be bi-modal because life expectancy of new plant is about fifty years. This possibility was sidestepped by allocating all ages above 30 years to the 1929 price category, so in effect the index applies only to equipment retirements.

TABLE 3.3

Retirement Index Weights

New Capital Goods Estimated Years Life	Fabricant Weights[1]	Smoothed Weights[2]
1	0.0	0.00
2	0.8	1.30
2.5	1.1	1.65
3	2.0	1.92
4	3.8	2.36
5	4.3	2.71
6	4.1	2.98
7	1.6	3.20
8	2.8	3.40
9	0.4	3.57
10	7.6	3.73
11	0.5	3.86
12	2.7	3.94
12.5	2.9	3.96
13	0.6	3.95
14	2.2	3.85
15	10.9	3.67
16	1.5	3.40
17	1.4	3.10
18	2.8	2.79
19		2.48
20	9.5	2.17
21		1.86
22	1.1	1.55
23		1.41
24		1.42
25	5.9	1.42
Over 25	29.4	29.40

Source: [1] Fabricant, *Capital Consumption and Adjustment*, p. 181.
       [2] Graphic interpolation, as explained in text.

The capital goods price index had to be modified to recognize that the "prices" applicable to the asset life distribution would vary according to the cyclical impact on asset purchases. The modifications to be described could equally well have been applied directly to the asset life distribution, since in either case the effect would be to give high weights to prices in years of heavy purchases and small weights to prices in years of negligible acquisitions. First, a weighted average capital goods price index was constructed by weighting the price index for each individual year by that year's value of non-farm producers plant and equipment purchases in order to get at average prices corresponding to the year intervals used in the Fabricant age distribution. For instance, the weight given 1929 is much larger in the average price for the period 1929–1933 than the weight given to the price in 1933 when the quantity of purchases was so much lower. Ordinarily intervals of five years were used although when very large increases in the price index occurred, the interval was shortened to two or four years. Second, the fractions of the age distribution corresponding to particular sets of years were used to weight the price average just described.

In envisaging what we have done, one can imagine Fabricant's asset life distribution being applied to a different set of prices as each new year of data becomes available. If prices are thirty percent higher this year than they were, say, ten years ago, and on the average seven percent of our equipment is 9–10 years old, we would multiply the seven percent by 1.30 in order to estimate in current dollars of what we would expect to be retiring, revalued in terms of constant (1953) dollars. The only modification to this straightforward procedure was described in step one where we weighted the price index to indicate that even though on the average we would retire seven percent of our ten year old equipment, very little equipment, might have been purchased in that year, for example, so that the price index has been adjusted for variability in acquisitions. Seen in this light, step one would have been unnecessary if the quantity of purchases was constant in each and every year.

Table 3.4 contains the retirement cost index in terms of 1953 dollars, computed for the post-war period of rapid price increases, at a time when retirements had originally been purchased in years of much lower prices. Throughout the 1930's and early 1940's, it was assumed, retirements were in 1929 prices, since so little investment took place during the 1930's and what was invested probably was not retired during the same period. A replacement cost index, computed by dividing the current price index by the retirement cost index, is shown alongside as a matter of general interest although it has no application to the present problem. This shows, for instance, that it would cost 68% more in 1955 to purchase assets retired during that year, according to our estimates.

The Department of Commerce has calculated a replacement cost index for producers durable equipment. Their results in a rough way support some of our calculations. For one thing, the replacement cost index fluctuated between 1.02 and 1.06 for the years 1934–1940. We assumed that all retirements were at the same price level during this period. For 1941 however there were some price increases—they report

TABLE 3.4

Post-war Capital Goods Retirement Cost Index
1953 = 1000[a]

Year	Retirement Index	Replacement Cost Index[b] Given Year = 1000	Dept. of Commerce[c] Estimates for Producers Durable Equipment: Ratio of Current Cost to Original Cost
1946	513	1288	1380
1947	521	1478	1570
1948	528	1591	1680
1949	568	1530	1750
1950	545	1626	1740
1951	560	1720	1810
1952	575	1701	1760
1953	590	1695	1720
1954	625	1632	
1955	624	1683	

[a] Source: See Text. In this context, 1953 = 1000 means that capital goods retired from a firm's property account were valued in 1953 dollars.

[b] Obtained by dividing the retirement index for a given year by the capital goods price index, Table 3.2, for the same year.

[c] Source: RAYMOND NASSIMBENE and DONALD G. WOODEN, "Growth of Business Capital Equipment, 1929–55," *Survey of Current Business*, Vol. 34, No. 12, December, 1954, Table 1, Private Producers Durable Equipment: Ratio of Current Cost to Original Cost for Depreciation and Retirement, 1929–1953, page 21.

that the ratio of current cost to original cost for depreciation and retirements was 1.11 in this year. For the postwar years, when comparisons are made between the Department of Commerce figures and our own, rough correspondence prevails, although their index increased more rapidly than mine and reached a somewhat higher value.[9]

Ideally, we would have preferred the actual age distribution of

[9] RAYMOND NASSIMBENE and DONALD G. WOODEN, "Growth of Business Capital Equipment, 1929–55," *Survey of Current Business*, Vol. 34, No. 12, December, 1954, pp. 18–26.

purchases and retirements for each firm instead of the aggregate distribution for an average year two decades ago. Regrettably, this information remains permanently closeted in the dusty archives of individual firms. Even though one might accurately specify the expected life of a piece of machinery or equipment, there will be substantial variance around this expectation. Retirements tend to be correlated with current levels of economic activity, more assets being replaced as output expands, other replacements being postponed as economic activity declines. Furthermore, different firms can have different life expectation for the same type of equipment, as maintenance and intensity of utilization of the original capital good are varied. Having outlined the severe limitations of this index, I still believe that it is one of the more acceptable retirement cost indexes that might be contrived. As a rule, gross additions far exceed retirements so that some inaccuracies in this index often will have slight effect on capital stock estimates.

The final step in computing a constant dollar estimate of fixed assets is to reconstitute the change in the gross property account in constant dollars by adding in deflated investment and subtracting out deflated (estimated) retirements. This net quantity is added to the previous year's constant dollar gross property account which, is either (a) the initial year-end of 1934 expressed in 1929 dollars or, in each year thereafter, (b) the accumulation of adjusted changes. The next year's original dollar change in the property account is split into current cost additions on the one hand and original cost retirements on the other, these components are deflated and then reconstituted into the change of gross property accounts in constant dollars and this amount is then added to the "real" gross property account, etc.

D. *Dollar Measures Versus Physical Measures in the Study of Investment Behavior*

Alternative types of data available for the study of firm or industry investment behavior have been used in several different ways. One approach has been to use physical data on capacity and output for an industry to derive estimated changes in the net capital stock for the dependent variable, investment, and the net physical capital stock as an explanatory variable.[10] The advantages of physical units for both

---

[10] HOLLIS CHENERY, "Overcapacity and the Acceleration Principle," *Econometrica*, 20, January, 1952, pp. 1–28; J. M. CLARK, "Business Acceleration and the Law of Demand; A Technical Factor in Economic Cycles," *Journal of Political Economy*,

outputs and capital stock are self-evident. While the need for price level corrections can be sidestepped, some severe drawbacks nevertheless remain. Far from all equipment in place is economically "useful" and indeed, serious questions must be raised about the precise economic content of a physical capital stock composed of widely different technologies, and hence different cost implications. This observation is not intended to invalidate the usefulness of this approach; indeed it is a highly valuable method because the quality of economic data at best is seldom good. The quality of physical data can, sometimes, approach the best data available.

The most widely used alternative approach depends on original dollar accounting figures.[11] Some pitfalls of accounting data have already been dwelt on at length while the advantages of accounting data require some further defense. Most firms produce a diversity of products which do not lend themselves to meaningful physical aggregation. At the same time, within the firm, decisions about overall capital expenditures are most often centrally determined. Hence, the firm's total activity ought to be used to represent the decision-influencing variables. Even if we had the greatest detail for the information regarding individual outputs and corresponding capital stock capacities, it would be the net aggregative effect of these individual components that would be relevant for a firm investment function, since capital expenditure decisions are made at the center. However, we do not have the best, highly detailed information. With lamentably few exceptions, and these are usually limited to the producers of predominantly intermediate materials such as cement, petroleum, and primary metals,

25: 217–235, March, 1917; Simon Kuznets, "Relation Between Capital Goods and Finished Products in the Business Cycle," in *Economic Essays in Honour of Wesley Clair Mitchell* (New York, 1935); Alan S. Manne, "Some Notes on the Acceleration Principle," *Review of Economics and Statistics*, 27: 93–99 (May, 1945); A. Kisselgoff and Franco Modigliani, "Private Investment in the Electric Power Industry and the Acceleration Principle," *The Review of Economics and Statistics*, Vol. 29, No. 4, November, 1957, pp. 363–379.

[11] Lawrence R. Klein, "Studies in Investment Behavior," in *Conference on Business Cycles*, National Bureau of Economic Research, Inc., New York, 1951; Ta Chung Liu and Ching-Gwan Chang, "U.S. Consumption and Investment Propensities: Prewar and Postwar," *American Economic Review*, 40: 565–582 (September, 1950); Robert Eisner, "Expectations, Plans and Capital Expenditures: A Synthesis of Ex-Post and Ex-Ante Data," paper delivered at joint meeting of the American Economic Association, Econometric Society and American Statistical Association (December 1953); John Meyer and Edwin Kuh, *The Investment Decision: An Empirical Study*, Cambridge, 1957.

no such information is available. Either one must completely give up the attempt to measure investment behavior for firms (other than for these exceptions), or resort to accounting information.

While it has been argued that accounting data represent the relevant capital budgeting information, particularly for the multi-product firm, the fact nevertheless remains that such data are really "proxy information". Most applied economic calculations actually deal with proxies since observed sample data rarely have a one-to-one correspondence with the magnitudes which the investigator would actually prefer. It is a belief that the correspondence between the actual and the ideal data is sufficiently close to validate any empirical work whatsoever. Indeed, the possibilities of fruitfully doing empirical work depend upon the extent to which meaningful relationships can be obtained using the best information available. If meaningful and useful relationships cannot be obtained, so much the worse.

3.4 Equation Forms

Equations will be defined here whose estimated parameters are the substance of this study. Full explanations will be deferred in some instances, but orderly procedure demands a unified presentation at least once. Because computational difficulties arose at several points, it did not prove possible to estimate all statistics for all equations. However, in every instance at least one representation of each equation type was calculated so that across-the-board comparisons, while not complete, are still feasible. Broadly speaking, there are five different equation categories, each containing several variants. The main classes are distinguished in Table 3.5 by capital letters. As shown in Part A of Table 3.5 variables in the first equation class are measured in arithmetic units, for a capital intensity measure, capital stock, sales and gross retained profit as explanatory variables. These appear with different lags and in different combinations. Equation 3.9 is the first difference of Equation (3.10) which contains no lags for sales or profits. Equation (3.11) has lagged sales and/or profits and Equation (3.12) assumes that investment behavior is governed by the average of current and past sales and/or profits. Finally, Equation (3.13) assumes that the average level of investment is predicted by the average level of sales and/or profits for a two year period.

Two separate reasons dictated the inclusion of the first difference

Equation (3.9). First, in most prediction situations it is desired to predict the change in the variable so that an evaluation of the predictive capacity of the model makes it desirable to estimate a first difference form. Second, the statistical properties of first differenced equations are affected by this transformation, a matter to be taken up in the next chapter. Equations (3.10), (3.11), and (3.12) involve two sorts of hypotheses about determinants of the current rate of investment. On *a priori* grounds, current sales, lagged sales or some combination could dominate the actual rate of investment. In order to get initial even though only crude ideas about the dynamic structure of investment functions of this general class, it seemed desirable not to prejudge the issue and hence these various alternatives were estimated. Quite obviously, within each equation number the sales equation, the profit equation, and the combined sales and profit equation represent the major theoretical constructs described in Chapter 2. Equation (3.13) evaluates the possibility that investment reactions should be viewed in a longer term context. That is, will aggregating over time periods more correctly portray the comparatively long-run nature of the investment process? Some time aggregation problems are dealt with in Chapter 7 at greater length.

The next set of equations shown in part B of Table 3.5 are straightforward logarithmic transformations of equations (3.9), (3.10), (3.11), and (3.12).[12] The log form has several advantages over arithmetic scale. First, the exponentiated form is a direct counterpart to the capacity models that were developed in Chapter 2. Second, log transformations can correct cross-section heteroscedasticity which is likely to occur when the individual firms are of greatly different size. The desirability of such measures will be taken up in the next chapter. It is evident that profits could not be used here since profits can range over negative values.

Several ratio models appear in Part C of Table 3.5. The ratio models bear a certain resemblance to the log models although several important differences should clearly be discerned. From the analytical point of view, in certain simple cases the two models are equivalent. In particular, when $\alpha_1 + \alpha_2 = 1$ in the following relationship, the correspondence between the ratio equation follows at once.

$$Y = A \, X_1^{\alpha_1} \, X_2^{\alpha_2} \qquad (3.1)$$

---

[12] (3.19) is the first difference version of (3.20), not the logarithm of (3.9).

TABLE 3.5

Equation forms

I_t = Gross Investment	P_t = Gross Retained Profits
C = Capital Intensity Index	$\hat{\beta}$ = Capital Coefficient: Reci-
K_t = Capital Stock	procal of C
S_t = Sales	D_t = Dividends

Part A

$$\Delta I_t = \alpha_0 + \alpha_1 C + \alpha_2 \Delta K_t + \alpha_3 \Delta S_t \tag{3.9S}$$
$$\Delta I_t = \alpha_0 + \alpha_1 C + \alpha_2 \Delta K_t + \alpha_4 \Delta P_t \tag{3.9P}$$
$$\Delta I_t = \alpha_0 + \alpha_1 C + \alpha_2 \Delta K_t + \alpha_3 \Delta S_t + \alpha_4 \Delta P_t \tag{3.9SP}$$

$$I_t = \alpha_0 + \alpha_1 C + \alpha_2 K_t + \alpha_3 S_t \tag{3.10S}$$
$$I_t = \alpha_0 + \alpha_1 C + \alpha_2 K_t + \alpha_4 P_t \tag{3.10P}$$
$$I_t = \alpha_0 + \alpha_1 C + \alpha_2 K_t + \alpha_3 S_t + \alpha_4 P_t \tag{3.10SP}$$

$$I_t = \alpha_0 + \alpha_1 C + \alpha_2 K_t + \alpha_3 S_{t-1} \tag{3.11S}$$
$$I_t = \alpha_0 + \alpha_1 C + \alpha_2 K_t + \alpha_4 P_{t-1} \tag{3.11P}$$
$$I_t = \alpha_0 + \alpha_1 C + \alpha_2 K_t + \alpha_3 S_{t-1} + \alpha_4 P_{t-1} \tag{3.11SP}$$

$$I_t = \alpha_0 + \alpha_1 C + \alpha_2 K_t + \alpha_3[(S_t + S_{t-1}) \div 2] \tag{3.12S}$$
$$I_t = \alpha_0 + \alpha_1 C + \alpha_2 K_t + \alpha_4[(P_t + P_{t-1}) \div 2] \tag{3.12P}$$
$$I_t = \alpha_0 + \alpha_1 C + \alpha_2 K_t + \alpha_3[(S_t + S_{t-1}) \div 2] + \alpha_4[(P_t + P_{t-1}) \div 2]$$
$$\tag{3.12SP}$$

$$[(I_t + I_{t-1}) \div 2] = \alpha_0 + \alpha_1 C + \alpha_2 K_t + \alpha_3[(S_t + S_{t-1}) \div 2] \tag{3.13S}$$
$$[(I_t + I_{t-1}) \div 2] = \alpha_0 + \alpha_1 C + \alpha_2 K_t + \alpha_4[(P_t + P_{t-1}) \div 2] \tag{3.13P}$$
$$[(I_t + I_{t-1}) \div 2] = \alpha_0 + \alpha_1 C + \alpha_2 K_t + \alpha_3[(S_t + S_{t-1}) \div 2] + \alpha_4[(P_t + P_{t-1}) \div 2]$$
$$\tag{3.13SP}$$

Part B

$$\Delta\log I = \alpha_0 + \alpha_1 \log C + \alpha_2 \Delta\log K_t + \alpha_3 \Delta\log S_t \tag{3.19}$$
$$\log I = \alpha_0 + \alpha_1 \log C + \alpha_2 \log K_t + \alpha_3 \log S_t \tag{3.20}$$
$$\log I = \alpha_0 + \alpha_1 \log C + \alpha_2 \log K_t + \alpha_3 \log S_{t-1} \tag{3.21}$$
$$\log I = \alpha_0 + \alpha_1 \log C + \alpha_2 \log [(K_t + K_{t-1}) \div 2] + \alpha_3 \log [(S_t + S_{t-1}) \div 2] \tag{3.22}$$

In this special case, we have a linear homogeneous function in the variables X_1 and X_2 so that the only coefficients to be estimated are the scale factor A and either α_1 or α_2. While this assumption may seem unnecessarily strong, the theoretical constructions strongly suggest that the coefficient on the capital stock should be negative so that putting it in the denominator of the ratios forces it to be negative. A further requirement is that the ratio form should have no additive intercept term. However, when we look at an equation with ratio variables, the analytical correspondence disappears and the ratios must be interpreted as variables "with a life of their own" quite apart from the log models. In this light then, we can view Equations (3.30) and (3.31) as containing different lags for profit rates combined with different lags

TABLE 3.5 (*continued*)

Part C

$$\frac{I_t}{K_t} = \alpha_0 + \alpha_1 \frac{P_t}{K_t} + \alpha_2 \frac{S_{t-1}}{C \cdot K_{t-1}} \tag{3.30A}$$

$$\frac{I_t}{K_t} = \alpha_0 + \alpha_1 \frac{P_t}{K_t} + \alpha_2 \frac{S_{t-1}}{C \cdot K_{t-1}} + \alpha_3 \frac{S_t}{C \cdot K_t} \tag{3.30B}$$

$$\frac{I_t}{K_t} = \alpha_0 + \alpha_1 \frac{S_t}{C \cdot K_t} \tag{3.30C}$$

$$\frac{I_t}{K_t} = \alpha_0 + \alpha_1 \frac{S_t}{C \cdot K_t} + \alpha_2 \frac{S_{t-1}}{C \cdot K_{t-1}} \tag{3.30D}$$

$$\frac{I_t}{K_t} = \alpha_0 + \alpha_1 \frac{P_t + P_{t-1}}{K_t \cdot 2} + \alpha_2 \frac{S_{t-1}}{C \cdot K_{t-1}} \tag{3.31A}$$

$$\frac{I_t}{K_t} = \alpha_0 + \alpha_1 \frac{P_t + P_{t-1}}{K_t \cdot 2} + \alpha_2 \frac{S_{t-1}}{C \cdot K_{t-1}} + \alpha_3 \frac{S_t}{C \cdot K_t} \tag{3.31B}$$

Part D

$$I_t = \alpha_0 + \alpha_1(\hat{\beta}S_t - K_t) \tag{3.34A}$$

$$I_t = \alpha_0 + \alpha_1(\hat{\beta}S_t - K_t) + \alpha_2(\hat{\beta}S_{t-1} - K_{t-1}) \tag{3.34B}$$

$$I_t = \alpha_0 + \alpha_1\{[\hat{\beta}(S_t + S_{t-1}) \div 2] - K_t\} \tag{3.35A}$$

$$I_t = \alpha_0 + \alpha_1\{[\hat{\beta}(S_t + S_{t-1}) \div 2] - K_t\} + \alpha_2\{[\hat{\beta}(S_{t-1} + S_{t-2}) \div 2] - K_{t-1}\} \tag{3.35B}$$

If $\hat{\beta}S_t < K_t$, and similarly for other variables of Equations 34 and 35 of the same form, these variables are set equal to zero in calculating the regression estimates.

Part E

$$D_t = \alpha_0 + \alpha_1 P_t + \alpha_2 D_{t-1} \tag{3.40}$$

$$D_t = \alpha_1 P_t + \alpha_2 D_{t-1}, \qquad \alpha_0 \equiv 0 \tag{3.41}$$

Note: Time series estimating equations differ from cross-section since C, the capital intensity variable, is a constant for each firm.

for rates of capacity utilization.

The variable $S_t/C \cdot K_t$ (or its lagged counterpart) is the index of capacity utilization. Recall from the earlier description of C in this chapter that $1/C = \hat{\beta}$ whose $\hat{\beta}$ is an estimate of the firm's capital coefficient. When the firm operates at just this rate, $S_t/C \cdot K_t = K^D \cdot S_t/S^D \cdot K_t = 1$, and when the ratio is less than unity, the firm has excess capacity. Equations (3.30C) and (3.30D) represent "pure" acceleration models without any profit influence included.

The next set of equations, in Part D of Table 3.5, is derived directly from the capacity model discussed in the previous chapter. In this instance the capital coefficient is not implicit in the sales variable coefficient estimate but instead has been obtained from "direct information" as the reciprocal of the capital intensity index. What we have done is to define a new variable. The new variable is the desired capacity increment. It is obtained by multiplying the output level by our estimated capital coefficient and subtracting from this product the capital stock at the beginning of the period. Therefore, all that remains for the statistician to do is to estimate the reaction coefficient from the sample input series just described, and investment, according to Equation (3.34A). The lagged capacity requirement variable has also been included as shown in Equation (3.34B). Equations (3.35A) and (3.35B) are similar except that current sales are replaced by averaged current and previous year's sales. The previous chapter describes how the irreversibility conditions can be weakened when there are several periods. In the present case, however, a complicated estimation procedure would have to be devised to satisfy the inequality conditions in the multiple lag case as well as the canons of sound estimation. We therefore adopted a restriction criticized earlier on theoretical grounds, namely that a variable was set equal to zero when negative capital outlays were predicted by that particular variable. Hence, these equations include positive variable values when the capacity requirement value is a positive, the remaining entries being zeros.

The last equations are two different formulations of the Lintner dividend hypothesis. Equation (3.40) presents the Lintner hypothesis in its original version, namely with the intercept term as a parameter to be estimated. Equation (3.41) on the other hand has been fitted where the coefficients are estimated subject to the restriction that the intercept term is zero. The implications of this particular restriction are indicated in Chapter 10.

3.5 The Economic Environment

Certain aggregate data in Table 3.6 provide a backdrop for our own particular sample of capital producing firms, for which analogous data are shown in Table 3.7.

The economic environment will be defined in two quite different ways. First, the major movements of the aggregate counterparts of the variables which directly or indirectly influence the individual firm behavior will be indicated. Second, sub-aggregated counterparts from our sample of firms are shown for comparison in order to establish how typical this particular sample is, since the selection procedure

TABLE 3.6

Indicators of Aggregate U.S. Economic Activity

	Indexes: 1947 = 100					($ billions) Constant Dollars: 1953 = 100			
Year	GNP	Plant and Equipment	Net Profits	Gross Retained Earnings	F.R.B. Index Durable Goods Component	GNP	Plant and Equipment	Net Profits	Gross Retained Earnings
1935	55	33	21	45	38	152.1	13.5	5.1	14.0
1936	61	46	42	49	49	169.6	18.6	10.0	15.2
1937	66	54	42	48	55	182.7	21.8	10.1	14.9
1938	62	43	20	41	35	173.6	17.4	4.9	12.8
1939	67	51	45	58	49	187.4	20.6	10.3	18.0
1940	73	61	58	66	63	204.2	24.6	13.7	20.6
1941	85	70	78	82	91	235.9	28.1	18.6	25.7
1946	100	80	85	85	86	278.2	31.9	20.2	26.6
1947	100	100	100	100	100	276.3	39.8	23.6	31.0
1948	105	110	102	105	104	290.2	43.8	24.1	32.6
1949	104	102	76	91	95	287.4	40.8	18.1	28.4
1950	113	124	105	112	116	314.9	49.6	24.9	34.8
1951	121	121	82	100	128	336.7	48.4	19.4	31.0
1952	126	120	69	92	136	349.5	48.0	16.4	28.7
1953	131	126	70	99	153	363.3	50.2	16.7	30.7
1954	129	127	66	100	137	358.5	50.5	15.6	31.0
1955	139	139	84	116	155	384.1	55.4	20.0	36.2

Sources:

GNP. *Economic Report of the President*, January, 1958, p. 121, Total Gross National Product in Table F-4, "Gross National Product or Expenditure, in 1947 Prices, 1929–57."

Plant and Equipment. *Economic Report of the President*, January, 1958, p. 121, New Construction plus Producers' Durable Equipment in Table F-4, "Gross National Product or Expenditure in 1947 Prices, 1929–57."

Net Profits. *Economic Report of the President*, January, 1958, p. 179, Total Corporate Profits After Taxes in Table F-56, "Profits Before and After Taxes, All Private Corporations, 1929–57," divided by Durable Goods Price Index, Chapter 3, Table 3.1.

Gross Retained Earnings. *Economic Report of the President*, January, 1958, Undistributed Profits in Table F-56, "Profits Before and After Taxes, All Private Corporations, 1929–57," p. 179 plus Depreciation Expense in Table F-10, "Relation of Gross National Product and National Income," p. 127, minus Dividend Payments in Table F-56, "Profits Before and After Taxes, All Private Corporations, 1929–57," p. 179, divided by Durable Goods Price Index.

was independent of the relation of these firms to the broad aggregates.

Aggregate figures presented for the entire economy include real GNP, real investment and real gross retained profit. The index of durable goods production, a component of the Federal Reserve Board Index of Industrial Production, provides an alternative measure of

TABLE 3.7

Average Investment, Sales, Profits and Capital Stock for Sample Firms

	Indexes: 1947 = 100				Constant Dollars: 1953 = 100			
Year	Invest-ment	Sales	Re-tained Profit	Capital Stock	Invest-ment	Sales (1000)	Retained Profit (1000)	Capital Stock (1000)
1935	38	37	44	75	601	15,560	1,154	15,165
1936	52	52	54	76	824	21,772	1,402	15,359
1937	74	59	57	78	1,160	24,876	1,489	15,860
1938	36	38	13	80	566	16,044	337	16,243
1939	38	49	52	81	601	20,654	1,340	16,390
1940	62	63	69	81	981	26,522	1,791	16,490
1941	86	99	87	84	1,349	41,727	2,257	17,012
1946	102	83	68	95	1,604	34,997	1,772	19,210
1947	100	100	100	100	1,570	42,175	2,595	20,239
1948	121	100	95	106	1,893	42,121	2,474	21,491
1949	82	83	63	110	1,292	34,870	1,624	22,268
1950	69	97	98	113	1,090	40,700	2,546	22,792
1951	99	120	88	116	1,554	50,697	2,293	23,385
1952	112	122	78	120	1,753	51,374	2,028	24,367
1953	112	129	85	125	1,761	54,347	2,206	25,333
1954	104	108	79	129	1,635	45,469	2,040	26,138
1955	121	119	102	135	1,902	53,221	2,636	27,292

general activity. In Chart 3.1, indexes of the output measures, real GNP, the durable goods production index and constant dollar sales for our sample firms are shown together. All have been put on the base 1947 = 100. The major similarities and differences are self-evident. Real GNP contains many non-durable goods and services which fluctuate much less year to year than does durable output. Hence, the comparatively violent fluctuations in the sales of our sample firms are more closely paralleled by the index of durable goods production. However, it should be noted that, while the pre-war configurations of the two series are rather similar, postwar, our particular industries did not increase sales beginning in 1951 to the same extent as did the durable index.

This divergence originates in the history peculiar to our firms. The sample is heavily weighted with tool makers, who make capital goods for capital goods producers, the latter having a much heavier weight in the durable goods index than the machine tool manufacturing firms. The tool making industries came out of World War II with substantial capacity and indeed, throughout much of the post-war period they operated with some spare plant and equipment. In part then, due to initial conditions different from those governing capacity utilization for the capital goods producers selling direct to final goods manufactuers, the rate of sales increase was not nearly so marked for our firms.

Chart 3.2, showing gross retained profits for the total economy and our sample set of firms again reveals characteristics similar to the first series on output. Greater variability for the sample firms is once again evident. The real investment figures for the whole economy also are

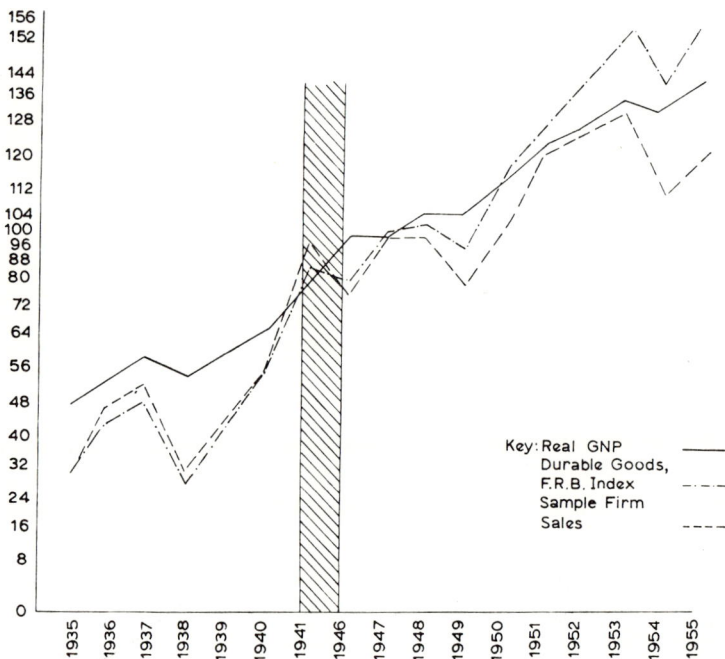

Chart 3.1 Output Indexes

subject to much less violent fluctuations than the sample firms, as shown in Chart 3.3. Indeed, it is obvious that capital goods producers sales and investment are most closely paralleled by the durable goods component of the Federal Reserve Board Index of Industrial Production.

Some indexes of firm behavior have been recorded in Table 3.8 and Chart 3.4: the ratio of gross investment to capital stock, the ratio of gross retained earnings to capital stock, and finally the ratio of sales to capital stock for each year, the latter put on base 1947 = 100. The profit rate exceeds the investment rate in every year except 1938, although the excess in many years is not substantial. A second indicator which characterizes our firms is shown by the sales to capital stock ratio, an index of capacity utilization. The peak capacity years cluster around the Korean and immediate post-Korean period, although it is interesting to note that 1941 was a year of even higher utilization. Indeed, it is worth noting that the percentage increase in capacity utilization from 1940 to 1941 is the largest of any year in the sample period. The durable goods production index also shows the largest percentage in-

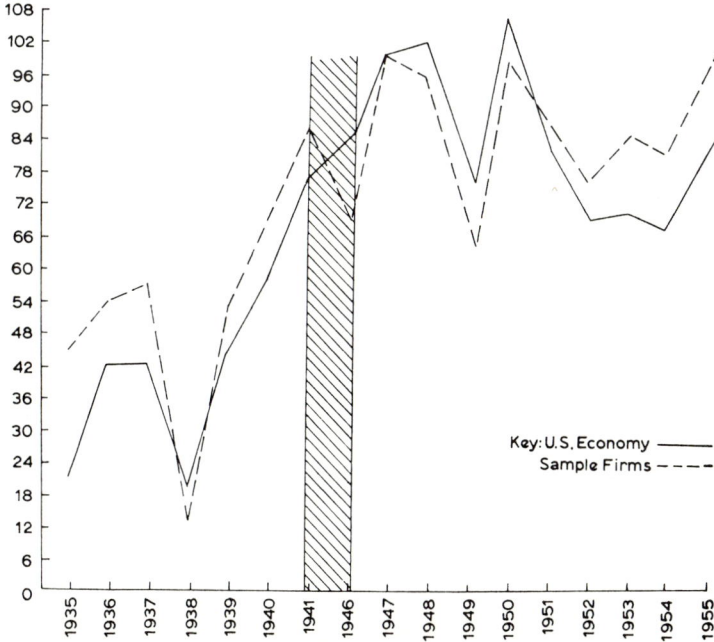

Chart 3.2 Gross Retained Profit Indexes

crease from 1940 to 1941. One might surmise that during this period, when there was a highly elastic labor supply, large-scale increases in demand could be met with existing capital stock through intensive utilization since material or labor bottle-necks would not thwart these rapid desired rates of growth. By the same token, it may well be imagined that the apparent low rates of capacity utilization in 1946, 1947, and 1948 were due in some measure to material or labor shortages, although the extensive acquisition of capital by many of these firms during the war put many of them in a strong position to meet orders subject only to minor capacity restrictions.

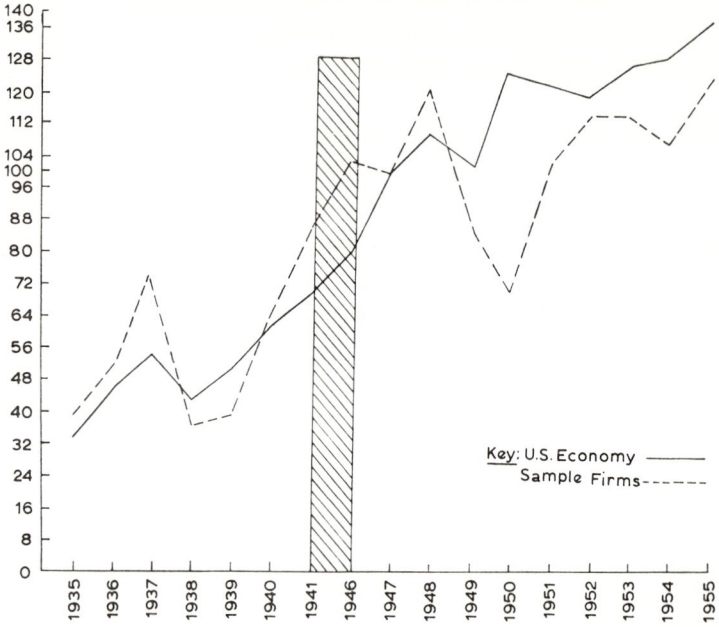

Chart 3.3 Real Investment Indexes

Key: U.S. Economy ———
Sample Firms ------

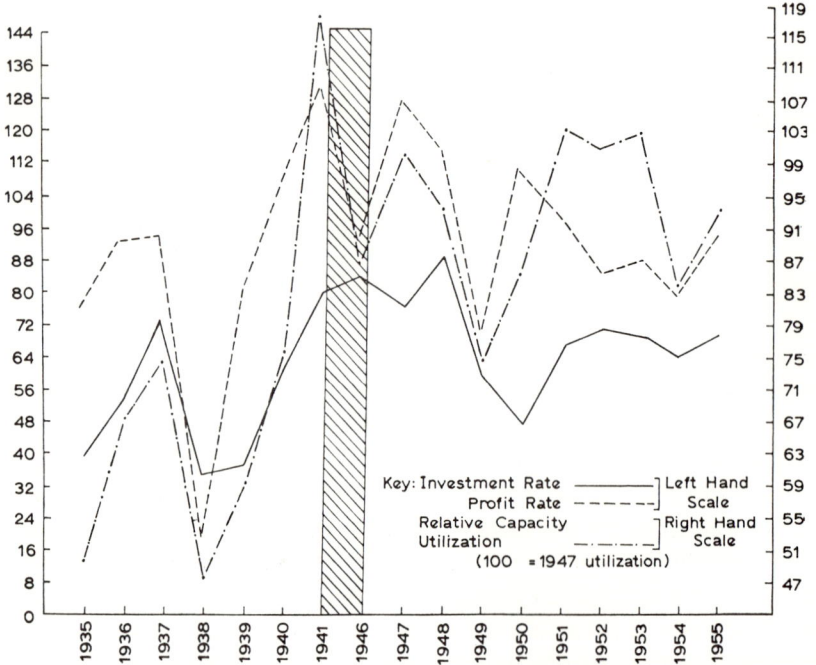

Key: Investment Rate ——— ⎤ Left Hand
Profit Rate ------ ⎦ Scale
Relative Capacity ⎤ Right Hand
Utilization —·—·— ⎦ Scale
(100 = 1947 utilization)

Chart 3.4 Sample Firm Indexes of Investment, Profit, and Capacity Utilization

TABLE 3.8

Rates of Investment, Retained Profits and Output for Sample Firms

Year	Investment Rate	Retained Profit Rate	Relative Capacity Utilization 1947 = 100
1935	0.039	0.076	0.492
1936	0.053	0.091	0.680
1937	0.073	0.093	0.752
1938	0.034	0.020	0.473
1939	0.036	0.081	0.604
1940	0.059	0.108	0.771
1941	0.079	0.132	1.177
1946	0.083	0.092	0.874
1947	0.077	0.128	1.000
1948	0.088	0.115	0.940
1949	0.058	0.072	0.751
1950	0.047	0.111	0.856
1951	0.066	0.098	1.040
1952	0.071	0.083	1.012
1953	0.069	0.087	1.029
1954	0.062	0.078	0.834
1955	0.069	0.096	0.936

Note: Columns 1 and 2 are rates which have *not* been standardized with base 1947 = 100. Column 3, however, is a capacity utilization rate obtained by dividing a sales-capital stock rate of every year by the 1947 rate. All underlying data measured in constant 1953 = 100 dollars.

3.6 Summary

The sixty firms in this study were primarily selected from among a group of capital goods producing industries, so that a complete time series on each would be available for the period 1935 to 1955. Once the firms had been selected, a number of data corrections were made, the most important being price level corrections. A particularly complex price deflation procedure was required for the fixed capital assets of the firm. The different equation forms used throughout the remainder of the study are also reported. When combined in different ways, these variables reflect either capacity-accelerator behavior or internal fund flows, with various lags. Further transformations such as logarithms, ratios, and first differencing were calculated on the basis of theoretical or statistical interest. Finally, the economic environment in which the firms operated has been characterized by aggregative measures of the entire economy. In general, the sixty sample firms' output pattern paralleled that of aggregate durable goods producers.

3.7 Appendix

Basic Sample Firms

No.	No.

(1) *Steel producers with Blast Furnaces*
Sharon Steel Corporation

(2) *Steel Producers without Blast Furnaces*
Keystone Steel and Wire Co.
Vanadium–Alloys Steel Co.

(4) *Rolling Mills without Steel Making Facilities*
Acme Steel Company
Eastern Stainless Steel Corp.
Signode Steel Strapping Co.
Superior Steel Corporation

(2) *Iron and Steel Foundry Products*
Byers Comapny, A.M.
Warren Foundary and Pipe Corp.

(7) *Non-Ferrous Metal Products: Producers and Fabricators*
Anaconda Wire and Cable Co.
Bridgeport Brass Company
Driver-Harris Company
General Cable Corporation
Hoskins Manufacturing Company
Mueller Brass Company
Revere Copper and Brass, Inc.

(3) *Steel-Wire, Springs and Rope*
Consolidated Electronics Industries
    Corporation
National Standard Company
Young Spring and Wire Corp.

(9) *Metal Working Machinery*
Allied Products Corporation
Black and Decker Company
The Bullard Company
Mesta Machinery Company
Monarch Machine Tool Co.
Starret (L.S.) Company
Sundstrand Machine Tool Co.
Union Twist Drill Company
Van Norman Machine Tool Co.

(2) *Bolts, Nuts and Rivets*
Aero Supply Mfg. Co., Inc.

Pittsburgh Screw and Bolt Corporation

(15) *General Industrial Machinery and Equipment*
American Chain and Cable Company, Inc.
American Machine and Metals, Inc.
Binks Manufacturing Company
Chicago Pneumatic Tool Company,
Fairbanks, Morse and Company
Gardner Denver Company
Harneschfeger Corporation
Ingersoll-Rand Company
Link-Belt Company
Lunkenheimer Company
Neptune Meter Company
Torrington Co. (of Maine)
Veeder Root
Walworth Company
Worthington Corporation

(5) *Electrical Supplies and Equipment*
Century Electric Co.
Cutler Hammer, Inc.
Gamewell Corp.
Minneapolis-Honeywell Co.
Sangamo Electric Company

(4) *Construction, Mining and Related Equipment*
Bucyrus-Erie Company
Emsco Manufacturing Co.
Jaeger Machine Co.
Reed Roller Bit Company

(2) *Engines and Turbines*
Cooper-Bessemer Corporation
Waukesha Motors

(3) *Special Industry Machinery*
American Laundry Machine Co.
Lynch Corporation
National Rubber Machinery Co.

(1) *Iron and Steel Forgings*
Transue and Williams Steel Forging
    Corporation

CHAPTER 4

SOME STATISTICAL PROBLEMS

4.1 Introduction

The technique of regression analysis will be exploited here in two forms. First, simply as regression equations and second, in an analysis of covariance procedures that will be described in Chapter 5.[1] The analysis in both instances will be predicated on the usual assumptions of the Fisher regression model:

(1) The explanatory variables are fixed in the sense that no probabilistic mechanism is postulated for generating them. Further, the error term is uncorrelated with any of the explanatory variables,

(2) the dependent variable is the sum of a linear function of the explanatory variables and an error term with constant variance,

(3) the samples are independent, that is, each observation of the error term is an independent drawing from a normal universe,

(4) and in particular, the error term is distributed independently in time.

---

[1] ALEXANDER M. MOOD, *Introduction to the Theory of Statistics*, New York, 1950, and MAURICE G. KENDALL, *The Advanced Theory of Statistics*, Vol. 2, 5th edition, New York, 1952, DONALD A. S. FRASER, *Statistics: An Introduction*, New York, 1959, Chapter 14, Henry Scheffé, *The Analysis of Variance*, New York, 1959, Chapter 6. One of the most complete writeups of the analysis of covariance in relation to testing the stability of structure will be found in GREGORY CHOW, "Tests of Equality Between Sets of Coefficients in Two Linear Regressions," *Econometrica*, Vol. 28, No. 3, July, 1960, pp. 591–605. Also see C. R. RAO, *Advanced Statistical Methods in Biometric Research*, New York, 1952. An interesting and thorough application of the analysis of covariance to an economic problem appears in DAVID DURAND, "Bank Stocks and the Analysis of Covariance," *Econometrica*, Vol. 23, No. 1, January, 1955, pp. 30–45. Numerous pitfalls and limitations of economic data used within a covariance model are indicated and discussed by Durand, in a frame of reference similar in some respects to my own. Another valuable reference will be found in *Biometrics*, Vol. 13, No. 3, September, 1957, especially in the article by H. FAIRFIELD SMITH, "Interpretation of Adjusted Treatment Means and Regressions in Analysis of Covariance," pp. 282–308.

Each assumption will be scrutinized in the context of this study while test statistics and other relevant estimates bearing on the applicability of the fundamental assumptions will be incorporated here, except for those related to specialized aspects of this study.

4.2 Identification and Bias

When coefficients of econometric models are estimated with micro data, this choice of data can often overcome "the" identification problem which arises when errors are correlated with explanatory variables because of simultaneous determination, thereby biasing least squares estimates.[2] In the context of investment behavior simultaneous equation bias could arise, for instance, because sales might not only (in conjunction with the firm's capital stock) determine investment but investment could equally well determine sales, in a manner described by familiar multiplier-accelerator models.

In the case of individual firms following a comparatively rigid price policy, behavior frequently observed in the manufacturing sector, quantities sold and hence (given the price) sales revenues will be determined by shifts in customer demand functions. The direction of causality is clear cut so that simultaneous equations' feedback common to macro economic models is unlikely to affect even the largest firms that behave in this way. Least squares bias could arise even when there was no causal link of the sort described if the micro exogenous time series were nevertheless significantly correlated with the macro exogenous time series. While not explicitly tested, it seems unlikely that this would be a major source of least squares bias in the present context. Exceptions to this proposition will occur only in a few post war years when backlog demand could be satisfied through additions to the firm's capital stock "unaccounted for" by the included variables. However, the *biased* estimates will exist when abnormal backlogs exist, not when they are eliminated through additions to capital stock, so that the assumed correlation between the error term and sales arising in the manner just indicated serves to re-establish the structural sales-investment relation, rather than distort it. Lagged variables such as capital stock are predetermined and therefore should be uncorrelated with the current value of the error term. Exceptions arise, however, when there is substantial autocorrelation in the lagged endogenous variables.

[2] J. MEYER and E. KUH, *op. cit.*, pp. 81–83.

This should not bias cross-sections but might create difficulties in time series.

The possibility of correlation between excluded variables and profits can arise for other reasons. Thus, when profits are high it is likely that research and development outlays will be increased. The increase in research and development outlays can result in an increased flow of innovations, and therefore, a greater investment demand. The net effect of all this will be a positive correlation between profits and the excluded (research and development) variables so that the profit regression coefficients will tend to be overstated, and similarly for the sales regression coefficients, through the correlation of sales with profits. However, this effect should not be impressively strong because of a considerable delay in the effect of increased research and development outlays on investment: the final outcome more often than not will be an increase in unexplained variance rather than bias.

Certain specific problems of bias arise from both the time series nature of the data and the particular structure of the estimating equation which will frequently be used. In the general case, when a series of observations has been generated by a stationary Markoff process, Hurwicz has shown that maximum-likelihood estimates and least squares estimates will be subject to small sample bias. For one particular model, Hurwicz found that small sample bias could be quite severe although the relative bias went to zero as the sample size increased; however, the bias becomes small as the Markoff parameter, α, tends towards unity. The last observation holds for extremely short samples of three and four observations. In a second model Hurwicz has shown that for samples of size 17 the relative bias will not exceed 10 percent and that for samples of size 50, the relative bias is no more than 4 percent.[3] In the absence of any other alternative estimation technique, it must be recognized that such biases can exist and in all cases will lead to downward biases, although highly autocorrelated errors may, curiously enough, decrease the relative bias.

The seriousness of a second type of bias peculiar to the type of model evolved by Koyck depends on the nature of a particular transfor-

[3] LEONID HURWICZ, "Least-Squares Bias in Time Series" in *Statistical Inference in Dynamic Economic Models*, edited by Tjalling C. Koopmans, Cowles Commission Monograph No. 10, New York, 1950, pp. 365–384. The first case is when the initial condition in the first order stochastic difference equation is a fixed, known number and the second case arises when the initial condition is a random drawing. The Markoff process is described in more detail in Section 4.5 of this chapter.

mation. The bias whose existence Koyck[4] described is such that the estimated coefficients are inconsistent estimates, since the lagged error term of the original equation, assumed to be independently distributed in time appears in the least squares error term of the Koyck transformation along with the lagged dependent variable. However, when the multiple correlation of the estimated equation is quite high the bias will be negligible and in particular, if it is high relative to the correlation among the explanatory variables, for instance, sales and capital stock. If the multiple correlation is low and/or the inter-correlation is high, by simply viewing the coefficients and their standard errors in the normal "classical" regression sense, we will tend to "distrust" the estimates in any event, since both these conditions will cause large standard errors of the estimated regression coefficients. Hence, this particular source of bias should not catch us unaware, even though autocorrelation introduced by the transformation will bias the standard error of estimate downward.

Lawrence Klein has recently described an appropriate theoretical construction underlying alternative estimation procedures in the case of estimating coefficients of distributed lags following the Koyck scheme.[5] Klein shows that when the original error term is uncorrelated or the autocorrelation is known, the appropriate regression for consistent estimates is a special case of diagonal regression, analogous to a method previously suggested by Koyck. In an example, Klein estimates the marginal propensity to consume when consumption follows a distributed lag pattern, a proposition based on habit persistent theories of consumer behavior. In this instance, his consistent estimates were similar to least squares estimates, since the multiple correlation was quite high in both instances.[6]

In this section several possible sources of bias have been enumerated that can arise either because certain variables are excluded from the estimating equation or because of the particular estimating equation used and the time series context. Some of the biases discussed are inherent in the sort of problem that we have been dealing with, for instance, those treated in Hurwicz. Others depend upon the specifica-

---

[4] LEENDERT M. KOYCK, *Distributed Lags and Investment Analysis*, 1954, Amsterdam, pp. 32–39.

[5] LAWRENCE R. KLEIN, "The Estimation of Distributed Lags," *Econometrica*, Vol. 26, No. 4, October, 1958, pp. 553–565.

[6] LAWRENCE R. KLEIN, "The Friedman-Becker Illusion," *The Journal of Political Economy*, Vol. 66, No. 6, December, 1958, pp. 539–545.

tion of the equation to be estimated, particularly those pertaining to autocorrelation, and these can and will be subject to test.

4.3 Heteroscedasticity

Error variances for large firms will substantially exceed those of small firms in the normal course of events. The possibility that the cross-section within-cell regression functions in the analysis of covariance might have unequal error variances must therefore be considered, a possibility that can be handled in two ways. The first is to test for the existence of heteroscedasticity among firms and eliminate the statistically significant outliers. The second alternative is to transform variables so that the error variances will be homogeneous. The log transformations, which equalize error variances on the assumption that these variances are strictly proportional to the size of the independent variable, or ratios, are popular transformations to achieve this end. Because logarithms change the theoretical interpretation of the resulting estimates, these will soon be discussed in more detail. Both alternatives have been used.

A test statistic devised by H. A David was applied to the error variances for 73 different firms that originally were considered for inclusion in the complete analysis.[7] Error variances of each firm were ranked from smallest to largest. When the ratio between two successive variances exceed the critical test statistic value at the 1 per cent level, a decision had to be made about how to treat firms in the two groups. Very conveniently it turned out there were two firms which had significantly smaller variances than the main group of firms, which on the basis of this test statistic could be treated as homogeneous, and there were also three large firms at the other extreme. On this basis, the five firms were eliminated both from time series and cross-section calculations. The David test statistic was also applied to cross-sections to determine whether there were significant inter-year differences in variances. Even if a given group of firms had equal error variances through time (within acceptable sampling error) the errors could be correlated so that in years of exceptionally large errors for one firm, exceptionally large errors for other firms would also exist. The results

[7] H. A. DAVID, "The Ranking of Variances in Normal Populations," *Journal of the American Statistical Association*, Vol. 51, No. 276, December, 1956, pp. 621–626.

of these inter-year tests will be presented shortly. There are two main effects of intra-year heteroscedasticity. First, the efficiency of the estimated coefficients is less than it would have been had weighted regression techniques been used. Second, prediction intervals and error variances based upon the assumption of constancy are imprecise estimates. The limitations imposed by these possibilities will be evaluated in due course when we examine the actual test statistics.

Here I must call attention to a warning by G. E. P. Box about limitations of tests such as this. In a paper which studied the effect of departures from the normality assumption on various tests, Box reports:

> "The present research suggests that when, as is usual, little is known of the parent distribution, this practice (testing for homogeneity of variance before testing for homogeneity of means in the analysis of variance) may well lead to more wrong conclusions than if the preliminary test was omitted. It has been shown... that in the commonly occurring case in which the group sizes are equal, or not very different, the analysis of variance test is affected surprisingly little by variance inequalities. Since this test is also known to be very insensitive to non-normality, it would be best to accept the fact that it can be used safely under most practical conditions. To make the preliminary test on variances is rather like putting to sea in a rowing boat to find out whether conditions are sufficiently calm for an ocean liner to leave port."[8]

While this warning must certainly be taken into account, there are such strong *a priori* reasons to suppose that variances could be unequal that it is well to run the risk of incorrect results rather than adopt Box's advice.

An advantage of the linear-in-logarithm or Cobb-Douglas form beyond its influence on error variance homogeneity,[9] is that in differential form it represents a dynamic formulation which should yield coefficients similar to those that one would get in regressions whose variables are percentage changes.[10] Thus when viewed in differential form the estimated coefficients reflect responses to percentage changes; in

---

[8] G. E. P. Box, "Non-Normality and Tests on Variances," *Biometrika*, Vol. 40, Parts 3 and 4, 1953, pp. 333.

[9] Examination of cross-section scatter diagrams showed that considerable heteroscedasticity was in fact eliminated by using logarithms. While I deplore references in the work of others to "priceless" information hidden in the author's drawer, the cost of reproducing the graphs was not thought to be warranted by the value of the information.

[10] Some preliminary estimates on percent changes were wholly unsatisfactory, to the extent that non-zero correlations occurred less frequently than one would obtain by chance when drawing samples from a normal distribution with parent correlation zero. In short, strong downward biases exist, probably attributable to errors of observation.

short, the coefficients are estimates of constant elasticities. The Cobb-Douglas form also directly represents a version of the capacity-pressure model akin to the linear (in original units) model described in Chapter 2:[11]

$$I_t = A \ X_t^{\alpha} \ K_t^{-\beta} = A \ \frac{X_t^{\alpha}}{K_t^{\beta}} \ \text{or} \ \frac{dI}{I} = \alpha \ \frac{dX}{X} - \beta \ \frac{dK}{K}. \qquad (4.1)$$

Extreme value problems are mitigated since extremely large or small values are given a relatively less weight. Even though the largest and smallest firms originally considered were eliminated, a substantial size difference among independent variable values remains. Such influences are reduced in a logarithmic formulation.[12] Profit variables cannot be used in this type of relationship because of occasional negative values. However, profits tend to be positively correlated with sales so that observed behavior of both sales and profit models could reveal rough qualitative similarities.

Ratio models offer an alternative to logarithms to control or eliminate heteroscedasticity. As illustrated elsewhere, simple deflation proves to be a special case of weighted regression when the deflator is proportional to error variance size.[13] Appropriate weighted regression estimates are most efficient in regression estimates with unequal error variance. In cross-section applications where error variance is often roughly proportional to the value of the explanatory variables, size adjustment through gross fixed assets deflation has a separate and independent justification quite apart from straightforward interpretation of the ratios which are interesting in themselves. It has been pointed out that, if the intercept of the undeflated equation differs from zero, the resulting estimates will be biased. An examination of the original equations, i.e., those in undeflated form, indicated that in fact the time series intercept was typically negligible so that this particular transformation has substantial validity in time series applications.

The principal test for homoscedasticity, the David statistic, was

---

[11] A more complete interpretation of logarithmic models is reserved for Chapter 9, which discusses capacity models in finer detail.

[12] Obviously, extreme values increase the efficiency of estimation when experimentally selected independent variables have deliberately been widely spaced. For non-experimental data, the suspicion usually exists that extreme values dominate the observed outcomes and might have arisen from the accidental inclusion of heterogeneous data.

[13] See "Correlation and Regression Estimates When the Data are Ratios," EDWIN KUH and JOHN R. MEYER, *Econometrica*, Vol. 23, No. 4, October, 1955, pp. 406–408.

TABLE 4.1

Summary of David Test Statistics on Time Series Error Variance Homogeneity

Equation Number	Number of Breaks Significance Level		Number of Homogeneous Firms Above and Below Heterogeneous Firm Pairs			
	5%	1%	First Break		Second Break	
			Above	Below	Above	Below
(3.9S)	none					
(3.9P)	none					
(3.9SP)	none					
(3.10S)	1	0	4	54		
(3.10P)	none					
(3.10SP)	1	0	5	53		
(3.11S)	none					
(3.11P)	none					
(3.11SP)	none					
(3.12S)	none					
(3.12P)	none					
(3.12SP)	none					
(3.19)	none					
(3.22)	none					
(3.30A)	1	1	57	1		
(3.30B)	1	1	57	1		
(3.31A)	2	0	0	56	56	1
(3.31B)	2	1	0	56	56	1

used to eliminate several firms from time series Equation (3.10) so that only slight interest attaches to the error variance homogeneity properties of the other original units time series estimates [Equations (3.11) and (3.12)] shown in Table 4.1. However, a few significant breaks came to the surface when the data were further transformed. Interestingly enough, the first difference model showed no time series break whatsoever. The ratio models of Equations (3.30) and (3.31) showed a few breaks, but none occurred for logarithms.

For cross-sections, however, a glance at Table 4.2 shows different and more interesting behavior. Even though the firms on the test statistical basis have been selected to have homogeneous error variances it does not follow that in particular years the error variances will inevitably follow the same pattern: in some years the cross-section variances may "blow up" because of uncertainty or the impact of widely distributed unincluded, exogenous forces whereas in other years the excluded factors may be negligible.

TABLE 4.2

Summary of David Test Statistics on Cross-Section Error Variance Homogeneity

Equation Number	Number of Breaks Significance Level		Number of Homogeneous Years Above and Below Heterogeneous Year Pairs					
			First Break		Second Break		Third Break	
	5%	1%	Above	Below	Above	Below	Above	Below
(3.9S)	3	3	2	2	2	5	5	1
(3.9P)	3	2	0	0	0	3	3	7
(3.9SP)	2	2	2	2	2	7	none	
(3.10S)	2	1	0	2	2	12	none	
(3.10P)	1	1	3	12	none		none	
(3.10SP)	2	1	0	2	2	12	none	
(3.11S)	3	1	0	1	1	1	1	2
(3.11P)	2	1	0	1	1	11	none	
(3.11SP)	3	3	0	1	1	2	2	8
(3.12S)	3	2	0	1	1	1	1	9
(3.12P)	2	1	0	1	1	11	none	
(3.12SP)	2	2	0	1	1	11	none	
(3.13S)	2	1	5	7	7	0	none	
(3.13P)	2	0	4	0	0	8	none	
(3.13SP)	1	1	5	8	none		none	
(3.19)	0	0	none		none		none	
(3.21)	0	0	none		none		none	
(3.30A)	2	1	9	3	3	0	none	

That, indeed, is what happened to Equation Set (3.10). First, a break occurs between the years with the two smallest variances and second, between 1941 and the next smaller pre-war year. In general, the error variances after World War II were substantially larger than pre-war. Two different reasons, the first essentially economic, the second statistical, might be adduced to explain the observed pre-war, post-war shift in error variance structure. Error variances are smaller because firms follow the induced pattern of investment most closely with underutilized capacity and great uncertainty about the future. When high levels of confidence and internal liquidity characteristic of the postwar period dominated, it was more feasible and less risky for individual firms to deviate from the recent values of the independent variables, to invest more independently of the current scene. Second, the error variance may be an increasing function of the independent variables.[14] In such instances no breaks should be expected with loga-

---

[14] When independent variables are not positively correlated with time, this particular construction would be incomplete. This condition suffices for the present study.

rithmic transformations where errors proportional to size will be more homogeneous, an implication borne out by the evidence. Logarithmic Equation (3.21) and Equation (3.22) are homogeneous at the five percent level. Nevertheless, the cyclical characteristics of the error variances, even in this case do lend some support to the economic interpretation, although it appears that both the economic and statistical causes were at work. In years when exogenous influences on investment expectations were greatest, namely 1951 and 1952, when the Korean War dominated the investment planning for capital goods producers in our sample, error variances were largest. The structure of errors will typically be strongly influenced by annual cross-section correlation. In addition, significance tests will have greatest validity on logarithmic transformations, which tend to minimize the influence of cross-section error variance correlations.

The behavior of Equation Sets (3.11) and (3.12) is generally similar, although Equation Set (3.11) has one more break per equation. These remarks apply to the sales equations, while the profit equations nearly always had one less break. This suggests that changes in the factors excluded from sales have a more important influence on investment than the factors excluded from profits. This inference will be useful in subsequent interpretations of the more fundamental factors affecting investment behavior. Equation Set (3.12), not surprisingly, acts in general very much like an average of Equation Sets (3.10) and (3.11).

4.4 Sample Independence

The third assumption in the standard regression model is that of sample independence. Because the same firms appear in numerous different samples it is quite conceivable that each firm's within-cell error form will be consistently positive or negative, because there may be unmeasured individual firm investment propensities. In this way different year sample error terms will be dependent.

To illustrate the point, let us start with a simple linear relationship between a dependent variable, Y, and two independent variables, X_1 and X_2.

$$Y_{jt} = \beta_1 X_{1jt} + \beta_2 X_{2jt} + \alpha_j + \varepsilon_{jt}, \qquad (4.2)$$

$j = 1,2,...J$, a firm index,
$t = 1,2,...T$, a time index.

Notice that the subscripts indicate a different intercept for each firm although for now the same regression slope coefficients are assumed for each firm in different periods. If these α_j are not explicitly introduced into the pooled regressions, the unincluded firm intercepts create sample inter-dependence, since this element would be common to all residuals for the same firm.

A. H. Carter has shown that an adaptation of the general linear hypothesis which includes the "firm effects" by introducing dummy variables, one for each firm, will lead to unbiased estimates of variances.[15] Carter assumes that the errors are randomly and independently distributed but that the "correlation effects" (as he calls them) arise through the repeated occurrence of the same items in the different samples, in much the same way that we have illustrated above. Literal application of this technique may cause large-scale computational problems; estimating regression coefficients where the variance-covariance matrices are of order sixty, seventy, or possibly larger, will often prove cumbersome.[16]

A second procedure leads to similar results but lacks the rigorous support of the general linear hypothesis. However, this method possesses real computational advantages over Carter's proposed method. Returning to equation (4.2) shown above, it might be possible to estimate the value of α_j, provided we have a large number of different cross-sections containing the same firms, so that the average value of each firm's residual across time could be calculated. For instance, the more aggressive firms would have a positive deviation within each cross-section while the less aggressive ones would have a negative average residual, when the residuals for the different firms are averaged for different year-cross-sections in the manner just described. With one such average residual for each firm taken as an estimate of α, we can compute the error sum of squares associated with this systematic component and extract it from the residual sum of squares, leaving an independent component to be applied in the analysis of covariance. This

---

[15] A. H. CARTER, "The Estimation and Comparison of Residual Regressions where there are Two or More Related Sets of Observations," *Biometrika*, Vol. 36, 1949, pp. 26–46. An alternative approach proposed by F. Yates treats the more intractable problem of assuming that the true errors are correlated. A clear exposition of the general linear hypothesis will be found in OSCAR KEMPTHORNE, *The Design and Analysis of Experiments*, New York, 1952, pp. 39–67.

[16] Availability of high speed computers with adequate storage capacity has reduced the computational difficulties to manageable proportions.

procedure will be described more completely in Chapter 6 and justified in a related context. By elementary algebra it follows that the average residual over cells from the within-cell regressions will be identically zero when the transformed observations are used. The same number of degrees of freedom are used up (one per firm) as in the Carter method, the computational burden is significantly reduced and the same general results are achieved, although, it is important to note, without the strong theoretical support offered by the general linear hypothesis.

An alternative is to first difference the data. When equation (4.2) is differenced with respect to time we have:

$$\frac{\Delta Y_{jt}}{\Delta t} = \beta_1 \frac{\Delta X_{1jt}}{\Delta t} + \beta_2 \frac{\Delta X_{2jt}}{\Delta t}. \tag{4.3}$$

First differencing with respect to time has annihilated the "firm effect", that is the intercept coefficient α_j, a hypothesis that actually can be tested using a firm's residuals in different cross-sections as defining a sample. Had equation (4.2) contained an additional term, for the sake of simplicity defined to be a linear trend, the process of differencing would have left equation (4.3) with a new intercept, namely the trend coefficient itself.[17] Furthermore, it is possible to test just how important these individual trends are in the sample. If the residuals from within cell regressions for a given firm differ insignificantly from zero in this first difference model, then the trend effects are unimportant.

4.5 Autocorrelation

Autocorrelation obviously can arise in time series and in less obvious fashion can also affect cross-sections.[18] In the latter case intra-cross-section errors are not affected if we are considering a single, isolated estimate. However, when information in the various cross-sections (which includes the same firms in different cross-sections) are pooled, the existence of autocorrelation should be recognized explicitly for two reasons. First, the standard errors of a pooled regression coefficient

[17] Cf. RICHARD STONE, *The Measurement of Consumers' Expenditure and Behavior in the United Kingdom, 1920–1938*, Cambridge, England, 1954, pp. 306–308.

[18] A comprehensive review of many points mentioned in this section will be found in R. L. ANDERSON, "The Problem of Autocorrelation in Regression Analysis," *Journal of the American Statistical Association*, Vol. 49, No. 265, March, 1954, pp. 113–129.

should be modified.[19] Second, evaluation of variance ratios will be biased since interdependent firm error terms imply that the effective degrees of freedom have been overstated.

A substantial literature on the effects of autocorrelated error terms and how to cope with them has been rapidly accumulating in recent years. Most of the proposed corrections depend upon exact knowledge of the variance-covariance matrix of the errors which seldom will be known. If on the other hand there is considerable serial correlation, it is known that t and F tests will be invalid since the error variance will be systematically underestimated and the efficiency of estimation will be less than when the errors are distributed independently in time.[20]

Because the denominator mean square is too small (since its degrees of freedom have been exaggerated), the hypothesis of no significant difference between the numerator and denominator of the F-ratio will be rejected too frequently. A standard asymptotic approximation formula for effective degrees of freedom is $N\{(1 - \varrho_1\varrho_2)/(1 + \varrho_1\varrho_2)\}$ where N is the sample size and ϱ_1 and ϱ_2 are first order serial correlations of two series. If, for instance , $\varrho_1 = \varrho_2 = 0.7$ the effective degrees of freedom will be one-third the number of observations actually used.[21]

Still another autocorrelation problem arises in the estimation of distributed lags, when, in our case, for instance, K_t is estimated as a weighted average of past sales. Marc Nerlove has shown that in the estimation of distributed lags, a maximum likelihood procedure requires stepwise maximization in which the geometric weighting factor, like $(1 - b)$ in Equation (2.5) of Chapter 2, rewritten as

$$K_t = \gamma + \alpha b \sum_{T=1}^{t} (1 - b)^{t-T}X_T + U_t$$

is allowed to vary systematically while the coefficients γ and α are estimated in a manner such that correlation is maximized, or what amounts to the same thing, the error sum of squares $(\Sigma\, U_t^2)$ is minim-

[19] See HERMAN WOLD, *Demand Analysis*, 1953, pp. 211–13.

[20] An easily accessible and well written summary of much of this literature will be found in Richard J. FOOTE, *Analytical Tools for Studying Demand and Price Structures*, Agricultural Handbook No. 146, Washington, D.C., 1949, pp. 158–169, a section written by Marc Nerlove. The disadvantages of using serial correlation coefficients estimated from sample data are developed by F. H. C. MARRIOT and J. A. POPE, "Bias in the Estimation of Autocorrelations," *Biometrika*, Vol. 41, 1954, pp. 390–404.

[21] See equation (4) at the bottom of Table 4.3 for an application of this proposition.

ized.[22] He also shows that unless the error term in the likelihood function follows a relatively complicated autoregressive structure similar in form to that of the solution to the difference equation whose coefficients are being estimated, the error term of the estimated equation will itself be autocorrelated. Nerlove concludes that "as suggested in our discussion of estimation procedures, all the difficulties so far presented in this part may, in theory, be obviated by assuming that the residuals of the original demand equations follow more-or-less complicated autoregressive schemes. In view of the nature of most economic time series, to assume these autoregressive schemes is neither better nor worse than to assume that the residuals in the original equations are independently distributed. On the other hand, false specification of any kind may lead to serious errors."[23] It should be observed that, contrary to Koyck's scheme, Nerlove's estimation processes require the assumption of autocorrelation in the original equation in order to arrive at uncorrelated disturbances in the transformed equation. Nerlove's estimation procedures are maximum likelihood procedures for evaluating distributed lags directly while Koyck's procedure estimates the distributed lag coefficients indirectly.

In an interesting treatment of the effects of error serial correlation on estimated coefficients in distributed lag models, Griliches has shown that the estimated reaction coefficient will be biased downward when the error term follows a first order Markoff process and serial correlation is positive. As noted previously, the bias will be greater, the higher the correlation among independent variables and the worse the goodness of fit. Griliches presents a number of tables showing what the expected value of the bias will be under a variety of different assumptions about true parameter values.[24]

Test statistics for cross-section autocorrelation will be computed when the residual variance has been defined in terms of the "private" residual variance of a particular firm, i.e., the sum of squared deviations from the individual firm's average (across cross-section) residual divided by degrees of freedom. Test statistics for autocorrelation in time series generated residuals were also computed. In both instances

[22] MARC NERLOVE, *Distributed Lags and Demand Analysis for Agricultural and Other Commodities*, Agricultural Handbook No. 141, Agricultural Marketing Service. U.S. Department of Agriculture, June, 1958, pp. 48–51.

[23] NERLOVE, *Ibid.*, p. 82.

[24] ZVI GRILICHES, "A Note on Serial Correlation Bias in Estimates of Distributed Lags," *Econometrica*, January, 1961, pp. 65–73.

the Durbin-Watson statistic was used, which is currently one of the most accurate available test statistics when the alternative hypothesis is a first order Markoff process generated error term. Two alternative serial correlation tests were rejected. The precursor of the Durbin-Watson test, the von Neumann test statistic, has certain biases that have been corrected in the Durbin-Watson statistic, in particular a bias for acceptance of the null hypothesis of no serial correlation as the number of regression coefficients estimated increases. Second, there is a test proposed by E. J. Hannan.[25] The Hannan test has the principal advantage over the Durbin-Watson statistic of possessing a completely determined distribution, i.e. it does not contain a zone of indecision. This exactitude, however, is obtained at the expense of estimating nearly twice as many parameters as appear in the original equation which, with the short time series we are forced to deal with, would lead to extremely inefficient estimates.

While it is sometimes correct to interpret findings of positive serial correlation in the residuals as a reflection of both a correctly specified regression equation and a truly autocorrelated residual, strong autocorrelation often indicates that the regression equation was improperly specified and that there are systematic, excluded factors which should explicitly be taken into account. The alternative to including other variab͞   changing the equation form, of course, is to increase the efficiency of estimation through a transformation such as first differencing that eliminates autocorrelation.

When autocorrelation is substantial, simple considerations indicate that first differencing can overcome this difficulty. Assume that the error term ε_t is generated by a Markoff process, in which v_t is a random variable distributed independently in time, and $|\alpha| < 1$, as in (4.4):

$$\varepsilon_t = \alpha \, \varepsilon_{t-1} + v_t \, , \qquad\qquad (4.4)$$

$$\Delta \varepsilon_t = (\alpha - 1)\varepsilon_{t-1} + v_t \, . \qquad\qquad (4.5)$$

If α equals 1, the first differencing process leaves only the random

[25] J. DURBIN and G. S. WATSON, "Testing for Serial Correlation in Least Squares Regression, I," *Biometrika*, Vol. 37 (December, 1950), pp. 409–428, and "Testing for Serial Correlation and Least Squares Regression, II," *Biometrika*, Vol. 38 (June, 1951), pp. 159–178; E. J. HANNAN, "Exact Tests for Serial Correlation," *Biometrika*, Vol. 42, Pts. 1 and 2, June, 1955, pp. 133–142 and "An Exact Test for Correlation Between Time Series," *op. cit.*, Vol. 42, Pts. 3 and 4, pp. 316–326, December, 1955.

term v_j for the residual. [26] Clearly from (4.5), if $\alpha < 1$, inverse correlation will be created. To anticipate later results, it turned out that the first differencing operation eliminated some slight positive autocorrelation. [27]

In some recent developments on another highly relevant aspect of autocorrelation, first difference estimation relations, E. J. Hannan has shown that the efficiency of the estimated regression coefficients depends on the independent variable's autocorrelations, in addition to previously known results that efficiency depends on autocorrelation in the true error. In a simple regression model where both error term and independent variable have been generated by a stationary simple Markoff process, it is possible to evaluate the asymptotic relative efficiency of the estimated parameters when the observations have been first differenced, and when they have not. These relative efficiencies, shown in Table 4.3, were calculated from theorems of Hannan and Wold. They clearly show, for highly plausible combinations of autocorrelation coefficients, that first differencing could lead to substantial increases in estimation efficiency.

Since economic time series are not usually generated from controlled experiments, the existence of autocorrelation shown by several studies on the autoregressive nature of time series should be taken into account in both estimation and hypothesis testing. This should not be construed to mean that "errors of observations" should be attributed to the independent variables on the specific ground of autocorrelation. [28]

Table 4.4 summarizes, as simple averages, the serial correlations obtained from the present sample. The serial correlation properties of the original variables, shown in Equation (3.10), have certain noteworthy properties. The capital stock variable has extemely high autocorrelations of both first and second order. The sales figures are slightly

---

[26] GUY H. ORCUTT and D. COCHRANE, "Application of Least Squares Regression to Relationships Containing Autocorrelated Error Terms," *Journal of the American Statistical Association*, Vol. 44, September, 1949, pp. 32–61.

[27] While existence of time series autogressive structure is not open to serious question, the precise nature and interpretation of the structure remains open to dispute. See especially JOHN GURLAND, "An Example of Autocorrelated Disturbances in Linear Regression," *Econometrica*, Vol. 22, No. 2, April, 1954, pp. 218–227.

[28] See GUY H. ORCUTT, "A Study of the Autoregressive Nature of the Time Series Used for Tinbergen's Model of the Economic System of the United States, 1919–1932," *Journal of the Royal Statistical Society*, Series B, Vol. X, No. 1, 1948, pp. 1–35, and ARTHUR J. GARTAGANIS, "Autoregression in the United States Economy – 1870–1929,', *Econometrica*, Vol. 22, 1954, pp. 228–243.

TABLE 4.3

Relative Efficiency of Estimation with Autocorrelation of the Errors

Ratio of asymptotic variance of estimated slope regression coefficient by least squares from original values to that estimated from first differences when both independent variable and error term have been generated by a stationary Markoff process, for some alternative autocorrelation values.

$\varrho_1 \backslash \varrho$	0	0.2	0.4	0.6	0.8	0.9	0.95
0	0.666	0.893	1.282	2.083	4.545	9.524	19.417
0.2	0.571	0.813	1.241	2.154	5.043	10.977	22.940
0.4	0.462	0.698	1.137	2.114	5.351	12.179	25.875
0.6	0.308	0.538	0.939	1.889	5.286	12.833	28.545
0.8	0.182	0.315	0.595	1.321	4.316	11.862	28.160
0.9	0.095	0.172	0.338	0.802	2.966	9.231	24.800
0.95	0.049	0.090	0.181	0.449	1.796	6.200	19.000

1. Assumed population characteristics and definitions:

$$Y_t = \alpha + \beta X_t + \varepsilon_t$$
$$\varepsilon_t = \varrho \varepsilon_{t-1} + V_t \qquad \text{var } \varepsilon = \sigma^2$$
$$X_t = \varrho_1 X_{t-1} + U_t \qquad \text{var } X = \sigma_x^2$$

2. Assume V, U are random independently distributed variables, and also that $|\varrho| < 1$ and $|\varrho_1| < 1$.

3. α and β are population parameters to be estimated by least squares when X and Y are in original units on the one hand and first differences on the other. Denote the asymptotic variance of the estimated β in original units as var $\hat{\beta}$ and the asymptotic variance on first differences as var $\hat{\beta}_{FD}$, and the sample size as N.

4. $\text{var } \hat{\beta} = \dfrac{1}{N} \dfrac{\sigma^2 (1 + \varrho \varrho_1)}{\sigma_x^2 (1 - \varrho \varrho_1)}.$

5. $\text{var } \hat{\beta}_{FD} = \dfrac{1}{2N} \dfrac{\sigma^2}{\sigma_x^2} \dfrac{(1 - \varrho)(3 - \varrho \varrho_1 - \varrho - \varrho_1)}{(1 - \varrho_1)(1 - \varrho \varrho_1)}.$

6. $\dfrac{\text{var } \hat{\beta}}{\text{var } \hat{\beta}_{FD}} = \dfrac{2(1 + \varrho \varrho_1)(1 - \varrho_1)}{(1 - \varrho)(3 - \varrho \varrho_1 - \varrho - \varrho_1)}.$

The table was computed from (6) for various combinations of ϱ and ϱ_1. The relation for var $\hat{\beta}$(4) is ascribed to HERMAN WOLD, *Demand Analysis*, 1953, p. 211 and that for var β_{FD}(5) was obtained by E. J. HANNAN in "Exact Tests for Serial Correlation," *Biometrika*, Vol. 42, Parts 1 and 2, June, 1955, p. 141. Both formulations are contained in the Hannan article.

less serially correlated. Since these are price corrected figures, one important trend element has been removed. Somewhat surprisingly, at least to the author, is the fact that gross retained profits are so much less autocorrelated than sales. The relative capacity variable has less autocorrelation than the others. Since this variable has been normalized, trend factors have been essentially removed so that autocorrelation for this normalized variable is negligible.

TABLE 4.4

Average Serial Correlations for Sample Firms

Equation		$S_t/C \cdot K_t$	K	S	P
(3.9)	Lag 1	−0.0874	0.0487	−0.0733	−0.2945
	Lag 2	−0.0762	−0.0011	−0.2022	−0.1258
(3.10)	Lag 1	0.4873	0.9190	0.7060	0.3287
	Lag 2	0.0902	0.8625	0.5215	0.1357
(3.11)	Lag 1	—	—	0.7413	0.3123
	Lag 2	—	—	0.5700	0.1211
(3.12)	Lag 1	—	—	0.8393	0.6283
	Lag 2	—	—	0.6425	0.2002
Serial Correlation Standard Deviations					
(3.9)	Lag 1	0.2627	0.3148	0.2743	0.2094
	Lag 2	0.2812	0.2794	0.2626	0.3291
(3.10)	Lag 1	0.2547	0.1399	0.1912	0.2968
	Lag 2	0.3661	0.1862	0.3018	0.3494
(3.11)	Lag 1	—	—	0.1818	0.3306
	Lag 2	—	—	0.2727	0.3862
(3.12)	Lag 1	—	—	0.1260	0.2117
	Lag 2	—	—	0.2752	0.4527
Coefficient of Variation					
(3.9)	Lag 1	−3.004	6.460	−3.741	−0.7109
	Lag 2	−3.686	−242.7	−1.298	−2.614
(3.10)	Lag 1	0.5226	0.1522	0.2708	0.9028
	Lag 2	4.058	0.2159	0.5787	2.575
(3.11)	Lag 1	—	—	0.2452	1.059
	Lag 2	—	—	0.4784	3.189
(3.12)	Lag 1	—	—	0.1501	0.3369
	Lag 2	—	—	0.4283	2.260

First differences completely annihilate whatever serial correlation existed in the original values and created an inverse relationship for the first lagged serial correlation coefficient, particularly strong in the case of profits. Even sales for firms now have negligible serial correlation and indeed the second order serial correlation coefficient is noticeably negative. Furthermore, when we view the first difference in the capital stock as a rough approximation to investment, for which no serial correlation coefficients were directly computed, it appears that investment is little correlated with itself on a year to year basis.

Potentially large advantages of first differences include the increased likelihood of sample independence through the elimination of individual firm constant effects and reduction in time series of error term autocorrelation. A potentially important disadvantage of the first differencing procedure is that errors of observation in the independent variables may be magnified. Consider the case where the observational errors in an independent variable are independently distributed in time. When the variable is first differenced, its error variance will double. However, if the errors of observation are positively correlated, first differencing can successfully reduce the error variance of the independent variable or variables. For example, if the error term is generated by the Markoff process then the variance of ε_t in equation (4.4) is greater than the variance of v_t; in fact,

$$\sigma_\varepsilon^2 = \frac{1 - \alpha^2}{\sigma_v^2}. \tag{4.6}$$

When first differencing reduces autocorrelation in the error of observation, this source of error variance will be less. Hence, the effects of first differencing are sensitive to the actual process generating the error term in the independent variable.

Bias will also result from such errors and must be carefully distinguished from biases originating from correlations between included and excluded variables which have been discussed previously. Even when the "observation" errors are uncorrelated with the included independent variables, the usual estimated regression coefficients (i.e., unweighted estimates) will be biased toward zero. This sort of bias will therefore be exaggerated if the errors are independent and reduced if the errors are autocorrelated, the ultimate importance depending on the variance of the error term in the estimating equation relative to the variance of the related independent variable. If the latter is large relative to the former, bias will be unimportant and *vice versa*. A certain grim satisfaction might be had from a conjecture that excluded variables influencing investment are often of such importance that observation error bias will be negligible, despite considerable errors of observation.

With only a few minor reservations, it is perhaps somewhat surprising to note in Table 4.5, which summarizes Durbin-Watson statistics, how infrequently time series autocorrelation in the error terms arises. It should be observed that the first difference model, Equation (3.9), has substantially less autocorrelation than any of the other time series,

TABLE 4.5

Durbin-Watson Test Summary: Time Series

| | Significance Level | | | | | |
| | Five Percent | | | One Percent | | |
Equation	No Serial Correlation	Indeter- minate	Serial Correlation	No Serial Correlation	Indeter- minate	Serial Correlation
(3.9S)	51	7	2	57	3	0
(3.9P)	51	9	0	57	3	0
(3.9SP)	45	15	0	52	8	0
(3.10S)	39	16	5	46	13	1
(3.10P)	37	21	2	46	12	2
(3.10SP)	39	19	2	43	17	0
(3.11S)	42	16	2	53	7	0
(3.11P)	40	17	3	50	8	2
(3.11SP)	40	20	0	51	9	0
(3.12S)	42	14	3	50	10	0
(3.12P)	40	16	4	52	5	2
(3.12SP)	39	20	1	50	10	0
(3.19)	55	4	1	58	2	0
(3.22)	35	23	2	53	6	1
(3.30A)	40	15	5	49	10	1
(3.30B)	37	19	4	43	16	1

an outcome reinforcing findings from other studies. Few firms had significant serial correlation in the time series computations, although a number, typically around 15, were in the indecisive middle range. At the five percent significance level, however, it should be noted that the smallest number of firms without serial correlation is recorded for Equation (3.10), which has no lagged values sales or profits. Equations (3.11) and (3.12) which do have lagged values typically have about 4 or 5 more in the "no serial correlation" category for the five percent level and 4 to 8 more at the one percent significance level. The evidence clearly suggests that autocorrelation is at least in part attributable to the exclusion of lagged variables. This particular reason has been cited by Nerlove as one of the most fundamental sources of autocorrelation, for which further evidence has now been adduced.[29]

[29] NERLOVE, *op. cit.* H. THEIL and A. L. NAGAR, "Testing the Independence of Regression Disturbances," *Journal of the American Statistical Association*, December, 1962, pp. 793–806, show that when independent variables first and second differences are small relative to the range of the variables, the correct significance level is the upper limit of the indeterminate range. For all except first difference equations and possibly the

How well the sales model behaves, in contrast to the profit model, cannot be clearly ascertained from time series evidence. Except for the first differenced model, the sales model contains less serial correlation than the profit model. The difference is not very marked and, indeed, some contradictory evidence is contained in Equation (3.10), the unlagged model, in which there is more positive serial correlation in the sales model than in the profit model but the profit model has many more undecided values. On Equations (3.11) and (3.12) there is no such ambiguity. There is some evidence that the inclusion of sales with profits reduces serial correlation slightly. Equation sets (3.10SP) and (3.11SP) have less serial correlation at the 5 percent level than (3.10P) or (3.11P), although the differences are small.

The hypothesis of no serial correlation cannot be rejected most of the time at the one percent significance level with the exception of Equation (3.10) which shows the greatest serial correlation of any of the equations. Invariably between 50 and 55 firms, a substantial majority of the sixty firms included, fall in this category. Hence, in the above analysis serial correlation tests reflect that even these simple investment models have not been inappropriately specified in this relevant aspect. While the absence of serial correlation offers grounds for encouragement, it is obvious that this is necessary but far from a sufficient condition for a validly specified model.

The Durbin-Watson statistic was also computed for firms in cross-sections. In this instance the error term is that for each firm in different years, a summary of which appears in Table 4.6. Each such error term, it will be recalled, is a deviation from its "private mean," defined as the average of cross-section residuals for the particular firm across all years,

$$\bar{\varepsilon}_j = \sum_{t=1}^{T} \varepsilon_{jt}/T \, . \qquad (4.7)$$

and this newly defined firm time series residual was correspondingly analyzed. Two alternatives, with conflicting outcomes, might be used to rationalize finding substantially more correlation for one data source than the other. Because the cross-section regressions had different intercepts, so the first argument runs, serial correlation in the inter-

ratio models these conditions will prevail. When first and second differences are small, the indeterminate column should be read as indicating autocorrelation at the stated significance level.

cepts, reflecting the common time series error effect, would cause cross-section data generated residual autocorrelations to be less than straight time series, since the cross-section intercept absorbs the common, autocorrelated effect.[30]

In contrast to the previous reason the second reason would support a contrary finding, where time series generated data would have less autocorrelation than cross-section generated data. For the sake of argument, assume that each firm has time series with the following characteristics. First, the dependent variable time series has strong serial correlation, due to continuity in investment programs, internal to the firm, the business cycle, and to some extent, trend. Second, the error term is uncorrelated. If all firms had similar slope coefficients and also possessed time series with the characteristics just described, we would expect to find relatively uncorrelated residuals once the regression effects from the cross-section had been taken out. Then the first proposition would dominate so that there would be less autocorrelation on the cross-section. But suppose instead that regression coefficients were in fact not homogeneous and that the estimated cross-section regression slopes are actually weighted averages of unlike, nonhomogeneous coefficients. In this case the dependent variable for each firm would "not be explained so well" as in the case of each firm with its own coefficients, for individual time series. When the regression explanation for each individual series is attenuated in this manner, autocorrelation in the dependent variable time series will become more pronounced. In such circumstances we would expect to find more autocorrelation on cross-sections than on time series. Which of the two conflicting possibilities prevailed is clear from an examination of Tables 4.5 and 4.6. The cross-sections show substantially more serial correlation, or more precisely, substantially fewer firms with no significant serial correlation than do the time series. It is particularly interesting to note on Equation (3.10) that the relative difference between the degree of explanation on cross-section and time series is considerably less than for the others. Although cross-sections are more serially correlated than the time series, on the first difference model, the difference is relatively small, much less than with nearly all the other equations. Anticipating the results of a later chapter, we observe that Equation (3.9) also has the most homogeneous slopes of all the regression equations. It thus appears that the heterogeneity among

---

[30] Chapter 5 goes further into the underlying concepts briefly presented here.

TABLE 4.6

Durbin-Watson Test Summary: Cross-Sections

| | Significance Level | | | | | |
| | Five Percent | | | One Percent | | |
Equation	No Serial Correlation	Indeter- minate	Serial Correlation	No Serial Correlation	Indeter- minate	Serial Correlation
(3.9S)	41	19	0	51	9	0
(3.9P)	45	15	0	47	13	0
(3.9SP)	41	19	0	50	10	0
(3.10S)	21	31	8	32	26	2
(3.10P)	16	40	4	28	30	2
(3.10SP)	11	48	1	23	37	0
(3.11S)	21	35	4	34	25	1
(3.11P)	19	40	1	33	27	0
(3.11SP)	17	42	1	24	36	0
(3.12S)	22	34	4	32	26	2
(3.12P)	16	41	3	28	32	0
(3.12SP)	13	47	0	22	38	0
(3.13S)	4	35	21	8	42	10
(3.13P)	3	36	21	10	42	8
(3.13SP)	1	43	16	3	54	3
(3.20)	19	27	14	29	28	3
(3.21)	19	31	10	27	30	3
(3.30A)	27	18	15	42	14	4
(3.30B)	23	27	10	31	27	2

regression coefficients could be the major source of the substantially higher serial correlation observed on the cross-sections.

The principal difference between the time series and cross-section Durbin-Watson statistics is the very large increase in the number of firms in the "undecided," middle column for the cross-section statistics. There is not a very large increase in the number of positive serial correlations and there must therefore, of course, be a substantial reduction in the number of firms in the "definitely no serial correlation" category.

A somewhat different way of looking at the Durbin-Watson statistics is to array the results according to size of firm. In Tables 4.7 and 4.8 the 60 firms were divided into three groups of twenty each according to average gross fixed assets in 1948. There is little room for comment on Equation (3.9), where in most cases serial correlation was negligible. On Equations (3.10) and (3.10SP) the largest number of insignificant serial correlations occurs for the largest firms. Without remark-

TABLE 4.7

Durbin-Watson Test: Size Categories for Time Series

	Significance Level					
	Five Percent			One Percent		
	No Serial Corre- lation	Indeter- minate	Serial Corre- lation	No Serial Corre- lation	Indeter- minate	Serial Corre- lation
Equations (3.9S)						
Smallest 20 firms	17	2	1	18	2	0
Middle 20 firms	16	3	1	19	1	0
Largest 20 firms	18	2	0	20	0	0
Total	51	7	2	57	3	0
Equation (3.9P)						
Smallest 20 firms	17	3	0	18	2	0
Middle 20 firms	16	4	0	19	1	0
Largest 20 firms	18	2	0	20	0	0
Total	51	9	0	57	3	0
Equation (3.9SP)						
Smallest 20 firms	13	7	0	17	3	0
Middle 20 firms	15	5	0	16	4	0
Largest 20 firms	17	3	0	19	1	0
Total	45	15	0	52	8	0
Equation (3.10S)						
Smallest 20 firms	12	6	2	15	4	1
Middle 20 firms	10	7	3	12	8	0
Largest 20 firms	17	3	0	19	1	0
Total	39	16	5	46	13	1
Equation (3.10P)						
Smallest 20 firms	9	10	1	15	4	1
Middle 20 firms	13	6	1	14	5	1
Largest 20 firms	15	5	0	17	3	0
Total	37	21	2	46	12	2
Equation (3.10SP)						
Smallest 20 firms	11	8	1	13	7	0
Middle 20 firms	11	8	1	12	8	0
Largest 20 firms	17	3	0	18	2	0
Total	39	19	2	43	17	0
Equations (3.11S)						
Smallest 20 firms	12	8	0	17	3	0
Middle 20 firms	12	6	2	16	4	0
Largest 20 firms	18	2	0	20	0	0
Total	42	16	2	53	7	0
Equation (3.11P)						
Smallest 20 firms	10	8	2	16	3	1
Middle 20 firms	12	7	1	14	5	1
Largest 20 firms	18	2	0	20	0	0
Total	40	17	3	50	8	2

TABLE 4.7 (*continued*)

Durbin-Watson Test: Size Categories for Time Series

	Significance Level					
	Five Percent			One Percent		
	No Serial Corre-lation	Indeter-minate	Serial Corre-lation	No Serial Corre-lation	Indeter-minate	Serial Corre-lation
Equation (3.11SP)						
Smallest 20 firms	11	9	0	16	4	0
Middle 20 firms	14	6	0	16	4	0
Largest 20 firms	15	5	0	19	1	0
Total	40	20	0	51	9	0
Equation (3.12S)						
Smallest 20 firms	14	6	0	17	3	0
Middle 20 firms	12	5	3	13	7	0
Largest 20 firms	17	3	0	20	0	0
Total	43	14	3	50	10	0
Equation (3.12P)						
Smallest 20 firms	10	8	2	17	2	1
Middle 20 firms	14	4	2	16	3	1
Largest 20 firms	16	4	0	20	0	0
Total	40	16	4	52	5	2
Equation (3.12SP)						
Smallest 20 firms	13	6	1	15	5	0
Middle 20 firms	11	9	0	15	5	0
Largest 20 firms	15	5	0	20	0	0
Total	39	20	1	50	10	0
Equation (3.19)						
Smallest 20 firms	18	1	1	18	2	0
Middle 20 firms	18	2	0	20	0	0
Largest 20 firms	19	1	0	20	0	0
Total	55	4	1	58	2	0
Equation (3.22)						
Smallest 20 firms	12	8	0	18	2	0
Middle 20 firms	10	8	2	15	4	1
Largest 20 firms	13	7	0	20	0	0
Total	35	23	2	53	6	1
Equation (3.30A)						
Smallest 20 firms	11	6	3	15	5	0
Middle 20 firms	12	6	2	15	4	1
Largest 20 firms	17	3	0	19	1	0
Total	40	15	5	49	10	1
Equation (3.30B)						
Smallest 20 firms	11	7	2	13	7	0
Middle 20 firms	10	8	2	12	7	1
Largest 20 firms	16	4	0	18	2	0
Total	37	19	4	43	16	1

TABLE 4.8

Durbin-Watson Test: Size Categories for Cross-Sections

	Significance Level					
	Five Percent			One Percent		
	No Serial Corre-lation	Indeter-minate	Serial Corre-lation	No Serial Corre-lation	Indeter-minate	Serial Corre-lation
Equation (3.9S)						
Smallest 20 firms	14	6	0	18	2	0
Middle 20 firms	12	8	0	16	4	0
Largest 20 firms	15	5	0	17	3	0
Total	41	19	0	51	9	0
Equation (3.9P)						
Smallest 20 firms	16	4	0	16	4	0
Middle 20 firms	13	7	0	14	6	0
Largest 20 firms	16	4	0	17	3	0
Total	45	15	0	47	13	0
Equation (3.9SP)						
Smallest 20 firms	14	6	0	18	2	0
Middle 20 firms	12	8	0	15	5	0
Largest 20 firms	15	5	0	17	3	0
Total	41	19	0	50	10	0
Equation (3.10S)						
Smallest 20 firms	7	10	3	9	9	2
Middle 20 firms	6	10	4	10	10	0
Largest 20 firms	8	11	1	13	7	0
Total	21	31	8	32	26	2
Equation (3.10P)						
Smallest 20 firms	2	17	1	10	9	1
Middle 20 firms	6	12	2	9	11	0
Largest 20 firms	8	11	1	9	10	1
Total	16	40	4	28	30	2
Equation (3.10SP)						
Smallest 20 firms	1	18	1	7	13	0
Middle 20 firms	5	15	0	7	13	0
Largest 20 firms	5	15	0	9	11	0
Total	11	48	1	23	37	0
Equation (3.11S)						
Smallest 20 firms	6	13	1	12	8	0
Middle 20 firms	7	11	2	10	9	1
Largest 20 firms	8	11	1	12	8	0
Total	21	35	4	34	25	1
Equation (3.11P)						
Smallest 20 firms	5	15	0	12	8	0
Middle 20 firms	7	13	0	10	10	0
Largest 20 firms	7	12	1	11	9	0
Total	19	40	1	33	27	0

TABLE 4.8 (*continued*)

Durbin-Watson Test: Size Categories for Cross-Sections

	Significance Level					
	Five Percent			One Percent		
	No Serial Corre- lation	Indeter- minate	Serial Corre- lation	No Serial Corre- lation	Indeter- minate	Serial Corre- lation
Equation (3.11SP)						
Smallest 20 firms	4	16	0	8	12	0
Middle 20 firms	7	12	1	8	12	0
Largest 20 firms	6	14	0	8	12	0
Total	17	42	1	24	36	0
Equation (3.12S)						
Smallest 20 firms	8	11	1	11	9	0
Middle 20 firms	7	11	2	9	10	1
Largest 20 firms	7	12	1	12	7	1
Total	22	34	4	32	26	2
Equation (3.12P)						
Smallest 20 firms	3	17	0	9	11	0
Middle 20 firms	7	11	2	9	11	0
Largest 20 firms	6	13	1	10	10	0
Total	16	41	3	28	32	0
Equation (3.12SP)						
Smallest 20 firms	3	17	0	8	12	0
Middle 20 firms	5	15	0	8	12	0
Largest 20 firms	5	15	0	6	14	0
Total	13	47	0	22	38	0
Equation (3.13S)						
Smallest 20 firms	1	14	5	1	16	3
Middle 20 firms	2	9	9	3	13	4
Largest 20 firms	1	12	7	4	13	3
Total	4	35	21	8	42	10
Equation (3.13P)						
Smallest 20 firms	0	16	4	4	13	3
Middle 20 firms	2	10	8	2	15	3
Largest 20 firms	1	10	9	4	14	2
Total	3	36	21	10	42	8
Equation (3.13SP)						
Smallest 20 firms	0	17	3	0	19	1
Middle 20 firms	1	12	7	2	17	1
Largest 20 firms	0	14	6	1	18	1
Total	1	43	16	3	54	3
Equation (3.21)						
Smallest 20 firms	4	14	2	7	13	0
Middle 20 firms	6	6	8	8	9	3
Largest 20 firms	9	11	0	12	8	0
Total	19	31	10	27	30	3

TABLE 4.8 (*continued*)

Durbin-Watson Test: Size Categories for Cross-Sections

	Significance Level					
	Five Percent			One Percent		
	No Serial Correlation	Indeterminate	Serial Correlation	No Serial Correlation	Indeterminate	Serial Correlation
Equation (3.20)						
Smallest 20 firms	6	7	7	1	10	9
Middle 20 firms	7	8	5	2	10	8
Largest 20 firms	1	12	7	0	8	12
Total	14	27	19	3	28	29
Equation (3.30B)						
Smallest 20 firms	7	11	2	9	11	0
Middle 20 firms	6	7	7	9	9	2
Largest 20 firms	10	9	1	13	7	0
Total	23	27	10	31	27	2
Equation (3.30A)						
Smallest 20 firms	8	6	6	12	7	1
Middle 20 firms	8	5	7	13	4	3
Largest 20 firms	11	7	2	17	3	0
Total	27	18	15	42	14	4

ing in detail on the subsequent patterns which evolved (and Equation (3.12) is somewhat ambiguous in this regard) it seems evident that the larger firms consistently show less serial correlation than do the smaller firms. Hence, to this extent, the specification happens to be superior for large firms than for small. While the differences are not so pronounced on the cross-sections, the time series distributions in Table 4.7 are more striking. For every equation the difference between the smallest twenty firms with no serial correlation and the largest twenty firms with no serial correlation is larger than on cross-sections, ordinarily exceeding three or four.

4.6 Summary

Several hypotheses about data generating structures and how these affect the least squares estimating procedure were reviewed. First, the possibility of least squares bias does not appear as troublesome in the context of individual firm estimation as it does in macro-economic models, the principal context in which the simultaneous equation problem has been discussed. Second, the problems posed by heterogeneous error variances were taken up. Sets of data with extremely heterogeneous inter-firm variances were excluded. No attempt was made to eliminate variance heterogeneity in the cross-sections, and as a consequence, the error variances post-war typically turned out to be larger than those measured for the pre-war period. Third, autocorrelated error terms were discussed and the Durbin-Watson test applied to individual firms. First differencing effectively removed autocorrelation, while the error terms for the remaining equations showed that, by and large, the assumption of independent errors would not be far wrong.

CHAPTER 5

THE TEMPORAL STABILITY OF CROSS-SECTIONS
AND THE SPECIFICATION OF VARIABLES

5.1 Introduction

The thesis to be developed here is that the possibilities of correctly specifying a behavior equation can be improved by using many cross-sections at the same time. After a series of cross-section regression equations are estimated and evaluated, one may refuse to accept an initial working hypothesis of correct specification and thereafter respecify the equation more accurately.[1] While time series and cross-section parameters will in general not be the same, many of the influences which enter into the determination of one will affect the other as well. The existence of these common causes permits inferences to be made about behavior over time from cross-section studies.

Variables can display one of three types of variation. First, variables that are the same for each individual in a cross-section but which vary from cross-section to cross-section will be called time variables. Second, variables which differ among individuals at a point of time but which are constant through time will be called section variables. Third, a variable can differ among individuals in a cross-section at a given point of time and also exhibit variations through time. Such variables will, for short, be dubbed time-section variables.

As examples of variables likely to occur in an investment study which exhibit these different kinds of behavior, one can readily conceive of "time-section" variables such as profits, sales and capital stock which change through time and differ among individuals. Section variables would include attributes of individual firm management which influence investment behavior, or inter-firm difference in capital inten-

---

[1] The same analysis could be usefully applied to time series with different cyclical behavior. For a concrete example, see E. KUH, *Profits, Profit Markups, and Productivity*, Study Paper No. 15, Joint Economic Committee, 1960, pp. 88–92.

sity. However, many of these variables which are treated as constant for an individual but which differ among them will occasionally change. For instance, a firm's capital intensity may change through time but as a rule only slowly. As examples of the third category, variables which are the same for individuals at a point of time but which vary through time, there are such things as prices, interest rates, and widespread optimism or pessimism. These are idealized cases since individual firms in a cross-section will often pay somewhat different prices and will face different interest rates or will be subject to different degrees of optimism and pessimism. Hence, even these variables are not "pure types" although the nature of the variation is characteristically of the sort described.[2]

These different sorts of variations apply, of course, to both included and excluded variables, i.e., shift variables or error terms. Throughout, attention will be concentrated on relations between excluded time variables and included time-section variables. For the sake of simplicity only two included variables will be considered. Initially it will be assumed that these two variables are of the time-section variety and that the relationship is approximately linear in both parameters and variables within a given cross-section. Finally, it will be assumed that the error variance is the same in each cross-section.

Let

$$Y_{jt} = \alpha + \beta X_{jt} + \varepsilon_{jt} \qquad (5.1)$$

where

Y_{jt} is the dependent variable; investment,
X_{jt} the independent variable; output,
ε_{jt} the error term,
$j = 1,2, .. J$ firm index,
$t = 1,2, .. T$ cell year index.

Certain varieties of the intertemporal behavior of this relationship that might be encountered can be described. The ultimate goal will be to use all available information through combining all single period cross-section observations in a single regression which will be termed the pool regression, that is, a single regression based on all observations through time. To do so there are two necessary conditions. First, the

[2] We could formally define section and time variables as limiting cases of time-section variables when the ratio of variance attributable to one or the other is negligible relative to the total variance of a particular variable.

cross-section regression parameters must come from the same universe. If both slope and intercept among different cross-sections are the same (within sampling error), this condition will have been met. If, however, the hypothesis that the intercept is constant among cross-sections has been rejected, but the hypothesis of constant slope has not, some useful information can be found in every cross-section. Parameters satisfying conditions of this sort will be called slope constant relationships. Second, the estimated cross-section parameters must not be related in a systematic way to excluded time variables such as trend, or cyclical variables. This comes down to saying that the excluded time variables must be random or we are in fact estimating an incorrectly specified structure. In some instances though, the true time error variable *is* autocorrelated, but in practice systematic behavior of the sort described will often arouse suspicions about the original specification.

The remainder of this section will suggest ways in which dynamic mis-specification can cause cross-section relations to differ and how the initial cross-section specification should consequently be modified in order to use numerous cross-sections efficiently. Areas surrounded with a dashed line represent the point scatter for a single period cross-section while the dashed straight line represents the single period cross-section regression. Solid lines serve the same purposes for the pool regression.

5.2 Constant Slope and Constant Intercept

Take the simplest situation first—the one in which both conditions have been met. Thus, slopes and intercepts are the same in each cross-section and their estimates are randomly distributed in time.

Case 5.2.1—Zero Time Effect.

This case is one where the passage of time has no effect whatsoever. Graphically, we envisage results similar to the following:

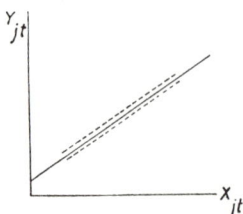

Fig. 5.1

The means of each variable are approximately the same for each set of annual observations. Pooling is permissible since by hypothesis the cross-section parameters are homogeneous estimates of the universe parameters, for the cross-sections are alike. Partitioning by time is wasteful since the pool regression will supply more reliable parameter estimates than any of the constituent annual regressions.

Case 5.2.2—Level Effect.

Complete constancy of structure may prevail, yet the passage of time yields more information than that contained in the situation just depicted. Many time-section variables undergo substantially greater variation over time than they exhibit in any one period, for instance, as shown in Figure 5.2. Once more, by hypothesis, pooling is permissible

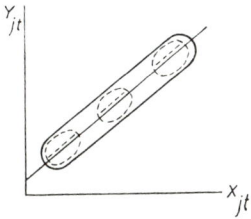

Fig. 5.2

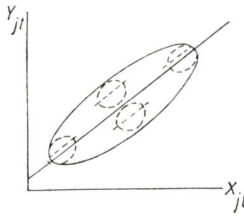

Fig. 5.3

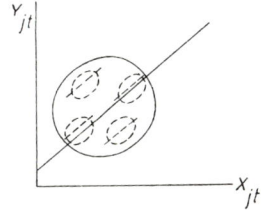

Fig. 5.4

and is additionally desirable since a much wider range of experience has been incorporated into the regression.

5.3 Slope Constant Structure

The conditions assumed in this section are that the slopes are equal within sampling error, but the intercepts differ between cross-sections. Where the influence of excluded time variables is random and large enough to cause the intercept term for the cross-section regressions to be heterogeneous, pool correlation and pool parameter homogeneity can be affected in numerous ways.

Case 5.3.1—Homogeneous Pool Slope, No Pool Correlation Effect.

It is possible that the pool slope parameter will be unbiased and the pool correlation will be the same as the (similar) cross-section correlations, as shown in Figure 5.3. In Figure 5.4, though, the pool correlation is less than the cross-section correlation.

Case 5.3.2—Homogeneous Pool Slope, Changed Pool Correlation

In the circumstances portrayed by Figures 5.3 and 5.4 we would be justified in using the pool slope parameter, but because of large inter-temporal errors in Case 5.3.2 (see Figure 5.4), our confidence associated with any particular prediction would, quite correctly, be lower than that associated with any one year. For example, external shocks such as wars could shift the level of the relation from period to period, leaving inter-firm (cross-section) errors unaffected. This possibility serves as a warning against exclusive reliance on a pool regression (or for that matter on a single period's cross-section) for extrapolative purposes without careful prior examination.

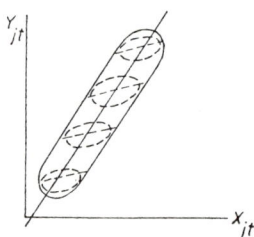

Fig. 5.5

The case opposite to the one portrayed here is the one conventionally discussed in statistics textbooks, when high correlation between the joint means is introduced through one or more extreme values. This would occur, in terms of the present exposition, if one or more cross-sections are widely separated from the other cross-sections.

Case 5.3.3—Heterogeneous Intercepts, No Pool Correlation Effect, Biased Pool Slope.

The possibilities, indeed likelihood, of bias in both pool parameters and pool correlation with heterogeneous intercepts are manifold. Parameter bias but no correlation effect could occur under the scatter conditions shown in Figure 5.5, where, of course, the pool slope parameter should never be used.

Case 5.3.4—Heterogeneous Intercepts, Reduced Correlation, Biased Pool Slope.

The extreme case of bias would be exemplified by a vertical or horizontal mean array of the single period cross-section regressions.

In the most extreme case (of which Case 5.3.3 is a less extreme example) the correlation would be driven toward zero and the pool slope parameter bear no relation whatsoever to the single period cross-section slope parameter.

The vertical and horizontal shift cases illustrated in Figures 5.6 and 5.7 imply that there are a number of important variables shifting inter-temporally that have been excluded from the estimating equation. Here the time variables are the important ones but, since by hypothesis the shifts are random, very little can be done about prediction. By using dummy variables or equivalent methods, one could estimate cross-section slope coefficients, not that these would be useful for time series prediction.

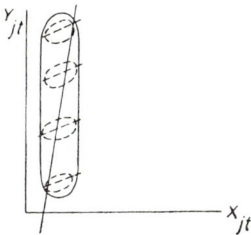

Fig. 5.6

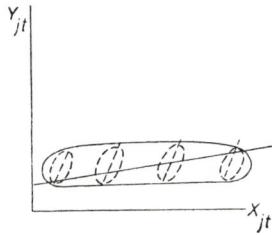

Fig. 5.7

5.4 Inter-Temporal Systematic Change of Structure: Different Slopes and Intercepts

Since estimation is meaningful only if the underlying structure is stable, this section heading is somewhat misleading. More accurately, functions that are intra-temporally approximately linear will often exhibit more complex but systematic behavior over time that will permit estimation of the more complicated intertemporal relation. This implies, once the hypothesis of randomness in the intertemporal error term has been rejected, that the systematic component must be extracted from the excluded variable category and be included explicitly in the inter-temporal or pool estimating equation. The alternative possibility of an autocorrelated error should also be borne in mind. Different estimation procedures are required in such instances.

Three major categories of systematic behavior over time will be analyzed: trend, cycles, and irreversibilities. While this is certainly not intended to be an exhaustive listing, these classifications probably include the more important types of behavior that occur in economic phenomena. A fourth variety of behavior, curvilinearity, is not systematically related to time, and might only be discovered with passage of the years.

Non-random behavior of the excluded variables manifested in apparently unstable estimated coefficients suggests that the simple intertemporal linear hypothesis is inadequate. In what follows, the implications of various important types of non-randomness are explored. The point scatters will not be shown on the following graphs. In the remainder of this section the circled numbers in the graphs signify the periods whose regressions have been included in the analysis.

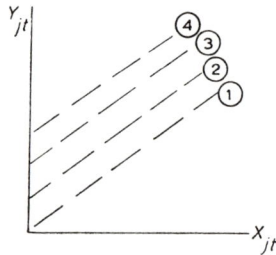

Fig. 5.8

Case 5.4.1—Slope Constancy with Systematic Trend Component in Intercepts of Cross-Section Regressions.

The situation envisaged in this section can be represented by Figure 5.8.

In the estimating equation

$$Y_{jt} = \alpha + \beta X_{jt} + \varepsilon_{jt}, \qquad (5.2)$$

we have:

$$\beta_1 = \beta_2 = \beta_3 = \beta_4,$$

and

$$\alpha_t = \alpha_1 + kt \ , \ t = 1, \dots 4; k \text{ is a constant.}$$

Here, the α_t differ by some constant plus a random error and an appropriate inter-temporal pool function might be:

$$Y_{jt} = \alpha_1 + \beta X_{jt} + kt + \varepsilon_{jt}. \qquad (5.3)$$

Here, t stands for time (or some variable related to time) and has been represented as a simple linear function although a more complicated relation might be more appropriate. The single cross-section slope coefficients in this case could be correctly estimated in isolation while the pool would have the additional variable t, which is constant between firms in a given period but varies systematically between periods.

Case 5.4.2—Systematic Trend in Cross-Section Slope Coefficients—No Level Effects.

Where the joint means remain approximately constant a systematic trend in the slope would yield results akin to those in Figure 5.9.

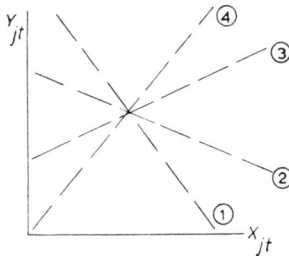

Fig. 5.9

Straight-forward pooling would, naturally enough, lead to nonsense results.

The correct function combination of individual cross-sections would treat the parameter β as some function of time (or other similar trend variable), e.g., $\beta = \gamma t$. Thus, we would have as our final estimating equation:

$$Y_{jt} = \gamma t \, X_{jt} + \alpha_t + \varepsilon_{jt}. \qquad (5.4)$$

Case 5.4.3—Systematic Trend in Slope Coefficients—Level Effects and Curvilinearity.

Where the cross-section slope parameters systematically differ at different levels, there are two alternative possibilities for inferring the correct structural relation. First, if the slopes differ systematically at different levels but the time ordering is not related to the levels (and hence the slopes), there is a strong presumption that the correct pool function is curvilinear. That is, the assumption of linearity within each cross-section turns out to be only an approximation.

When the cross-sections are juxtaposed on the same graph it becomes clear that the function is not linear over its entire range. It might be possible under highly favorable conditions to determine whether the pool relationship is curvilinear with only one cross-section at each level—usually, several such cross-sections will be required. Thus,

$$Y_{jt} = \alpha + \beta X_{jt}^{\pi} + \varepsilon_{jt} \qquad (5.5)$$

would be one possible correct pool function.

Case 5.4.4—Level Effects and "Changing Structure".

Changing structure at different levels could be distinguished from curvilinearity only if there were repeated observations at each (joint)

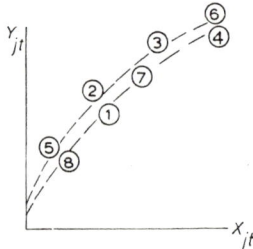 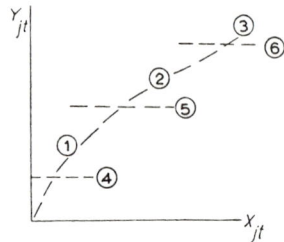

Fig. 5.10   Fig. 5.11

level of the variables when the cross-section parameters change in conjunction with both level and time. Here, the outcome would differ from that envisaged in Figure 5.10 as the slopes in later time periods would consistently differ from those in earlier time periods, as in Figure 5.11. The correct estimating procedure would be to estimate the parameters of:

$$Y_{jt} = \beta t X_{jt} + \alpha + \varepsilon_{jt}. \qquad (5.6)$$

This is the same relation as Equation (5.4), and has been shown separately in this context to indicate the dangers of confounding when level effects are present, unlike the situation portrayed in Equation (5.4).

Case 5.4.5—Level Effects and Cyclical Behavior.

Cross-section slopes may change through time in a cyclical manner. Systematic time ordering within cycle determined time blocks would be a necessary condition for a cyclical effect. Should the cycle phases occur at the same levels, the cross-section regressions might resemble the configuration of a curvilinear pool function. If the two were indistinguishable it would not do any particular harm: the appropriate pool regression is the same.

Distinct cyclical behavior would be revealed where the cyclical time blocks occur at different levels, and when each cyclical time block includes a complete cycle (Figure 5.12). Parameters of the two cyclically different functions might each be separately estimated or a dummy cycle variable be introduced and the pool function estimated as a single entity.

It would be necessary to have several complete cycle phases to be sure that the constants fitted to the several different cycles behaved

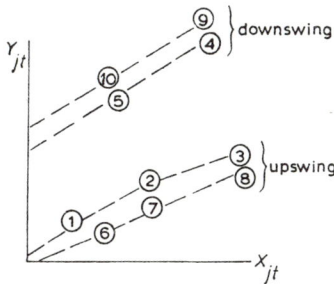

Fig. 5.12

randomly and were not in fact different by some systematic trend component alone.

Case 5.4.6—Level Effects and Irreversibilities.

The detection of irreversibilities will be closely related to cyclical patterns; often the distinction will prove unnecessary. If a reversal in direction led to different and non-random slopes at each level, irreversibilities could be shown to exist provided there were at least three observations at each level. If there were only two at each level, it would be impossible to distinguish irreversibilities from trend changes in slope such as those shown in Figure 5.11.

Case 5.4.7—Structural Breaks.

It is not infrequent for the statistician to have a hunch that the underlying behavior structure has undergone radical change. He might decide to split the data into two parts believed to be homogeneous, estimate parameters in the two segments of data and then test for significant differences. Most time series data, however, are so insensitive (i.e., have so few effective degrees of freedom) that the results of the test are likely to be inconclusive. Examination of a series of cross-sections might yield strong evidence concerning a structural break. As one obvious and relevant example that comes to mind, many behavioral patterns are thought to have changed radically from the twenties to the thirties, or from pre-World War II to post-World War II. Checking for a structural break can sometimes be relatively simple. Where the slope (or intercept) parameter estimates do not come from a homogeneous population but, say from two time subsets, the following patterns might be revealed.

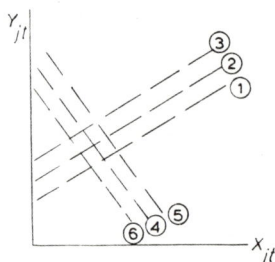
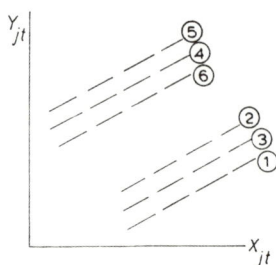

Fig. 5.13   Fig. 5.14

More elaborate patterns than those surveyed throughout this section are, of course, likely to occur. As the configurations become more elaborate detection also becomes increasingly difficult. Nevertheless, it should be clear that in the use of time series alone or in setting up pooled cross-section observations, full exploitation of the data and minimization of *a priori* assumptions call for procedures analogous to those heuristically described above.[3] Equally, use of a single period cross-section unsupported by evidence from other cross-sections at different points of time is likely to be a dangerous procedure.

5.5 Inter-Temporal Changes in Excluded Variables: The Correlation Problem

In the previous two sections the question of what happens to error variance within cross-sections with the passage of time has been ig-

---

[3] Analytical and statistical content is provided by the analysis of covariance explained later in this chapter.

nored. For expository purposes it was assumed that all cross-section error variances were constant. The major possibilities depend upon many of the analytical concepts used in connection with regression. The only new problems concern inter-temporal homoscedasticity.

Case 5.5.1—Zero Time Effects on Errors.

Should the error distributions come from a single population and they are random in time, there are no problems.

Case 5.5.2—Level Effects on Errors.

Where the intra-temporal error variances change systematically as a function of level but are random in time, the pool regression will have residuals which do not have a constant variance, i.e., are heteroscedastic. Once recognized, this should be taken into account in setting confidence or prediction intervals around the regression. Weighted regression techniques should be used to estimate parameters, or variables should be transformed to homogenize the error variances.

Case 5.5.3—Systematic Effects on Errors.

The cross-section correlations may exhibit a decreasing or increasing trend. A superficial way to manage this would be to take this fact into account in prediction intervals, as set out in the previous paragraph.

A trend in the individual correlation implies that variables excluded in the original estimating equation for cross-sections are gradually becoming more important or less important relative to the included variables. If the latter, so much the better. If the former is the case, that the excluded variables are of increasing relative importance, it suggests that there are other variables that should be included in the equation. Equally, systematic behavior in error variances of a cyclical or irreversible nature suggests that additional variables should be included in the cross-section estimating equation.

5.6 Covariance Tests for Regression Coefficient Homogeneity

Prior graphic presentation on the economics of cross-section variability turns out to have an exact statistical counterpart, the analysis of covariance for the homogeneity of regression coefficients. While the analysis is generalizable to several dimensions, only one-way analysis of covariance was essential for our purposes. The main variables of classification are years for cross-sections and individual firms for time series.

The most appropriate analysis for our use has been developed by M. G. Kendall and A. Mood.[4] Two aspects of the estimated regression coefficients can be tested: first, the homogeneity of regression slope coefficients (for the same variable, but different cells), and second, differences among cell regression intercept coefficients. It should be noted that, as constructed, this analysis can only determine that not all the slope coefficients (for the same variable) collectively are homogeneous. This analysis cannot indicate that one or several variables have heterogeneous coefficients while possibly the remainder are homogeneous, should the results indicate heterogeneity. Other adaptations of the general linear hypothesis discussed at the end of this section could achieve this end however.[5]

The test procedure has three main steps. The first, over-all test is meant to discover if slopes and intercepts simultaneously are homogeneous among cells. Slope homogeneity is required for the same variable in different cells, while differences among different variable slopes are perfectly acceptable. Should this hypothesis (that of overall homogeneity) be accepted, quite obviously the testing procedure would not go further. However, should the over-all homogeneity hypothesis be rejected, the second step of the analysis is to decide if the regression slopes collectively are the same in the different cells. If this hypothesis of homogeneity is not rejected, one then proceeds to the third and final test that determines the inter-cell equality of regression intercepts. In principle, step one is separable from steps two and three.

Four types of regressions and five residual sums of squares are computed. The calculations summarized in Table 5.1 require further explanation to be elucidated by reference to the analysis of covariance in which the cells are year cross-sections.[6] The main indicial and other notation will be this:

---

[4] MAURICE G. KENDALL, *Advanced Theory of Statistics*, 3rd Edition, 1951, Vol. 2, pp. 237–245 and ALEXANDER M. MOOD, *Introduction to the Theory of Statistics*, pp. 350–356. An excellent general treatment relating analysis of covariance and prediction intervals will be found in GREGORY C. CHOW, "Tests of Equality Between Two Sets of Coefficients in Two Regressions," *Econometrica*, July, 1960. Also see DONALD A. S. FRASER, *Statistics: An Introduction*, 1958, pp. 356-360.

[5] It would be possible if the hypothesis of homogeneity were rejected to proceed systematically to try many combinations of included variables and determine which variable or variable combinations were associated with the largest F values. This trial and error approach could raise havoc with the usual interpretations placed upon significance levels.

[6] This notation is set up in a way that will rapidly enable the reader to understand

Notation:

Cells (years)	$t = 1, 2, \ldots T,$
Observations within cell (firms)	$j = 1, \ldots J,$
Total sample size	$N = TJ,$
Independent variables X_i or X_s, i, s	$= 1, 2 \ldots K,$
Residual sum of squares	$= S^2,$
Within cell mean	$= \bar{X}_{ti}$ or $\bar{X}_{ts},$
Over-all mean	$= \bar{X}_i$ or $\bar{X}_s.$

The first type of regression shown in equation (5.7) is called the unrestricted cell regression.

$$Y_{jt} = \alpha_t + \sum_{s=1}^{k} \beta_{ts} X_{tsj} \qquad \text{Type A. (5.7)}$$

There are "T" of these regressions, one for each year. This is simply the within cell, standard cross-section regression. The second type of regression, called the restricted or cell mean corrected regression, has slope coefficients that are computed as a weighted average of the within-cell slope coefficients. The weights are the sums of squared deviations from the mean for the independent variable in the bivariate case.[7] In a least squares sense such estimates represent averages of the slope coefficients uninfluenced by differences in the mean values of the explanatory variables among different cells. It is an average regression which has minimum residual variance subject to the restriction that the slopes are the same in all cells. The total sum of squares from the first regression type will, of course, be smaller because there is no restriction about regression slope uniformity. While it is inconvenient (short of setting up a general matrix notation for regression models which has been well presented several places) to portray this for several variables, the slope β' in (5.8) for the bivariate case illustrates the nature of this parameter estimate.

$$\beta' = \frac{\sum_{t,j} (X_{jt} - \bar{X}_t)(Y_{jt} - \bar{Y}_t)}{\sum_{t,j} (X_{jt} - \bar{X}_t)^2} \qquad \text{Type B. (5.8)}$$

the notation in a setting where the cells are years containing cross-section samples. In the next chapter this notation will be applied to data where the *firm* is the cell containing time series sample observations.

[7] See MOOD, *op. cit.*, p. 355.

The third regression, the cell mean regression, is shown in equation (5.8). Within each cell all observations for firms are averaged to construct a new observation so that if there are, for instance, seventeen years (cells), seventeen values per variable constitute this regression's sample observations.

$$\bar{Y}_t = \alpha'' + \sum_{s=1}^{k} \beta_s'' \bar{X}_{ts} \qquad \text{Type C. (5.8)}$$

The last regression will be called the "grand regression." It is obtained by combining all the individual observations into a single regression, ignoring the cell boundaries. This regression corresponds to the single regression shown by the solid line in the diagrams of the preceding sections.

$$Y_{jt} = \alpha''' + \sum_{stj} \beta_s''' X_{stj} \qquad \text{Type D. (5.10)}$$

To perform the over-all test, the total sum of squares from the within-cell or unrestricted regressions (divided by appropriate degrees of freedom) provides a variance ratio denominator that is to be tested against the residual variation from the grand regression not otherwise taken into account. Should this F ratio, designated F_1, prove insignificant (i.e., should we reject the hypothesis of significant differences) we can then proceed on the assumption that slopes for the same variable and intercepts are the same in different cells. In general, we would proceed no further. If, however, the hypothesis of homogeneity is rejected, the attempt would be made to find out if the non-homogeneity could be attributed to the slope coefficients.

Isolation of heterogeneous slopes (as the cause of over-all non-homogeneity indicated by F_1) also relies upon the within-cell error variance for the denominator of the test statistic F_2. The difference between the sums of squares obtained from the weighted average, or Type B regression and the within-cell Type A sum of squares (divided by degrees of freedom) provides the F_2 numerator. Should this ratio prove insignificant, we can then determine the extent to which non-homogeneities could arise in the intercepts. It is important to note here, however, that the test sequence would halt should the slope homogeneity hypothesis be rejected. The test logic is such that we cannot test for heterogeneous intercepts if the slopes are not equal. If one thinks about the matter, it soon becomes apparent that it is seldom a meaningful question to ask if intercepts are the same when slopes are unequal.

Two steps are needed in order to test for homogeneity of regression intercepts. The first is to decide whether the cell mean or Type C equation significantly reduces the residual sum of squares around the mean of the dependent variable. If so, and this can be evaluated by F_3 defined in Table 5.1, we would proceed to the final step. If there is not a significant, (and by hypothesis) linear relationship in the coefficients, then, as will become apparent, it is impossible to check on intercept homogeneity.

The final test objective is to estimate the equality of the Type B and Type C regression coefficients. If there is a meaningful cell mean regression (which has been tested by F_3), it follows that all the cross-sections are juxtaposed on one another with approximately the same intercept, provided that F_4 is insignificant. This outcome implies that the hypothesis of equality between cell mean regression and weighted average regression coefficients cannot be rejected.[8]

Two cautions about this procedure should be voiced, the first relating to the internal logic and the second to the formal statistical propriety of the proposed test sequence. Taking up these propositions in reverse order it should be observed that the tests are not independent. Provided that the full testing sequence must be completed to discover the sources of non-homogeneity, four test statistics will have been used, three of which could be construed to depend upon the acceptance or rejection of the immediately prior test. At present, little is known about how to combine such tests in order to arrive at the correct conditional inference, so that a purist would perhaps argue we could go no further. A bolder individual might reply that if the tests indicate extreme instability, then it is unlikely that we have been greatly misled by their inter-independence, which would ordinarily bias results in

[8] There is a second case not considered by Mood and Kendall in which the intercepts might be approximately equal. Should the hypothesis of linearly related cell means be rejected as could easily happen, and yet the means of the variables are about equal, and on the other hand, the within-cell slopes are approximately equal, it would be misleading to follow the Mood and Kendall procedures. In this situation, even if the linear relation between means has been rejected, the appropriate test would be for the significant differences between means for the dependent and/or the independent variables. If neither of these sets of hypotheses can be rejected, it follows, on the assumptions that the within-cell regression slopes are the same, that the intercepts are about equal. A difficulty with the proposed procedure as given above is the absence of fully appropriate ways of combining the different sets of tests.

TABLE 5.1

Covariance Tests for Regression Homogeneity

F Ratios	Test Description	Mean Square Ratio	Sums of Squares	Mean Squares
F_1	Overall Test	$\dfrac{MS_5}{MS_1}$	$S_a^2 = \sum\limits_{t=1}^{T} S_{at}^2$	$S_a^2/[N - T(K + 1)] = MS_1$
F_2	Cell Slope Homogeneity	$\dfrac{MS_2}{MS_1}$	$S_e^2 = S_b^2 - S_a^2$	$S_e^2/[K(T - 1)] = MS_2$
			S_b^2	Not used directly in analysis of covariance.
F_3	Cell Mean Significance	$\dfrac{MS_3}{MS_1}$	S_c^2	$JS_c^2/(T - K - 1) = MS_3$
			$S_f^2 = S_{\bar{d}}^2 - JS_c^2 - S_b^2$	$S_f^2/K = MS_4$
F_4	Cell Mean Slope Equality with Individual Cell Slopes	$\dfrac{MS_4}{MS_1}$	$S_{\bar{d}}^2$	Not used directly in analysis of covariance.
			$S_g^2 = S_{\bar{d}}^2 - S_a^2$	$S_g^2/(T - 1)(K + 1) = MS_5$

Explanation

1. *Notation:*

Cells (years)	$t = 1, 2, \ldots T$
Observations within cell (firms)	$j = 1, \ldots J$
Total sample size	$= N$
Independent variables X_i or X_s,	$i, s = 1, 2, \ldots K$
Residual sum of squares	$= S^2$
Within cell mean	$= \bar{X}_{ti}$ or $\bar{X}_{ts}$
Overall mean	$= \bar{X}_i$ or $\bar{X}_s$

2. *Regressions*

There are four types of regressions:

A. Unrestricted cell regressions:
moment matrix $= \| \sum\limits_j (X_{jts} - \bar{X}_{ts})(X_{jti} - \bar{X}_{ti}) \|$.

B. Restricted (or cell mean corrected) regression:
moment matrix $= \| \sum\limits_t \sum\limits_j (X_{jts} - \bar{X}_{ts})(X_{jti} - \bar{X}_{ti}) \|$.

C. Cell mean regression:
moment matrix $= \| \sum\limits_t (\bar{X}_{ts} - \bar{X}_s)(\bar{X}_{ti} - \bar{X}_i) \|$.

D. Grand Regression:
moment matrix $= \| \sum\limits_{t,j} (X_{jts} - \bar{X}_s)(X_{jti} - \bar{X}_i) \|$.

3. *Residuals*

Each regression has an associated residual sum of squares designated by S_{at}^2, S_b^2, S_c^2 and $S_{\bar{d}}^2$. In addition to these residual sums of squares there are others used in the analysis which are obtained from the previous ones:
(i) $S_e^2 = S_b^2 - S_a^2$ (ii) $S_f^2 = S_{\bar{d}}^2 - JS_c^2 - S_b^2$ (iii) $S_g^2 = S_{\bar{d}}^2 - S_a^2$.

Sources: M. G. KENDALL, *Advanced Theory of Statistics*, Vol. II, and A. M. MOOD, *Introduction to the Theory of Statistics*.

favor of hypothesis acceptance. On the other hand, should we find a substantial amount of apparent stability, we should perhaps take this as encouraging evidence that, however, must be viewed with some reserve. For the purpose of this investigation, we can rephrase the previous sentence to state that we are much more anxious to avoid Type II than we are to avoid Type I errors. This will be the case in much academic research.[9]

In perusing the internal test logic, the question may be asked: can we legitimately follow two parallel procedures, by first testing for combined heterogeneity according to F_1 and then going through steps that involve F ratios 2, 3, and 4? The uncomfortable possibility exists, for instance, that according to F_1 we might find homogeneous slopes and intercepts, yet this finding could be compatible with an indication of opposite results according to F_2, F_3, and F_4 because the alternative hypotheses are somewhat different in the two cases. Worse still, we might reject the hypothesis of over-all homogeneity using the test ratio F_1, but then find according to F_2, F_3, and F_4 that we cannot reject the null hypothesis, so that the existence of heterogeneity indicated by F_1 cannot be traced.

While the same general class of hypothesis is under test, however, the alternative hypotheses are explicitly different. In the first instance the total residual sum of squares is split into two components in the F_1 test while in the second instance the same residual variance is split into four different parts in order to carry out test procedures indicated by F_2, F_3, and F_4. Thus, incompatible and apparently inconsistent inferences can arise in the manner indicated above. This outcome is quite proper at a formal statistical level, although at the less formal but important level of interpreting test statistics, it is an annoyance.

A different but related set of hypotheses about homogeneity of regression slope coefficients must be tested when explicit account is taken of individual firm effects discussed in the previous chapter, Section 3, on Sample Independence. Based on Carter's application of the general linear hypothesis to the particular problem at hand, this test requires that dummy variables, one for each firm, be introduced into a single general regression equation which, however, will also have

[9] W. ALLAN WALLIS, "Compounding Probabilities from Independent Significance Tests," *Econometrica*, Vol. 10, Nos. 3 and 4, July–October, 1942, pp. 229–248, indicates the nature of the problem where tests are assumed independent. The case of non-independence is trickier and to date is still largely an unsolved problem.

different within-cell slopes (as with the multi-equation A regressions), one for each variable in each year when cross-section estimation is the objective. The test structure is the same as for the F_1 test shown in Table 5.1. The following equation, using previously established notation is extended only by the inclusion of the firm dummy variables represented by Z_j.

$$Y_{jt} = \sum_{s=1}^{K} \beta_{st} X_{sjt} + \alpha_j + \alpha_0.$$ (5.11)

An example using two independent variables for three years with five individual firms is written out below to enable the reader to familiarize himself quickly with a simple example of the equation structure of (5.11), above.

$$\left. \begin{array}{l} Y_{j1} = \beta_{11} X_{11j} + \beta_{21} X_{21j} \\ Y_{j2} = \beta_{12} X_{12j} + \beta_{22} X_{22j} \\ Y_{j3} = \beta_{13} X_{13j} + \beta_{23} X_{23j} \end{array} \right\} + \left\{ \begin{array}{l} \alpha_1 \\ \alpha_2 \\ \alpha_3 \\ \alpha_4 \\ \alpha_5 \end{array} \right\} + \alpha_0.$$ (5.12)

Here, β_{11} is the regression coefficient for the first independent variable in period 1, β_{12} is the regression coefficient for the first independent variable in period 2, etc. while α_1 through α_5 represent the dummy variable firm effects. The objective will be to test the hypothesis that $\beta_{11} = \beta_{12} = \beta_{13}$ and the hypothesis that $\beta_{21} = \beta_{22} = \beta_{23}$. To test both hypotheses simultaneously, simply compute the analogue to the A regressions discussed previously in which a single regression coefficient per cross-section is estimated, in the present example six regression coefficients, three for each variable, in addition to simultaneous estimates of the α's. Second, compute the analogue to the D regression described previously, based on a variable in which the same slope is used for all years, i.e., has a single coefficient which will be estimated for variable X_1 using pooled data of all years, while variable X_2's coefficient will be estimated similarly. The sum of squares computed in the first instance will be smaller than the sum of squares from the second, D-type regression. When this A Type error sum of squares is subtracted from the D type sum of squares and divided by degrees of freedom, it will provide a valid F test numerator. The denominator mean square is based on the sum of squares associated with the A Type regression, and its associated degrees of freedom.

If we had wished only to test the assumption that the β's associated with X_1 were the same within cross-sections, but believed that the slope coefficients associated with X_2 were equal and therefore do not intend to test the possibility, we would go through similar procedures to those described above except that in each and every case the same slope would be computed for X_2 in every cross-section for *both* A- and D-type regressions. Then the differences in residual sums of squares would reflect only variations in the X_1 cross-section regression coefficients.

Using the notation of Table 5.1, we can now set up in Table 5.2 test F_5 for the case when it is believed that all slopes could differ.

TABLE 5.2

Covariance Test for Regression Homogeneity

	Test Description	Mean Square Ratio	Sums of Squares	Mean Square
F_5	Slope homogeneity, firm effects included	$\dfrac{MS_7}{MS_6}$	$S_{a'}^2$ $S_{d'}^2$ $S_{g'}^2 = S_{d'}^2 - S_{a'}^2$	$S_{a'}^2/[N-(J+TK+1)] = MS_6$ Not used directly in analysis $S_{g'}^2/[K(T-1)] = MS_7$

A' Regression

Define

$$M_{xxt} = \sum_j (X_{jts} - \bar{X}_{ts})(X_{jti} - \bar{X}_{ti})$$

$$M_{xz} = \sum_j (X_{jts} - \bar{X}_{ts})(Z_j - \bar{Z})$$

$$Z_{mj} = 1 \text{ for } m = j$$

$$Z_{mj} = 0 \text{ for } m \neq j$$

Then,

$$
\begin{Vmatrix}
M_{xxT} & 0 & \cdots & 0 & \cdots & \cdots & 0 & M_{xzT} \\
0 & \ddots & & \vdots & & & \vdots & \vdots \\
\vdots & & \ddots & \vdots & & & \vdots & \vdots \\
0 & \cdots & \cdots & M_{xxt} & \cdots & \cdots & 0 & M_{xzt} \\
\vdots & & & & \ddots & & \vdots & \vdots \\
0 & \cdots & \cdots & 0 & \cdots & 0 & M_{xx1} & M_{xz1} \\
M_{xzT} & \cdots & \cdots & M_{xzt} & \cdots & \cdots & M_{xz1} & 1
\end{Vmatrix}
$$

defines the product-moment matrix of independent variables for the A regression.

Recalling that we have K regular independent variables, J firm dummy independent variables and T cells, the upper left hand corner submatrix has $(TK)^2$ elements (the off diagonal elements are null), the lower right hand corner identity sub-matrix (which arises by definition from M_{zz}) has J^2 elements while the minor diagonal sub-matrices have $TK \times J$ elements. The entire matrix has $(J + TK)^2$ elements.

D' Regression

Define $\quad m_{xx} = \left\| \sum_j (X_{jts} - \bar{X}_s)(X_{jti} - \bar{X}_i) \right\| \quad$ Then, $\quad \left\| \begin{array}{c|c} m_{xx} & m_{xz} \\ \hline m_{xz} & 1 \end{array} \right\|$

$$m_{xz} = \left\| \sum_j (X_{jts} - \bar{X}_s)(Z_j - \bar{Z}) \right\|$$

defines the product-moment matrix for the D' regression. The upper left submatrix has K^2 elements, the lower right identity submatrix has J^2 elements and the minor diagonal matrices have $(K \times J)$ elements. The entire matrix has $(K + J)^2$ elements.

5.7 Cross-Section Analysis of Covariance

A. *Over-all Homogeneity*

Dynamic instability in the estimated regression coefficients is a strong possibility when cross-sections have been improperly or incompletely specified. Column (1f) of Table 5.3, the F test statistic for the over-all test on both slope and intercept homogeneity, appears to confirm the suspicions discussed in the early parts of this chapter.[10] In every instance, significant heterogeneity at the 1 per cent level is indicated.

The main conclusions from the over-all test are these. The smallest F_1 value, for original units, just significantly different from zero at the 1 per cent level, is recorded for Equation (3.12SP). Equation (3.12S) has a similar F_1 statistic. When just unlagged independent variables appear, which is the case for Equation (3.10), the F_1 statistics are definitely larger. Hence, the treatment of lags, however crude the

[10] These "suspicions" were generated by the apparent volatility of cross-section estimates in the Meyer-Kuh investment study. The graphical scheme explaining the types of gyrations that might be expected was completed several years prior to the covariance analysis calculations.

TABLE 5.3

Cross-Sections: Analysis of Covariance for Regression Coefficient Homogeneity[1]

Equation	F_1 Over-All Test						F_2 Slope Homogeneity					
	Degrees of Freedom		Critical F's			Actual F's	Degrees of Freedom		Critical F's			Actual F's
	Numerator	Denominator	0.10 level	0.05 level	0.01 level		Numerator	Denominator	0.10 level	0.05 level	0.01 level	
	(1a)	(1b)	(1c)	(1d)	(1e)	(1f)	(2a)	(2b)	(2c)	(2d)	(2e)	(2f)
(3.9S)	52	784	1.34	1.46	1.71	2.45***	39	784	1.38	1.51	1.80	2.36***
(3.9P)	52	784	1.34	1.46	1.71	3.04***	39	784	1.38	1.51	1.80	2.64***
(3.9SP)	65	770	1.32	1.42	1.65	2.55***	52	770	1.34	1.46	1.71	2.49***
(3.10S)	64	952	1.32	1.42	1.65	2.01***	48	952	1.36	1.48	1.74	1.97***
(3.10P)	64	952	1.32	1.42	1.65	2.75***	48	952	1.36	1.48	1.74	2.45***
(3.10SP)	80	935	1.30	1.40	1.62	1.91***	64	935	1.32	1.42	1.65	1.82***
(3.11S)	56	840	1.33	1.44	1.69	2.30***	42	840	1.37	1.50	1.78	2.11***
(3.11P)	56	840	1.33	1.44	1.69	2.83***	42	840	1.37	1.50	1.78	2.75***
(3.11SP)	70	825	1.31	1.42	1.64	2.25***	56	825	1.33	1.44	1.69	2.13***
(3.12S)	56	840	1.33	1.44	1.69	1.80***	42	840	1.37	1.50	1.78	1.80***
(3.12P)	56	840	1.33	1.44	1.69	2.30***	42	840	1.37	1.50	1.78	2.30***
(3.12SP)	70	825	1.31	1.42	1.64	1.70***	56	825	1.33	1.44	1.69	1.74***
(3.13S)	56	840	1.33	1.44	1.69	2.08***	42	840	1.37	1.50	1.78	2.11***
(3.13P)	56	840	1.33	1.44	1.69	2.66***	42	840	1.37	1.50	1.78	2.37***
(3.13SP)	70	825	1.31	1.42	1.64	1.81***	56	825	1.33	1.44	1.69	1.76***
(3.19)	56	840	1.33	1.44	1.69	3.67***	42	840	1.37	1.50	1.78	2.85***
(3.20)	64	952	1.32	1.42	1.65	1.51**	48	952	1.36	1.48	1.74	1.14
(3.21)	56	840	1.33	1.44	1.69	2.34***	42	840	1.37	1.50	1.78	1.04
(3.22)	56	840	1.33	1.44	1.69	2.29***	42	840	1.37	1.50	1.78	2.03***
(3.30A)	42	855	1.37	1.50	1.78	4.13***	28	855	1.42	1.57	1.89	5.01***
(3.30B)	56	840	1.33	1.44	1.69	2.88***	42	840	1.37	1.50	1.78	3.12***
(3.31A)	42	855	1.39	1.53	1.82	3.80***	28	855	1.45	1.62	1.96	4.62***
(3.31B)	56	840	1.36	1.48	1.74	3.51***	42	840	1.39	1.53	1.82	4.00***

* = 10% Significance Level   ** = 5% Significance Level   *** = 1% Significance Level

Table 5.3 (*Continued*)

	F_3 Cell Mean Significance						F_4 Cell Mean Slope Equality					
	Degrees of Freedom		Critical F's				Degrees of Freedom		Critical F's			
Equation	Numerator	Denominator	0.10 level	0.05 level	0.01 level	Actual F's	Numerator	Denominator	0.10 level	0.05 level	0.01 level	Actual F's
	(3a)	(3b)	(3c)	(3d)	(3e)	(3f)	(4a)	(4b)	(4c)	(4d)	(4e)	(4f)
(3.9S)	10	784	1.65	1.91	2.47	2.89***	3	784	2.13	2.68	3.95	2.22*
(3.9P)	10	784	1.65	1.91	2.47	4.97***	3	784	2.13	2.68	3.95	1.90
(3.9SP)	9	770	1.68	1.96	2.56	3.23***	4	770	1.99	2.45	3.48	1.90
(3.10S)	13	952	1.58	1.80	2.29	2.43***	3	952	2.13	2.68	3.95	0.83
(3.10P)	13	952	1.58	1.80	2.29	3.41***	3	952	2.13	2.68	3.95	4.79***
(3.10SP)	12	935	1.60	1.83	2.34	2.66***	4	935	1.99	2.45	3.48	0.92
(3.11S)	11	840	1.62	1.87	2.40	3.66***	3	840	2.13	2.68	3.95	0.03
(3.11P)	11	840	1.62	1.87	2.40	3.13***	3	840	2.13	2.68	3.95	2.85**
(3.11SP)	10	825	1.65	1.91	2.47	3.53***	4	825	1.99	2.45	3.48	0.60
(3.12S)	11	840	1.62	1.87	2.40	1.72*	3	840	2.13	2.68	3.95	2.16*
(3.12P)	11	840	1.62	1.87	2.40	1.79*	3	840	2.13	2.68	3.95	4.23***
(3.12SP)	10	825	1.65	1.91	2.47	1.42	4	825	1.99	2.45	3.48	1.85
(3.13S)	11	840	1.62	1.87	2.40	2.21**	3	840	2.13	2.68	3.95	1.21
(3.13P)	11	840	1.62	1.87	2.40	2.87***	3	840	2.13	2.68	3.95	5.78***
(3.13SP)	10	825	1.65	1.91	2.47	2.35**	4	825	1.99	2.45	3.48	1.09
(3.19)	11	840	1.62	1.87	2.40	3.10***	3	840	2.13	2.68	3.95	17.27***
(3.20)	13	952	1.58	1.80	2.29	0.80	3	952	2.13	2.68	3.95	1.75
(3.21)	11	840	1.62	1.87	2.40	1.99**	3	840	2.13	2.68	3.95	0.12
(3.22)	11	840	1.62	1.87	2.40	2.05**	3	840	2.13	2.68	3.95	6.87***
(3.30A)	12	855	1.60	1.83	2.34	2.47***	2	855	2.35	3.07	4.79	1.64
(3.30B)	11	840	1.63	1.87	2.40	2.56***	3	840	2.13	2.68	3.95	0.82
(3.31A)	12	855	1.65	1.91	2.47	1.61***	2	855	2.35	3.07	4.79	5.33***
(3.31B)	11	840	1.68	1.96	2.56	1.71**	3	840	2.13	2.68	3.95	3.31***

[1] Based on Table 5.1 Critical F values were obtained from A.M. Mood, *Introduction to Statistics*, Tables V, pp. 426–427. Linear interpolation was employed except for degrees of freedom exceeding 120. The critical F values in every case have been recorded for 120 degrees of freedom for each denominator sum of squares even though the actual degrees of freedom were at least four times as great. The approximation error in this case is negligible.

present attempt, has a major bearing on the heterogeneity observed. On logarithms, however, unlagged Equation (3.20) had the greatest homogeneity.

B. *Slope Homogeneity*

Since the over-all test reveals disappointingly large total heterogeneity, the next step in the test procedure calls for the slope homogeneity test. Logarithmic model Equations (3.20) and (3.21), have F_2 statistics of about unity, indicating highly homogeneous cross-section slopes. The remaining slopes reject the homogeneity hypothesis at the 1 per cent level. Equations (3.12S) and (3.12SP) have the smallest values in the remaining equations. This confirms the observation on the over-all test, where the combined lag model had smaller F's than either the simple lag or the current values of sales and/or profits. Those for Equation (3.10) are only slightly larger, however.

Comparing the F statistic within each equation set for the profit and sales equation indicates that heterogeneity for the profit model is always greater than that of the sales model. On the basis of coefficient homogeneity, the profit equation would be abandoned in favor of the sales, acceleration model. However, if the option of utilizing both variables remained open, the homogeneity indicated for the combined profit and sales equation is ordinarily greater than for either of the equations separately. This is not universally true, however, nor are the differences large.

C. *Intercept Homogeneity*

The test for intercept homogeneity is valid only when slopes are approximately homogeneous. Since only Equations (3.20) and (3.21) had homogeneous slopes, strict interpretation should be restricted to these two alone. In both instances intercept heterogeneity is not especially noticeable. In the remaining equations, therefore, intercept and slope variability cannot be rigorously separated.

However, at a less formal level of observation, the F_3 or F_4 statistics are often larger than either F_1 or F_2. Hence the impact of dynamic factors constant to individuals at a point of time, the so-called pure time series variables, are fundamentally important in disturbing cross-section relations. Such variables push about cross-section intercepts, making it impossible to pool cross-section estimates, even should the slopes be the same. More concretely, since the cross-section intercept term includes an exogenous element of reaction to investment opportunities, different cyclical situations might lead to different cyclical reactions: for instance, the intercept term might be low when capacity utilization is low or decreasing and the intercept term might be high when capacity utilization is high or increasing. This particular point will be explored more fully in Chapter 9, when capacity models are discussed in some detail.[11]

5.8 Time Series Analysis of Covariance

A. *Over-all Homogeneity*

The time series results of Table 5.4 do not correspond closely to cross-section test statistics for the same equation since the excluded variables are so different. This point arises repeatedly and should be construed as a warning against drawing uncritical inferences from one type of data for the other.

The most striking fact recorded for time series is the over-all homogeneity of Equation (3.9). Equation (3.9S) shows insignificant departures from the null hypothesis at the 10 per cent level and Equation (3.9SP) has a variance ratio equal to about unity for the over-all test. Slope heterogeneity on Equation (3.9SP) is only significant at the 5 per cent level. Despite these encouraging results the heterogeneity for Equation (3.9) was pronounced on cross-sections. First differencing of time series eliminates the intercept in each individual firm equation so that the first difference equation intercept now represents a trend. Since the trend effects are weak, intercept homogeneity becomes a real possibility on time series. For cross-sections the intercept represents an average firm trend *plus* the average pure time series error term, whose large variance prevented over-all homogeneity.

Lag structure does not differentiate among the original units equations, although Equations (3.10S) and (3.10SP) appear relatively most homogeneous according to F_1. Variable, transformations into logarithms or ratios do not affect homogeneity to any great extent.

B. *Slope Homogeneity*

Evidence for slope homogeneity, too, is different from cross-sections, once more providing a warning that the differential quantitative im-

---

[11] Intercepts for Equations (3.9) to (3.12), similar in economic interpretation, are treated in Chapter 9.

TABLE 5.4

Time Series: Analysis of Covariance for Regression Coefficient Homogeneity[1]

Equation	F_1 Over-All Test						F_2 Slope Homogeneity					
	Degrees of Freedom		Critical F's			Actual F's	Degrees of Freedom		Critical F's			Actual F's
	Numerator	Denominator	0.10 level	0.05 level	0.01 level		Numerator	Denominator	0.10 level	0.05 level	0.01 level	
	(1a)	(1b)	(1c)	(1d)	(1e)	(1f)	(2a)	(2b)	(2c)	(2d)	(2e)	(2f)
(3.9S)	177	660	1.26	1.35	1.53	1.25	118	660	1.26	1.35	1.53	1.75***
(3.9P)	177	660	1.26	1.35	1.53	1.40**	118	660	1.26	1.35	1.53	1.94***
(3.9SP)	236	600	1.26	1.35	1.53	1.13	177	600	1.26	1.35	1.53	1.42**
(3.10S)	177	840	1.26	1.35	1.53	2.28***	118	840	1.26	1.35	1.53	1.58***
(3.10P)	177	840	1.26	1.35	1.53	2.34***	118	840	1.26	1.35	1.53	1.75***
(3.10SP)	236	780	1.26	1.35	1.53	2.24***	177	780	1.26	1.35	1.53	1.76***
(3.11S)	177	720	1.26	1.35	1.53	2.46***	118	720	1.26	1.35	1.53	1.95***
(3.11P)	177	720	1.26	1.35	1.53	2.50***	118	720	1.26	1.35	1.53	1.97***
(3.11SP)	236	660	1.26	1.35	1.53	2.49***	177	660	1.26	1.35	1.53	2.11***
(3.12S)	177	720	1.26	1.35	1.53	2.46***	118	720	1.26	1.35	1.53	1.75***
(3.12P)	177	720	1.26	1.35	1.53	2.60***	118	720	1.26	1.35	1.53	2.14***
(3.12SP)	236	660	1.26	1.35	1.53	2.94***	177	660	1.26	1.35	1.53	2.49***
(3.19)	177	720	1.26	1.35	1.53	1.92***	118	720	1.26	1.35	1.53	2.59***
(3.20)	177	840	1.26	1.35	1.53	4.04***	118	840	1.26	1.35	1.53	2.70***
(3.21)	177	720	1.26	1.35	1.53	5.45***	118	720	1.26	1.35	1.53	4.20***
(3.22)	177	720	1.26	1.35	1.53	4.68***	118	720	1.26	1.35	1.53	3.17***
(3.30A)	177	720	1.26	1.35	1.53	3.64***	118	720	1.26	1.35	1.53	3.14***
(3.30B)	236	660	1.26	1.35	1.53	3.38***	177	660	1.26	1.35	1.53	2.71***
(3.31A)	177	600	1.26	1.35	1.53	3.11***	118	600	1.26	1.35	1.53	2.72***
(3.31B)	236	540	1.26	1.35	1.53	2.90***	177	540	1.26	1.35	1.53	2.40***

* = 10% Significance Level   ** = 5% Significance Level   *** = 1% Significance Level

Table 5.4 (*continued*)

Equation	F_3 Num. (3a)	Denom. (3b)	0.10 (3c)	0.05 (3d)	0.01 (3e)	Actual (3f)	F_4 Num. (4a)	Denom. (4b)	0.10 (4c)	0.05 (4d)	0.01 (4e)	Actual (4f)
(3.9S)	57	660	1.33	1.44	1.68	0.12	2	660	2.35	3.07	4.79	3.75**
(3.9P)	57	660	1.33	1.44	1.68	0.11	2	660	2.35	3.07	4.79	6.67***
(3.9SP)	56	600	1.33	1.44	1.69	0.10	3	600	2.13	2.68	3.95	2.72**
(3.10S)	57	840	1.33	1.44	1.68	3.64***	2	840	2.35	3.07	4.79	5.10***
(3.10P)	57	840	1.33	1.44	1.68	3.23***	2	840	2.35	3.07	4.79	9.24***
(3.10SP)	56	780	.133	1.44	1.69	3.57***	3	780	2.13	2.68	3.95	6.07***
(3.11S)	57	720	1.33	1.44	1.68	3.57***	2	720	2.35	3.07	4.79	1.60
(3.11P)	57	720	1.33	1.44	1.68	3.31***	2	720	2.35	3.07	4.79	10.29***
(3.11SP)	56	660	1.33	1.44	1.69	3.69***	3	660	2.13	2.68	3.95	2.33*
(3.12S)	57	720	1.33	1.44	1.68	3.66***	2	720	2.35	3.07	4.79	10.52***
(3.12P)	57	720	1.33	1.44	1.68	3.57***	2	720	2.35	3.07	4.79	4.84***
(3.12SP)	56	660	1.33	1.44	1.69	4.18***	3	660	2.13	2.68	3.95	6.76***
(3.19)	57	720	1.33	1.44	1.68	0.55	2	720	2.35	3.07	4.79	1.24
(3.20)	57	840	1.33	1.44	1.68	0.39	2	840	2.35	3.07	4.79	10.86***
(3.21)	57	720	1.33	1.44	1.68	6.32***	2	720	2.35	3.07	4.79	53.91***
(3.22)	57	720	1.33	1.44	1.68	7.36***	2	720	2.35	3.07	4.79	1.77
(3.30A)	57	720	1.33	1.44	1.68	3.66***	2	720	2.35	3.07	4.79	32.31***
(3.30B)	56	660	1.33	1.44	1.69	4.07***	3	660	2.13	2.68	3.95	29.79***
(3.31A)	57	600	1.33	1.44	1.68	3.22***	2	600	2.35	3.07	4.79	23.05***
(3.31B)	56	540	1.33	1.44	1.69	3.60***	3	540	2.13	2.68	3.95	19.57***

F_3 Cell Mean Significance; F_4 Cell Mean Slope Equality. Columns: Degrees of Freedom (Numerator, Denominator); Critical F's (0.10 level, 0.05 level, 0.01 level); Actual F's.

[1] Based on Table 1. Critical F values were obtained from A. M. Mood, *Introduction to Statistics*, Table V, pp. 426–427. Linear interpolation was employed except for degrees of freedom exceeding 120. The critical F values in every case have been recorded for 120 degrees of freedom for each denominator sum of squares even though the actual degrees of freedom were at least four times as great. The approximation error in this case is negligible.

pact of excluded variables makes drawing inferences about one body of data from the other a hazardous undertaking.

Most slope homogeneity prevails on Equation (3.9SP). The F_2 ratio for Equation (3.12), which showed most homogeneity among the original units equations on cross-sections, turns out to be inferior to Equation (3.10) in a time series context, although somewhat superior (except for (3.11SP)) to the lag model, Equation (3.11). In short, the response to the current sales level is slightly more homogeneous than when lags are taken into account.

Interestingly, greater heterogeneity among coefficients is to be observed on time series when sales and profits are included in the same regression equation, except for the first differenced model. F_2 ratios for Equations (3.10SP), (3.11SP), and (3.12SP) (particularly the latter) are noticeably larger than for either the sales or the profit equations alone. This result, too, contradicts cross-section findings.

In sharp contrast to cross-sections, the logarithmic models showed the greatest time series heterogeneity on slope coefficients. Ratio models likewise showed much time series heterogeneity.

C. *Intercept Homogeneity*

On F_3, and particularly on F_4, extremely large variance ratios prevail. F_3 is small only for Equations (3.9), and (3.19), and (3.20). It should not have been unexpected to find that the intercept terms, representing "autonomous investment" in the arithmetic models, differ greatly among firms. Frequently large firms will have large intercepts (either negative or positive), while small firms would tend to have more moderate intercepts, so that heterogeneity and correspondingly large variance ratios should be anticipated.[12] Since intercepts in the original units are annihilated by first differencing, only large trends would cause large F ratios in this context. Because trends were negligible, however, the first difference model intercepts were comparatively small as revealed in the covariance analysis. Hence, no profound importance attaches to the heterogeneity in inter-firm intercepts, although intercept heterogeneity in cross-sections has substantial economic interest. In short, if time series slopes were homogeneous and one

---

[12] The test design would have been more powerful if this belief had been taken into account in designing the covariance analysis. However, there were abundant degrees of freedom for the error variance so that perhaps not a great deal would have been gained.

wished to predict using micro equations, it would only be necessary to sum the constant terms and predict from the slope part of the equation rather than pool such equations.

One outcome on time series consistent with cross-sections is that, within a given equation lag form, the variance ratio for slopes on the profit equation is noticeably larger than the sales equation alone. Were uniform reactions to be used as a criterion and one had to choose either the sales model or the profit model, the final choice would favor the sales model.

5.9 Possible Causes of Heterogeneity in Estimated Cross-Section Coefficients

Cross-section coefficients can be studied further to establish whether some important systematic excluded variables influenced the regression coefficients or instead the heterogeneity arose from random events. In Equation (3.10), for instance, there are 17 cross-section regression equations, so that each cross-section coefficient can be treated as one observation in a 17-item time series. This series can then be related to important economic variables which might explain the observed instabilities. The procedure adopted was to rank correlate the five economic indicators described in Chapter 2 using Kendall's Rank Correlation Coefficient τ.[13]

The expected value of Kendall's Rank Correlation Coefficient is about two-thirds that of the more commonly used Spearman coefficient. It is also approximately normally distributed in the case of independent ranks when the sample size exceeds 10. The indicators selected are real GNP, the durable goods component of the Federal Reserve Board Index of Industrial Production, the gross rate of growth of the capital stock, the gross retained profit rate, and the rate of capacity utilization where the last three indexes are for the aggregate of sample firms. These five indicators have quite different characteristics, already described in Chapter 3. Real GNP and the Durables Index have a noticeable trend over the sample period, whereas the ratios or rates do not. Table 5.5 records simple rank correlations among the selected indicators. Real GNP and the Durables Index are highly correlated with each other. None of the other correlations exceed 0.60, so

---

[13] M. G. KENDALL, *The Advanced Theory of Statistics*, 3rd edition, 1951, Vol. 1, Chapter 16.

TABLE 5.5

Rank Correlations among Indicators

	Real GNP	Durable Index	$\bar{I}_t/\bar{K}_t$	$\bar{P}_t/\bar{K}_t$	$\bar{S}_t/\bar{K}_t$
Real GNP	1.00	0.897	0.279	0.088	0.471
Durable Index		1.000	0.324	0.191	0.574
$\bar{I}_t/\bar{K}_t$			1.000	0.412	0.544
$\bar{P}_t/\bar{K}_t$				1.000	0.529
$\bar{S}_t/\bar{K}_t$					1.000

Note: $\sigma_\tau = 0.179$, where $\sigma_\tau = \sqrt{\dfrac{2(2n+5)}{9n(n-1)}}$ for sample size $n = 17$. τ is approximately normally distributed for sample sizes of 10 or more. See KENDALL, op. cit., Chapter 16.

that independent information can by obtained from each indicator.

The capital intensity coefficient on Equation (3.9) is inversely correlated with the three rates—investment rate, profit rate, and capacity utilization rate—sometimes significantly so. For instance, when the investment rate is high, the capital intensity effect (which on *a priori* grounds is negative) will have its strongest influence, and similarly for the other two rates. Although the correlations are not significant on the capital stock coefficient (which may be interpreted as an estimate of "the" reaction coefficient), all the larger rank correlation coefficients indicate that the reaction coefficient is larger (the coefficient on capital stock is more negative) at times when real GNP and durable goods and the investment rate are highest.

The correlations of the indicators with the capital stock and profit coefficients are positive on Equation (3.10), while the correlations with sales are uniformly negative. When interpreting the sales model as a capacity acceleration model, the negative correlation of the indicators with the capital stock coefficient in Equation (3.9) was taken to mean that the rate of reaction was faster (i.e., the slope coefficient of capital stock more negative) during periods of highest activity either absolutely or relatively, depending on the indicator. Here the reverse is true. This reversal might be explained in two ways. First, a large part of the variability in the explanatory variables is considered by firms to be transitory. Therefore, during periods of high investment rates, the rate of reaction slows down because it is expected the rate of investment will soon decelerate to more normal levels. Conversely, when durable goods production is low, the rate of reaction is high because

TABLE 5.6

Cross-Section Parameter Estimate Rank Correlations with Indicators

Equation (3.9S)

Rank Correlation With:	Slope Coefficients			Intercept	RPE	Multiple Correlation
	C	ΔK_t	ΔS_t			
Real GNP	0.187	-0.187	-0.143	-0.099	0.143	-0.341*
Durable Goods Production Index	0.209	-0.143	-0.143	-0.099	0.099	-0.385*
Investment Rate $= I_t/K_t$	-0.407**	-0.121	0.341*	0.406**	0.033	0.121
Profit Rate $= \bar{P}_t/K_t$	-0.253	0.033	0.297	0.253	-0.055	0.143
Capacity Utilization Rate $= \bar{S}_t/K_t$	-0.143	0.033	0.033	0.209	0.055	-0.121

Equation (3.9P)

Rank Correlation With:	Slope Coefficients			Intercept	RPE	Multiple Correlation
	C	ΔK_t	ΔP_t			
Real GNP	0.143	-0.099	0.033	-0.033	0.099	-0.187
Durable Goods Production Index	0.143	-0.055	0.077	-0.033	0.055	-0.231
Investment Rate $= I_t/K_t$	-0.319	-0.165	0.121	0.406**	0.121	0.055
Profit Rate $= \bar{P}_t/K_t$	-0.209	0.033	0.187	0.319	-0.033	-0.055
Capacity Utilization Rate $= \bar{S}_t/K_t$	-0.121	0.121	0.077	0.319	0.143	-0.275

Equation (3.9SP)

Rank Correlation With:	Slope Coefficients				Intercept	RPE	Multiple Correlation
	C	ΔK_t	ΔS_t	ΔP_t			
Real GNP	0.121	-0.209	-0.165	-0.099	-0.055	0.099	-0.319
Durable Goods Production Index	0.121	-0.143	-0.165	-0.099	-0.055	0.077	-0.363*
Investment Rate $= I_t/K_t$	-0.385*	-0.033	0.143	0.055	0.363*	0.099	0.121
Profit Rate $= \bar{P}_t/K_t$	-0.275	0.033	0.275	-0.055	0.165	-0.055	0.099
Capacity Utilization Rate $= \bar{S}_t/K_t$	-0.143	0.033	-0.033	-0.099	0.209	0.121	-0.055

Note: 1. $\sigma_\tau = 0.201$, where $\sigma_\tau = \sqrt{\dfrac{2(2n+5)}{9n(n-1)}}$ for sample size $n = 14$. τ is approximately normally distributed for sample size of 10 or more. See KENDALL, op. cit., Chapter 16.

2. $*$ = 10% significance, $**$ = 5% significance, $***$ = 1% significance.

Table 5.6 (*continued*)

Equation (3.10S)

Rank Correlation With:	Slope Coefficients			Intercept	RPE	Multiple Correlation
	C	K_t	S_t			
Real GNP	−0.250	0.118	−0.235	0.220	−0.030	0.088
Durable Goods Production Index	−0.235	0.147	−0.221	0.206	−0.088	0.147
Investment Rate $= I_t/\bar{K}_t$	−0.015	0.265	−0.221	—	−0.353**	0.412**
Profit Rate $= \bar{P}_t/\bar{K}_t$	−0.103	—	−0.147	0.118	−0.191	0.088
Capacity Utilization Rate $= \bar{S}_t/\bar{K}_t$	−0.088	0.176	−0.324*	0.074	−0.368**	0.235

Equation (3.10P)

Rank Correlation With:	Slope Coefficients			Intercept	RPE	Multiple Correlation
	C	K_t	P_t			
Real GNP	−0.397**	0.176	0.250	0.103	−0.162	0.353**
Durable Goods Production Index	−0.353**	0.191	0.250	0.118	−0.206	0.382**
Investment Rate $= I_t/\bar{K}_t$	−0.059	0.368**	0.162	−0.059	−0.412**	0.515**
Profit Rate $= \bar{P}_t/\bar{K}_t$	−0.191	−0.088	0.235	0.103	−0.221	0.324*
Capacity Utilization Rate $= \bar{S}_t/\bar{K}_t$	−0.191	0.176	0.324*	0.015	−0.382**	0.500***

Equation (3.10SP)

Rank Correlation With:	Slope Coefficients				Intercept	RPE	Multiple Correlation
	C	K_t	S_t	P_t			
Real GNP	−0.235	0.206	0.265	0.191	0.220	—	0.088
Durable Goods Production Index	−0.206	0.206	−0.294	0.191	0.206	−0.074	0.162
Investment Rate $= I_t/\bar{K}_t$	—	0.279	−0.294	0.220	−0.044	−0.338*	0.338*
Profit Rate $= \bar{P}_t/\bar{K}_t$	−0.088	0.044	−0.280	0.235	0.088	−0.176	0.147
Capacity Utilization Rate $= \bar{S}_t/\bar{K}_t$	−0.059	0.265	−0.397**	0.294	0.044	−0.309*	0.206

Note: 1. $\sigma_\tau = 0.179$ where $\sigma_\tau = \sqrt{\dfrac{2(2n+5)}{9n(n-1)}}$ for sample size $n = 17$. τ is approximately normally distributed for sample sizes of 10 or more. See KENDALL, *op. cit.*, Chapter 16.

2. * = 10% significance, ** = 5% significance, *** = 1% significance.

Table 5.6 (*continued*)

Equation (3.11S)

Rank Correlation With:	Slope Coefficients			Intercept	RPE	Multiple Correlation
	C	K_t	S_{t-1}			
Real GNP	−0.086	0.390**	−0.238	0.124	0.010	0.048
Durable Goods Production Index	−0.086	0.371*	−0.200	0.162	−0.067	0.124
Investment Rate $= I_t/R_t$	0.105	0.448***	−0.124	−0.105	−0.410**	0.505***
Profit Rate $= \bar{P}_t/R_t$	0.143	0.219	−0.010	−0.105	−0.143	0.124
Capacity Utilization Rate $= \bar{S}_t/R_t$	0.029	0.448***	−0.143	0.010	−0.333*	0.314

Equation (3.11P)

Rank Correlation With:	Slope Coefficients			Intercept	RPE	Multiple Correlation
	C	K_t	P_{t-1}			
Real GNP	−0.333*	0.143	0.276	0.181	0.029	0.371*
Durable Goods Production Index	−0.295	0.105	0.314	0.219	0.029	0.371*
Investment Rate $= I_t/R_t$	−0.181	0.333*	0.162	−0.010	−0.276	0.486***
Profit Rate $= \bar{P}_t/R_t$	−0.181	−0.048	0.314	0.105	−0.048	0.333*
Capacity Utilization Rate $= \bar{S}_t/R_t$	−0.219	0.181	0.238	0.143	−0.276	0.562***

Equation (3.11SP)

Rank Correlation With:	Slope Coefficients				Intercept	RPE	Multiple Correlation
	C	K_t	S_{t-1}	P_{t-1}			
Real GNP	−0.048	0.390**	−0.333*	0.181	0.105	0.086	−0.010
Durable Goods Production Index	−0.086	0.352*	−0.257	0.181	0.143	0.010	0.067
Investment Rate $= I_t/R_t$	−0.010	0.352*	−0.067	0.105	0.029	−0.352*	0.486***
Profit Rate $= \bar{P}_t/R_t$	0.143	0.314	−0.257	0.390**	−0.200	−0.181	0.219
Capacity Utilization Rate $= \bar{S}_t/R_t$	−0.048	0.352*	−0.295	0.219	0.067	−0.295	0.257

Note: 1. $\sigma_\tau = 0.192$, where $\sigma_\tau = \sqrt{\dfrac{2(2n+5)}{9n(n-1)}}$ for sample size $n = 15$. τ is approximately normally distributed for sample sizes of 10 or more. See KENDALL, *op cit.*, Chapter 16.

2. * = 10% significance, ** = 5% significance, *** = 1% significance.

Equation (3.12S)

Rank Correlation With:	Slope Coefficients			Intercept	RPE	Multiple Correlation
	C	K_t	$[(S_t + S_{t-1}) \div 2]$			
Real GNP	−0.257	0.124	−0.181	0.181	0.010	0.086
Durable Goods Production Index	−0.257	0.124	−0.105	0.181	−0.086	0.181
Investment Rate = I_t/R_t	0.162	0.333*	−0.257	−0.162	−0.352	0.486***
Profit Rate = $\bar{P}_t/R_t$	−0.067	0.048	−0.067	−0.010	−0.162	0.162
Capacity Utilization Rate = $\bar{S}_t/R_t$	−0.067	0.238	−0.219	0.029	−0.390**	0.257

Equation (3.12P)

Rank Correlation With:	Slope Coefficients			Intercept	RPE	Multiple Correlation
	C	K_t	$[(P_t + P_{t-1}) \div 2]$			
Real GNP	−0.352*	0.162	0.181	0.257	0.029	0.333*
Durable Goods Production Index	−0.352*	0.124	0.219	0.295	−0.010	0.333*
Investment Rate = I_t/R_t	−0.086	0.390**	0.029	−0.048	−0.314	0.448***
Profit Rate = $\bar{P}_t/R_t$	−0.200	−0.105	0.295	0.067	−0.086	0.257
Capacity Utilization Rate = $\bar{S}_t/R_t$	−0.200	0.162	0.181	0.105	−0.276	0.410**

Equation (3.12SP)

Rank Correlation With:	Slope Coefficients				Intercept	RPE	Multiple Correlation
	C	K_t	$[(S_t + S_{t-1}) \div 2]$	$[(P_t + P_{t-1}) \div 2]$			
Real GNP	−0.276	0.257	−0.257	0.238	0.200	0.029	0.029
Durable Goods Production Index	−0.276	0.219	−0.219	0.238	0.238	−0.048	0.067
Investment Rate = I_t/R_t	0.105	0.333*	−0.219	0.048	−0.067	−0.409**	0.410**
Profit Rate = $\bar{P}_t/R_t$	0.067	0.086	−0.410**	0.352*	−0.048	−0.162	0.143
Capacity Utilization Rate = $\bar{S}_t/R_t$	−0.048	0.295	−0.390**	0.200	0.086	−0.314	0.143

Note: 1. $\sigma_\tau = 0.192$, where $\sigma_\tau = \sqrt{\dfrac{2(2n+5)}{9n(n-1)}}$ for sample size $n = 15$. τ is approximately normally distributed for sample sizes of 10 or more. See KENDALL, op. cit., Chapter 16.

2. * = 10% significance, ** = 5% significance, *** = 1% significance.

Table 5.6 (*continued*)

Equation (3.13S)

Rank Correlation With:	Slope Coefficients			Intercept	RPE	Multiple Correlation
	C	K_t	$[(S_t + S_{t-1}) \div 2]$			
Real GNP	−0.390**	0.333*	−0.314	0.182	−0.105	0.219
Durable Goods Production Index	−0.276	0.333*	−0.314	0.143	−0.143	0.333*
Investment Rate $= I_t/\bar{K}_t$	0.219	0.505***	−0.390**	−0.162	−0.181	0.295
Profit Rate $= \bar{P}_t/\bar{K}_t$	0.200	0.276	−0.295	−0.029	−0.162	0.124
Capacity Utilization Rate $= \bar{S}_t/\bar{K}_t$	−0.105	0.428**	−0.372*	0.067	−0.314	0.276

Equation (3.13P)

Rank Correlation With:	Slope Coefficients			Intercept	RPE	Multiple Correlation
	C	K_t	$[(P_t + P_{t-1}) \div 2]$			
Real GNP	−0.257	0.333*	0.086	0.105	−0.162	0.314
Durable Goods Production Index	−0.219	0.371*	0.086	0.105	−0.257	0.352*
Investment Rate $= I_t/\bar{K}_t$	0.086	0.600***	−0.333	−0.048	−0.162	0.219
Profit Rate $= \bar{P}_t/\bar{K}_t$	0.010	0.162	0.029	0.010	−0.219	0.162
Capacity Utilization Rate $= \bar{S}_t/\bar{K}_t$	0.010	0.428**	−0.010	0.048	−0.333*	0.314

Equation (3.13SP)

Rank Correlation With:	Slope Coefficients				Intercept	RPE	Multiple Correlation
	C	K_t	$[(S_t + S_{t-1}) \div 2]$	$[(P_t + P_{t-1}) \div 2]$			
Real GNP	−0.372*	0.333*	−0.276	−0.143	0.238	0.067	0.105
Durable Goods Production Index	−0.333*	0.333*	−0.276	−0.105	0.200	0.029	0.181
Investment Rate $= I_t/\bar{K}_t$	0.086	0.486***	−0.238	−0.295	−0.067	0.029	0.143
Profit Rate $= \bar{P}_t/\bar{K}_t$	0.105	0.200	−0.181	−0.124	−0.048	−0.067	0.086
Capacity Utilization Rate $= \bar{S}_t/\bar{K}_t$	−0.162	0.390**	−0.219	−0.238	0.105	−0.105	0.124

Note: 1. $\sigma_\tau = 0.192$, where $\sigma_\tau = \sqrt{\dfrac{2(2n+5)}{9n(n-1)}}$ for sample size $n = 15$. τ is approximately normally distributed for sample sizes of 10 or more. See KENDALL, *op cit.*, Chapter 16.

2. * = 10% significance, ** = 5% significance, *** = 1% significance.

Table 5.6 (*continued*)

Equation (3.19)

Rank Correlation With:	Slope Coefficients			Intercept	Multiple Correlation
	$\log C$	$\Delta \log K_t$	$\Delta \log S_t$		
Real GNP	-0.276	-0.162	0.105	0.086	0.181
Durable Goods Production Index	-0.238	-0.105	0.086	0.143	0.181
Investment Rate $= I_t/K_t$	-0.048	-0.105	-0.181	-0.238	0.010
Profit Rate $= \bar{P}_t/K_t$	0.010	-0.162	-0.048	-0.219	0.143
Capacity Utilization Rate $= \bar{S}_t/K_t$	-0.067	-0.048	-0.124	-0.276	0.124

Test statistics are the same as for Equation (3.9).

Equation (3.20)

Rank Correlation With:	Slope Coefficients			Intercept	Multiple Correlation
	$\log C$	$\log K$	$\log S_t$		
Real GNP	-0.412**	-0.176	0.073	0.132	-0.059
Durable Goods Production Index	-0.412**	-0.206	0.015	0.191	-0.088
Investment Rate $= I_t/K_t$	-0.147	-0.015	-0.117	0.059	0.147
Profit Rate $= \bar{P}_t/K_t$	-0.088	-0.162	0.206	0.059	-0.191
Capacity Utilization Rate $= \bar{S}_t/K_t$	0.397**	-0.044	-0.088	0.103	0.044

Test statistics are the same as for Equation (3.10).

Equation (3.21)

Rank Correlation With:	Slope Coefficients			Intercept	Multiple Correlation
	$\log C$	$\log K_t$	$\log S_{t-1}$		
Real GNP	-0.238	0.162	-0.143	0.200	0.428**
Durable Goods Production Index	-0.295	0.086	-0.105	0.181	0.505***
Investment Rate $= I_t/K_t$	-0.124	0.010	0.010	-0.124	0.314
Profit Rate $= \bar{P}_t/K_t$	-0.200	-0.029	0.010	0.029	0.086
Capacity Utilization Rate $= \bar{S}_t/K_t$	-0.200	0.238	-0.257	0.067	0.390**

Test statistics are the same as for Equation (3.11).

Table 5.6 (continued)

Equation (3.22)

Rank Correlation With:	Slope Coefficients			Intercept	Multiple Correlation
	$\log C$	$\log K_t$	$\log [(S_t + S_{t-1}) \div 2]$		
Real GNP	−0.181	−0.028	0.010	0.314*	0.505***
Durable Goods Production Index	−0.238	−0.067	0.067	0.333*	0.524***
Investment Rate = I_t/K_t	0.105	0.238	−0.105	−0.067	0.276
Profit Rate = $\bar{P}_t/K_t$	−0.105	−0.200	0.257	0.124	0.162
Capacity Utilization Rate = $\bar{S}_t/K_t$	0.028	0.181	−0.085	0.200	0.428**

Test statistics are the same as for Equation (3.12).

Equation (3.30A)

Rank Correlation With:	Slope Coefficients		Intercept	Multiple Correlation
	P_t/K_t	$\dfrac{S_{t-1}}{C \cdot K_{t-1}}$		
Real GNP	−0.124	−0.067	0.028	−0.219
Durable Goods Production Index	−0.105	−0.048	0.010	−0.238
Investment Rate = I_t/K_t	−0.142	−0.124	0.371*	−0.200
Profit Rate = $\bar{P}_t/K_t$	−0.028	−0.200	0.181	−0.028
Capacity Utilization Rate = $\bar{S}_t/K_t$	−0.180	−0.333*	0.333*	−0.219

Equation (3.30B)

Rank Correlation With:	Slope Coefficients			Intercept	Multiple Correlation
	P_t/K_t	$\dfrac{S_{t-1}}{C \cdot K_{t-1}}$	$\dfrac{S_t}{C \cdot K_t}$		
Real GNP	−0.181	−0.162	0.086	0.124	−0.181
Durable Goods Production Index	−0.181	−0.162	0.124	0.067	−0.162
Investment Rate = I_t/K_t	−0.181	−0.200	0.086	0.333*	−0.162
Profit Rate = $\bar{P}_t/K_t$	−0.029	−0.276	0.238	0.105	−0.010
Capacity Utilization Rate = $\bar{S}_t/K_t$	−0.219	−0.276	0.048	0.371*	−0.200

Test statistics for (3.30A) and (3.30B) are the same as for Equation (3.12).

Table 5.6 (continued)

Equation (3.31A)

Rank Correlation With:	Slope Coefficients		Intercept	Multiple Correlation
	$[(P_t + P_{t-1}) \div 2]/K_t$	$\dfrac{S_{t-1}}{C \cdot K_{t-1}}$		
Real GNP	−0.238	0.028	0.010	−0.352*
Durable Goods Production Index	−0.200	0.048	0.028	−0.352*
Investment Rate = I_t/K_t	−0.124	0.048	0.200	−0.200
Profit Rate = $\bar{P}_t/K_t$	0.010	−0.162	0.219	−0.048
Capacity Utilization Rate = $\bar{S}_t/K_t$	−0.162	−0.238	0.276	−0.200

Equation (3.31B)

Rank Correlation With:	Slope Coefficients			Intercept	Multiple Correlation
	$[(P_t + P_{t-1}) \div 2]/K_t$	$\dfrac{S_{t-1}}{C \cdot K_{t-1}}$	$\dfrac{S_t}{C \cdot K_t}$		
Real GNP	−0.333*	−0.181	0.257	0.047	−0.333*
Durable Goods Production Index	−0.295	−0.219	0.333*	−0.028	−0.314*
Investment Rate = I_t/K_t	−0.200	−0.142	0.086	0.238	−0.085
Profit Rate = $\bar{P}_t/K_t$	−0.066	−0.314*	0.181	0.047	0.028
Capacity Utilization Rate = $\bar{S}_t/K_t$	−0.181	−0.257	0.105	0.276	−0.142

Test Statistics for (3.31A) and (3.31B) are the same as for Equation (3.12).

the low level of production is considered temporary.[14] This unfortunately provides two quite opposite explanations for the observed results
which ought to be resolved in some manner. My own inclination is to
favor the interpretation originally devised for the first differenced
model. In addition if there are autocorrelated observational errors that
appear in original units but which are eliminated by first differencing,
the two different results are reconcilable. Of all the cross-section models, this one contains the information most relevant to the effect of
changes in variables on investment. By definition this is what is being
measured, since the purely cross-sectional characteristics are largely
suppressed by first differencing so that the more dynamic, average
inter-firm response to changes in the various independent variables is
measured.

In Equation (3.10P) the indicators, particularly capacity utilization
rate, strongly influence the profit regression coefficient. In short, as
might have been expected, the higher the rate of capacity utilization,
the greater is the investment response to profits among firms. As usual,
the characteristics of the individual coefficients displayed in sets (3.10S)
and (3.10P) are effectively reproduced in the combined set (3.10SP).

Of all the indicators, only the investment rate has a statistically
significant correlation with any Equation (3.10S) parameter, and that
is with multiple correlations, not the regression coefficients. All the
indicators are highly correlated with profit model parameter estimates
in (3.10P). Such differential behavior reveals that the factors included
in sales but excluded from profits satisfactorily account for investment
variation. Hence, the profit coefficients are strongly influenced by sales,
capacity utilization, while the sales coefficient is systematically unrelated to the profit rate. Thus the sales model is distinctly better specified
on cross-sections than the profit model in this significant respect.

Equation (3.11) rank correlations contain only one significant change
from the results reported for Equation (3.10). For Equation (3.11S)
the indicators, with one exception, correlate highly with the capital

[14] The familiar distinction between permanent and transient income changes on
consumption behavior provides a direct parallel. Edwin Mansfield has suggested that
costs of change are an increasing function of the size of the change so that reaction
coefficients decline as the gap increases. Combining the "foregone opportunity" result
with the "cost of change" result plus temporary *vs.* permanent expectations could lead
to a unimodel distribution of the reaction coefficient as a function of the gap between
actual and desired stock. The curve would rise until cost disadvantages outweighed
profits foregone.

stock coefficient, but in a relatively negligible manner on the profit model capital stock coefficient. Lagged sales contain less explicit "cyclical" information pertinent to current investment, so far as this reacts upon the capital stock coefficient, than is true for lagged profits. The multiple correlation pattern, however, follows that of Equation (3.10), strongly implying the superiority of the sales, accelerator version. Equation (3.12) behaves much like Equation (3.10). It appears from prior evidence that the weight of statistical explanation is heavily dependent on current independent variables, so that comments on Equation 10 apply virtually unaltered to this equation.

Equation (3.13) possesses different characteristics. The most notable departure from patterns of Equations (3.10) to (3.12) is that the multiple correlation no longer correlates much with any of the indicators. This supports an inference that the investment planning period is longer than a year, so that averaging the two year investments and explaining them by concurrent average explanatory values (except for capital stock which is not averaged) provides a more accurate specification of the investment decision mechanism.

Equations (3.20)–(3.22) in logarithms have different correlation properties than their arithmetic counterparts. The multiple correlation is significantly correlated with real GNP and the durable goods index of industrial production for Equations (3.21) and (3.22), although not for Equation (3.20). Thus the cross-section explanation of investment is effectively randomized only when current output is the primary output variable. While all equations have negative correlations with the capital intensity variable, indicating *ceteris paribus* that more will be invested by the more capital intensive firm, this is statistically significant only for Equation (3.20). Since this is a minor contributor to the total statistical explanation of investment, the small correlations with the remaining slope coefficients reconfirm a covariance analysis finding for Equations (3.21) and (3.22) which had highly homogeneous slopes, that the "moving cross-section" approach aids specification. Although strong cyclical variation exists in the proportion of variance explained, cyclical patterns followed by our indicators have been fully included in this cross-section specification for the various logarithmic equations. The correlations between nearly all the indicators and the intercept are positive, although small in most cases, except in Equation (3.22), showing not at all surprisingly that this autonomous cross-section investment component is cyclically positively related.

On the whole, the ratio model parameter correlations with the cyclical indicators are scattered and low, indicating effective cross-section specifications. The only distinct correlation patterns show up in Equation (3.30) where the investment rate and capacity utilization rate tend to be positively correlated to the intercept, again showing the cyclical variability of this autonomous cross-section investment determinant. Neither of the trend output variables, namely real GNP and the production index, had correlations with the intercept at all so that it is apparently rates which are important in this context rather than trend factors. On Equation (3.31) when the lagged profit variable is averaged along with the current profit variable, this being the only change from Equation (3.30), the effect is moderately attenuated.

The introduction of lagged profits in Equation (3.31) doubles the inverse correlation between the cross-section multiple correlation coefficients and real GNP or the industrial production index. Thus, the lower are profits over the current and previous period the higher the proportion of variance actually explained. This seems to be mainly a trend effect because the rate variables have very much lower correlations.

Finally, for both Equations (3.30) and (3.31), profit rate and capacity utilization effects are uniformly negatively correlated with all the five indicators while the current capacity variable is positively related to the cyclical indicators. Since the correlations are weak, not much importance attaches to this particular uniformity.

5.10 Summary

Consideration was given to the principal types of systematic behavior that cross-sections might be expected to exhibit when time series influences on them have not been explicitly treated. The analysis of covariance is the most appropriate device to discover incorrect specifications of this sort.

The analysis of covariance has been applied to numerous different cross-sections for adjacent years, with the same firms included in each cross-section. With few exceptions, cross-sectional parameter stability did not exist. The main source of heterogeneity among cross-sections was attributable to the highly variable intercepts, indicating the omission of dynamic factors. The profit equation parameters were more closely related to cyclical indicators than sales parameters revealing the less adequate specification of the profit model in this context. The analysis of covariance applied to time series showed that the first differenced model displayed highly homogeneous responses for slopes. Otherwise, the slopes were quite heterogeneous although the sorts of heterogeneity found differed from those observed on cross-sections.

CHAPTER 6

SPECIFICATION IN CROSS-SECTIONS AND TIME SERIES

6.1 Introduction

When specifying a regression equation, it is usual to stipulate that the error term is a random variable distributed independently in time and uncorrelated with the explanatory variables. Numerous aspects of these specifications were explored in Chapter 4 in the context of our particular problem. Here the same question will be approached, but from a somewhat different point of view. In particular, some implications of partitioning the error term into two parts will be studied, one of which behaves according to the standard properties enumerated above, the other part being a constant. For cross-sections the latter is a constant firm attribute unaccounted for by the included cross-section variables. In time series it is a constant equal in value for each firm within a given time period, but which differs from period to period.

How time series are related to cross-sections will be a major theme of this chapter. This has been a topic of widespread, though inconclusive, study. Some current views about the differences between the two sorts of estimates can be summarized. First, the source of estimation bias often differs. As an example, one will typically find an income elasticity coefficient on cross-sections higher than on time series because high income is associated with high consumption levels and is also correlated with age. Unless age is introduced as another independent variable in the estimated cross-section function, the income coefficient will jointly measure the effects of age and income on consumption. In time series the age composition of the population is either constant or subject to gradual, slow change so that the age-income correlation would be negligible. Such inter-individual variables which change little over time must be included explicitly in cross-section regressions to make cross-section and time series regression coefficients on the dynamic variables equivalent, or biases of the sort illustrated can seriously distort the estimates.

While the bias mentioned could lead to over or under-estimates, a second major possible source of bias will ordinarily cause estimated coefficients to be larger on cross-sections than time series. This will be so since cross-sections more nearly represent adjusted long-run equilibrium than annual time series, a point to be developed at greater length later in this chapter.

It is a premise of the analysis in the remainder of this chapter that individual observations included in one cross-section should appear in every other cross-section. Until a great deal more is known about cross-section, time series relations, I believe it is essential to have rectangular arrays of data to permit study of the systematic inter-relations at different periods of time. Indeed, many "one-shot" or several period cross-sections are of dubious value because of the likely existence of inter-period instability soon to be described more fully. The amount and type of instability cannot be ascertained unless the investigator has a number of consecutive cross-sections. Furthermore, the extent of individual or "pure cross-sectional" effects can only be ascertained from an orthogonal array of data.

Increasing reliance upon cross-section data by econometricians has been motivated by three factors.[1] First, because of large sample sizes and apparent unimportance of serial correlation in a cross-section, severe problems of collinearity in time series did not appear to be so serious a handicap in cross-sections. Second, many demographic attributes which affect economic behavior are often cross-sectional. Thus it is essential to go to micro-economic information of a demographic sort, which can be done most conveniently on cross-sections. Third, the availability of high-speed computers and the increased flows of sample survey information challenged the ingenuity of many investigators who were eager to exploit any sort of data in order to understand behavior better.

While at one time it was too readily assumed that estimates obtained from cross-sections would be equally applicable in time series applications, merely because a behavior equation had the same func-

---

[1] Most of the ideas in the introduction through Sections 5.2, 5.4 B and the summary, appeared in *Econometrica*, April, 1959, pp. 1–18. Gregory Chow, Jean Crockett, Guy Orcutt, John Meyer, Robert Solow, and the Harvard Seminar in Quantitative Economics made helpful criticisms on an earlier version of that paper.

tional form, the last five or six years have witnessed increasing of skepticism about this presumed symmetry. The following appraisal of regression coefficients and error variance estimates from cross-sections and time series offers partial documentation on the side of the skeptics. Since the identical group of firms appears in both cross-sections and time series, extraneous influences arising out of sample differences do not obscure the analysis.

Subsequent remarks fall into two categories. In the first, some results are presented on the error variances and how these differ between cross-sections and time series. In the second, contrasts are drawn between estimates of cross-section and time series coefficients, and some of the more pertinent reasons for the observed discrepancies are indicated.

6.2 Error Variance Composition

Because the independent errors will tend to cancel each other and thereby eliminate much of the cross-section error variance, it is sometimes thought that the translation of cross-section estimates into useful aggregate predictions should be quite easy. Therefore, the relative error variance will decrease as more and more firms are included in the aggregate. Even though individual variances are additive (plus or minus covariance terms), the relative prediction error is given by $\sigma_e/\bar{Y}$ $= \sigma_{ej}/\sqrt{N}\bar{Y}_j$, where N is the sample size, σ_e is the regression standard error of estimate, $\bar{Y}_j$ is the mean of the dependent variable and σ_{ej} is constant for each firm. When observations are averaged, it follows directly that $\sigma_e = \sigma_{ej}/\sqrt{N}$. These presumptions break down if the errors in fact are not independent but instead are persistent, auto-correlated characteristics of the individual firms in the sample. If much of the unexplained variance is systematic and non-random, the relative cross-section prediction error will not be a decreasing function of the number of firms according to the square-root relation, and the cross-section error variance will systematically overstate the variability of the time series.

With a rectangular array of data available, we can estimate these persistent individual firm effects and their influence on the cross-section error variance. A regression equation is ordinarily specified to be of the following form:

$$Y_{jt} = \alpha + \beta_1 X_{1jt} + \beta_2 X_{2jt} + \ldots + \beta_k X_{kjt} + \varepsilon_{jt}, \qquad (6.1)$$

$j = 1, \ldots J$ individual firms,

$t = 1, \ldots T$ time, in years.

In this regression equation the error term ε_{jt} is usually assumed to be a random independently distributed variable. Sometimes no further attention is paid to specification of the error term. However, the results presented in Chapter 5 on specification and cross-section stability suggested that one ought to expand the variable classifications into three categories: section variables which are constant for a particular firm (or individual) through time but which differ among firms, time variables which are the same for each firm at a given time but vary through time, and time-section variables which differ among firms both at a point in time and also through time. Since these categories apply to included variables, they should also apply to excluded or error term variables. Hence, redefine ε_{jt} as follows:

$$\varepsilon_{jt} = \gamma_j + \tau_t + \nu_{jt}. \qquad (6.2)$$

These three additive error components are the firm effect γ_j, the pure time effect τ_t, and the time-section variable represented by ν_{jt}. The squared residual can be further broken up into the following components.

$$\varepsilon_{jt}^2 = 2\gamma\,\tau_j + 2\tau_t\nu_{jt} + 2\gamma_j\nu_{jt} + \gamma_j^2 + \tau_j^2 + \nu_{jt}. \qquad (6.3)$$

With no loss of generality we may assume that γ_j, τ_t, and ν_{jt} each have zero means. Furthermore, because the variables γ and τ have been defined to be orthogonal, their cross-product terms drop out. Hence the sum of squares associated with a given sample would be represented according to equation (6.4) below:

$$\sum_{t=1}^{T} \sum_{j=1}^{J} \varepsilon_{jt}^2 = 2 \underset{t}{\sum}\underset{j}{\sum} \gamma_j\nu_{jt} + 2 \underset{j}{\sum}\underset{t}{\sum} \tau_t\nu_{jt} + \underset{t}{\sum}\underset{j}{\sum} \gamma_j^2 + \underset{t}{\sum}\underset{j}{\sum} \tau_t^2 + \underset{t}{\sum}\underset{j}{\sum} \nu_{jt}^2. \quad (6.4)$$

One of the first things to notice is that the error sum of squares associated with the cross-section will include only the first, third and fifth terms, while the error sum of squares associated with the time series will include the second, fourth and fifth terms, since τ_t is a constant in cross-sections and hence has a zero covariance with any cross-section variable, while γ_j is a constant in time series and therefore will not correlate with time series. Hence, we can break the sum of squares of (6.4) down into a cross-section error sum of squares and a time series error sum of squares according to Equations (6.5a) and (6.5b).

Cross-Section $\quad \sum\limits_{t=1}^{T} \sum\limits_{j=1}^{J} \varepsilon_{jt}^2 = 2 \sum\limits_{t}^{T}\sum\limits_{j}^{J} \gamma_t \nu_{jt} + T \sum\limits_{j}^{J} \gamma_j^2 + \sum\limits_{t}^{T}\sum\limits_{j}^{J} \nu_{jt}^2 .$ (6.5a)

Time Series $\quad \sum\limits_{t}^{T}\sum\limits_{j}^{J} \varepsilon_{jt}^2 = 2 \sum\limits_{t}^{T}\sum\limits_{j}^{J} \tau_t \nu_{jt} + J \sum\limits_{t}^{T} \tau_t^2 + \sum\limits_{t}^{T}\sum\limits_{j}^{J} \nu_{jt}^2 .$ (6.5b)

The question next arises about how best to estimate the components γ and τ. It is of course possible to estimate these coefficients directly through the use of dummy variables as recommended in Chapter 5. At this stage, however, a slightly different technique will be adopted which has computational simplicity to recommend it, although not the theoretical elegance of the general linear hypothesis treatment. On the assumption that the same firms appear in all periods, the average residual for a particular firm can be computed by averaging that firm's residuals across cross-section year regressions to supply an estimate of γ_j. Similarly, one could define, as the average residual for a given year, the average across all firm error terms from time series regressions[2] and thus obtain an estimate of τ_t. By using the arithmetic mean in the previous operations, it immediately follows that the covariance terms in (6.5a) and (6.5b) will be identically zero, a result of some importance, so that we are finally left with cross-section and time series combined error sum of squares as defined in equations (6.6a) and (6.6b).

Cross-Section $\quad \sum\limits_{t}^{T}\sum\limits_{j}^{J} \varepsilon_{jt}^2 = T \sum\limits_{j}^{J} \gamma_j^2 + \sum\limits_{t}^{T}\sum\limits_{j}^{J} \nu_{jt}^2 ,$ (6.6a)

Time Series $\quad \sum\limits_{t}^{T}\sum\limits_{j}^{J} \varepsilon_{jt}^2 = J \sum\limits_{t}^{T} \tau_t^2 + \sum\limits_{t}^{T}\sum\limits_{j}^{J} \nu_{jt}^2 .$ (6.6b)

The individual firm effects to which reference has been made in the initial paragraphs of this chapter can be measured by the F distribution. Given the usual assumptions of normality and equality of within cell variances the total sum of squares can be partitioned into two independently distributed sums of squares according to equation (6.6a): the first is attributable to individual firm effects and the second to the error sum of squares. Accordingly, equation (6.7) is an F statistic

---

[2] It is obvious that the double summation over all individual observations in all years will be identically zero if the residuals have been computed from least squares regressions.

which evaluates the statistical importance of these individual firm effects.

$$F = \frac{T \, \Sigma \, \gamma_j^2 / J}{\sum\limits_{t}^{T}\sum\limits_{j}^{J} \nu_{jt}^2 / T(J - k - 1) - J}.$$
(6.7)

A second device, which contains a good deal of heuristic information, is simply to divide the firm effect sum of squares by the total sum of squares to evaluate straightforwardly what fraction of the total cross-section error sum of squares is attributable to individual firm effects, as shown in (6.8).

$$\frac{T\Sigma\gamma_j^2}{\sum\limits_{t}^{T}\sum\limits_{j}^{J} \varepsilon_{jt}^2} = \frac{T\Sigma\gamma_j^2}{T\Sigma\gamma_j^2 + \Sigma\Sigma\nu_{jt}^2}.$$
(6.8)

Since it is my intent to study time series behavior, it is essentially correct to designate the fraction of variance attributable to individual firm effects as extraneous because the cross-section variance estimates may seriously overestimate the time series variability through the inclusion of individual firm effects. One component of time series variability not present here, of course, is the time constant effect, so that a comparison of unexplained variance really depends upon the relative importance of the individual firm effect sum of squares and the year effect sum of squares. These comparisons will be presented in due course.

Several other measures of some interest can also be derived from the decomposed residuals beside the summary information contained in the two previous statistical constructs all presented in Table 6.1. First, within each year one can partition the variance into the fraction attributable to firm effects Column (5), and that attributable to time varying errors Columns (9–11). Second, it is also instructive to evaluate the patterns of the simple correlation between the individual firm effect and the time varying error, although it should be remembered that the correlation over all sample years is identically zero.

6.3 Cross-Sections and Firm Effects

A. *Analysis of Variance*

The test statistic results summarized in Column (4) tell in a precise way a story that might have been expected. To begin, it is worth noting

TABLE 6.1

Firm Effects

Equation	Degrees of Freedom Numerator (1)	Denominator (2)	Critical F 0.01 level (3)	Actual F's (4)	$T\sum_{j=1}^{J}\gamma_j^2 / \dfrac{\sum\sum\varepsilon_{jt}^2}{TJ}$ (5)	Average $\sum_{j=1}^{J}\gamma_j^2 / \sum_{j=1}^{J}v_{jt}^2$ Pre-war (6)	Post-war (7)	All Yrs. (8)	Average Correlation of γ_{jt} with v_{jt} Pre-war (9)	Post-war (10)	All Yrs. (11)
(3.9S)	60	1024	1.66	0.3617	0.0291	0.1027	0.0257	0.0532	−0.1372	0.0236	−0.0338
(3.9P)	60	710	1.66	0.5116	0.0407	0.1324	0.0352	0.0699	−0.0481	0.0008	−0.0166
(3.9SP)	60		1.66	0.3965	0.0324	0.1139	0.0285	0.0590	−0.1237	0.0129	−0.0359
(3.10S)	60	892	1.66	3.185***	0.1765	0.6286	0.1411	0.3419	−0.4276	0.1873	−0.0659
(3.10P)	60	875	1.66	3.057***	0.1706	0.5346	0.1376	0.3011	−0.3409	0.1457	−0.0547
(3.10SP)	60		1.66	2.931***	0.1673	0.6142	0.1333	0.3314	−0.4227	0.1771	0.0699
(3.11S)	60	840	1.66	3.058***	0.1904	0.7138	0.1430	0.3713	−0.4540	0.1810	−0.0730
(3.11P)	60	765	1.66	2.835***	0.1791	0.5861	0.1379	0.3172	−0.3992	0.1698	−0.0578
(3.11SP)	60		1.66	2.851***	0.1828	0.7064	0.1365	0.3645	−0.4790	0.1906	−0.0772
(3.12S)	60	840	1.66	3.111***	0.1931	0.7175	0.1472	0.3753	−0.4418	0.1793	−0.0692
(3.12P)	60	765	1.66	2.850***	0.1798	0.6201	0.1391	0.3315	−0.3966	0.1677	−0.0580
(3.12SP)	60		1.66	2.818***	0.1810	0.7061	0.1367	0.3644	−0.4600	0.1860	−0.0724
(3.13S)	60	840	1.66	4.977***	0.2769	0.7517	0.2088	0.4260	−0.4679	0.2329	−0.0474
(3.13P)	60	765	1.66	4.648***	0.2634	0.6432	0.2015	0.3782	−0.4012	0.2042	−0.0380
(3.13SP)	60		1.66	4.511***	0.2613	0.7486	0.1952	0.4166	−0.4893	0.2396	−0.0520
(3.20)	60	892	1.66	5.500***	0.3700	0.2070	0.4157	0.3298	−0.2234	−0.1926	−0.0213
(3.21)	60		1.66	5.503***	0.2974	0.2343	0.4453	0.3609	0.2864	−0.2361	−0.0271
(3.30A)	60	892	1.66	2.918***	0.1833	0.2795	0.2801	0.2799	−0.0814	−0.0328	−0.0522

*** = 1% level of significance.

that the first difference model Equation (3.9) was remarkably success-ful in eliminating the individual firm constant effect. For each equa-tion the F ratio was considerably less than unity. While the firm con-stant effect remaining in the profit Equation (3.9P) was somewhat greater than that in either Equation (3.9S) or (3.9SP), in all cases a theoretically predictable consequence of first differencing has been empirically verified. If enough firms had significant and different trend terms, however, a significant average error or firm effect would have appeared in the first difference model. It appears that this is not the case.

For the remaining equations the firm constant effects are substan-tial. There is little basis for expressing a preference among Equations (3.10), (3.11), and (3.12). All three show extremely large F's relative to the stringent 1 per cent critical significance level. On Equations (3.13) where the data were averaged, the firm effects were especially prominent. Even though certain other desirable consequences may happen as a result of the averaging process, it appears that the aver-aging process exaggerates individual firm effects. By far the largest F statistic was recorded in Equation (3.21), which is the logarithmic model recorded here. From the point of view of coefficient stability, Equation (3.21) showed the most stable temporal structure, but an undesirable characteristic is present, namely, an exaggeration of the individual firm effects. For many purposes these firm effects can be accommodated in an estimation scheme so that this particular defect should not, by itself, weigh especially heavily in a final assessment.

The second way to evaluate the firm constant influence on cross-section error variances is to divide the firm constant sum of squares by the total sum of squares, according to Table 6.1, Column (5). While this provides qualitatively similar information to that in the analysis of variance, this measure is an index of the relative importance of the firm effects instead of a significance test. The first difference model individual firm effects are between 3 and 4 per cent of the total sum of squares or what we might intuitively suppose to be a negligible fraction. Equations (3.10) through (3.12), allocate between 16 and 20 per cent of the total error sum of squares to firm constant effects and the remainder to time varying errors. The fraction of total variance accounted for by the firm effect is as high as 30 to 40 per cent on Equations (3.20) and (3.21). A slightly different arrangement of the data, essentially partitioning the time varying effects into pre-war and post-war periods, is shown in Columns 6 and 8 where firm sums of squares are divided by the within error sum of squares. For Equations (3.10)–(3.13), it is clear pre-war that individual firm characteristic were more than half as great as the pure error variance. It would have been most misleading to have extrapolated pre-war behavior into the present using cross-section error variances because the relative importance of the different types of errors shifted radically. Post-war, for the same set of equations, the average of the error variance accounted for by this component was between 10 per cent and 15 per cent. Hence, the excluded firm variables in the post-war period were less crucial to time series error variance estimation. When these excluded individual firm effects are dominant, serious biases of the wrong sort could prevail— wrong in the sense that utilization of these behavior equations in time series applications, with primarily cross-sectional, static errors, would be inappropriate to a time series forecast.

A structural shift between the pre-war and post-war period evidently took place. In Columns (9) and (10) for the pre-war and post-war, respectively, the sub-period averages of simple correlations within each year between the firm effect, γ_j, and the time-varying error, v_{jt}, are shown. These correlations are strongly negative pre-war and moderately positive in the post-war period. The first difference model offers an exception with negligible correlations in both periods. Over the entire period the average correlation was small. This bimodal distribution, not surprisingly, led to very large Chi-square values and strong indications, therefore, of inter-period heterogeneity. The main economic implication seems to be that in periods of underutilized capacity which characterized the pre-was economy, errors of the two kinds specified are off-setting in their effects. In the boom periods characterizing the post-war scene, the excluded forces (both firm effects and dynamic "shocks") were mutually reinforcing. This conclusion follows directly from the additional proposition that the regressions corresponding to these correlations are homogeneous. Because $\sigma^2_{\gamma j}$ is constant in every year and $\Sigma \gamma_j v_{jt} = 0$, interpretation of these correlations must be undertaken cautiously.

B. *Actual Effects of Averaging*

Next an evaluation of how the averaging of observations can actually reduce the standard error of estimate will be attempted, an effect which depends largely on the extent of autocorrelated individual

TABLE 6.2

Predicted and Actual Reductions in Standard Errors of Estimate Attributable to Averaging of Observations: Typical Unaveraged $\hat{\sigma}_e$

Equation	Unaveraged Data "Typical" $\hat{\sigma}_e$ (1)	Predicted $\hat{\sigma}_e$ (2)	Actual $\hat{\sigma}_e$ (3)	Difference (4)=(3)−(2)	Difference ÷ Unaveraged $\hat{\sigma}_e$ (5)=(4)÷(1)	Actual $\hat{\sigma}_e$ ÷ Predicted $\hat{\sigma}_e$ (6)=(3)÷(2)
			A. Cross-Sections			
(3.9S)	1175	151.7	109.3	−42.4	−0.0361	0.7205
(3.9SP)	1159	149.6	103.3	−46.3	−0.0399	0.6905
(3.9P)	1186	153.1	105.3	−47.8	−0.0403	0.6878
(3.10S)	1023	132.1	443.9	311.8	0.3048	3.3600
(3.10SP)	1013	130.8	426.0	295.2	0.2914	3.2570
(3.10P)	1044	134.8	431.8	297.0	0.2845	3.2030
(3.11S)	1079	139.3	482.4	343.1	0.3180	3.4630
(3.11SP)	1063	137.2	468.8	331.6	0.3119	3.417
(3.11P)	1085	140.1	473.2	333.1	0.3070	3.378
(3.12S)	1066	137.6	478.6	341.0	0.3199	3.478
(3.12SP)	1051	135.7	466.4	330.7	0.3147	3.437
(3.12P)	1069	138.0	472.4	334.4	0.3128	3.423
(3.30A)	0.0642	0.0083	0.0293	0.0210	0.3273	3.534
(3.30B)	0.0643	0.0083	0.0295	0.0212	0.3304	3.558
			B. Time Series			
(3.9S)	1195	319.3	245.8	−73.5	−0.0615	0.7698
(3.9SP)	1205	322.0	255.0	−67.0	−0.0556	0.7919
(3.9P)	1208	322.8	325.7	2.9	0.0024	1.0090
(3.10S)	960.0	232.8	198.4	−34.4	−0.0358	0.8522
(3.10SP)	929.4	225.4	205.3	−20.1	−0.0216	0.9108
(3.10P)	990.7	240.3	239.6	−0.7	−0.0007	0.9971
(3.11S)	989.4	255.5	255.3	−0.2	−0.0002	0.9992
(3.11SP)	945.4	244.1	245.7	1.6	0.0017	1.007
(3.11P)	1008	260.3	237.0	−23.3	−0.0231	0.9105
(3.12S)	969.4	250.3	172.9	−77.4	−0.0798	0.6908
(3.12SP)	883.7	228.3	153.8	−74.5	−0.0843	0.6737
(3.12P)	967.9	249.9	176.8	−73.1	−0.0755	0.7075
(3.30A)	0.0549	0.0133	0.0139	0.0005	0.0098	1.041
(3.30B)	0.0522	0.0127	0.0141	0.0015	0.0286	1.118

firm effects in cross-section errors. To compute the error reduction effects, calculations based on the standard error of estimate were made from the annual cross-sections and from the time series based on individual firm observations on the one hand, and the standard errors of estimate based on both types of averaged data on the other. The averaged data are, first, averages of firm observations over time which

Table 6.2 (*continued*)

Equation	Ratio of Cross-Section to Time Series Differences (Column 4CS number divided by corresponding element in Column 4TS) (7)	Ratio of Cross-Section to Time Series Relative Difference (Column 5CS number divided by corresponding element in Column 5TS) (8)	Ratio of Cross-Section to Time Series Actual $\hat{\sigma}_e \div$ Predicted $\hat{\sigma}_e$ (Column 6CS number ÷ by corresponding element in Column 6TS) (9)
(3.9S)	0.577	0.587	0.936
(3.9SP)	0.691	0.718	0.872
(3.9P)	−16.48	−16.79	0.673
(3.10S)	−9.064	−8.514	3.944
(3.10SP)	−14.69	−13.49	3.575
(3.10P)	−424.3	−406.4	3.213
(3.11S)	−1716.	−1590.	3.466
(3.11SP)	207.2	183.5	3.393
(3.11P)	−14.30	−13.29	3.712
(3.12S)	−4.406	−4.009	5.033
(3.12SP)	−4.439	−3.733	5.099
(3.12P)	−4.574	−4.143	4.835
(3.30A)	38.91	33.40	3.395
(3.30B)	14.25	11.55	3.182

can then be used for a cross-section regression, and second, annual averages across firms to be used in time series estimation. The actual "typical" standard error of estimate reported in Column (1) of Table 6.2, represents an error estimate using unaveraged data. It was computed by averaging individual (firm or year) variances. When divided through by the square root of the number of items in the aggregated observations, we obtain a prediction, shown in Column (2), of the regression standard error that would be observed if the individual errors were truly independent. In Column (3) are the actual results, where the standard error is from the regression equation estimated from averaged data. These results are shown for both cross-section and time series, and the difference between the predicted and the actual standard errors of estimate are shown in Column (4).

Instead of using the total sum of squares in order to arrive at a typical figure, the median estimates were used for unaveraged data and exactly the same procedures were repeated. When divided through by the square root of the number of items in the sample, we obtained a prediction, shown in Column (2A) of the regression standard error that would be observed if the individual errors were independently

TABLE 6.3

Predicted and Actual Reductions in Standard Errors of Estimate Attributable to Averaging of Observations: Median $\hat{\sigma}_e$

Equation	Unaveraged Data, Median $\hat{\sigma}_e$ (1A)	Predicted σ (2A)	Actual $\hat{\sigma}_e$ (3A)	Difference (4A)=(3A)−(2A)	Difference ÷ Unaveraged $\hat{\sigma}_e$ (5A)=(4A)÷(2A)	Actual $\hat{\sigma}_e$ ÷ Predicted $\hat{\sigma}_e$ (6A)=(3A)÷(2A)
			A. Cross-Sections			
(3.9S)	1136	146.6	109.3	—37.3	—0.0328	0.7456
(3.9SP)	1124	145.1	103.3	—41.8	0.0372	0.7119
(3.9P)	1190	153.6	105.3	—48.3	—0.0406	0.6855
(3.10S)	924.5	119.4	443.9	324.5	0.3510	3.718
(3.10SP)	926.6	119.6	426.0	306.4	0.3307	3.562
(3.10P)	946.7	122.2	431.8	309.6	0.3270	3.534
(3.11S)	1026	132.4	482.4	350.0	0.3411	3.644
(3.11SP)	1034	133.5	468.8	335.3	0.3243	3.512
(3.11P)	1065	137.5	473.2	335.7	0.3152	3.441
(3.12S)	1013	130.8	478.6	347.8	0.3433	3.659
(3.12SP)	1021	131.8	466.4	334.6	0.3277	3.539
(3.12P)	1041	134.4	472.4	338.0	0.3247	3.515
(3.30A)	0.0523	0.0637	0.0293	0.0226	0.4318	0.4344
(3.30B)	0.0526	0.0068	0.0295	0.0227	0.4324	0.4350
			B. Time Series			
(3.9S)	671.7	179.5	245.8	66.3	0.0987	1.369
(3.9SP)	667.8	178.5	255.0	76.5	0.1146	1.429
(3.9P)	724.8	193.7	325.7	132.0	0.1821	1.681
(3.10S)	506.1	122.8	198.4	75.6	0.1494	1.616
(3.10SP)	491.9	119.3	205.3	86.0	0.1748	1.721
(3.10P)	559.4	135.7	239.6	103.9	0.1857	1.766
(3.11S)	545.5	140.8	255.3	114.5	0.2099	1.813
(3.11SP)	537.3	138.7	245.7	107.0	0.1991	1.771
(3.11P)	580.6	149.9	237.0	87.1	0.1500	1.581
(3.12S)	534.3	138.0	172.9	34.9	0.0653	1.253
(3.12SP)	499.5	129.0	153.8	24.8	0.0497	1.192
(3.12P)	557.6	144.0	176.8	32.8	0.0588	1.228
(3.30A)	0.0348	0.0084	0.0139	0.0054	0.1561	1.643
(3.30B)	0.0303	0.0073	0.0141	0.0068	0.2242	1.924

distributed. In Column (3A) the results are the same as in Column (3) where the standard error is from the regression equation estimated from averaged data. Hence, Table 6.2 and Table 6.3 are the same except that medians, instead of averages, define the typical firm standard error of estimate.

There are several ways to compare the difference between the pre-

Table **6.3** (*continued*)

Equation	Ratio of Cross-Section to Time Series Differences (Column 4CS number divided by corresponding element in Column 4TS)	Ratio of Cross-Section to Time Series Relative Difference (Column 5CS number divided by corresponding element in Column 5TS)	Ratio of Cross-Section to Time Series Actual $\sigma_e \div$ Predicted σ_e (Column 6CS number $\div$ by corresponding element in Column 6TS)
	(7A)	(8A)	(9A)
(3.9S)	−0.562	−0.333	0.545
(3.9SP)	−0.546	−0.325	0.498
(3.9P)	−0.366	−0.223	0.408
(3.10S)	4.292	2.349	2.301
(3.10SP)	3.563	1.892	2.070
(3.10P)	2.980	1.761	2.001
(3.11S)	3.057	1.625	2.010
(3.11SP)	3.134	1.629	1.983
(3.11P)	3.854	2.101	2.176
(3.12S)	9.966	5.257	2.920
(3.12SP)	13.49	6.607	2.969
(3.12P)	10.30	5.522	2.862
(3.30A)	4.155	2.766	2.644
(3.30B)	3.349	1.929	2.261

dicted and actual $\hat{\sigma}_e$ which are shown in the raw by Column (4). These relative errors are indicated in Columns (7) to (9) for the typical standard error and Columns (7A) to (9A) for the median standard error. In Column (9) appears the ratio of the difference between predicted and actual $\hat{\sigma}_e$ for cross-sections and time series. That is, it is the cross-section difference shown in Part I, Column (4) divided by the time series difference shown in Part II, Column (4). Column (8) or (8A) shows the ratio of the relative differences for cross-sections and time series; that is, it is Column (5) for cross-sections divided by the corresponding time series entry also from Column (5). Finally, Columns (9) and (9A) present a final comparison, the ratio of actual to predicted $\hat{\sigma}_e$ for cross-sections divided by the corresponding time series number, i.e., it is the ratio of cross-section to time series elements for Column (6) or (6A).

Columns (5) to (9) are simply different ways of making comparisons between predicted and actual standard error reduction when averaging has been performed. Instead of a tedious column-by-column commentary, attention will be restricted to comparisons which make the point most directly, leaving the reader free to choose the comparisons most appealing to him. The first regularity to be noticed is that the actual reduction is substantially less than that predicted for cross-sections. The discrepancy for Equations (3.10), (3.11), and (3.12) is in the vicinity $300 to $350. For Equation (3.9), the difference is very slight and indeed goes a bit in the other direction. This result is consistent with annihilation of the intercept term through first differencing. Second, for time series it is to be noted that the difference between predicted and actual is very small for Equations (3.10) to (3.12), ranging between essentially 0 and 75. In Table 6.3, the differences for cross-sections are extremely similar to Table 6.2 findings. The ratio of the actual averaged standard error to the predicted standard error when averaged data are used is typically around three for cross-sections, a fact reflected by Column (6) of Table 6.2 and Column (6A) of Table 6.3. For time series the ratio is about unity according to Columns (6) and (6A). For the sake of comparison, the division of time series by actual cross-section value for these ratios is contained in Columns (9) and (9A).

The negative conclusion must be drawn that, for Equations (3.10) through (3.12), simply increasing the sample size or averaging will be relatively ineffectual in increasing the precision of cross-section estimation. For these equations, at least, (and quite probably for a very much larger set of equations) the averaging process will not reduce the variance because of the powerful influence of the excluded individual firm effects. These results indicate firm effects tend to nullify the desirable results of increasing sample size and/or averaging. Presuming "errors will cancel out in the aggregate" for cross-sections can indeed be dangerously incorrect. Of course, the inclusion of dummy variables to measure individual firm effects would eradicate the basis for this particular objection. But then the investigator is obliged to have a panel of moving cross-sections which indeed seems very desirable for a great many purposes including the present one. Time series too have autocorrelation but in the present case, of a sufficiently weak nature so that the persistent firm effect type of autocorrelation has adverse cross section consequences which appear to be much the greater cause for concern.[3]

[3] When we compare Tables 6.2 and 6.3 and in particular the results they indicate in Columns (5) and (6), the following observations seem to hold. First, for cross-sections the relative results are strikingly similar except for Equation (3.30) on cross-sections in which case the median result for Columns (5A)–(6A) are 20 to 30 per cent greater than the "typical" results for Columns (5)–(6). Second, because in many cases the results for Column (5) are extremely small, the ratio of Column (5A) to (5) is extremely

Equation (3.12) which has the least desirable cross-section characteristics in the sense that the relative reduction from averaging is least, (an effect noted earlier in connection with the individual firm effects) has superior specification properties in other respects. Once again, individual firm effects on cross-sections have been so efficiently annihilated on Equation (3.9) that the firm-constant effect goes quite the other way, i.e. a greater error variance reduction is obtained from averaging on cross-sections than for time series, although in either case the effects are negligible. The statistical benefits from destroying individual firm effects are considerable.

6.4 Time Series and Time Constant Effects

The time constant variables, whether explicitly included as independent variables or in the error term are, by definition, the effects which are the same to all firms in a given period but which may change from one period to the next. Such factors might include events which affect a particular industry or possibly the entire economy such as unusual optimism or a major strike. Table 4 contains the analysis of variance for the importance of such time constant effects. The analysis of variance is formally identical to that contained in equation (6.1), although in the present instance the cells are firms instead of years. Initially, it is obvious that first differencing had no such beneficial effects on time series as it had on the cross-sections. It was the firm constants which created cross-section difficulties that were eliminated by first differencing in cross-sections. Firm constant effects are absorbed into the intercept term on time series so that they do not provide any component of the unexplained variance. Hence, one can only conclude that the time constant element in the error term, although small in percentage terms, was still large enough to materially influence the error variance, as shown by the significant F ratio.

While Equation (3.10S) displays marginal significance at the 1 per

erratic. However, if we compare either (6A) to (6) or (4A) to (4), the answer is clear: in the case of median estimates, the predicted change typically overestimates the actual change, i.e., in the ordinary course of events, Column (3) exceeds Column (2) often by a moderate to large amount in time series. Typically then the value for (6A) exceeds the value in Column (6) by about 75 per cent. The highly skewed nature of the error variance lends support to the proposition that perhaps more faith should be put in the median rather than the typical values. However, no choice need be made since the relative differences between time series and cross-sections have a rather consistent rank ordering.

TABLE 6.4

Measurement of the Importance of Time Constant Effects

Equation	Degrees of Freedom		Critical F's			Actual F's	$J\Sigma_t^T\tau_t^2/\Sigma_t^T\Sigma_j^J\varepsilon_{jt}^2$
	Numerator (1)	Denominator (2)	0.10 level (3)	0.05 level (4)	0.01 level (5)	(6)	(7)
(3.9S)	14	646	1.56	1.80	2.24	2.000**	0.0465
(3.9SP)	14	586	1.56	1.80	2.24	2.481***	0.0510
(3.10S)	17	823	1.52	1.71	2.13	2.144***	0.0456
(3.10P)	17	823	1.52	1.71	2.13	3.797***	0.0727
(3.10SP)	17	763	1.52	1.71	2.13	2.223***	0.0439
(3.11S)	15	705	1.54	1.75	2.19	3.152***	0.0628
(3.11P)	15	705	1.54	1.75	2.19	3.005***	0.0601
(3.11SP)	15	645	1.54	1.75	2.19	2.607***	0.0572
(3.12S)	15	705	1.54	1.75	2.19	1.464	0.0302
(3.12P)	15	705	1.54	1.75	2.19	2.656***	0.0541
(3.12SP)	15	645	1.54	1.75	2.19	1.710*	0.0383
(3.22)	15	705	1.54	1.75	2.19	4.016***	0.0787
(3.30A)	17	823	1.52	1.71	2.13	1.859**	0.0381
(3.30B)	17	823	1.52	1.71	2.13	1.477	0.0332
(3.31A)	15	765	1.54	1.75	2.19	1.982**	0.0420
(3.31B)	15	765	1.54	1.75	2.19	1.333	0.0318

* = 10% significance level
** = 5% significance level
*** = 1% significance level

cent level, Equation (3.10P) shows highly significant departures from the null hypothesis with an F ratio almost twice as large as that of (3.10S). Column (7), which records the fraction of the total error variance accounted for by the common time constant effect is about 8 per cent for the profit model and only $4\frac{1}{2}$ per cent for the sales model. Sales seem, therefore, to include critical time-correlated elements common to a large number of firms which, when not taken explicitly into account, lead to a substantial increase in the variance attributable to such time constant factors. It should be noted that error variances are relatively much closer to each other. Second, the lagged model, Equation (3.11), has considerably more excluded time constant factors in either (3.11P) or (3.11S) than Equation (3.10), but in combination the extent of the omission is considerably reduced as shown by (3.11SP). Nevertheless, the lagged model by itself does poorly in comparison with Equation (3.10).

Third, when lagged and current values for sales or profits are combined in Equation (3.12), the picture changes markedly. In particular, the combined lag in Equation (3.12S) indicates that even at the 10 per cent level of significance, the time constant effects are not significant. The combined model Equation (3.12SP), has a larger fraction of total variance attributable to the time constant variable, just registering significance at the 10 per cent level. Finally, Equation (3.12P) shows significant effects at the 1 per cent level, even though the combined lag for profits alone shows more homogeneity than either Equations (3.10S) or (3.11P), which do not combine both time periods. The relatively low F statistic, to which corresponds a low fraction of variance attributable to time constant effects (about 3 per cent) provides further corroborative evidence of the importance of the lag structure in making the correct specification. This analysis also indicates that the sales model has a much greater capability of annihilating this particular excluded variable effect than the profit model, a finding of real significance for this study.

The ratio model including only lagged values of capacity utilization and current profit rates, (3.30A), is just above the level of 5 per cent significance. When only the lagged values are included in (3.30A) however, the F ratio is just below the 10 per cent level. This particular result coincides with the earlier finding that, including the average in Equation (3.12) in contrast to either Equation (3.10) or (3.11) alone, reduces the variance ratio. Equation (31B), which has an average of past and present profits as well as separate lags for capacity utilization rates has the lowest F ratio of all equal to 1.3 which is clearly insignificant at the 10 per cent level. In this model then, we find that both lagged profits and, in different ways, lagged capacity utilization interact favorably. This equation successfully encompasses the major common effects, so that for all practical purposes the remaining residuals are independent in the sense defined here.

The logarithmic models, represented by Equation (3.22), performed badly, much as on the cross-sections with regard to this particular attribute. For reasons which do not seem immediately obvious, logarithmic models exaggerate the influence of common effects.

6.5 Relations Between Cross-Section and Time Series Estimates

A. *Comparison of Coefficients*

Regression coefficients from cross-sections and from time series will be compared next and then some reasons for the observed sources of divergence will be outlined. Actual comparisons between cross-sections and time series appear in Table 6.5, where the estimates have been computed in three different ways. The most obvious way to compare regression coefficients from cross-sections and time series is to use average data. This has been done in the first pair of estimates within each equation set. A second, somewhat more complicated way can also be used to eliminate some (but not all) aggregation bias when comparing cross-section and time series coefficients. This method depends upon using estimates from the weighted or B regressions originally computed for the analysis of covariance. Third, the A regression coefficients (i.e. the individual cell regressions) have been recorded by taking a weighted average of these coefficients, where the weight is Fisher's information measure, i.e. the reciprocal of each coefficient's estimated variance. Standard errors of the coefficients have been recorded in parentheses.

Table 6.6 contains results for t tests to establish the significance of differences between cross-section and time series estimated coefficients for B and C regressions. The cross-section and time series estimates are independently distributed even though computed from the same body of data provided that the error term is distributed independently in time. Error term autocorrelations were in general low. Still, the test statistics must be interpreted bearing in mind the usual reservations about the remaining assumptions. The coefficient variance estimates have been pooled according to procedures explained in the notes to Table 6.6.

Three main results, which are extremely similar on both the B and C regressions, emerge from the analysis. First, the profit variable is relatively homogeneous when measured on cross-sections or time series. In every case the t statistic is less than 0.60, an indication of considerable homogeneity by ordinary significance standards. Second, the sales variable is ordinarily quite heterogeneous when cross-section and time series tests are made, with one exception. Equation (3.11SP) has a homogeneous sales coefficient. Third, the sales coefficient shows a

TABLE 6.5

Comparison of Cross-Section and Time Series Estimates

	C	K	S	P	Multiple Correlation
.Equation (3.9S)					
Average Data Regression					
Cross-Section		0.0152 (0.0252)	0.0205 (0.0063)		0.5375
Time Series		0.1031 (0.1913)	0.0347 (0.0096)		0.7371
Weighted Regression					
Cross-Section	−18.90 (44.40)	−0.1450 (0.0235)	0.0229 (0.0038)		0.2844
Time Series		−0.1638 (0.0276)	0.0246 (0.0037)		0.3298
Weighted Average					
Cross-Section	34.00	−0.1276	0.0219		
Time Series		−0.0841	0.0232		
Equation (3.9P)					
Average Data Regression					
Cross-Section		0.0268 (0.0213)		0.4140 (0.1040)	0.5832
Time Series		0.0812 (0.2538)		0.2324 (0.1414)	0.4452
Weighted Regression					
Cross-Section	−7.10 (45.06)	−0.1341 (0.0238)		0.1030 (0.0328)	0.2269
Time Series		−0.1610 (0.0283)		0.1148 (0.0332)	0.2568
Weighted Average					
Cross-Section	−12.40	−0.1170		0.0046	
Time Series		−0.0878		0.0489	
Equation (3.9SP)					
Average Data Regression					
Cross-Section		0.0050 (0.0241)	0.0121 (0.0067)	0.3206 (0.1144)	0.6135
Time Series		0.0978 (0.1988)	0.0392 (0.0139)	−0.0722 (0.1548)	0.7436
Weighted Regression					
Cross-Section	−18.8 (44.8)	−0.1445 (0.0237)	0.0221 (0.0044)	0.0127 (0.0373)	0.2846
Time Series		−0.1638 (0.0290)	0.0246 (0.0046)	−0.00002 (0.0422)	0.3298
Weighted Average					
Cross-Section	−30.7	−0.1404	0.0256	−0.0328	
Time Series		−0.0889	0.0233	0.0064	

Table 6.5 (*continued*)

	C	K	S	P	Multiple Correlation
Equation (3.10S)					
Average Data Regression					
Cross-Section		0.0169	0.0204		0.9085
		(0.0057)	(0.0031)		
Time Series		−0.0057	0.0332		0.9134
		(0.0261)	(0.0082)		
Weighted Regression					
Cross-Section	−147.0	0.0053	0.0261		0.7056
	(45.9)	(0.0038)	(0.0019)		
Time Series		−0.0010	0.0286		0.5152
		(0.0076)	(0.0023)		
Weighted Average					
Cross-Section	−110.6	−0.0021	0.0265		
Time Series		−0.0149	0.0282		
Equation (3.10P)					
Average Data Regression					
Cross-Section		0.0185		0.4143	0.9137
		(0.0052)		(0.0588)	
Time Series		0.0547		0.3402	0.8708
		(0.0193)		(0.1306)	
Weighted Regression					
Cross-Section	56.3	0.0282		0.2919	0.6827
	(41.0)	(0.0028)		(0.0255)	
Time Series		0.0461		0.2536	0.4493
		(0.0062)		(0.0280)	
Weighted Average					
Cross-Section	60.3	0.0196		0.2791	
Time Series		0.0286		0.1305	
Equation (3.10SP)					
Average Data Regression					
Cross-Section		0.0155	0.0089	0.2656	0.9177
		(0.0055)	(0.0056)	(0.1094)	
Time Series		0.0031	0.0307	0.0450	0.9139
		(0.0287)	(0.0125)	(0.1640)	
Weighted Regression					
Cross-Section	−139.4	0.0058	0.0206	0.1155	0.7104
	(46.0)	(0.0038)	(0.0024)	(0.0323)	
Time Series		0.0018	0.0255	0.0587	0.5176
		(0.0081)	(0.0030)	(0.0362)	
Weighted Average					
Cross-Section	−109.5	−0.0042	0.0226	0.1050	
Time Series		−0.0150	0.0257	0.0194	

Table 6.5 (*continued*)

	C	K	S	P	Multiple Correlation
Equation (3.11S)					
Average Data Regression					
Cross-Section		0.0193	0.0204		0.8980
		(0.0061)	(0.0035)		
Time Series		0.0072	0.0262		0.8454
		(0.0486)	(0.0155)		
Weighted Regression					
Cross-Section	−101.2	0.0117	0.0242		0.6845
	(51.7)	(0.0043)	(0.0022)		
Time Series		0.0040	0.0252		0.4511
		(0.0093)	(0.0028)		
Weighted Average					
Cross-Section	−88.2	0.0016	0.0282		
Time Series		−0.0098	0.0207		
Equation (3.11P)					
Average Data Regression					
Cross-Section		0.0208		0.4092	0.9021
		(0.0057)		(0.0674)	
Time Series		0.0510		0.3323	0.8680
		(0.0212)		(0.1454)	
Weighted Regression					
Cross-Section	79.9	0.0320		0.2630	0.6683
	(45.5)	(0.0031)		(0.0293)	
Time Series		0.0470		0.2252	0.4147
		(0.0070)		(0.0321)	
Weighted Average					
Cross-Section	96.6	0.0239		0.2454	
Time Series		0.0293		0.0834	
Equation (3.11SP)					
Average Data Regression					
Cross-Section		0.0178	0.0092	0.2587	0.9058
		(0.0060)	(0.0064)	(0.1240)	
Time Series		0.0327	0.0080	0.2786	0.8701
		(0.0504)	(0.0199)	(0.2011)	
Weighted Regression					
Cross-Section	−95.4	0.0120	0.0188	0.1139	0.6890
	(51.9)	(0.0043)	(0.0028)	(0.0365)	
Time Series		0.0085	0.0205	0.0869	0.4570
		(0.0100)	(0.0037)	(0.0412)	
Weighted Average					
Cross-Section	−63.1	0.0031	0.0226	0.1114	
Time Series		−0.0023	0.0162	0.0285	

Table 6.5 (*continued*)

	C	K	S	P	Multiple Correlation
Equation (3.12S)					
Average Data Regression					
Cross-Section		0.0191	0.0197		0.8997
		(0.0060)	(0.0033)		
Time Series		−0.0577	0.0504		0.9321
		(0.0335)	(0.0112)		
Weighted Regression					
Cross-Section	−164.5	0.0047	0.0272		0.6982
	(51.9)	(0.0043)	(0.0022)		
Time Series		−0.0150	0.0337		0.5044
		(0.0093)	(0.0029)		
Weighted Average					
Cross-Section	−112.6	−0.0013	0.0279		
Time Series		−0.0291	0.0344		
Equation (3.12P)					
Average Data Regression					
Cross-Section		0.0216		0.3897	0.9024
		(0.0056)		(0.0639)	
Time Series		0.0263		0.6009	0.9289
		(0.0176)		(0.1380)	
Weighted Regression					
Cross-Section	5.7	0.0237		0.3605	0.6881
	(45.8)	(0.0033)		(0.0319)	
Time Series		0.0353		0.3710	0.4685
		(0.0070)		(0.0379)	
Weighted Average					
Cross-Section	52.3	0.0163		0.3477	
Time Series		−0.0206		0.2255	
Equation (3.12SP)					
Average Data Regression					
Cross-Section		0.0181	0.0095	0.2346	0.9068
		(0.0059)	(0.0060)	(0.1170)	
Time Series		−0.0351	0.0306	0.3423	0.9512
		(0.0318)	(0.0139)	(0.1679)	
Weighted Regression					
Cross-Section	−157.6	0.0052	0.0189	0.1789	0.7060
	(51.8)	(0.0043)	(0.0030)	(0.0423)	
Time Series		−0.0081	0.0257	0.1510	0.5137
		(0.0099)	(0.0041)	(0.0519)	
Weighted Average					
Cross-Section	−86.4	0.0022	0.0208	0.1844	
Time Series		−0.0295	0.0289	0.0600	

Table 6.5 (*continued*)

	P_t/K_t	E_{t-1}	E_t	Multiple Correlation
Equation (3.30A)				
Average Data Regression				
Cross-Section	0.3835	−0.0755	−0.0696	0.6260
	(0.0705)	(0.1183)	(0.1852)	
Time Series	0.1479	0.0101	0.0348	0.6242
	(0.2539)	(0.0435)	(0.0472)	
Weighted Regression				
Cross-Section	0.1521	−0.0023	0.0634	0.3546
	(0.0226)	(0.0157)	(0.0145)	
Time Series	0.0752	0.0097	0.0631	0.3617
	(0.0263)	(0.0123)	(0.0114)	
Weighted Average				
Cross-Section	0.1437	0.0053	0.0287	
Time Series	0.0431	0.0243	0.0339	
Equation (3.30B)				
Average Data Regression				
Cross-Section	0.3748	−0.1143		0.6248
Weighted Regression				
Time Series	0.1395	0.0515		0.3004
	(0.0231)	(0.0095)		
Weighted Average				
Time Series	0.1229	0.0396		

much lower t value (even though in many cases a significantly high one by usual significance standards) in combination with the profit variable. On the B regressions for (3.9SP), (3.11SP), and (3.12SP) and for all the C regressions, the sales coefficients show smaller t statistics in the SP than in the S equation set. A final minor point is that the capital stock coefficient behaves irregularly, with insignificance in about half the cases and significance in the others, although the heterogeneity is somewhat more evident on the B than the C regressions. The sales slope on the B regressions is invariably greater on time series than cross-sections since all the t statistics are positive. The reverse, however, is true when aggregation bias is more pronounced in the C regressions where on Equations (3.10), (3.11SP), and both (3.12S) and (3.12SP) we find the cross-section sales slope exceeding the time series slope.

The greater homogeneity for profits than sales reflected by the t tests is not in accord with a non-probabilistic measure of percentage differences shown in Table 6.7. For Equation (3.10) the percentage difference for the C regression is greater for sales than profits in comparing

TABLE 6.6

Significance Tests for Differences between
Cross-Section, Time-Series Estimated Coefficients

	K	S	P	Degrees of Freedom Time series	Cross-section
		B Regression			
(3.9S)	1.0917	7.2778***		660	784
(3.9SP)	0.5216	3.0156***	0.3509	600	770
(3.9P)	0.7270		0.5723	660	784
(3.10S)	0.7241	2.1724***		840	952
(3.10SP)	0.4494	3.333***	0.0833	780	935
(3.10P)	−2.6324***		−0.4711	840	952
(3.11S)	0.7476	2.1389**		720	840
(3.11SP)	0.3271	0.7609	0.0636	660	825
(3.11P)	−1.9737**		−0.3750	720	840
(3.12S)	1.9126*	5.3243***		720	840
(3.12SP)	1.2430	2.6600***	0.1985	660	825
(3.12P)	−1.5065		−0.2320	720	840

	K	S	P	Degrees of Freedom Time Series	Cross-Section
		C Regression			
(3.9S)	0.8746	6.370***		11	57
(3.9SP)	0.9234	5.8734***	0.3576	10	56
(3.9P)	0.4423		0.1869	11	57
(3.10S)	−0.7410	−2.2828**		14	57
(3.10SP)	−0.2362	−0.8552	−0.0605	13	56
(3.10P)	1.8660*		0.2595	14	57
(3.11S)	−0.2574	−0.8067		12	57
(3.11SP)	0.3041	0.7450	0.0648	11	56
(3.11P)	1.3727		0.1888	12	57
(3.12S)	−1.7067*	−5.1200***		12	57
(3.12SP)	−1.1565	−2.5333***	−0.1970	11	56
(3.12P)	0.2043		0.0247	12	57

Note:

1. * 10% significance, two tail test,
   ** 5% significance, two tail test,
   *** 1% significance, two tail test.

2. For averaged data (C. Regression) estimates, the standard error of the difference is:

$$\hat{\sigma}_{\hat{\beta}_1^* - \hat{\beta}_1} = \frac{\hat{\beta}_1^* - \hat{\beta}_1}{\sqrt{\left[\dfrac{C_{11}}{J} + \dfrac{C_{11}^*}{T}\right]\hat{\sigma}_p^2}}$$

where

$\hat{\beta}_1$ = cross-section estimate of x_1's coefficient.

$\hat{\beta}_1^*$ = time-series estimate of x_1's coefficient.

C_{11} = element in inverse of product-moment matrix corresponding to x_1 for cross-section.

C_{11}^* = element in inverse of product moment matrix corresponding to x_1 for time-series.

$\hat{\sigma}_p^2$ = pooled estimate of β_1's variance.

$\hat{\sigma}^2$ = cross-section estimate of variance.

$\hat{\sigma}_*^2$ = time-series estimate of variance.

n = cross-section degrees of freedom.

n^* = time-series degrees of freedom.

$$\hat{\sigma}_p^2 = \frac{nJ\hat{\sigma}^2 + n^*T\hat{\sigma}_*^2}{n + n^*}$$

3. The same formula applies to B regressions except that J and T are set equal to unity.

4. The test statistic is $t = \dfrac{\hat{\beta}_1^* - \hat{\beta}_1}{\hat{\sigma}_{\hat{\beta}_1^* - \beta_1}}$.

(3.10S) and (3.10P) while the percentage difference between time series and cross-section for the B regression is less for sales than for profits. The same observation holds generally for (3.10SP) although curiously enough, the percentage error is increased for sales. On Equation (3.9) a quite similar story is evident from a quick perusal and Equations (3.11) and (3.12) differ only in minor details.

By definition therefore the difference between the two alternative ways of measuring homogeneity is the greater variability in the variance of the estimated profit coefficients. Even though the numerator of the t statistic is larger, i.e., the difference between time series and cross-section is greater for the profit coefficient than for the sales coefficient, the greater variance of the difference more than offsets the difference in the numerator. Since the t statistic is the only probability measure at our disposal, from the point of view of experimental evidence greatest reliance should be placed on it.

B. *Sources of Discrepancies*

One of the first facts to note in this comparison of cross-sections and time series, is that the capital stock regression coefficient is nearly always positive and larger on time series than on cross-sections. It was suggested earlier that there are two conflicting forces regarding the capital stock coefficient. The first factor, the depreciation effect, tends to make the coefficient positive while the coefficient ought to be negative when interpreted as a reaction coefficient. Thus, the more pronounced positive tendency on time series might reflect the greater impact of the depreciation effect through time than that observed on cross-sections at a given point of time.

Putting Equation (3.9) momentarily to the side, the profit coefficient in the clear majority of instances is larger on cross-sections than on time series. Sales, however, tend to behave in an opposite fashion, namely to have larger coefficients on time series than on cross-sections.

One reason the estimates differ (and in this study one cannot point to the fact that the estimates depend upon different information with different quantitative implications) is that cross-sections typically will reflect long-run adjustments whereas annual time series will tend to reflect shorter run reactions.[4] Because disequilibria among firms tend

---

[4] In the case of food demand functions, a discussion can be found about the difficulties inherent in combining qualitatively different data and some problems of different response mechanisms in EDWIN KUH and JOHN R. MEYER, "How Extraneous Are

TABLE 6.7

Relative Difference between Cross-Section and Time Series Estimates

	K	S	P	Multiple Correlation
Equation (3.9S)				
Average Data Regression	5.783	0.693		0.371
Weighted Regression	0.130	0.074		0.160
Weighted Average	−0.341	0.059		
Equation (3.9P)				
Average Data Regression	2.030		−0.439	−0.237
Weighted Regression	0.201		0.115	0.132
Weighted Average	−0.250		9.630	
Equation (3.9SP)				
Average Data Regression	18.560	2.240	−1.225	0.212
Weighted Regression	0.134	0.113	−1.002	0.159
Weighted Average	−0.367	−0.090	−1.195	
Equation (3.10S)				
Average Data Regression	−1.3383	−0.6298		0.049
Weighted Regression	−1.1859	0.0965		−0.270
Weighted Average	6.0000	0.0657		
Equation (3.10P)				
Average Data Regression	1.9583		−0.178	−0.047
Weighted Regression	0.6358		−0.131	−0.342
Weighted Average	0.4616		−0.532	
Equation (3.10SP)				
Average Data Regression	−0.8026	2.4417	−0.8306	−0.004
Weighted Regression	−0.6924	0.2386	−0.4916	−0.271
Weighted Average	2.5714	0.1354	−0.8154	

to be synchronized in response to mutual market forces and the business cycle, many disequilibrium effects wash out (or appear in the regression intercept) so that the higher cross-section slope estimates can be interpreted as predominantly reflecting long-run equilibrium behavior. The fully adjusted response will typically show a higher coefficient than an incompletely adjusted response. Since the cross-section data will also contain some short-run disturbances, however, these coefficients will only approximate fully adjusted long-run coefficients. As Koyck has shown, one can interpret short-run elasticities or responses in terms of the first few terms of the geometric series which are the weights placed on the previous level of sales. Nerlove has also shown how estimates of

Extraneous Estimates?," *Review of Economics and Statistics*, November, 1957, pp. 380–93.

Table 6.7 *(continued)*

	K	S	P	Multiple Correlation
Equation (3.11S)				
Average Data Regression	−0.632	0.2834		−0.059
Weighted Regression	−0.6593	0.0418		−0.341
Weighted Average	−7.0122	−0.2657		
Equation (3.11P)				
Average Data Regression	1.4510		−0.188	−0.038
Weighted Regression	0.4701		−0.144	−0.379
Weighted Average	0.2270		−0.660	
Equation (3.11SP)				
Average Data Regression	0.831	−0.130	0.077	−0.039
Weighted Regression	−0.292	0.096	−0.237	−0.337
Weighted Average	−1.767	−0.283	−0.744	
Equation (3.12S)				
Average Data Regression	−4.016	1.5574		0.036
Weighted Regression	−4.171	0.2380		−0.277
Weighted Average	21.384	0.2334		
Equation (3.12P)				
Average Data Regression	0.2157		0.542	0.029
Weighted Regression	0.4882		0.029	−0.319
Weighted Average	−2.2607		−0.351	
Equation (3.12SP)				
Average Data Regression	−2.9387	2.2210	0.459	0.049
Weighted Regression	−2.5667	0.3626	−0.185	−0.272
Weighted Average	−14.1696	0.3908	0.674	
Equation (3.30)				
Average Data Regression	−0.614	−1.134	−1.500	−0.003
Weighted Regression	−0.505	−5.163	−0.005	0.020
Weighted Average	−0.700	3.6285	0.1828	

Note: Each coefficient is computed as $\dfrac{\hat{\beta}^* - \hat{\beta}}{\hat{\beta}}$, where

β = Cross-section estimate,
$\hat{\beta}^*$ = Time series estimate.

distributed lags can be used to evaluate short-, intermediate-, and long-run reactions, when, however, the coefficients have been estimated on time series.[5]

[5] L. KOYCK, *Investment Analysis and Distributed Lags*, and M. NERLOVE, "Distributed Lags and Demand Analysis," *Agricultural Handboek* 141, U.S. Department of Agriculture, Washington, D.C., 1958. A worthwhile addition to this discussion, based however on somewhat restrictive assumptions, will be found in Y. GRUNFELD, "The Interpretation of Cross Section Estimates in a Dynamic Model, "*Econometrica*, July, 1961, pp. 397–404.

Thus, dynamic specification errors that bias time-series estimates downward will be less observable in cross-sections. Suppose that the explanatory variables operate according to a pattern of distributed lags:

$$I_t = a + b_0 X_t + b_1 X_{t-1} + \ldots b_n X_{t-n} + c K_{t-1} + \varepsilon_t.$$

If, for example, terms beyond b_1 are neglected, b_1, which represents only a part of the reaction, will be a small number compared to the total long-run reaction coefficient. Least-squares bias, which arises from high partial correlations between the excluded and included variables should not ordinarily be large, since the X_{t-1} are likely to have almost equally strong simple correlations with both X_t and K_{t-1}. On cross-sections, behavior is less explicitly dynamic: inter-firm variability is reflected by the observed variables and their coefficients so that inter-firm excluded factors rather than intra-firm dynamic factors are most likely to dominate. That is, inter-firm dynamic specification difficulties will be less since market or cyclical factors faced in common by all firms in an industry will not affect inter-firm variability and therefore will exert a minor influence on cross-section estimates. In particular, we should expect *a priori* the cross-section negative reaction coefficient to be larger than the shorter-run time series estimate, a proposition that perhaps explains much of the observed phenomenon that the time-series capital stock coefficients are typically more positive than the corresponding cross-section estimates, given a similar depreciation effect on both cross-sections and time series.

These observations on differential cross-section, time series behavior lend support to the rather obvious proposition that the biases from excluded variables can be strikingly different in time series and cross-sections. Therefore, the propriety of applying in one context behavior relations estimated in another context is to be questioned. If these biases are inherent in the time reaction mechanism, we shall want to preserve estimation biases, and we could cause positive damage by importing static inter-firm bias into a time series frame of reference.[6] In short, sources of biases differ and often may be rather stable. We should, therefore, preserve such biases until more appropriate specification can reduce bias in its relevant temporal context.

---

[6] An important exception to this proposition arises in the study of stabilization policy where the central purpose is to change or analyze the structure of dynamic processes.

Cross-section and time series estimates will usually differ for the reasons given above. For prediction purposes, however, it is most important that the numerical value of differences between estimates be ascertained. If the time series estimate is some function of the typical cross-section estimate, one estimate can be translated into the other irrespective of the causal factors that determined the discrepancy. When such systematic relations can be found, the predicting statistician will have an extremely valuable tool. In this connection, cross-sections have two advantages. First, should the relations which generated the observations undergo a structural change, the estimates could be revised immediately upon discovery that the cross-section relationships had altered, unless the function translating cross-section into time series estimates changed at the same time. Time series could not be used so efficiently for this purpose because of the necessarily long time interval that must pass before assurance can be given that a change had occurred. The more variable are the cross-section estimates, however, the weaker does this proposition become. Second, cross-sections typically have many more degrees of freedom than time series and often the independent variation is greater.

What should be stressed, however, is that cross-sections cannot be used successfully to make time series predictions unless a systematic relationship between the cross-section and time series estimates has been firmly established. Only when joint information is available and empirical relations are established between the two types of information will it be possible to make inferences from one type of data to the other without other major sources of variation (e.g., quality of data, type of data) obscuring the cause of observed discrepancies.

6.6 Summary

Throughout this chapter I have tried to demonstrate that a proper understanding of time series implications of a single cross-section requires sequential observations on the same individuals in a number of different time periods. Other possible data compositions that frequently arise in practice include those with different individuals in a number of consecutive time periods for sample surveys, and cross-section samples at separate points of time linked by aggregates for the intervening periods. Until a great deal more has been learned about cross-section, time series relations, a rectangular array of data is essential to the full understanding of the systematic inter-relations between the different sample types. Observations on individuals at only one or a few points of time will often be structurally incomplete because the observations in a given cross-section are likely to be affected by prior observations.[7] More important, with a rectangular array of data, inference from time series residuals about the cross-section behavior can be drawn, and *viceversa*. Many relevant hypotheses about the structure of error distributions in cross-sections and hence about the joint time series, cross-section structure depend upon completeness of information.

In addition, the biases which influenced the cross-section estimates are highly unlikely to be qualitatively or quantitatively of the same sort that affect the time series estimates. Because, in any realistic situation, estimating equations typically will be incorrectly specified, certain time series biases will do no damage if the underlying structure does not change, and they therefore ought to be preserved. We are almost certain to be misled if the incorrectly specified cross-section estimates with their particular, and often irrelevant, biases are utilized in a time series context.

These generalizations were based on evidence already presented. More concrete empirical propositions also emerged. First, the error variances in cross-sections overestimate the variability actually present in the independent time series error. The extent of over-estimation is difficult to ascertain unless we have a rectangular set of observations. In the present case, as reported in Table 6.1, it is seen that irrelevant, "pure cross-section" variability amounts to slightly more than one-quarter of the time-varying unexplained variance. While this source of variability will not affect the time series variance, we cannot evaluate how much cross-section errors will in fact diminish through increased sample size or aggregation unless both time series and cross-section information have been used according to suggested procedures.

Second, the cross-section estimates of the profit coefficient are typically about twice as large as the corresponding time series estimates, for the investment functions considered, while the capital stock coefficients are substantially smaller. Large differences, too, were noticeable for the sales and capital stock coefficients. Although differences

---

[7] This point has been explicitly recognized in the late 1940' studies of consumption behavior by James Duesenberry and Franco Modigliani and also in the more recent work of Modigliani and Brumberg and of Milton Friedman.

among coefficients were found in estimates from aggregate data, it is shown that the differences could not be attributed to certain biases, since the weighted or B regression coefficients, which do not suffer as much from dangers inherent in the aggregation process, displayed similar behavior.

In general, dynamic coefficients cannot be estimated from cross-sections with any degree of confidence unless there is supporting time series information to provide assurance that the biases analyzed throughout this chapter do not distort the estimated coefficients and variances in the particular cross-section. Only when supporting time series are at hand can cross-sections be used safely in a time series context. It must be concluded that estimates of micro- or macrodynamic effects cannot typically rely upon cross-section estimates. This does not reduce or eliminate the usefulness of cross-sections for testing some hypotheses: the estimated coefficients, however, must be used with the greatest circumspection in their application to time series processes.

CHAPTER 7

AGGREGATION

7.1 Introduction

While the importance of utilizing micro-economic information in the solution of econometric problems has led to concentration on the direct analysis of micro-observations, information available in this study also can shed light on some aggregation effects. This important subject will be explored here by treating the aggregated micro observations on the dependent variable as an aggregate, to be predicted from either the micro equations or by a simple aggregated macro-economic equation. Because the micro-economic estimates are available, results from both methods can be compared. The capability to look beneath the surface of an aggregate is not often available.

This chapter is concerned with a limited aspect of problems that arise in interpreting estimates from macro-economic information because of aggregation effects. These arise first, as the conventional problem of aggregating over individuals, and second, as effects that alternative choices of time period aggregates or averages have upon estimated coefficients.

7.2 Aggregates of Observations

A. *Aggregation Bias*

Since individual firm and other micro data will ordinarily be unavailable or prohibitively expensive, aggregate independent variables will often be the data base used to predict an aggregate dependent variable. Analytical links between micro and macro estimates have been studied by H. Theil, who has made an important methodological contribution in the theory of aggregation. The principal benefit from Theil's work has been to make explicit the sources of aggregation bias and its measurement rather than to suggest ways of coping with the problem.[1]

One of Theil's main conclusions for aggregation theory is this: In general, regression coefficients estimated by least squares from aggregated observations of the independent variables will differ from the average of the individual micro parameters by an amount termed the "aggregation bias" whose extent depends on certain covariance terms. Definition of these terms is not essential to subsequent exposition. In several circumstances, however, aggregation bias will be zero.

First, appropriately weighted linear aggregates of the independent variables will eliminate aggregation bias; by construction, predictions from these weighted aggregates will yield the same prediction as the sum of the micro predictions using micro variables and micro parameters. A basic limitation to the application of this prescription lies in the nature of the weights which Theil has shown to be the appropriate ones. These weights are the individual micro parameters. Of course, if these were known, no difficulties would have arisen in the first place, since these micro coefficients rather than a macro estimate would be employed.

Second, the summed micro predictions will equal the macro prediction when two conditions hold simultaneously: the micro variables for each individual must vary proportionally with the simple, unweighted aggregate or macro variables and relative changes in the micro variables must be the same for each individual. This condition is unlikely to be met in practice. However, both conditions will automatically be fulfilled if the micro-independent variables grow at the same relative rate. Thus, even if the individual micro parameters differ, similar micro and macro predictions will be made if individual firms are split up into groups with equal growth rates in the independent variables, a criterion which could easily have practical applications.[2]

Third, even when aggregation bias is nil, different micro parameters will cause the macro prediction to differ from the summed micro prediction when the homogeneity condition of the previous paragraph is

[1] H. THEIL, *Linear Aggregation of Economic Relations*, Amsterdam, 1954. A highly useful exposition and commentary are to be found in R. G. D. ALLEN, *Mathematical Economics*, pp. 694–719, and the excellent review by JOHN S. CHIPMAN which appeared in *The Review of Economics and Statistics*, Vol. 39, May, 1957, No. 2, pp. 233–235.

[2] More far reaching implications of this result have been derived by HERBERT A. SIMON and ALBERT K. ANDO, "Aggregation of Variables in Dynamic Systems," *Econometrica*, Vol. 29, No. 2, April, 1961.

violated, unless all individual micro-variable changes are equal. Such an occurrence strikes one as rather improbable, to say the least.

Fourth, when all "non-corresponding" micro parameters are equal or all non-corresponding micro variables are equal, aggregation bias will be zero. This also is highly implausible. Another unlikely situation, that really amounts to the same thing, occurs when the "non-corresponding" micro variables have zero partial correlations with the macro variable under consideration.

The fifth, and final possibility of realizing zero aggregation bias also does not hold generally, but it is extremely important to observe that to some degree it is within the investigator's power to bring about this result: all corresponding parameters must be equal. This intuitively acceptable theorem has been known for many years in the literature on aggregation theory. What does this mean for the practical task of aggregation? Since no exact way exists to make all micro parameters within a given group equal, we will stipulate in obvious fashion that the regression coefficients must be equal within prescribed statistical error limits according to the analysis of covariance. More often than not, individual time series are unavailable so that finely divided sub-aggregates would be used instead, but the central proposition nevertheless remains: that within any given *a priori* construction or theoretical behavior equation the sub-aggregates or at the lowest level, the individuals, must be divided into groups reflecting homogeneous behavior coefficients in order to minimize aggregation bias.

The definition of aggregation bias proposed by Theil, the difference between the slopes estimated from aggregate data and the unbiased estimate or average of the corresponding micro parameters can now be given empirical content. The results for Equations (3.9) through (3.12) for both time series and cross-section results have been summarized in Table 7.1. The first column is the slope coefficient estimated from aggregate data. The second column is the average of the micro parameters. The third column is the difference between the two, while the fourth column presents a measure of relative bias to assist making comparisons across equations, namely column (3) $\div$ (2).

One of the most noticeable effects for the capital stock slope is that in most instances there is less relative aggregation bias in the profit set of equations than in the sales equations. In most instances, however, the aggregation bias is severe: it is regrettable that estimation of this important structural parameter is particularly obscured in aggregated

AGGREGATION

TABLE 7.1

Evaluation of Aggregation Bias
Time Series Slope Estimates:

Equation	Aggregate Estimate[1] (1)	Micro Estimate Average (2)	Aggregation Bias (3) = (1) − (2)	Relative Aggregation Bias (4) = (3) ÷ (2)
		Capital Stock Slope		
(3.9S)	0.10305	−0.23266	0.33571	−1.44294
(3.9SP)	0.09777	−0.24661	0.34437	−1.39645
(3.9P)	0.08125	−0.23637	0.31761	−1.34374
(3.10S)	−0.00570	−0.00280	−0.00290	1.03651
(3.10SP)	−0.00305	−0.01574	0.01269	−1.80622
(3.10P)	0.05470	0.03779	0.01691	0.44742
(3.11S)	0.00719	0.01200	−0.00481	−0.40071
(3.11SP)	0.03269	0.01307	0.01962	1.50094
(3.11P)	0.05098	0.04224	0.00873	0.20667
(3.12S)	−0.05765	−0.02202	−0.03636	1.65150
(3.12SP)	−0.03509	−0.03273	−0.00236	0.07219
		Sales Slope		
(3.9S)	0.03468	0.02294	0.01174	0.51189
(3.9SP)	0.03922	0.03022	0.00901	0.29814
(3.10S)	0.03320	0.03451	−0.00131	−0.03789
(3.10SP)	0.03070	0.04143	−0.01074	−0.25910
(3.11S)	0.02622	0.02997	−0.00375	−0.12522
(3.11SP)	0.00801	0.02755	−0.01953	−0.70906
(3.12S)	0.05038	0.04679	0.00359	0.07683
(3.12SP)	0.03060	0.04477	−0.01417	−0.31647
		Profit Slope		
(3.9P)	0.23237	0.09918	0.13319	1.34294
(3.9SP)	−0.07224	−0.06116	−0.01109	0.18130
(3.10P)	0.34016	0.19051	0.14965	0.78556
(3.10SP)	0.04500	−0.07010	0.11510	−1.64197
(3.11P)	0.33232	0.19982	0.13251	0.66313
(3.11SP)	0.27861	0.04281	0.23580	5.50822
(3.12P)	0.60091	0.32881	0.27210	0.82752
(3.12SP)	0.34230	0.03964	0.30267	7.63588

[1] Estimates from the C Regression have been recorded in Column 1.

data relatively more than any of the other parameters. While perhaps this finding originated in sample peculiarities, it should serve as a caution to individual investigators working with aggregative data. A second quite striking point about the capital stock slope is that the relative

TABLE 7.2

Evaluation of Aggregation Bias
Cross-Section Slope Estimates;

Equation	Aggregate Estimate[1] (1)	Micro Estimate Average (2)	Aggregation Bias (3) = (1) − (2)	Relative Aggregation Bias (4) = (3) ÷ (2)
	Capital Stock Slope			
(3.9S)	0.01520	−0.17189	0.18709	−1.08843
(3.9SP)	0.00500	−0.17643	0.18144	−1.02835
(3.9P)	0.02684	−0.17573	0.20257	−1.15277
(3.10S)	0.01685	0.00305	0.01380	4.52713
(3.10SP)	0.01545	0.00274	0.01272	4.65032
(3.10P)	0.01849	0.02470	−0.00609	−0.25138
(3.11S)	0.01930	0.01026	0.00904	0.88125
(3.11SP)	0.01780	0.01141	0.00639	0.56055
(3.11P)	0.02077	0.02836	−0.00759	−0.26774
(3.12S)	0.01914	0.00512	0.01402	2.73714
(3.12SP)	0.01810	0.00522	0.01288	2.46992
(3.12P)	0.02155	0.02159	−0.00004	−0.00178
	Sales Slope			
(3.9S)	0.02050	0.02253	−0.00203	−0.09021
(3.9SP)	0.01205	0.02115	−0.00910	−0.43044
(3.10S)	0.02037	0.02838	−0.00802	−0.28251
(3.10SP)	0.00892	0.02291	−0.01399	−0.61081
(3.11S)	0.02043	0.02738	−0.00695	−0.25381
(3.11SP)	0.00920	0.01788	−0.00869	−0.48568
(3.12S)	0.01970	0.02829	−0.00858	−0.30346
(3.12SP)	0.00050	0.01803	−0.00852	−0.47274
	Profit Slope			
(3.9P)	0.41398	0.08767	0.32631	3.72182
(3.9SP)	0.32056	0.02467	0.29589	11.99309
(3.10P)	0.41433	0.28804	0.12629	0.43845
(3.10SP)	0.26563	0.12163	0.14399	1.18384
(3.11P)	0.40917	0.28998	0.11918	0.41101
(3.11SP)	0.25871	0.17727	0.08145	0.45947
(3.12P)	0.38967	0.35204	0.03763	0.10689
(3.12SP)	0.23459	0.20581	0.02878	0.13985

[1] Estimates from the C Regression have been recorded in Column 1.

bias is by far smallest for Equation Set (3.12). It also may be significant that this shows the largest correct *a priori* (i.e., negative) sign. In particular, the relative aggregation bias is only 7 per cent for the combined sales, profit set which would show a reaction coefficient of about 0.033, which, when corrected for the depreciation factor, would be about 0.07. Interestingly enough, the most consistent large bias in this coefficient occurs in the first differenced model. When both profits and sales are included in the same equation, aggregation bias ordinarily increases.

Relative aggregation bias for the sales slope is typically less than that for the profit slope. The lowest relative aggregation bias for the sales model occurs in (3.12S), while the least aggregation bias for profits occurs in (3.9SP). The marginal propensity to invest out of gross retained earnings is 0.34 according to aggregate data, but when the individual micro parameters have been averaged, the marginal propensity to spend on investment from gross retained earnings is only 0.19 for Equation (3.10). At the same time, the 0.34 slope coefficient for profits is closer to magnitudes encountered on aggregative industry data. Quite possibly, then, this coefficient may have been overrated when estimated from aggregative data. The same overestimation occurs in Equation (3.12P), where the relative aggregation bias is 82 per cent and the marginal propensity to spend is 0.60 on aggregate data but only 0.33 for the average of the micro coefficients. The relative aggregation error is a massive 760 per cent on Equation (3.12SP). Here the average marginal propensity to spend is about 0.04 while from aggregative data we would take it to be almost eight times that amount. It is evident that aggregation can lead to severe distortions. This conclusion is extremely disturbing for policy purposes. Finally, contrary to the case of profits, aggregation tends to bias downward the estimated sales slope coefficient. For Equations (3.10S), (3.10SP), (3.11S), (3.11SP) and (3.12SP), the arithmetic mean of the individual coefficients is greater than the estimate obtained from aggregated data.

Cross-section aggregation bias is especially severe for the capital stock slope coefficient except on (3.12P). The absolute differences are sometimes quite large, especially for Equation (3.9). Both relative bias and absolute bias appear to be less on cross-sections than on time series. The other absolute differences between the aggregate estimate and the average of the micro parameters are small, although the relative errors are frequently quite large. The absolute differences for the sales slope turn out to be negligible for almost every equation, but the relative biases range between 10 per cent and 60 per cent.

As with time series, both the absolute differences and the relative differences for the profit equations are considerable. The bias again is in favor of exaggerating the influence of profits when aggregate data are used (especially on the first differenced model) although the differences are slight for Equation (3.12).

B. *Prediction*

The process of subdivision within a given behavior relationship according to micro behavior coefficient homogeneity will cause some practical difficulties. In some cases, despite the fact that the aggregation bias in the estimated coefficient is large, the *effects* on prediction will be small if the distribution among individuals within the aggregation of independent variable values follows certain restrictive patterns previously mentioned. In such cases one could aggregate all the way to one individual behavior equation for predictive purposes. For policy purposes this would not be satisfactory, a point that will be developed immediately.

To arrive at a criterion for an appropriate aggregation level, we must define the error terms for aggregated micro predictions, and macro estimates.

There is a set of J micro equations:

$$y_{jt} = a_j + b_j x_{jt} + \varepsilon_{jt}, \qquad \begin{aligned} j &= 1, \ldots J \\ t &= 1 \ldots T. \end{aligned} \qquad (7.1)$$

The aggregate micro error for period t is simply:

$$E_t = \sum_{j=1}^{J} \varepsilon_{jt}. \qquad (7.2)$$

An equation estimated from aggregated data,

$$X_t = \sum_{j=1}^{J} x_{jt} \text{ and } Y_t = \sum_{j=1}^{J} y_{jt}$$

has an error term which differs in general from E_t because of aggregation bias effects so that in the macro equation:

$$Y_t = \alpha + \beta x_t + V_t, \quad V_t \neq E_t. \qquad (7.3)$$

Prediction that is based on (7.1) is free of aggregation bias. V_t, on the other hand, will in general be subject to aggregation bias. The difference between these two can be defined as the aggregation error, U_t:

$$V_t \equiv E_t + U_t. \qquad (7.4)$$

Hence, the aggregate error sum of squares can be separated into three components:

$$\sum_{t=1}^{T} V_t^2 = \sum_{t=1}^{T} E_t^2 + \sum_{t=1}^{T} U_t^2 + 2 \sum_{t=1}^{T} E_t U_t. \qquad (7.5)$$

When error terms have been obtained from least squares estimates, the following properties for U_t hold:

$$\bar{U} = 0, r_{ux} = 0, \text{ and } \Sigma E_t U_t \neq 0 \text{ (in general)}. \qquad (7.6)$$

Thus, there exists a "pure" aggregation error component of the macro error sum of squares ΣU_t^2, and a covariant element,

$$2 \sum_{t=1}^{T} E_t U_t.$$

Because the two error components are not independently distributed, no statistical test on the importance of the aggregation bias is *directly* possible. Heuristic information relevant to policy formation can be derived quite simply from the relation (7.5), since the proportion of error attributable to aggregation is:

$$\text{Per cent aggregation error} = \frac{\sum_{t}^{T} U_t^2 + 2 \sum_{t}^{T} E_t U_t}{\Sigma V_t^2}. \qquad (7.7)$$

This proportion could be evaluated according to whatever criteria a policymaker might desire.

An evaluation of a few time-series estimation equations, using this measure of relative aggregation bias, is shown in Table 7.3 for Equations (3.10) and (3.11)[3]. Equation (3.10S) has a small, negative aggregation bias—that is, one would be slightly better off predicting from the macro equation, although not much, since the negative covariance terms are small. In the case of the profit equation, however, a fairly large negative relative aggregation bias exists: we are "much better off" for prediction purposes to use the aggregated equation, although the standard error of estimate, even for the aggregate, is substantially greater than that for the sales equation. When both profits and sales

---

[3] Only these two equations are available since programming difficulties caused the loss of the summed micro errors for the other equations.

TABLE 7.3

Aggregation Errors: Equation (3.10)

Year	Error Terms (3.10S) V_t (1)	E_t (2)	U_t (2)-(1)	Error Terms (3.10SP) V_t (1)	E_t (2)	U_t (2)-(1)	Error Terms (3.10P) V_t (1)	E_t (2)	U_t (2)-(1)
1935	-139	-39	100	-95	-45	51	-370	-170	200
1936	-112	-21	91	-93	-23	70	-173	-42	131
1937	144	215	71	95	216	121	147	238	91
1938	-128	-84	44	-163	-54	109	-220	14	234
1939	-228	-201	27	-156	-206	-49	-387	-300	87
1940	-13	-15	-3	59	-26	-84	-84	-79	5
1941	-119	-149	-30	-136	-144	-8	151	102	-49
1946	331	342	11	287	346	60	386	402	16
1947	26	76	49	-17	58	76	100	32	-68
1948	321	354	33	359	338	-21	314	273	-41
1949	52	57	5	-20	59	80	-89	-27	62
1950	-327	-341	-14	-319	-367	-48	-437	-572	-135
1951	-219	-206	13	-217	-196	20	56	-54	-110
1952	52	-23	-75	65	-3	-68	279	182	-97
1953	23	-109	-132	55	-91	-146	189	76	-112
1954	183	65	-118	147	66	-82	66	-37	-103
1955	153	80	-73	150	70	-80	74	-37	-110
$\sum x^2$	566,320	551,137	72,989	511,880	547,964	101,570	999,463	803,373	215,949
Aggregation Error $\sum U_t^2 + 2\sum E_t U_t =$		-15,335			36,084			-195,977	
Relative Aggregation Error $\dfrac{\sum U_t^2 + \sum E_t U_t}{\sum V_t^2} =$		-3%			6%			-24%	
Standard Error of Estimate	201	198	—	198	205	—	267	240	—

V_t = Average Micro Error E_t = Average Macro Error U_t = Aggregation Error

TABLE 7.4
Aggregation Errors: Equation (3.11)

Year	Error Terms (3.11S)			Error Terms (3.11SP)			Error Terms (3.11P)		
	V_t (1)	E_t (2)	U_t (2)-(1)	V_t (1)	E_t (2)	U_t (2)-(1)	V_t (1)	E_t (2)	U_t (2)-(1)
1936	-29	42	71	-54	10	64	-233	-12	221
1937	135	212	76	139	211	72	108	217	109
1938	-522	-467	56	-466	-445	21	-416	-426	-10
1939	-207	-202	5	-150	-24	126	-191	-16	175
1940	36	57	21	54	37	-17	-62	26	88
1941	235	267	32	202	215	13	177	217	40
1947	192	243	51	168	268	100	300	281	-20
1948	279	315	36	204	210	6	279	212	-67
1949	-252	-237	16	-207	-329	-123	-228	-335	-107
1950	-181	-247	-66	-250	-252	-2	-274	-281	-7
1951	99	55	-45	45	-112	-158	-46	-154	-107
1952	-14	-15	-2	23	45	22	200	80	-120
1953	4	-32	-36	50	90	40	242	127	-116
1954	-113	-241	-128	-33	-135	-102	-13	-99	-86
1955	336	249	-87	274	211	-63	158	163	5
Σx^2	738,240	780,102	51,351	561,978	664,182	92,647	731,740	674,018	163,685

Aggregation Error
$\Sigma U_t^2 + 2\Sigma E_t U_t =$

		41,862			102,204			-57,722	

Relative Aggregation Error
$\dfrac{\Sigma U_t^2 + \Sigma E_t U_t}{\Sigma V_t^2} =$

		5%			15%			-9%	

Standard Error of Estimate

	248	255	—	226	246	—	247	237	—

V_t = Average Micro Error E_t = Average Macro Error U_t = Aggregation Error are included in the equation, the relative aggregation proportion is slightly positive.

Qualitatively similar results hold for Equation (3.11). In Equation (3.11), the aggregation bias is negative for the profit equation and positive for the sales equation, although the per cent aggregation bias for the lagged profit model is much less than it was for Equation (3.10). The positive aggregation bias of 15 per cent in (3.10SP) is large enough to be bothersome. In this particular equation the macro error estimate for profits alone is smaller than either estimate for the sales equation below. In part, then, the "good" performance of profits on the aggregate series is attributable to the fortuitous circumstance of negative covariance terms. Should these persist into the future, and remain part of the error-generating structure, this property could be utilized to advantage, although for purposes of structural estimation such behavior is less desirable.

A valuable contribution to the study of aggregation and specification error can be found in an article by Griliches and Grunfeld.[4] They go well beyond the simple calculations presented here to derive the relationships between macro estimates and micro estimates in terms of the micro-distribution error correlations. They conclude that if the correlations between the micro-error terms are negative, the macro estimate will be superior to the summed micro estimates. Further, when specification error exists, there is a good possibility that the macro estimate will be superior to the summed micro estimates. The examples given above show that there is no empirical presumption that leads one to suppose that the micro-error term will always behave nicely and thus improve the macro prediction based upon the aggregate instead of the summed micro predictions. The rhetorical question: "Is aggregation necessarily bad?" must be answered in the negative, although at times aggregation *is* bad. However, even though aggregation "is not necessarily bad" for prediction purposes, it is nearly always bad from the point of view of estimating structural coefficients.

In a related study, J. C. G. Boot and G. M. de Wit[5] have further developed the Theil aggregation theorems to apply to an investment study for which micro-economic data were easily available. Unlike

---

[4] Z. GRILICHES and Y. GRUNFELD, "Is Aggregation Necessarily Bad?," *Review of Economics and Statistics*, January, 1960.

[5] "Investment Demand: An Empirical Contribution to the Aggregation Problem," *International Economic Review*, Vol. 1, 1960, pp. 1–30.

Griliches and Grunfeld, Boot and de Wit do not pay attention to the effects of specification error. However, they go further in the particular sense that many more implications of the variance-covariance properties of micro and macro errors are analyzed.

A different, statistically founded test procedure for minimizing aggregation bias exists, however, in some developments of the analysis of covariance. The analysis of covariance can be designed to test the homogeneity of regression coefficients. Should homogeneity exist at specified significance level, we have, as pointed out earlier, a sufficient condition for the absence of the aggregation bias. In general, however, there will be differences, i.e., shifts among the values of the independent variables facing the individual firms or individuals so that the goal must be to jointly minimize aggregation error and random or residual error. At the other extreme consider the case in which there was zero random error in individual behavior equations so that all prediction errors could be attributed to aggregation bias.

The criterion given above must be reconsidered carefully in the context of structural coefficient estimation, instead of prediction. Strictly speaking, in estimating behavior coefficients the whole emphasis should be on regression coefficient homogeneity. By their very nature, structural estimates cannot be correct if the individual micro coefficients differ. Hence the overriding criterion must be homogeneity of regression coefficients. The residual variance criterion relevant for prediction will fall out as an estimate after the homogeneity criterion has been satisfied.

The practical course of action is to separate firms into groups which have common behavior coefficients, described in terms of a probability model which indicates statistically insignificant divergences among the regression coefficients.[6] Firms within these groups constitute, if you will, a sub-industry.

Research should ultimately yield a more adequate representation of behavior so that revision of the initial behavior equation will permit the aggregation of previously dissimilar firms (or in some cases sub-industries). Clearly a major objective of economic research is to discover those characteristics which account for differences among firm parameters through the more accurate and complete specification of behavior.

---

[6] Because large firms are enumerated for the most part in studies like the present one, the probability model underlying these tests cannot be valid. For smaller size brackets, finite population corrections can be applied.

At the same time it is to be hoped that the observed stochastic component will gradually diminish. This is a corollary to the proposition that better specification will provide grounds for rendering the coefficients more homogeneous and should simultaneously reduce the error variance. Thus the idea of a stable error distribution is only a tentative working hypothesis. This very definitely does not rule out the possibility that much unexplained variation will remain. And spurious reductions will be created by generating hypotheses from a given sample more often than true reductions.

7.3 Aggregates of Time Periods

The choice of an appropriate time unit is another aspect of aggregation problems important in specification of behavior relations.[7] In this regard it is essential to realize that alternative choices of time periods will either suppress or magnify dynamic characteristics of the data, but in general they will not remain unaffected. A most familiar though narrow example is that annual, instead of monthly, data will eliminate seasonal and possibly other short-term variations. Only nonperiodic variations are to be observed when the observations are measured at or averaged over intervals equal to the period.

Policy requirements strongly affect the choice of behavior equation. It may be that the relation is to be used for the determination of short-term actions. In this case, the required data period would have to be very short, so that the "sticky" low frequency components in the included determining variables will be roughly constant and those subject to short-term variation and policy manipulation will carry the burden of explanation. Ordinarily, therefore, different sets of estimated coefficients and different error variances will be associated with different time periods, a view at odds with a frequently stated one that there is in fact a unique behavior relationship that ought to be measured.[8] The fluctuations of main interest can be measured in several ways, although averaging eliminates the possibility of estimating high frequency components, an effect which is often desirable.

If we wished to explain all the minute-to-minute or hour-to-hour

[7] See also L. R. KLEIN, *Econometrica*, 1953, pp. 313–322.

[8] Both aspects are taken into account in modern time series analysis of spectral density. While all good research strategy ultimately will encompass fluctuations of most frequencies, numerous econometric purposes are best served by concentrating research effort on only several parts of the spectrum.

variations in economic time series, we might conceivably be able to do so. However, it might require many years of study and a very large number of variables to explain all such short-term variations. But we simply may be uninterested in such short-term variations. When such short-term factors are excluded from the regression equation and also are independently distributed and uncorrelated with the variables which explain the longer term movements, averaging over time can filter out the short-term fluctuations. The possibility of studying some stabilization policies will be limited when primarily long-term parameters are estimated. If errors of observation in the independent variables are randomly and independently distributed, time aggregation will reduce observation error bias, although bias will be increased when, as often happens, time series observation errors are highly autocorrelated.

In the context of cross section consumption-income relationships,[9] some authors have suggested that actual observed annual income which is reported on a cross-section is incorrectly measured because long-run income, that to which current consumption is actually adjusted, is not represented in annual income, so that the slope estimate in an estimated consumption-income relationship will be biased downward. It may well be in the present study that the annual periods chosen are so short that the actually measured profit and sales are not those upon which expectations are formed, so that when we average over time, we may obtain a truer representation of the independent variables. This at least is one interpretation that can be put upon estimates for two-year averages.

Aggregates over time periods have been calculated only for Equation (3.13), where both independent and dependent variables have been averaged for concurrent two-year periods. Correlations are higher than for the unaggregated data. The median multiple correlation coefficient for Equation (3.13P) of 0.7359 compares with the median estimate for (3.10P) of 0.6993 and with (3.11P) of 0.6921. Similarly, the median multiple correlation for (3.13S) of 0.8001 contrasts with 0.7394 on (3.10S) and 0.7343 on (3.11S). Analogous results hold for the other quartile and extreme values. Averaging the independent variables should typically have the effect of reducing errors of observation and is less likely to affect multiple correlations. This turned out to be

[9] See especially MILTON FRIEDMAN, *A Theory of the Consumption Function*, National Bureau of Economic Research: Princeton, 1957.

the case for Equation (3.12) which has correlations similar to Equation (3.10). These findings coincide with those of Meyer and Kuh, where five-year averages showed remarkably larger partial correlations and multipe correlations than did the annual cross-section samples. When predictions are required for short periods the problem cannot be avoided by averaging, since the random element appears inevitably larger in these circumstances, which must be recognized for prediction purposes.

Part of what we intend to convey can be illustrated by the example of an individual firm's investment program. In a typical postwar situation, when firms were straining against capacity, and demand was rising swiftly, a firm might place orders for various sorts of capital goods, including, for instance, one large new plant. Should one look at a four or five year period, relative rates of increase in the capital stock in four of the five years that were in the neighborhood of 5 to 10 per cent would be observed, but in the year that the large plant was completed, the rate of fixed asset growth would have been as much as 30 per cent. This very large difference between the hypothetical fifth year and the other years might be explained in terms of a gestation and/or decision lag in a complete model, an objective that should ultimately be attained.[10]

There are three possible ways of treating the essentially nonlinear and/or distributed lag effects described above. The first is to average out the nonlinearity through averaging the data and thus spreading out the nonlinear effect over a number of periods. The second is to take the data on a year-by-year basis, obtain a different set of estimated coefficients and, in addition, a very large unexplained variance, which correctly represents one short-term reaction pattern. Ideally, one would estimate the lag which "truly" represented the cumulative effects of increasing output with respect to a strain on the capital stock which eventuated in the very large plant outlay in a given year, but it is the difficulty of achieving this third goal that often will force us to choose one or both of the other two.

---

[10] AVRAM KISSELGOFF and FRANCO MODIGLIANI, "Private Investment in the Electric Power Industry and the Acceleration Principle," *The Review of Economics and Statistics*, Vol. 39, No. 4, Nov. 1957, pp. 363-79, have built gestation lags into their capacity-acceleration model in an ingenious manner.

CHAPTER 8

TESTS OF SOME MAJOR HYPOTHESES

8.1 Introduction

This chapter surveys the main statistical results. Previous quantitative results report tests of some of the regression analysis assumptions (Chapter 4), the stability of estimated coefficients (Chapter 5), the relationship between time series and cross-section estimates (Chapter 6), and the evaluation of some aggregation effects (Chapter 7). These particular aspects of the study now are to be followed by tests of goodness of fit, the reliability of estimates and the general predictive merits of the equations selected. Subsequent comparisons will be of two sorts: first, comparisons between profit and sales equations for the same lag structure and second, comparisons of the different lag structures within a given equation. Most interpretation of Equations (3.30), (3.31), (3.34) and (3.35) will be reserved for the next chapter on acceleration models.

In addition to the ordinary goodness of fit measures, two other statistical devices have been employed to evaluate the estimated equations. First the analysis of variance is used to test whether the addition of a profit variable to a sales equation significantly reduces the unexplained variance. Second, a test statistic devised by Theil specifically to evaluate forecast success, has also been applied for the two post-regression data years 1956 and 1957.

Many different test statistics have been used. Should this abundance not prove too overwhelming, it is my belief that we will be much further along the path towards understanding of the models than often is the case. It happens in much econometric work that a particular test, or a narrow range of tests, is applied in a given study so that many important aspects of specification are left unexplored. While it is undeniably plodding to undertake a great many different tests, the minimum use of assumptions and the maximum use of test statistics should be at worst harmless and ordinarily will be helpful.

Interpretation of the significance tests is not always obvious. In most instances frequency distributions of estimated coefficients and the various test statistics are available. The straightforward textbook type of interpretation is either invalid or irrelevant, when we have access to the entire distribution, or at least an estimate of it. Much -more to the point, therefore, will be an examination of the central ten dencies as if they were approximations of population values. In this light the tabulations of the test statistics, for instance, t statistics for regression coefficients, are most appropriately viewed as reflecting the reliability of estimation. Thus, the sample t statistics reflect the variability of the estimates and not whether a given coefficient was drawn from a population whose mean was zero. It would be ridiculous to suppose, for example, that 60 estimates of a coefficient were in fact zero at some specified probability level, say 5 per cent, when the sample t statistics were less than 1.5 for every sample value but all were greater than one half. The correct interpretation for such a statistic would be that the parameter is positive and can only be estimated subject to large uncertainty for the sample sizes available.

Most of the basic data summarizing the regression estimates have been presented in an appendix to this chapter. Comments in the next sections are based upon this lengthy table, and compilations derived from it.

8.2 How Well Do the Equations Explain Investment?

A. *Cross-Sections*

By most ordinary standards the cross-section fit for the first difference model Equation (3.9) is quite low. The first and third quartiles of the multiple correlations are 0.34 and 0.40 respectively and at most half of the 14 multiple correlation coefficients register significance at the 5 per cent level.

The capital intensity coefficient is zero almost all the time at quite generous significance levels. On a one-tail test, the sales coefficient shows up strongly: at the 10 per cent level, 10 of the 14 coefficients are significant, 7 of them at the 5 per cent level. Similarly, on a one-tail basis, the capital stock change variable is significant at the 5 per cent level in about half the total number of cases. The profit variable does poorly, showing statistically significant coefficients in only 4 of the 14 cross-sections on a one-tail test basis. Finally, the intercept terms are small, indicating that homogeneity or near homogeneity prevails. In only four instances do the intercepts differ from zero at the 5 per cent level.

As should be expected, the goodness of fit for Equations (3.10)–(3.12) is superior to the first difference model. In all cases the multiple correlation in Equation (3.10) differs significantly from zero at the 1 per cent level and correspondingly, the multiple correlation first and third quartiles are roughly 0.70 and 0.80, indicating that half the variance is typically explained by the included variables. So far as specific variables are concerned, the capital intensity variable is the weakest, with only 5 of the 17 coefficients significant at the 10 per cent or better level for a one-tail test. The capital stock variable, on a one-tail test, does not reveal much independent strength. Only 5 of the 17 are statistically significant at the 10 per cent level or greater for (3.10S) and (3.10SP), whereas none show one-tailed significance on the profit model. Both sales and profits alone in (3.10S) and (3.10P), respectively, can be reliably measured: 15 or 16 show one-tailed significance at the 5 per cent level. A higher degree of reliability is indicated for the sales coefficient, however. The intercept term is "significantly" different from zero at the 10 per cent level 5 times on the sales model and not at all on the profit model. Equations (3.11) and (3.12) tell a similar story to Equation (3.10). Since sharp contrast in the context of overall goodness of fit and significance of individual coefficients is only revealed between Equations (3.10), (3.11), and (3.12) on one hand, and Equation (3.9) on the other, extensive comments on Equations (3.11) and (3.12) will be omitted in the present context.

On logarithmic Equations (3.20)–(3.22), the only independently significant variable is sales. While on the cross-section the independent variables are highly correlated in the original units, the inter-correlations seem to be sufficiently higher, so that the independent contribution of each variable is harder to discern. The median multiple correlation is higher than those observed in the original unit regressions (3.10) to (3.13). Equation (3.19) shows capital stock to be more important in the same fashion as did its original units counterpost, Equation (3.9).

Ratio model Equations (3.30A) and (3.30B) have fewer significant multiple correlations than the other models except for the first differenced model. Since the variables are ratios, however, the multiple correlation is in effect the partial correlation between investment and the other variables with the capital stock held constant. Profit is the one independent variable which shows pronounced influence. Eleven out of 15 profit partial regression coefficients differ significantly from zero at the 5 per cent level for (3.30B).

B. *Time Series*

Goodness of fit for the first difference model, Equation (3.9), on time series is also below that for the original units models. Only about one-third of the multiple correlations differ significantly from zero at the 5 per cent level. The median multiple correlation is 0.54, so that these regressions explain only one-quarter of the change in investment on the average. For only a quarter of the firms does the explanation equal or exceed half of the variability in the investment change. For another quarter of the firms, the explanation is 15 per cent or less. Both the change in capital stock and either change in sales or change in profit show significance at the 5 per cent level with the same relative frequency as the multiple correlation, approximately one-third of the time. One interesting contrast observable in time series is that the change in capital stock, which is one estimate of investment, is relatively more important in Equation (3.9) than its counterpart, the capital stock itself, which appears in the original unit models, Equations (3.10) to (3.12). Extremely few of the intercepts differ significantly from zero for the first differenced model, evidently because trend was a subsidiary influence on investment.

About half the multiple correlations for the original units models, Equations (3.10) to (3.12), differ significantly from zero at the 5 per cent level. The relative frequency with which the sales or profit variable differs from zero is much greater than for the capital stock variable.

On the logarithmic models, Equations (3.20)–(3.22), there are noticeably more significant regressions than on its original units counterpart, Equations (3.10S)–(3.12S). About forty of the regressions differ significantly from zero at the 5 per cent significance level for the log models, whereas only thirty do so on the original units models.

For the ratio model, an even larger number of significantly different multiple correlations show up ranging from 38 in model (3.30A) to 44 in model (3.30B),[1] even though these are to be interpreted as partial correlations.

The related "pure" capacity accelerator model, which is based upon a strict definition of capacity requirements, has 20 significant multiple correlations in (3.34B) and 15 in (3.34A). Many fewer large correlations appear for Equation (3.35). The low, yet substantial, frequency of significant correlations stems from the rigid specification which limits concomitant covariation with other variables from enlarging the degree of explanation claimed.

8.3 Profits or Sales ?

A. *Alternative Profit Theory Hypotheses*

The concrete form in which profit variables ought to be tested depends upon which of the several profit theories is of central interest. The two main branches are the "Expectational" school and the "Cash Flow" school.

As a matter of reasonably well established fact, which in turn is in agreement with reasonably well established theory, it seems that the expectational hypothesis for profits cannot, and perhaps should not, be distinguished from the sales level or capacity accelerator hypothesis. The main candidate variable for the expectational hypothesis is simply net income after tax, a secondary candidate being gross operating profit. Both variables will tend to have strong correlations with the level of sales. This is a structural relationship which evolves from conventional pricing policies in the manufacturing sector which, in conjunction with fairly constant short-run marginal costs, cause both these categories of profit to have strong linear correlations with the level of sales. This, of course, is a one way, structural relationship for the individual firms. When sales change, a given firm's profits will change proportionately in the same direction, and definitely not the other way around.[2] Hence, the pure expectational school is structurally linked to the level of sales hypothesis. This does not mean that the expectational school is "wrong". It does mean, though, that future expected profits are expected to come from future expected levels of

---

[1] As pointed out in Chapter 4, the high correlations for the ratio models cannot be attributed in the intercept term since these were generally negligible by ordinary statistical tests of significance.

[2] As a complicating factor, non-proportional changes will arise during periods of rapid price change from inventory valuation changes, an effect to which Tinbergen attributes important independent effects on real investment out lays.

output, which in turn are assumed to be related to current levels of output.

The cash flow school does have independent status which quantitatively is best represented by net retained income plus depreciation expense. For a given mix of physical assets and constant depreciation policies, depreciation expense will be roughly proportional to the capital stock, while retained earnings depend among other things upon (proportional) taxes, net income, and dividend policy. When all of these are mixed together to yield a gross retained earnings figure, the large positive correlation between this profit measure of liquidity flow and sales is likely to be weakened.

In summary then, the profit expectation school should be viewed as a variant of the sales level hypothesis. Therefore, no attempt has been made to distinguish between the profit expectation school and the level of sales or capacity accelerator hypothesis. The other main branch of the profit school is the liquidity flow hypothesis which asserts that cash flow will dominate the rate of investment. In this form, the almost complete linear dependence of profits (in this case gross retained earnings) on the level of sales is weakened so that the independent influences can be distinguished.

Dispute still exists about whether acceleration models or profit models alone better explain the level of investment, a matter that will be studied for the present set of regression estimates. At the end of this section, my findings will be related to those of other investigators. As remarked upon in the previous section, the individual regression coefficient tests, in most instances, indicated a larger fraction of significant sales coefficients than profit coefficients. Table 8.1 presents a summary for both one- and two-tail tests, when in both instances the one-tail test is *a priori* positive.

B. *Individual Coefficient Behavior*

Table 8.1 summarizes the significance of individual coefficients for sales and profits variables in Equations (3.10)–(3.13). It is evident on the basis of partial regression coefficients, that the sales coefficient has statistical significance much more frequently than the profit coefficient in Equation (3.9). Subsequently, attention will be focused exclusively on one-tail tests, although the two-tail test results are also recorded. There is little to choose between sales and profits individually in Equation (3.10). Yet when the two are combined in Equation (3.10SP), a

Table 8.1

Significant Regression Coefficients for Sales and Profit Variables: Cross-Sections

Number of Coefficients Significant at:	Equation (3.9S) Sales Coefficient		Equation (3.9P) Profit Coefficient		Equation (3.9SP) Sales	Profit	Sales	Profit
	one tail	two tail	one tail	two tail	one tail		two tail	
10%	3	2	0	0	1	1	1	0
5%	3	1	0	2	3	1	3	2
1%	4	5	4	3	4	1	3	1

Number of Coefficients Significant at:	Equation (3.10S) Sales Coefficient		Equation (3.10P) Profit Coefficient		Equation (3.10SP) Sales	Profit	Sales	Profit
	one tail	two tail	one tail	two tail	one tail		two tail	
10%	0	2	1	4	2	1	1	1
5%	3	2	5	2	3	3	5	2
1%	13	12	10	9	7	2	4	2

Number of Coefficients Significant at:	Equation (3.11S) Sales Coefficient		Equation (3.11P) Profit Coefficient		Equation (3.11SP) Sales	Profit	Sales	Profit
	one tail	two tail	one tail	two tail	one tail		two tail	
10%	1	2	1	1	2	2	0	1
5%	3	3	2	1	1	4	2	5
1%	10	8	8	8	5	2	4	1

Number of Coefficients Significant at:	Equation (3.12S) Sales Coefficient		Equation (3.12P) Profit Coefficient		Equation (3.12SP) Sales	Profit	Sales	Profit
	one tail	two tail	one tail	two tail	one tail		two tail	
10%	0	1	2	1	2	2	2	2
5%	2	3	2	1	2	5	0	6
1%	12	10	9	9	4	3	4	1

Number of Coefficients Significant at:	Equation (3.13S) Sales Coefficient		Equation (3.13P) Profit Coefficient		Equation (3.13SP) Sales	Profit	Sales	Profit
	one tail	two tail	one tail	two tail	one tail		two tail	
10%	0	1	0	1	1	2	2	1
5%	1	0	1	0	3	1	3	2
1%	13	13	12	12	7	3	5	1

Source: Appendix table.

different result emerges: the sales variable is obviously superior. It thus appears that the significance noted for the profit variable in Equation (3.10P) can be predominantly attributed to the correlation with sales.

In the simple lag model, Equation (3.11), moderate superiority exists for the sales variable in (3.11S) in contrast to (3.11P). However, the total number of equations significant at the 10 per cent level is the same for the variables in combined Equation (3.11SP), although a larger number of the sales coefficients is significant at the 1 per cent level than for the profit variable. In short, it would now appear that internal fund flows play their most important role when lagged — so important, indeed, that the superiority of sales so clearly visible in the unlagged model, has virtually been eliminated. Results even more strikingly in favor of the profit variables are evident for the average lag of Equation (3.12). At the 5 per cent level, there are eight significant profit coefficients and only six significant sales coefficients, although in Equations (3.10P) and (3.10S) at the 5 per cent level, there are, respectively, only eleven significant profit coefficients and fourteen significant sales coefficients.

Equation (3.13SP) strongly favors the sales variable. The difference between Equations (3.12) and (3.13) is that an average of current and lagged investment is the dependent variable in Equation (3.13) instead of current investment alone as in Equation (3.12). In both equations the independent variables are averages of current and previous sales or profits, and lagged capital stock. Averaging the dependent variable leads to a radical shift toward the sales variable and away from the profit variable: there are ten significant sales coefficients and only four significant profit coefficients at the 5 per cent significance level.

Considerable independent variation is to be observed for profits and sales, sufficient to discriminate between the two more readily than when net after-tax profit is the profit independent variable. In this light, it appears that both variables have an independent role to play, a proposition most clearly revealed by different lag structure estimates.

The time series results in Table 8.2 do not correspond to those reported for cross-sections. The main pattern observable in cross-sections, the changing importance of profits relative to sales as the lag structure was altered, is not evident. Time series results, in brief, show that no matter what the lag structure, the sales variable is clearly superior to the profit variable according to the significance tests utilized here.

TABLE 8.2

Significant Regression Coefficients for Sales and Profit Variables: Time Series

Number of Coefficients Significant at:	Equation (3.9S) Sales Coefficient		Equation (3.9P) Profit Coefficient		Equation (3.9SP)			
					Sales	Profit	Sales	Profit
	one tail	two tail	one tail	two tail	one tail		two tail	
10%	5	6	6	3	12	5	2	1
5%	10	7	8	5	4	2	2	1
1%	7	4	2	2	3	0	4	1

Number of Coefficients Significant at:	Equation (3.10S) Sales Coefficient		Equation (3.10P) Profit Coefficient		Equation (3.10SP)			
					Sales	Profit	Sales	Profit
	one tail	two tail	one tail	two tail	one tail		two tail	
10%	4	9	2	6	6	4	5	5
5%	13	13	7	8	9	3	7	4
1%	20	11	13	7	11	2	8	1

Number of Coefficients Significant at:	Equation (3.11S) Sales Coefficient		Equation (3.11P) Profit Coefficient		Equation (3.11SP)			
					Sales	Profit	Sales	Profit
	one tail	two tail	one tail	two tail	one tail		two tail	
10%	5	7	10	6	6	4	6	5
5%	11	9	10	5	12	4	11	3
1%	11	7	6	5	4	2	1	1

Number of Coefficients Significant at:	Equation (3.12S) Sales Coefficient		Equation (3.12P) Profit Coefficient		Equation (3.12SP)			
					Sales	Profit	Sales	Profit
	one tail	two tail	one tail	two tail	one tail		two tail	
10%	6	3	10	5	4	8	3	6
5%	7	9	9	7	10	5	11	6
1%	19	14	11	9	11	4	8	4

Note: The 10% significance level includes t statistics significant at the 10% level up to the 5% level, the 5% significance level includes t statistics significant at the 5% level up to the 1% level, etc. Hence, all t statistics significant at the 10% level would include the total number reported at 10%, 5% and 1%, while all t statistics significant at the 5% level would include the total number reported at 5% and 1%, etc.

Source: Appendix Table.

Twenty-two sales coefficients in (3.9S) show one-tail significance at the 10 per cent level in contrast to sixteen for profit coefficients in (3.9P). When the two are combined in (3.9SP) it appears that only seven profit coefficients are significant at the 10 per cent level, while a total of nineteen sales coefficients are significant. Quite patently, the majority of the significant profit coefficients show up only because of collinear relations with the sales variable. The same outcome appears in more exaggerated form in Equation (3.10), where, at the 5 per cent significance level, twenty profit coefficients are significant in (3.10P) yet only five are significant in Equation (3.10SP). The sales coefficient has many more reliable estimates in both situations. In Equation (3.12S), for instance, twenty-six significant sales coefficients appear and for Equation (3.12P) twenty significant profit coefficients at the 5 per cent significance level. In Equation (3.12SP), however, twice as many sales coefficients as profit coefficients are significant at the 5 per cent level while slightly less than a two-to-one superiority for sales exists even at the 10 per cent significance level.

Unfortunately, but perhaps not surprisingly, the inferences drawn about competing hypotheses are highly sensitive to the origins of the data. Since the major objective is to improve understanding of dynamic, time series behavior, it should be pointed out that no matter how the contrasts are drawn from time series, the acceleration sales model is superior to the internal fund flow, profit model.

B. *Goodness of Fit*

An alternative, more inclusive, method of comparing profit and sales is presented in Table 8.3, where multiple correlations from averaged data, the median individual year (or firm) multiple correlation, the median relative prediction error, and the median standard error have been arrayed for Equations (3.9) to (3.13). A blow-by-blow account is inessential, so that only a few impressions will be noted.

The standard errors of estimate for profit equations are generally larger than those for the sales model, and furthermore, the standard error of estimate for the combined sales and profit equation is seldom smaller than that for the sales equation alone. With one notable exception, this property applies to all the cross-section equations and time series. Equation (3.12SP) on time series has a median standard error of estimate, 499, substantially below the standard error of estimate, 534, for the sales equation and still further below the standard error of estimate for (3.12P) of 558. On goodness of fit criteria the sales model would generally be preferred to the profit model. With the sole exception noted, extremely little added predictive power would be gained

TABLE 8.3

Goodness of Fit Measures Cross Sections for Sales and Profit Equations

	Equation (3.9S)	Equation (3.9P)	Equation (3.9SP)
Cross-Sections			
.Average Data, Multiple Correlation	0.5375	0.5832	0.6135
Median Multiple Correlation	0.3720	0.3403	0.4040
Median R.P.E.	1.76	2.05	1.75
Median Standard Error	1140	1192	1120

	Equation (3.10S)	Equation (3.10P)	Equation (3.10SP)
Average Data, Multiple Correlation	0.9085	0.9137	0.9177
Median Multiple Correlation	0.7394	0.6993	0.7528
Median R.P.E.	0.7773	0.7721	0.7566
Median Standard Error	925	947	926

	Equation (3.11S)	Equation (3.11P)	Equation (3.11SP)
Average Data, Multiple Correlation	0.8980	0.9021	0.9058
Median Multiple Correlation	0.7343	0.6921	0.7437
Median R.P.E.	0.8113	0.7862	0.7807
Median Standard Error	1020	1070	1030

	Equation (3.12S)	Equation (3.12P)	Equation (3.12SP)
Average Data, Multiple Correlation	0.8997	0.9024	0.9068
Median Multiple Correlation	0.7460	0.6999	0.7579
Median R.P.E.	0.7876	0.7551	0.7544
Median Standard Error	1020	1040	1020

	Equation (3.13S)	Equation (3.13P)	Equation (3.13SP)
Average Data, Multiple Correlation	0.9387	0.9143	0.9416
Median Multiple Correlation	0.8001	0.7359	0.8081
Median R.P.E.	0.5733	0.6582	0.5705
Median Standard Error	880	937	887

Time Series

	Equation (3.9S)	Equation (3.9P)	Equation (3.9SP)
Average Data, Multiple Correlation	0.7371	0.4452	0.7436
Median Multiple Correlation	0.5430	0.4778	0.6014
Median R.P.E.	5.94	6.17	5.74
Median Standard Error	672	725	668

Table 8.3 (*continued*)

	Time Series		
	Equation (3.10S)	Equation (3.10P)	Equation (3.10SP)
Average Data, Multiple Correlation	0.9134	0.8708	0.9139
Median Multiple Correlation	0.6124	0.5419	0.6665
Median R.P.E.	0.5524	0.5726	0.5311
Median Standard Error	506	559	492
	Equation (3.11S)	Equation (3.11P)	Equation (3.11SP)
Average Data, Multiple Correlation	0.8454	0.8680	0.8701
Median Multiple Correlation	0.5745	0.5308	0.6373
Median R.P.E.	0.5391	0.5643	0.5369
Median Standard Error	545	581	538
	Equation (3.12S)	Equation (3.12P)	Equation (3.12SP)
Average Data, Multiple Correlation	0.9321	0.9289	0.9512
Median Multiple Correlation	0.6245	0.5583	0.7156
Median R.P.E.	0.5227	0.5388	0.4983
Median Standard Error	534	558	499

Source: Appendix Table.

from including profits with sales and the remaining explanatory variables.

A standard statistical procedure, the analysis of variance to test for the significance of adding a new variable to a regression equation, can provide related contrasts among equations. Table 8.4 summarizes results for Equations (3.9) to (3.13) for cross-sections and Equations (3.9) to (3.12) for time series. In the first instance, a test can determine whether adding profits to sales and the standard explanatory variables significantly reduces the unexplained variance at the stated significance level, and in the second instance, the test can be applied by adding sales to the profit equation, when, as before, the standard explanatory variables have already been included. The evidence again broadly confirms that presented earlier in this chapter since the tests are far from independent.

On cross-sections the addition of sales to an equation already incorporating profits significantly reduces the unexplained variance more often than when profits were introduced into an equation already containing sales and the remaining explanatory variables. This statement

TABLE 8.4

Added Variable Analysis of Variance for Sales and Profit Equations

Cross-Sections	Profit Added to Sales					Sales Added to Profit				
	Eq. (3.9)	Eq. (3.10)	Eq. (3.11)	Eq. (3.12)	Eq. (3.13)	Eq. (3.9)	Eq. (3.10)	Eq. (3.11)	Eq. (3.12)	Eq. (3.13)
10% Level	0	1	1	2	1	1	1	0	2	2
5% Level	2	2	5	6	2	3	5	2	0	3
1% Level	1	3	1	1	1	2	4	4	4	5
Time Series										
10% Level	1	4	6	5	–	2	5	6	2	–
5% Level	1	5	3	6	–	2	7	11	12	–
1% Level	1	1	1	4	–	3	8	1	8	–

Source: Appendix Table.

is especially true of Equations (3.9) and (3.10). There is a stand-off in Equations (3.11) and (3.12). Equation (3.13) on the other hand, definitely shows a preponderance in the direction of sales.

The change in explanatory power as the lag structure changes, noted for cross-sections above and also noted in an earlier context, once again is diminished on time series. In every case the addition of sales reduces the unexplained variance more frequently than the addition of profits, quite independently of the lag structure. However, relative to other profit equations, Equation (3.12) shows the independent, added contribution of profit most often. Generally speaking, sales significantly reduce the unexplained variance two to three times as often in contrast to the frequency with which reduction of equivalent significance occurs when profits are introduced into an estimating equation.

A last item of evidence on profit and sales equations to be derived from goodness of fit measures is based on paired comparisons between multiple correlations so that the entire distribution is considered, instead of just the upper tail. These calculations appear in Table 8.5. The results are further subdivided into the smallest and largest thirty firms in the time series estimates.[3] The first column shows the number of cases for time series estimates when multiple correlations for sales exceed the multiple correlation for profits (however small the differ-

[3] Firms have been arrayed according to gross fixed assets (un-price corrected) in 1948. While clearly firms would criss-cross from smaller to larger because of differential rates of growth, it is to be expected that at the mid-point of time, for this particular sample, we will have a rough split which will indicate larger and smaller firm reactions to sales or profits.

TABLE 8.5

Paired Comparisons of Sales and Profit Model Multiple Correlations

Time Series	$R_s > R_p$	$R_p > R_s$	Probability of $R_s > R_p$ if $R_s{}^* = R_p{}^*$
Equation (3.9)			
Smallest 30 firms	20	10	0.07
Largest 30 firms	24	6	0.01
Total	44	16	0.01
Equation (3.10)			
Smallest 30 firms	22	8	0.02
Largest 30 firms	21	9	0.03
Total	43	17	0.01
Equation (3.11)			
Smallest 30 firms	11	19	−0.15
Largest 30 firms	20	10	0.07
Total	31	29	—
Equation (3.12)			
Smallest 30 firms	13	17	−0.47
Largest 30 firms	17	13	0.47
Total	30	30	
Cross-Sections			
Equation (3.9)			
Total	6	8	−0.60
Equation (3.10)			
Total	11	6	0.33
Equation (3.11)			
Total	10	5	0.20
Equation (3.12)			
Total	8	7	0.38
Equation (3.13)			
Total	8	7	0.38

Note: Population correlations are symbolized by R^*. Sample correlations exclude the asterisk.

ence) while the second column shows how often profit multiple correlation exceeds the sales correlation. Binomial probabilities have also been calculated on the null hypothesis that profit equation multiple correlations exceed sales equation multiple correlations half the time. On Equation (3.10) for cross-sections, if the population multiple correlations were equal, the odds are one in three that we would have observed sales multiple correlations exceeding profit multiple correlations eleven out of seventeen times. For cross-sections approximate equality prevails in Equations (3.9), (3.12) and (3.13). However, Equations (3.10) and (3.11) indicate a higher correlation for sales than for profits in the clear majority of cases.

In time series, more than two-thirds of the firms show a higher correlation on sales than profits for Equations (3.9) and (3.10), and the relative importance to large and small firms alike is the same. The binomial probability calculation points toward a highly significant difference. On Equation (3.11) a significantly greater number of small firms is profit rather than sales oriented and the reverse is true for large firms. For the total, however, it is a stand-off. Each equation dominates with the same frequency on Equation (3.12). Furthermore, there is no such large-firm, small-firm disparity of behavior on Equation (3.12) so evident for Equation (3.11).

C. Ratio Models

Equations (3.30A) and (3.30B) explain variations in the gross rate of capital stock growth, (i.e., price corrected investment divided by price corrected capital stock) by the gross retained profit rate on capital stock and per cent capacity utilization of the previous and current period. These variables correspond to those used in the Meyer and Kuh study, since they are ratios with capital stock as the deflator, although several variable definitions are modified and, in the present instance, the profit variable is gross retained earnings instead of net income. Equation (3.30A) uses lagged capacity utilization and the current profit rate as explanatory variables. The underlying hypothesis can be briefly restated: there is a lagged response to capacity utilization of the previous period, and current gross retained earnings act as a restriction on those capacity demands generated during the previous period. The inclusion of the current capacity variable in (3.30B) is an obvious extension of the hypothesis.

One quite strikingly interesting result is that the profit rate variable is much more significant than the capacity utilization variable on cross-sections. At the 5 per cent level there are 12 significant profit rate variable coefficients and only 4 significant capacity utilization variables. Furthermore, when capacity utilization is added to the profit rate variable, only twice does it significantly reduce the unexplained variance, again at a 5 per cent level of significance. Equation (3.30B) reports similar statistics. The profit rate stands out as the dominant variable, and addition of the current capacity utilization to lagged capacity utilization and the gross retained profit rate does little to improve the explanation. The comparatively low multiple correlations arise from the fact that deflation by the capital stock implies that the influence on investment of profits and capacity utilization has been estimated net of the capital stock.

Time series lead to quite other conclusions. For one thing, the relative importance of the lagged capacity variable in Equation (3.30A) is much greater for individual firms—at the 5 per cent level, both the internal profit rate and the lagged capacity variable have the same number of significant coefficients, twentysix. Recall that on cross-sections the lagged capacity variable was relatively much less significant. Hence, the apparent influence of the capacity variable when measured in ratio form has either a bias in its favor on time series or an unfavorable bias against it on cross-sections. One cannot appeal to ratio bias as the fundamental source of the relatively more favorable results on time series, since an examination of the intercepts for Equations (3.10), (3.11), and (3.12) indicates that, for time series, intercepts significantly different from zero occur a very small fraction of the time.[4]

Results different from cross-sections also appear on time series when the current capacity utilization variable is added to lagged capacity utilization and the internal profit rate in Equation (3.30B). From either the median, weighted average, or B regression coefficients, the effect of adding the current capacity variable on the profit rate coefficient is extremely severe: the profit rate effect is very sharply diminished in importance when current capacity utilization is an additional explanatory variable. Similarly, the weight of lagged capacity utilization is somewhat diminished A one-tail test of significance reveals that the current capacity utilization variable has 18 coefficients significant at the 5 per cent level, the lagged capacity variable has 14 significant coefficients at the 5 per cent level, while only 11 profit coefficients are significant at the 5 per cent level. However, the number of significant profit coefficients at the 10 per cent level is roughly equal to those for both the lagged and current capacity utilization variables at the same significance level. The added variable analysis of variance test shows

[4] E. Kuh and J. R. Meyer, "Correlation and Regression when the Data Are Ratios," *Econometrica*, October, 1955 date 1957, pp. 400–16.

how strongly the inclusion of the current capacity variables reduces the unexplained variance.

The profit rate variable can be quite potent when the average of current and lagged profits is used to explain the current gross investment rate of growth. On (3.31A), there are 29 significant profit variables at the 5 per cent level and only 12 lagged capacity variable coefficients significant at the 5 per cent level. However, it appears that this formulation which so favors profits may also be partly spurious: when the current capacity variable is introduced into the estimating equation, there is a sharp diminution in the importance of the averaged profit variable, which now has only 13 coefficients at or beyond the 5 per cent significance level against 19 for the current capacity variable and only 4 for the lagged relative capacity variable. Again, at the 10 per cent significance level, the profit variable has about an equal number of significant coefficients as does the current capacity variable, while the lagged capacity variable still trails well behind the other explanatory variables. One can also see the importance of including the current capacity variable by noting the frequency with which adding current capacity to the other two variables reduces the unexplained variance. Further, when it is included, the median correlation increases from 0.612 to 0.694 in Equation (3.30) and from 0.607 to 0.720 in Equation (3.31).

These results can now be summarized. First, in a ratio formulation the profit variable appears to be a more powerfully independent force driving investment than in linear, original units form. It is not obvious where the source of this relative difference lies. Second, the influence of lagged capacity utilization on the rate of investment is weak relative to current capacity utilization. When only current internal profit rates are used, the lagged capacity utilization variable almost equals the influence of the current capacity utilization variable. Its independent significance is negligible when average profits are used. Third, the Meyer-Kuh cross-section investment study also using ratio variables, found profits to be important under certain circumstances. It appears that the equations using ratio variables are most likely to record outcomes favorable to profit hypotheses.

8.4 Which Lag Structure ?

Cross-section versions of Equations (3.10)–(3.12) offer little basis for discrimination, although the unlagged model is superior by a small margin. Corresponding logarithmic equations also tend to favor the unlagged version which can be seen from a comparison of the median standard errors of estimate.

On time series, it does not seem to matter which lag is used in the straightforward profit models while with sales alone Equation (3.11S) is slightly inferior to both Equations (3.10S) and (3.12S). A favorable interaction is apparent in the combined set (3.12SP) since the median multiple correlation exceeds either individual median multiple correlation by more than in either Equation (3.10SP) or (3.12SP). Logarithmic analogues Equations (3.20)–(3.22) do not reveal clearly discernible differences, the lag version of Equation (3.21) having about the same explanatory strength as the others.

8.5 Some Principal Economic Characteristics

A. *Elasticities*

Heretofore, numerous statistical attributes derived from alternative theories of investment behavior have been studied to the exclusion of primarily economic traits. This section remedies the shortcomings in part through a discussion of elasticities.

The estimated elasticities are recorded for each equation set when the elasticities have been evaluated at three points: the sample variable means, the sample means plus one standard deviation, and the sample means minus one standard deviation, according to horizontal divisions in Table 8.6. Calculations for Equations (3.9) to (3.13) are shown for sales, profit, and the combination in the three vertical partitions. As with previously recorded distributions of parameter estimates from A regressions, these have been listed according to extreme values, and in between, the two quartile and median values.

On cross-sections the original unit Equations (3.10) through (3.13) show substantially larger median elasticities for sales than for profits. Thus the median sales elasticity of investment in Equation (3.10) is 0.75 and the median profit elasticity in the profit model is 0.38. When both have been included in Equation (3.10SP), the profit elasticity is halved to 0.19, while the sales elasticity has been somewhat diminished

TABLE 8.6

Elasticities: Equation (3.9) Time Series

	$\bar{S} - \sigma_s$		$\bar{P} - \sigma_p$		$\bar{S} - \sigma_s, \bar{P} - \sigma_p$		
	K	S	K	P	K	S	P
Smallest	−2.88	−74.11	−33.89	−2.52	−1.16	−2.77	−2.06
First Quartile	0.02	0.50	0.03	0.38	0.02	0.54	0.47
Median	0.28	0.74	0.27	0.83	0.28	0.76	0.74
Third Quartile	0.60	1.05	0.59	1.29	0.61	0.95	0.87
Largest	6.79	10.26	2.19	85.18	6.04	14.79	6.41

	$\bar{S}$		$\bar{P}$		$\bar{S}, \bar{P}$		
	K	S	K	P	K	S	P
Smallest	−105.70	−56.28	−109.12	−19.56	−111.64	−24.26	−13.82
First Quartile	−2.90	−0.35	−3.19	−0.08	−3.08	−0.59	−0.45
Median	−0.54	0.40	−0.39	0.09	−0.73	0.44	−0.07
Third Quartile	0.66	1.19	0.80	0.38	1.03	1.76	0.20
Largest	99.72	19.66	102.53	5.70	95.27	24.11	4.72

	$\bar{S} + \sigma_s$		$\bar{P} + \sigma_p$		$\bar{S} + \sigma_s, \bar{P} + \sigma_p$		
	K	S	K	P	K	S	P
Smallest	−1.98	−0.35	−178.98	−27.68	−2.60	−7.91	−18.45
First Quartile	1.00	0.85	0.78	0.43	0.97	0.90	0.64
Median	1.61	1.07	1.57	0.85	1.65	1.11	1.18
Third Quartile	2.31	1.37	2.15	1.16	2.25	1.34	1.50
Largest	14.62	20.12	20.40	135.48	27.92	139.35	6.90

Elasticities: Equation (3.10) Time Series

	$\bar{S} - \sigma_s$		$\bar{P} - \sigma_p$		$\bar{S} - \sigma_s, \bar{P} - \sigma_p$		
	K	S	K	P	K	S	P
Smallest	−2.17	−6.13	−20.58	−0.60	−2.14	−211.73	−0.58
First Quartile	−0.60	0.11	−0.04	0.01	−0.67	0.11	−0.13
Median	−0.02	0.87	0.33	0.16	0.00	0.70	−0.02
Third Quartile	0.54	1.43	0.96	0.46	0.61	1.86	0.17
Largest	13.59	16.58	8.55	1.08	8.54	34.12	0.98

	$\bar{S}$		$\bar{P}$		$\bar{S}, \bar{P}$		
	K	S	K	P	K	S	P
Smallest	−5.88	−1.78	−3.72	−1.42	−5.72	−1.46	−1.83
First Quartile	−0.88	0.45	−0.03	0.07	−1.24	0.40	−0.28
Median	−0.02	0.98	0.46	0.33	−0.01	1.09	−0.10
Third Quartile	0.67	1.35	0.99	0.67	0.61	1.55	0.26
Largest	8.00	2.45	6.03	1.03	6.02	3.26	0.99

	$\bar{S} + \sigma_s$		$\bar{P} + \sigma_p$		$\bar{S} + \sigma_s, \bar{P} + \sigma_p$		
	K	S	K	P	K	S	P
Smallest	−9.17	−5.75	−7.61	−8.16	−29.43	−3.76	−84.28
First Quartile	−1.27	0.53	−0.06	0.09	−2.13	0.51	−0.69
Median	0.00	0.98	0.59	0.39	−0.03	1.06	−0.17
Third Quartile	0.73	1.22	1.08	0.74	0.67	1.33	0.40
Largest	41.53	1.77	4.77	1.02	49.71	2.17	1.00

Note: Elasticities have been evaluated at the mean of all variables in the middle row-blocks. In the top row-blocks, elasticities have been evaluated at the mean minus one standard deviation for each column, with the remaining variables still measured at their means. In the bottom row-blocks, elasticities have been evaluated at the mean plus one standard

Table 8.6 (*continued*)

Elasticities: Equation (3.11) Time Series

	$\bar{S} - \sigma_s$		$\bar{P} - \sigma_p$		$\bar{S} - \sigma_s, \bar{P} - \sigma_p$		
	K	S	K	P	K	S	P
Smallest	−2.59	−152.21	−3.15	−0.29	−4.72	−74.32	−0.77
First Quartile	−0.67	−0.12	−0.10	−0.05	−0.63	−0.29	−0.10
Median	0.12	0.42	0.32	0.12	0.10	0.17	0.03
Third Quartile	1.04	1.36	1.43	0.43	1.11	1.43	0.18
Largest	23.10	35.26	21.08	3.90	56.60	308.97	1.54

	$\bar{S}$		$\bar{P}$		$\bar{S}, \bar{P}$		
	K	S	K	P	K	S	P
Smallest	−3.49	−2.06	−4.79	−0.64	−5.71	−2.89	−1.54
First Quartile	−1.21	−0.05	−0.15	−0.02	−1.00	−0.45	−0.19
Median	0.42	0.86	0.66	0.38	0.29	0.86	0.20
Third Quartile	0.90	1.20	1.37	0.62	1.10	1.32	0.40
Largest	9.97	3.90	9.71	1.88	9.86	3.97	1.28

	$\bar{S} + \sigma_s$		$\bar{P} + \sigma_p$		$\bar{S} + \sigma_s, \bar{P} + \sigma_p$		
	K	S	K	P	K	S	P
Smallest	−12.29	−4.99	−8.57	−1.64	−494.90	−5.28	−17.77
First Quartile	−2.39	−0.20	−0.13	−0.08	−1.89	−0.09	−0.46
Median	0.12	0.69	0.43	0.40	0.21	0.56	0.19
Third Quartile	0.93	1.14	1.29	0.71	1.19	1.25	0.49
Largest	6.62	2.34	6.56	1.52	92.70	11.332	1.20

Elasticities: Equation (3.12) Time Series

	$\bar{S} - \sigma_s$		$\bar{P} - \sigma_p$		$\bar{S} - \sigma_s, \bar{P} - \sigma_p$		
	K	S	K	P	K	S	P
Smallest	−2.44	−273.61	−29.73	−0.68	−14.92	−74.18	−1.13
First Quartile	−0.91	0.21	0.17	0.08	−0.91	−0.29	−0.22
Median	−0.18	1.07	0.24	0.32	−0.34	0.30	0.05
Third Quartile	0.28	2.29	1.04	1.15	0.26	3.14	0.48
Largest	12.17	15.62	7.42	4.17	9.81	2526.62	4.18

	$\bar{S}$		$\bar{P}$		$\bar{S}, \bar{P}$		
	K	S	K	P	K	S	P
Smallest	−4.40	−1.32	−4.85	−1.93	−6.39	−1.77	−2.49
First Quartile	−1.89	0.54	−0.26	0.18	−1.57	0.00	−0.52
Median	−0.31	1.08	0.30	0.48	−0.64	0.92	0.10
Third Quartile	0.29	1.79	1.16	1.09	0.39	2.18	0.72
Largest	7.12	4.31	4.94	1.86	6.43	5.02	2.41

	$\bar{S} + \sigma_s$		$\bar{P} + \sigma_p$		$\bar{S} + \sigma_s, \bar{P} + \sigma_p$		
	K	S	K	P	K	S	P
Smallest	−22.04	−1.75	−8.75	−10.24	−14.74	−5.22	−77.19
First Quartile	−3.76	0.58	−0.45	0.21	−2.67	−0.04	−0.89
Median	−0.43	1.05	0.32	0.60	−0.41	0.96	0.15
Third Quartile	0.45	1.44	1.05	1.06	1.02	1.67	0.79
Largest	9.71	2.60	4.06	1.57	71.68	2.59	1.92

Note: Elasticities have been evaluated at the mean of all variables in the middle row-blocks
In the top row-blocks, elasticities have been evaluated at the mean minus one standard
deviation for each column, with the remaining variables still measured at their means. In
the bottom row-blocks. elasticities have been evaluated at the mean plus one standard

Table 8.6 *(continued)*

Elasticities: Equation (3.9) Cross-Section

	$\bar{S} - \sigma_s$			$\bar{P} - \sigma_p$			$\bar{S} - \sigma_s,\ \bar{P} - \sigma_p$			
	C	K	S	C	K	P	C	K	S	P
Smallest	−1.51	−6.87	−0.61	−194.32	−1.79	−7.43	−1.51	−7.76	−0.64	−12.69
First Quartile	−0.73	−0.09	−0.32	−0.95	−0.14	−0.06	−0.81	−0.06	−0.35	0.03
Median	−0.33	0.25	0.26	−0.59	0.26	0.18	−0.43	0.25	0.26	0.35
Third Quartile	0.09	0.45	0.92	−0.10	0.68	0.71	−0.03	0.45	0.71	0.75
Largest	6.95	0.85	5.18	0.40	6.70	12.11	75.84	0.84	3.49	2.07

	$\bar{S}$			$\bar{P}$			$\bar{S},\ \bar{P}$			
	C	K	S	C	K	P	C	K	S	P
Smallest	−9.79	−10.41	−10.22	−11.29	−12.29	−6.81	−23.07	−13.91	−10.24	−9.56
First Quartile	−2.32	−1.43	−0.33	−2.44	−1.45	−3.66	−3.11	−1.46	−0.80	−0.11
Median	−0.69	−0.31	0.36	−0.43	−0.34	−0.04	−0.81	−0.29	0.03	0.03
Third Quartile	0.15	0.19	0.88	0.40	0.17	0.26	0.16	0.19	0.45	0.59
Largest	15.46	1.30	1.53	17.11	1.31	1.36	15.45	1.31	8.84	1.59

	$\bar{S} + \sigma_s$			$\bar{P} + \sigma_p$			$\bar{S} + \sigma_s,\ \bar{P} + \sigma_p$			
	C	K	S	C	K	P	C	K	S	P
Smallest	−2.44	−0.62	−0.18	−18.03	−1.13	−35.51	−5.17	−0.50	−4.49	−0.61
First Quartile	−1.43	0.10	0.31	−1.05	0.25	−0.21	−1.90	0.03	0.27	−0.32
Median	0.17	1.08	0.69	0.34	1.08	0.24	−0.05	1.08	0.82	0.07
Third Quartile	6.91	5.54	1.56	5.56	2.61	1.19	5.46	5.56	2.10	1.10
Largest	68.41	13.89	14.17	99.41	46.40	1.95	39.22	16.61	3.49	2.04

Note: Elasticities have been evaluated at the mean of all variables in the middle row-block. In the top row-block, elasticities have been evaluated at the mean minus one standard deviation for each column, with the remaining variables still measured at their means. In the bottom row-block, elasticities have been evaluated at the mean plus one standard deviation for each column, with the remaining variables still measured at their means.

Table 8.6 (continued)

Elasticities: Equation (3.10) Cross-Section

	$\bar{S} - \sigma_s$			$\bar{P} - \sigma_p$			$\bar{S} - \sigma_s, \bar{P} - \sigma_p$			
	C	K	S	C	K	P	C	K	S	P
Smallest	-0.26	-0.05	-4.15	-0.16	-0.03	-0.38	-0.27	-0.04	-0.31	-0.13
First Quartile	-0.23	-0.02	-0.15	-0.04	0.00	-0.03	-0.20	-0.01	0.00	-0.01
Median	-0.16	0.00	0.01	0.03	0.02	-0.01	-0.18	-0.00	0.07	0.00
Third Quartile	-0.04	0.04	0.17	0.14	0.10	0.08	-0.05	0.05	0.42	0.04
Largest	0.03	0.47	1.00	0.53	0.57	0.25	0.03	0.43	0.82	0.15

	$\bar{S}$			$\bar{P}$			$\bar{S}, \bar{P}$			
	C	K	S	C	K	P	C	K	S	P
Smallest	-0.59	-0.51	0.17	-0.31	-0.02	-0.01	-0.60	-0.46	0.07	-0.25
First Quartile	-0.49	-0.27	0.56	-0.06	0.15	0.27	-0.41	-0.36	0.33	0.02
Median	-0.29	0.07	0.75	0.06	0.31	0.38	-0.33	-0.09	0.61	0.19
Third Quartile	-0.08	0.42	1.04	0.23	0.61	0.61	-0.10	0.30	0.95	0.36
Largest	0.05	0.17	1.19	0.67	0.91	0.77	0.05	0.85	1.26	0.57

	$\bar{S} + \sigma_s$			$\bar{P} + \sigma_p$			$\bar{S} + \sigma_s, \bar{P} + \sigma_p$			
	C	K	S	C	K	P	C	K	S	P
Smallest	-1.14	-1.71	0.28	-0.52	-0.04	-0.03	-1.17	-1.44	0.14	-0.73
First Quartile	-0.89	-1.07	0.70	-0.10	0.25	0.43	-0.73	-1.06	0.49	0.02
Median	-0.53	-0.37	0.83	0.07	0.45	0.54	-0.63	-0.35	0.74	0.27
Third Quartile	-0.11	0.47	1.04	0.30	0.74	0.77	-0.15	0.44	0.97	0.52
Largest	0.07	0.93	1.09	0.74	0.95	0.87	0.07	0.91	1.12	0.73

Note: Elasticities have been evaluated at the mean of all variables in the middle row-block. In the top row-block, elasticities have been evaluated at the mean minus one standard deviation for each column, with the remaining variables still measured at their means. In the bottom row-block, elasticities have been evaluated at the mean plus one standard deviation for each column, with the remaining variables still measured at their means.

Table 8.6 *(continued)*

Elasticities: Equation (3.11) Cross-Section

Top row-block

	$\bar{S} - \sigma_s$			$\bar{P} - \sigma_p$			$\bar{S} - \sigma_s, \bar{P} - \sigma_p$			
	C	K	S	C	K	P	C	K	S	P
Smallest	−0.26	−0.01	−2.25	−0.10	−0.02	−0.33	−0.26	−0.00	−0.00	−0.20
First Quartile	−0.18	−0.00	0.01	−0.08	0.00	−0.07	−0.15	−0.00	0.00	−0.03
Median	−0.10	0.01	0.04	0.07	0.08	−0.00	−0.07	0.01	0.02	0.00
Third Quartile	−0.02	0.03	0.20	0.20	0.17	0.03	0.01	0.04	0.17	0.02
Largest	0.11	1.09	0.44	0.77	0.37	0.15	0.06	0.57	0.84	0.09

Middle row-block

	$\bar{S}$			$\bar{P}$			$\bar{S}, \bar{P}$			
	C	K	S	C	K	P	C	K	S	P
Smallest	−0.58	−0.43	0.03	−0.20	−0.07	−0.21	−0.57	−0.53	−0.42	−0.37
First Quartile	−0.38	−0.13	0.47	−0.15	0.19	0.17	−0.31	−0.13	0.09	−0.05
Median	−0.19	0.04	0.67	0.11	0.40	0.28	−0.13	0.10	0.43	0.09
Third Quartile	−0.05	0.28	0.88	0.31	0.65	0.55	0.02	0.32	0.69	0.41
Largest	0.17	1.01	1.11	0.86	0.90	0.85	0.10	0.91	1.23	0.77

Bottom row-block

	$\bar{S} + \sigma_s$			$\bar{P} + \sigma_p$			$\bar{S} + \sigma_s, \bar{P} + \sigma_p$			
	C	K	S	C	K	P	C	K	S	P
Smallest	−1.12	−1.52	−0.94	−0.32	−0.15	−0.32	−1.08	−2.25	−1.39	−1.23
First Quartile	−0.65	−0.43	0.57	−0.23	0.30	−0.23	−0.52	−0.29	0.16	−0.11
Median	−0.30	−0.00	0.76	0.16	0.56	0.16	−0.19	0.17	0.60	0.27
Third Quartile	−0.07	0.56	0.93	0.40	0.77	0.40	0.02	0.47	0.80	0.48
Largest	0.23	1.01	1.05	0.90	0.94	0.90	0.14	0.95	1.10	0.87

Note: Elasticities have been evaluated at the mean of all variables in the middle row-block. In the top row-block, elasticities have been evaluated at the mean minus one standard deviation for each column, with the remaining variables still measured at their means. In the bottom row-block, elasticities have been evaluated at the mean plus one standard deviation for each column, with the remaining variables still measured at their means.

Table 8.6 (continued)

Elasticities: Equation (3.12) Cross-Section

Top row-block

	$\bar{S} - \sigma_s$			$\bar{P} - \sigma_p$			$\bar{S} - \sigma_s, \bar{P} - \sigma_p$			
	C	K	S	C	K	P	C	K	S	P
Smallest	−0.26	−0.04	−14.27	−0.14	−0.009	−0.23	−0.25	−0.03	−0.49	−0.09
First Quartile	−0.23	−0.02	−0.18	−0.12	−0.004	−0.02	−0.20	−0.01	−0.003	−0.02
Median	−0.14	−0.004	0.05	−0.02	0.03	0.02	−0.15	−0.002	0.03	0.01
Third Quartile	−0.07	0.05	0.24	0.11	0.13	0.13	−0.06	0.04	0.06	0.06
Largest	0.07	0.67	1.29	0.63	0.32	0.78	0.04	0.46	0.48	0.44

Middle row-block

	$\bar{S}$			$\bar{P}$			$\bar{S}, \bar{P}$			
	C	K	S	C	K	P	C	K	S	P
Smallest	−0.59	−0.40	−0.87	−0.28	−0.22	−0.12	−0.55	−0.52	−0.18	−0.31
First Quartile	−0.51	−0.29	0.49	−0.24	0.01	0.30	−0.41	−0.23	0.28	0.01
Median	−0.26	−0.18	0.65	−0.03	0.28	0.47	−0.30	−0.16	0.39	0.30
Third Quartile	−0.10	0.26	1.02	0.17	0.56	0.67	−0.10	0.30	0.66	0.47
Largest	0.11	0.94	1.10	0.75	0.81	0.98	0.07	0.86	1.24	0.92

Bottom row-block

	$\bar{S} + \sigma_s$			$\bar{P} + \sigma_p$			$\bar{S} + \sigma_s, \bar{P} + \sigma_p$			
	C	K	S	C	K	P	C	K	S	P
Smallest	−1.13	−1.35	0.18	−0.46	−0.54	−0.30	−1.04	−2.18	−0.43	−1.02
First Quartile	−0.93	−0.76	0.72	−0.38	0.03	0.47	−0.73	−0.59	0.43	0.00
Median	−0.47	−0.38	0.81	−0.05	0.43	0.69	−0.49	−0.38	0.56	0.45
Third Quartile	−0.21	0.44	1.01	0.23	0.70	0.87	−0.16	0.44	0.79	0.63
Largest	0.15	0.97	1.05	0.82	0.90	0.99	0.10	0.92	1.11	0.95

Note: Elasticities have been evaluated at the mean of all variables in the middle row-block. In the top row-block, elasticities have been evaluated at the mean minus one standard deviation for each column, with the remaining variables still measured at their means. In the bottom row-block, elasticities have been evaluated at the mean plus one standard deviation for each column, with the remaining variables still measured at their means.

Table 8.6 (continued)

Elasticities: Equation (3.14) Cross-Section

	$\bar{S}-\sigma_s$			$\bar{P}-\sigma_p$			$\bar{S}-\sigma_s, \bar{P}-\sigma_p$			
	C	K	S	C	K	P	C	K	S	P
Smallest	−0.29	−0.05	−0.86	−0.18	−0.02	−0.08	−0.28	−0.05	0.0001	−0.01
First Quartile	−0.22	−0.01	0.01	−0.03	−0.002	−0.02	−0.18	−0.009	0.01	−0.002
Median	−0.15	0.003	0.09	−0.004	0.01	0.03	−0.15	0.001	0.04	0.01
Third Quartile	−0.13	0.02	0.33	0.03	0.09	0.18	−0.09	0.05	0.24	0.06
Largest	−0.02	0.21	2.21	0.32	0.28	0.46	0.03	0.18	5.72	0.21

	$\bar{S}$			$\bar{P}$			$\bar{S}, \bar{P}$			
	C	K	S	C	K	P	C	K	S	P
Smallest	−0.66	−0.64	0.24	−0.37	−0.13	0.12	−0.65	−0.57	0.12	−0.04
First Quartile	−0.47	−0.29	0.58	−0.07	0.03	0.33	−0.37	−0.32	0.20	0.09
Median	−0.28	−0.21	0.85	−0.007	0.34	0.49	−0.31	−0.07	0.56	0.17
Third Quartile	−0.21	0.24	0.96	0.06	0.47	0.67	−0.18	0.11	0.79	0.42
Largest	−0.03	0.66	1.30	0.46	0.74	0.90	−0.05	0.62	1.06	0.60

	$\bar{S}+\sigma_s$			$\bar{P}+\sigma_p$			$\bar{S}+\sigma_s, \bar{P}+\sigma_p$			
	C	K	S	C	K	P	C	K	S	P
Smallest	−1.33	−2.65	0.39	−0.63	−0.27	0.22	−1.29	−2.14	0.21	−0.08
First Quartile	−0.88	−0.84	0.71	−0.10	0.06	0.49	−0.64	−0.94	0.32	0.17
Median	−0.47	−0.48	0.92	−0.01	0.49	0.64	−0.51	−0.14	0.72	0.29
Third Quartile	−0.33	0.38	0.99	0.07	0.63	0.79	−0.29	0.31	0.87	0.58
Largest	−0.04	0.78	1.14	0.55	0.84	0.94	−0.07	0.75	1.03	0.73

Note: Elasticities have been evaluated at the mean of all variables in the middle row-block. In the top row-block, elasticities have been evaluated at the mean minus one standard deviation for each column, with the remaining variables still measured at their means. In the bottom row-block, elasticities have been evaluated at the mean plus one standard deviation for each column, with the remaining variables still measured at their means.

to 0.61. On Equation (3.12), the strength of profits is more noticeable. Here, the sales elasticity alone is 0.65 and the profit elasticity
alone is 0.47. When both are included in the same regression the median
sales and profit elasticities are 0.39 and 0.30.

On the averaged data model, Equation (3.12), the strength of sales
relative to profits is even greater, as can be verified from Table 8.6. It is
also worth noting in connection with all equations that the profit
values are normally more compressed around their median than the
sales models, particularly in the upward direction.

One elasticity property worth noting is that the lower the value of
the independent variable, the lower are the elasticities. For instance, in
Equation (3.10SP), the sales elasticity falls from 0.61 to a median value
of 0.07 when evaluated at one standard deviation less than its average,
given that capital stock, capital intensity and profit are held at their
average values. Correspondingly, the profit elasticity moves from 0.19
to zero. Symmetrical results hold when sales and/or profits are moved
from their mean to the mean plus one standard deviation.

On time series, the domination of sales measured in terms of the estimated elasticities is unambiguous. According to Equation (3.10S), a
1 per cent change in sales induces about a 1 per cent change in investment for average values of the independent variables. A 1 per cent
change in profit from Equation (3.10P) will induce only a 1/3 per cent
increase in investment. When the two are combined in (3.10SP), the
sales elasticity is slightly increased, while the median profit elasticity
is a negligible (negative) number. The third quartile response of profits
is only 0.26 when these variables are evaluated at their mean, while it
is 1.55 for sales in (3.10SP). Even Equation (3.12), which showed profit
to such strong advantage on cross-sections, fails to improve the observed elasticity of investment with respect to profit. In Equation (3.12SP)
evaluated at means, it is seen that values about similar to those for the
unlagged model prevail, although this time the profit elasticity is
small and more appropriately a positive number.

The capital stock elasticities for median values are small. On the
profit model, they are large and positive (in (3.10P) the capital stock
elasticity is perversely positive and greater than the profit elasticity)
the median values being close to the neighborhood of zero in (3.10S)
and in (3.10SP). However, the median elasticity for the capital stock is
about −0.64 for Equation (3.12) a theoretically much more respect-
able number. In principle, it is to be supposed that the elasticity of

investment with respect to capital stock would be equal in magnitude and opposite in sign to the sales elasticity. That is, in general, decreases in excess capacity coming about through increases in sales or decreases in capital stock would be expected to have an equal impact on the desire to invest, and conversely. Since some capital outlays include expenditures for reasons other than capacity expansion, rationalization of even moderately large differences, in the elasticities is possible in the direction of a smaller elasticity for the capital stock than sales. The sales component presumably represents a pure capacity effect, whereas the capital stock elasticity represents a combined effect of capacity and other investment motivations.[5]

The policy implications of these results are clear. Other things equal, a small per cent increase in sales will have a greater effect on investment than a small per cent increase in internal funds. If the government seeks to stimulate investment and the objective is magnitude, not qualitative composition, it inexorably follows that the greatest investment effect will come from measures which increase demand rather than measures which increase internal funds. While obviously public policy issues touched on here have numerous ramifications beyond that of dollar volume and we are here concerned with a sample whose limitations are severe, these particular consequences may hold some general interest.

B. *Per Cent Errors*

Another way to evaluate the relative merits of profits and sales equations is to compare the residuals on a year-to-year basis and in a straightforward way judge relative merit. In Equation (3.10), the profit error exceeded the sales equation error in most years, although post-war, with the exception of 1946, 1950, and 1952, the sales errors exceeded the profit errors. Far and away the largest error occurred in 1950 when the acceleration motivations provided a much clearer picture of actual behavior than the profit equation. When lags are introduced, according to Equation (3.11), quite different behavior appeared. Lagged profits pre-war provided a much better explanation in every year except 1937 when the two are almost equally good. Post-

---

[5] A large amount of the discrepancy can be explained by neglecting to make depreciation adjustments on the capital stock coefficient, since these are quite large (at least equal in value to the median capital stock coefficient, or larger). This procedure is described fully at the beginning of the next chapter.

war, the lagged sales did better six times, while lagged profits were superior only three times.

Much of the observed per cent errors were concentrated in particular years. Equation (3.10) has one extremely bad year, 1950. This is especially so for (3.10P) but also for (3.10SP) as well. Equation (3.12S) on the other hand, did very well indeed in 1950 but not (3.12P), and the (3.12S) performance in 1938 showed a very large per cent error. Equation (3.11) had numerous bad years and was clearly the worst of all. It is interesting to observe how poorly the profit variable predicted investment in the Korean War year of 1950. There was a tremendous surge in output and large inventory profits were generated. Investment fell well short of predicted magnitudes, particularly according to the internally generated fund flow hypothesis.

Recession years were especially well predicted by Equation (3.10). The recovery year, 1938, was fairly well predicted by Equation (3.10) and (3.12P) but not by the average model on (3.12S). On the other hand, the lag model on both profits, sales and the combination did very poorly in 1938.

While not a great deal has been gleaned from these comparisons, in the majority of instances the profit residual is smaller in absolute value than the sales equation residual, although when error sums of squares are looked at, for instance those for Equation (3.10), sales do much better because of a few very large errors which appear in the profit equation, but not in the sales equation. Post-war, when capacity pressures were greatest, errors in the current profit equation are typically less than errors in the current sales equation. Conversely, on the lag equation, the post-war sales errors are typically much smaller than the profit errors.

The relatively poor ability of current compared with lagged profits, to explain investment suggests a reformulation of the decision process. Instead of treating profits as a "choke" on investment outlays that have been primarily generated by pressures on capacity, retained profits are most important as a source of *prior* finance. For a given level of capacity requirements, planned investment will be greater in the next year, the higher are current profits. These plans are then modified as the time for actual investment outlays approaches, mainly in response to current capacity pressures. This restatement of the investment decision process is not only consistent with the immediate statistical outcome but furthermore is broadly consistent with current knowledge about timing relations between aggregate investment and internal fund flows, a matter to be further developed in Chapter 12.

C. *Relation to Meyer-Kuh Study*

The preceding results bear on the Meyer-Kuh *Investment Decision* results in a variety of ways. The principal Meyer-Kuh empirical conclusions were these: During periods of high capacity utilization, acceleration forces were dominant and internal fund flows were secondary in the determination of investment rates. Contrarily, during periods of less than full capacity, the dominant guide to investment came from internal fund flows, primarily, it was thought, as a liquidity restraint. Finally, over the long run, investment will be geared to some desired capital-output relationship according to accelerator reasoning.[6] These empirical inferences were based upon data for 15 industry groups in cross-sections for the five individual years, 1946–1950, and the long-run accelerator inferences were based upon averaged data for the same period. The different industry coverage makes direct comparison of these results with the Meyer-Kuh findings most hazardous. In general, however, my results are less favorable to the internal liquidity, profit hypothesis than they are to the acceleration hypothesis. Here it seems that cross-sections are more favorable than time series in providing statistical support for profit effects. Apparently, inter-firm investment differentials are perhaps more closely related to internal fund flows than intra-firm investment variations in time series, although the Meyer-Kuh inferences were based upon differences in correlations among different periods and hence did contain time series information. Except for the ratio model, it appears that the orthogonal contribution of internal fund flows to the explanation of investment is comparatively slight, and considerably less than that for sales or acceleration.

8.6 Predictions for 1956 and 1957

A. *Relative Distribution of Prediction Errors*

Until now, some of the main implications about profit and sales models and different lag structures have been based on several statistics derived from regression estimates. The possibility of testing the equations further is opened by using data unavailable at the time the regressions were fitted, since the regressions terminated in 1955. A fre-

[6] J. R. MEYER and E. KUH., *The Investment Decision, op. cit.*, pp. 190–195.

quent danger in econometric work is to examine the data and the select functional forms which best describe it afterwards, thereby invalidating significance tests. There are two main alternatives that can be pursued to minimize this danger, in addition to the obvious but impractical recommendation not to examine the data in the first place. One approach followed throughout this study is to have so many subsamples of data that it is extremely ponderous to integrate all the sample information by visual inspection. In short, one way to avoid bias is to have so many observations that no one sample or small subset of samples is likely to contain a significant quantity of information about the universe whose characteristics are under investigation. Second, however, it is desirable to forecast beyond the sample period as an independent check. Indeed, for macro-economic relationships, where numerous sub-samples are unavailable, a most indispensable test lies in projections beyond the sample period.

Comparative performance for the prediction years 1956 and 1957 across equations will be evaluated in order to discover which lag structure predicts most accurately and to determine whether profit, sales, or the combination of the two produces the best forecasts. There was considerable attrition in the forecasting sample which started the regression analysis with 60 firms. For the same sort of reasons discussed in Chapter 3 in connection with selection for the original sample, seventeen firms were unavailable for both 1956 and 1957. It is to the records for the remaining hardy 43 firms that we must turn for evidence. Unknown biases may have been introduced through the loss of these seventeen firms.

Table 8.7 records the range, median and quartile values for the size frequency distribution of per cent forecast errors by firm for 1956 and 1957. Per cent errors have been reported as predicted investment minus actual investment divided by actual investment. It is evident that actual investment typically exceeded predicted investment, as indicated by the negative median values for all equations in both years. In almost three-quarters of the predictions, the per cent error was negative. Ideally, of course, the average error would be zero. The median per cent errors range from -0.083 to 0.289. Since individual firm behavior is the prediction objective here (although it is not the central objective of this inquiry), which should not be expected to be predictable with the utmost precision, the median errors do not seem grossly disappointing. Furthermore, the "bias" revealed by the consistent nega-

TABLE 8.7

Distribution of Algebraic Relative Errors by Firm

Equation (3.9)

	1956			1957		
	(3.9S)	(3.9P)	(3.9SP)	(3.9S)	(3.9P)	(3.9SP)
Largest	+2.38	+2.54	+3.39	+2.76	+4.34	+17.46
First Quartile	−0.34	−0.28	−0.12	−0.76	−0.77	−0.77
Median	−0.72	−0.77	−0.62	−0.94	−0.97	−0.94
Third Quartile	−0.88	−0.91	−0.86	−1.03	−1.07	−1.10
Smallest	−1.23	−1.38	−1.26	−3.39	−3.84	−3.06

Equation (3.10)

	1956			1957		
	(3.10S)	(3.10P)	(3.10SP)	(3.10S)	(3.10P)	(3.10SP)
Largest	+4.91	+4.89	+5.26	+7.00	+8.43	+7.57
First Quartile	+0.15	+0.15	+0.09	+0.18	−0.01	−0.12
Median	−0.14	−0.15	−0.11	−0.19	−0.24	−0.22
Third Quartile	−0.36	−0.43	−0.39	−0.47	−0.56	−0.53
Smallest	−0.85	−0.85	−0.85	−0.77	−0.86	−0.96

Equation (3.11)

	1956			1957		
	(3.11S)	(3.11P)	(3.11SP)	(3.11S)	(3.11P)	(3.11SP)
Largest	+4.15	+3.71	+4.15	+7.38	+8.05	+7.38
First Quartile	+0.06	+0.06	+0.03	+0.15	+0.08	+0.15
Median	−0.24	−0.20	−0.22	−0.22	−0.28	−0.28
Third Quartile	−0.44	−0.46	−0.48	−0.51	−0.49	−0.48
Smallest	−0.87	−0.93	−0.95	−0.81	−0.83	−0.86

Equation (3.12)

	1956			1957		
	(3.12S)	(3.12P)	(3.12SP)	(3.12S)	(3.12P)	(3.12SP)
Largest	+4.04	+3.80	+5.30	+6.31	+7.29	+6.91
First Quartile	+0.14	+0.19	+0.06	+0.35	+0.05	+0.32
Median	−0.15	−0.14	−0.08	−0.18	−0.17	−0.14
Third Quartile	−0.36	−0.49	−0.43	−0.44	−0.48	−0.46
Smallest	−0.85	−0.90	−0.91	−0.78	−0.83	−0.85

tive sign for the median values is probably related to the tremendous investment boom of that period. If "excessive" optimism did indeed prevail during this span of time, we should not be alarmed by the bias. However, this does make further testing desirable since a model obviously fails if a consistent bias or drift arises after the period of fit.

The results of primary interest can be simply stated. First, Equation (3.12) definitely appears to possess forecasting capacity superior to either (3.10) or (3.11). While minor exceptions exist, it can be seen from examination of the quartile values that the distribution around the median for Equation (3.12) is more tightly bunched than it is for the other two equations, although Equation (3.10) does almost as well in 1956. Second, the combination of profits and sales in Equation (3.12) leads to a substantially smaller median error than when either variable is used separately to predict investment. For the other equations this reinforcement does not appear. Equation (3.12SP) has a somewhat smaller median error than either (3.10S) or (3.10P) for 1956, while in 1957, Equation (3.10SP) acted roughly as though it were an average of (3.10S) and (3.10P), its median error falling about in the middle. The same held true for Equation (3.11). Only for Equation (3.12) in both 1956 and 1957 does a pronounced reinforcement exist in the sense that the profit-sales equation has a better prediction than the individual sales or profit equations. This outcome shows a certain stability of structure since similar results appear in the regression statistics.

Table 8.8. rank orders the relative errors for each firm across different lag structures for each particular set of included variables. 1956, it will be recalled, was a year of booming activity with investment at high levels. 1957 was also a year of large capital expansion but smaller output rate of growth, and during the last three months there was a rapid decline in the level of manufacturing activity.

It can be seen on the sales equation in 1956, for instance, that the current value of sales clearly did best in the sense that it ranked first 17 times, whereas the next best equation ranking first was Equation (3.11) with only ten first. If, however, we extend the rank comparisons to include the first two positions, it is seen that Equation (3.10) and Equation (3.12) do almost equally well. Equation (3.11) predicts poorly.

In 1957 the outcome is quite different. Both the current and lag equations, (3.10) and (3.11), do equally well considering the combined first or second rank whereas the combined lag structure of Equation (3.12) does almost as well on the first rank and dominates completely when the first two ranks are totaled. Thus, for sales, accelerator equations, the combined lag structure is a distinct improvement over just the current value at best, and is at least as good in the worst case.

For the profit equation alone, the superiority of current relative to lag information is not nearly as apparent, although a moderate difference can be discerned. In 1956, the lagged profit models behave similarly to the sales models, but in 1957, looking at the first two ranks, it is a matter of indifference which lag structure is used. Indeed, looking at the first rank alone, it is seen that the lag value of profits shows up most importantly here. The historical regressions also favored lagged over current profits, so that there has been continuity of structure into the forecast period.

The combined sales, profit equation for 1956 reveals that the current value is most important according to the first rank alone, but when the first two ranks are combined, the average lag is slightly superior. The lag value is clearly inferior to either the current or combined lag. In 1957 once again, Equation (3.12SP) is superior, but Equation (3.11SP) does distinctly better than (3.10SP) according to the first two ranks. In light of observations made in the preceding paragraph about the profit equation, it appears that when profits exert strong quantitative impact, the effect appears most prominently with a delay.

While nothing much conclusive emerged, the results in the forecast period correspond with those for the historical period of fit. While this outcome is not exciting, it provides some assurance about the stability of the estimated structures.

All three equations for a given lag—sales, profits or sales plus profits—are treated equally in the comparative forecast analysis recorded in Table 8.9. At the end of this section, paired comparisons are made for sales and profit equations alone. For the first differenced model of Equation (3.9) profits and sales strongly reinforce each other in 1956. Thus the combined equation comes out best, with the sales model a strong second and the profit model a weak third. The weakness of the profit model's relative prediction power carries over into 1957 when the current sales change variable proves superior. Equation (3.9SP) does quite well—probably because of the sales variable influence. In this instance the profit model has been decisively rejected and the sales model upheld.

The poorness of fit, however, for this particular equation, despite some advantages accruing to first difference formulations, renders these findings of doubtful value.

Equation (3.10S) in 1956 was relatively much stronger than Equation (3.10P). Equation (3.10SP) did slightly better observing the first

TABLE 8.8

Rank Order of Relative Error Across Equations

1956

Rank	Equations				Equations				Equations			
	(3.9S)	(3.10S)	(3.11S)	(3.12S)	(3.9P)	(3.10P)	(3.11P)	(3.12P)	(3.9SP)	(3.10SP)	(3.11SP)	(3.12SP)
1	7	17	10	9	8	13	9	13	6	19	5	13
2	2	11	8	22	2	13	12	16	1	11	15	16
3	0	11	21	11	0	12	19	12	6	9	15	13
4	34	4	4	1	33	5	3	2	30	4	8	1

1957

Rank	Equations				Equations				Equations			
	(3.9S)	(3.10S)	(3.11S)	(3.12S)	(3.9P)	(3.10P)	(3.11P)	(3.12P)	(3.9SP)	(3.10SP)	(3.11SP)	(3.12SP)
1	4	14	14	11	2	11	15	15	5	15	12	11
2	1	9	9	24	3	14	10	16	1	7	15	20
3	1	19	16	7	2	14	16	11	3	16	12	12
4	37	1	4	1	36	4	2	1	34	5	4	0

TABLE 8.9

Rank Order of Relative Errors for Firm Comparisons of Sales, Profit, and Sales-Profit Models in 1956 and 1957

1956

Rank	Equations				Equations				Equations			
	(3.9S)	(3.10S)	(3.11S)	(3.12S)	(3.9P)	(3.10P)	(3.11P)	(3.12P)	(3.9SP)	(3.10SP)	(3.11SP)	(3.12SP)
1	13	15	19	16	8	11	16	14	22	17	8	13
2	20	14	12	12	12	7	9	9	11	22	22	22
3	10	14	12	12	23	25	18	18	10	4	13	13

1957

Rank	Equations				Equations				Equations			
	(3.9S)	(3.10S)	(3.11S)	(3.12S)	(3.9P)	(3.10P)	(3.11P)	(3.12P)	(3.9SP)	(3.10SP)	(3.11SP)	(3.12SP)
1	17	16	16	15	16	13	14	15	10	14	13	13
2	21	12	11	11	7	16	17	17	15	15	16	16
3	5	15	16	16	20	14	12	12	18	14	14	14

rank alone and much better when the first two ranks are considered. That is, definite forecasting reinforcement was apparent in 1956, but the sales model by itself forecasts well. The profit model did relatively worst. In 1957, on the other hand, it is impossible to distinguish among these three equations. The first rank alone or the sum of the first two ranks is equal for the three equations.

Ranks for Equation (3.11) are unusually distributed in 1956. Restricting observation only to the first rank, the sales model is clearly best while the profit model is next best. However, according to the first two ranks, (3.11SP) comes in a strong second after the sales model. It is surprising that even with an additional variable included in the regression, the combined sales, profit variable did not do better. Again in 1957 it is impossible to distinguish the three forms of Equation (3.11) since the ranks are uniformly distributed.

Equation (3.12) shows sales to be slightly superior to profits in 1956 when the first two ranks are considered, although Equation (3.12S) and Equation (3.12SP) do almost as well. In 1957 the profit model comes out ahead in the ranking race, especially on the first rank alone, but even here the differences are relatively modest. Even so, (3.12P) comes out on the first two ranks with 32, Equation (3.12SP) with 29 and Equation (3.12S) with 26. If anything, this outcome slightly favors the profit equation alone, thereby lending mild support to the profit rationing hypothesis. This particular affirmation depends upon how much faith can be placed in the belief that substantial differential credit restrictions were operative in 1957 relative to 1956.

Paired comparisons of sales and profit coefficients are shown in Table 8.10. The joint sales, profit equation thus does not confuse binary comparisons. In Equation (3.9) sales dominates the profit model in both 1956 and 1957 in about two out of three instances in general agreement with the tripartite comparisons of Table 8.10. For Equation (3.10), however, the obvious sales dominance in 1956 gave way to approximate equality in 1957. Since the profit variable heavily measures internal liquidity flows, it may be supposed that the greater credit stringency in 1957 led to the relatively better performance of the profit model in 1957 compared to 1956. Equation (3.11) provides similar information although profits show up relatively better in both 1956 and 1957 than for the unlagged model. Finally, in Equation (3.12) a repetition of the previous outcomes is observable. Sales dominates profits in 1956, while in 1957 the profit variable was the more potent.

TABLE 8.10

*Rank Order of Profit, Sales Relative Error Comparisons
by Firm in 1956 and 1957*

1956

Rank	Equations				Equations			
	(3.9S)	(3.10S)	(3.11S)	(3.12S)	(3.9P)	(3.10P)	(3.11P)	(3.12P)
1	27	28	25	25	16	15	18	18
2	16	15	18	18	27	28	25	25

1957

Rank	Equations				Equations			
	(3.9S)	(3.10S)	(3.11S)	(3.12S)	(3.9P)	(3.10P)	(3.11P)	(3.12P)
1	26	22	20	19	17	21	23	24
2	17	21	23	24	26	22	20	19

The relative importance of the two variables thus changed between the two years. Since Equation (3.12) typically performs better than the others as shown in evaluation of relative errors, it seems that more weight ought to be given the results for this particular equation. Forecasting into 1956 reveals the dominance of accelerator motivation. When we turn to 1957, when both the rate of growth in final demand had tapered off and credit was tighter, we find that the profit variable has become relatively more influential. This conclusion is broadly consistent with the Meyer-Kuh cross-section results. It does not seem that either variable should be neglected—given the sort of markets in which these firms operate at least, some independent explanatory contributions from each hypothesis are discernible.

B. *Theil Inequality Coefficients*

Theil has devised a statistic to measure forecast errors called the inequality coefficient. This particular statistic, designated "U" by Theil, equals zero when no forecast errors have occurred and unity when the forecasts have, in a particular sense, proved completely inaccurate. It can be used to partition the forecast error into three components: The first, the partial coefficient of inequality, U^m, shows whether or not there is a bias in the prediction mechanism, reflected in a difference between the average actual outcome and the average prediction. The second partial coefficient of forecast errors, U^s, arises from differences in the standard deviations of the actual and predicted

TABLE 8.11

Theil Inequality Coefficients for Equations (3.9) to (3.12)
for 1956 and 1957

All Firms

Equation	1956			Equation	1957		
	S	P	SP		S	P	SP
(3.9)	0.63	0.64	0.57	(3.9)	0.80	0.83	0.85
(3.10)	0.26	0.26	0.24	(3.10)	0.32	0.34	0.34
(3.11)	0.28	0.27	0.26	(3.11)	0.31	0.26	0.28
(3.12)	0.26	0.25	0.24	(3.12)	0.29	0.27	0.28

Twenty-One Smallest Firms

Equation	1956			Equation	1957		
	S	P	SP		S	P	SP
(3.9)	0.64	0.69	0.56	(3.9)	0.80	0.82	0.80
(3.10)	0.23	0.29	0.23	(3.10)	0.31	0.33	0.31
(3.11)	0.35	0.38	0.37	(3.11)	0.32	0.34	0.34
(3.12)	0.31	0.34	0.32	(3.12)	0.32	0.33	0.32

Twenty-Two Largest Firms

Equation	1956			Equation	1957		
	S	P	SP		S	P	SP
(3.9)	0.63	0.64	0.57	(3.9)	0.80	0.83	0.85
(3.10)	0.26	0.25	0.24	(3.10)	0.32	0.34	0.34
(3.11)	0.28	0.26	0.25	(3.11)	0.31	0.25	0.27
(3.12)	0.26	0.24	0.23	(3.12)	0.29	0.26	0.28

series, while the third part of the forecast error, U^c, is attributable to lack of correlation between the predicted and the actual forecast values. The first two causes of inequality are systematic in nature, while the third is not. Theil has concluded: "It seems that we must draw the conclusion that, if the forecaster's ability does not allow him to attain perfection, the desirable distribution of inequality over the three sources is $U^m = U^s = 0$, $U^c = 1$."[7]

Our results are the following. The Theil U statistic unfortunately was not zero. Except for Equation (3.9) which was unhappily close to unity for most equations and years, the Theil statistic averages between 0.25 and 0.30 for all firms combined, according to Table 8.11. We might say very crudely that within this definition, the forecasts are "70 to 75 per cent accurate." These results are only mildly satisfac-

[7] H. THEIL, *Economic Forecasts and Policy*, Amsterdam, 1958, p.37.

tory. Fortunately, however, an outcome stated by Theil to be desirable, namely that the correlation component of the forecast, should be high and that the mean and standard deviation component should be low, has been very nearly satisfied. The correlation component accounts for 95 per cent or more of the Theil inequality statistic so that the mean and standard deviation terms representing systematic bias components are in fact negligible. Individual equation results, reported in Table 8.11, will be described in abbreviated fashion since these sample statistics do not strongly distinguish among the alternative hypotheses. The decomposition of the forecast error is not recorded since the correlation component always dominates the other influences.

In 1956, the profit equations do as well as or better than the sales equations, although the difference in the U statistic for the same equation between profit and sales is very slight. The combined sales, profit set does still better than either sales or profits individually. While the profit, sales differentials were moderate, measurement comparisons among the different lag structures lead to somewhat different conclusions from those previously cited. In 1956 the different lag structures perform about the same. The same was true in 1957 for the sales model. However, in the profit equations in 1957, a noticeable difference can be observed. Equation (3.11), the simple lag, does as well as or better than the combined lag, and contrary to previous findings, the current value for Equation (3.10) does distinctly worse than the others. The current value predicts noticeably worse with a U statistic of 0.34 than the simple lag with a U statistic of 0.28. The same result holds and probably for analogous reasons in the combined sales, profit set for which the simple lag does better than the combined lag.

8.7 Summary

The results of this chapter are so numerous that a summary can best serve by presenting a few of the principal highlights. Of central importance is the conclusion that the explanatory power of sales is much greater than profits. This generalization receives ambiguous support on cross-section data but the differences appear overwhelming on time series which are the most reliable data source for the class of hypotheses that this study is designed to test.

However, the statistical significance of profits is much greater when lagged or when the average lag is used, while lagged values for the level of output have the weakest statistical explanatory power. Because of the differential statistical influence of the lag structure, it seems desirable to reformulate the propositions about capital budgeting decisions orginally stated as working hypotheses. In light of the present findings, it seems that the cash flow effect is more important some time before the actual capital outlays are made than it is in actually restricting the outlays during the expenditure period. Hence the hypothesis of liquidity flow as primarily an active and current restraint is not tenable on this evidence. Instead, it is appropriate to view internal liquidity flows as a critical part of the budgeting process which later is modified, primarily in light of variations in the level of output and capacity utilization. Both capacity utilization and cash flow enter the budgetary decision, with capacity utilization having the far greater explanatory weight while deviations from the expectation or plan are most strongly influenced by capacity utilization and less so by actual cash flow.

When predictions are made for 1956 and 1957, a period after the regressions were fitted, the mean forecast error was quite large. The average lag equation was definitely the better predictor when any distinctions are to be discerned. Generally speaking, the results concerning sales and profits based on the historical regression data persisted into the forecast period, providing some confidence that the statistical results were not pure caprice. However, the average error was strongly negative in both forecast years. One departure in the forecast results from historical regression results occurred in 1957, a year of high level capacity utilization and one in which the current profit variable did about as well as the sales variable. In some equations it predicted with greater accuracy. From this, one might infer that the credit rationing hypothesis has a certain validity, although it should be noted that the profit effect is strongest when lagged so that the previous restatement of the hypothesis in expectational form seems most nearly correct.

APPENDIX

Summary of Regression Estimates

1. Significance tests reported at the bottom part of the table should be interpreted in the following way. The number of coefficients at the 1% level records values significant at 1% or greater levels of probability. Those recorded at the 5% level are significant at between 5% and 1% and those recorded at the 10% level are significant between the 10% and 5% level. Therefore *all* coefficients significant at the 10% level, for instance, would be the sum of all entries in the relevant column.

2. "Added Variable" analysis of variance appears in the right hand side of the significance test section. When no variable is mentioned in the heading, it is to be understood that the inclusion of the last variable in the equation has been tested on the null hypothesis that it does not significantly reduce the unexplained variance. Equations designated (SP) have been tested when the profits variable has been added to sales and the sales variable added to profits.

3. A (−) indicates that no test statistics were calculated for this particular significance level whereas a zero indicates that the test was performed but no test statistics were included in that range of significance.

4. The relative prediction error is defined as the ratio of the standard error to the mean of the independent variable, a concept described in Chapter 6.2.

5. The standard error of estimate is measured in units of $1000 and 1954 prices.

Summary of Estimates for Regression Equations
Cross-Section

Equation (3.9S): $\Delta I_t = \alpha_0 + \alpha_1 C + \alpha_2 \Delta K_t + \alpha_3 \Delta S_t$

Observations in A Regression = 60   Total A Regressions = 14

	Coefficient for Independent Variables			Intercept	Multiple Correlation	Relative Prediction Error	Standard Error of Estimate
	C	ΔK_t	ΔS_t				
A Regression[1]							
Smallest	−292.3	−0.4360	−0.0380	−760	0.1642	−34.95	509
First Quartile	−100.7	−27.0100	0.0041	−14	0.2905	−2.06	814
Median	−28.9	−0.1228	0.0291	150	0.3720	1.76	1140
Third Quartile	44.0	−0.0577	0.0460	370	0.4549	6.70	1410
Largest	239.5	0.0205	0.0649	1399	0.7460	177.64	1800
Weighted Average[2]	−34.0	−0.1276	0.0219				
B Regression	−18.9	−0.1450	0.0229	—	0.2844	—	1230
	(44.4)	(0.0235)	(0.0038)				
C Regression	—	0.0131	0.0347	−108	0.7371	4.18	258
		(0.1913)	(0.0096)	(153)			
D Regression	−20.8	−0.1382	0.0258	131	0.3211	20.88	1220
	(43.9)	(0.0227)	(0.0032)	(107)			

Significance Tests[3]

Test Structure[4]

Number of Coefficients Significant at:	One Tail	Two Tail	One Tail	Two Tail	One Tail	Two Tail	Two Tail	One Tail
	−	±	−	±	+	±	±	+
10% Level	2	0	1	1	3	2	1	−
5% Level	0	0	1	0	3	1	3	3
1% Level	0	0	5	5	4	5	0	4

[1] Size distributions were obtained for each estimated parameter, so that elements in each row generally refer to estimates from different regression equations.

[2] Weighted by reciprocal of regression coefficient estimated variance.

[3] For A regressions only.

[4] For one tail tests, the a priori sign selected is justified in detail in the text.

Summary of Estimates for Regression Equations
Cross-Section

Equation (3.9SP): $\Delta I_t = \alpha_0 + \alpha_1 C + \alpha_2 \Delta K_t + \alpha_3 \Delta S_t + \alpha_4 \Delta P_t$

Observations in A Regression = 60   Total A Regressions = 14

	Coefficient for Independent Variables				Intercept	Multiple Correlation	Relative Prediction Error	Standard Error of Estimate
	C	ΔK_t	ΔS_t	ΔP_t				
A Regression[1]								
Smallest	-303.8	-0.4510	-0.0428	-0.4270	-882	0.2360	-35.26	491
First Quartile	-103.3	-0.2727	-0.0142	-0.1747	-146	0.2963	-2.05	802
Median	-36.2	-0.1256	0.0305	-0.0661	136	0.4040	1.75	1120
Third Quartile	76.5	-0.0672	0.0472	0.1083	439	0.5360	6.52	1410
Largest	339.4	0.0205	0.0537	0.7078	1412	0.7460	176.57	1810
Weighted Average[2]	-30.7	-0.1404	0.0256	-0.0328				
B Regression	-18.8	-0.1445	0.0221	0.0127	-	0.2846	-	1240
	(44.8)	(0.0237)	(0.0044)	(0.0373)				
C Regression	-	0.0978	0.0392	-0.0722	-107	0.7436	4.34	269
		(.1988)	(0.0139)	(0.1548)	(159)			
D Regression	-20.8	-0.1381	0.0256	0.0026	131	0.3211	20.89	1230
	(43.9)	(0.0228)	(0.0038)	(0.0341)	(107)			

Significance Tests[3]

Test Structure[4]

Number of Coefficients Significant at:	C		ΔK_t		ΔS_t		ΔP_t		Intercept		Added Variable Test	
	One Tail −	Two Tail ±	One Tail −	Two Tail ±	One Tail +	Two Tail ±	One Tail +	Two Tail ±	Two Tail ±	One Tail +	P added to C	S to P
10% Level	2	0	1	1	1	1	1	0	0	-	0	1
5% Level	0	1	1	0	3	3	1	2	4	2	2	3
1% Level	0	0	5	5	4	3	1	2	0	5	1	2

[1] Size distributions were obtained for each estimated parameter, so that elements in each row generally refer to estimates from different regression equations.

[2] Weighted by reciprocal of regression coefficient estimated variance.

[3] For A regressions only.

[4] For one tail tests, the *a priori* sign selected is justified in detail in the text.

Summary of Estimates for Regression Equations
Cross-Section

$$\Delta I_t = \alpha_0 + \alpha_1 C + \alpha_2 \Delta K_t + \alpha_4 \Delta P_t \quad \text{Equation (3.9P)}$$

Observations in A Regression = 60   Total A Regressions = 14

	Coefficient for Independent Variables			Intercept	Multiple Correlation	Relative Prediction Error	Standard Error of Estimate
	C	ΔK_t	ΔP_t				
A Regression[1]							
Smallest	−287.8	−0.4680	−0.2020	−667	0.1679	−36.56	491
First Quartile	−123.6	−0.3493	−0.0635	−168	0.2398	−2.22	799
Median	−4.4	−0.1188	0.0496	250	0.3403	2.05	1192
Third Quartile	83.2	−0.0784	0.2548	594	0.4908	6.61	1410
Largest	277.0	0.0430	0.6040	1372	0.6250	176.85	1830
Weighted Average[2]	−12.4	−0.1170	0.0046				
B Regression	−7.1	−0.1341	0.1030	—	0.2269	—	1250
	(45.1)	(0.0238)	(0.0328)				
C Regression	—	0.0812	0.2324	−26	0.4452	5.54	342
		(0.2538)	(0.1414)	(199)			
D Regression	−7.9	−0.1271	0.1241	149	0.2343	21.43	1260
	(45.0)	(0.0233)	(0.0297)	(110)			

Significance Tests[3]

	Test Structure[4]							
	C		ΔK_t		ΔP_t		Intercept	
	One Tail	Two Tail	One Tail	Two Tail	One Tail	Two Tail	Two Tail	One Tail
Number of Coefficients Significant at:	−	±	−	±	+	±	±	+
10% Level	1	0	2	1	0	0	0	−
5% Level	0	0	2	1	0	2	4	1
1% Level	0	0	5	5	4	3	0	4

[1] Size distributions were obtained for each estimated parameter, so that elements in each row generally refer to estimates from different regression equations.

[2] Weighted by reciprocal of regression coefficient estimated variance.

[3] For A regressions only.

[4] For one tail tests, the *a priori* sign selected is justified in detail in the text.

Summary of Estimates for Regression Equations
Cross-Section

Equation (3.10S): $I_t = \alpha_0 + \alpha_1 C + \alpha_2 K_t + \alpha_3 S_t$

Observation in A Regression = 60 Total A Regressions = 17

	Coefficient for Independent Variables			Intercept	Multiple Correlation	Relative Prediction Error	Standard Error of Estimate
	C	K_t	S_t				
A Regression[1]							
Smallest	-448.6	-0.02935	0.00725	-159	0.5014	0.3815	386
First Quartile	-260.9	-0.01966	0.01993	243	0.6875	0.6159	617
Median	-125.0	0.00405	0.02797	563	0.7394	0.7773	925
Third Quartile	-56.1	0.02272	0.03890	965	0.7688	0.8286	1320
Largest	42.5	0.07440	0.04666	1351	0.9121	1.3090	1490
Weighted Average[2]	-110.6	-0.00213	0.02648				
B Regression	-147.0 (45.9)	0.00527 (0.00376)	0.02612 (0.00185)	-	0.7056	-	1060
C Regression	-	-0.00570 (0.02614)	0.03320 (0.00822)	210 (302)	0.9134	0.1527	206
D Regression	-160.3 (44.2)	0.00386 (0.00358)	0.02714 (0.00169)	591 (117)	0.7245	0.8122	1050

Significance Tests[3]

Test Structure[4]

Number of Coefficients Significant at:	C		K_t		S_t		Intercept	
	One Tail −	Two Tail ±	One Tail −	Two Tail ±	One Tail +	Two Tail ±	Two Tail ±	One Tail +
10% Level	4	1	3	1	0	2	4	−
5% Level	1	0	2	1	3	2	5	0
1% Level	0	0	0	2	13	12	0	17

[1] Size distributions were obtained for each estimated parameter, so that elements in each row generally refer to estimates from different regression equations.
[2] Weighted by reciprocal of regression coefficient estimated variance.
[3] For A regressions only.
[4] For one tail tests, the *a priori* sign selected is justified in detail in the text.

Summary of Estimates for Regression Equations
Cross-Section

Equation (3.10SP): $I_t = \alpha_0 + \alpha_1 C + \alpha_2 K_t + \alpha_3 S_t + \alpha_4 P_t$

Observations in A Regression = 60   Total A Regressions = 17

	Coefficient for Independent Variables				Intercept	Multiple Correlation	Relative Prediction Error	Standard Error of Estimate
	C	K_t	S_t	P_t				
A Regression[1]								
Smallest	−384.3	−0.03035	0.00324	−0.2039	−145	0.5101	0.3690	387
First Quartile	−226.2	−0.01586	0.01142	0.0501	237	0.6918	0.5892	606
Median	−119.5	−0.00992	0.02419	0.1447	531	0.7528	0.7566	926
Third Quartile	−65.8	0.02068	0.03068	0.2572	932	0.7860	0.8314	1320
Largest	41.9	0.07272	0.04862	0.4088	1079	0.9196	1.3100	1490
Weighted Average[2]	−109.5	−0.00420	0.02259	0.1050				
B Regression	−139.4 (46.0)	0.00582 (0.00380)	0.02058 (0.00241)	0.1155 (0.0323)	—	0.7104	—	1070
C Regression	—	0.00305 (0.02872)	0.03070 (0.01247)	0.0450 (0.1640)	162 (358)	0.9139	0.1580	214
D Regression	−153.6 (47.0)	0.00440 (0.00356)	0.02212 (0.00220)	0.1063 (0.0300)	547 (117)	0.7285	0.8077	1050

Significance Tests[3]

Test Structure[4]

	C		K_t		S_t		P_t		Intercept	Multiple Correlation	Added Variable Test	
	One Tail	Two Tail	One Tail	Two Tail	One Tail	Two Tail	One Tail	Two Tail	Two Tail	One Tail	P added to S	S to P
Number of Coefficients Significant at:	−	±	+	±	+	±	+	±	±	+		
10% Level	6	0	2	1	2	1	1	1	3	—	1	1
5% Level	0	0	2	2	3	5	3	2	3	0	2	5
1% Level	0	0	1	2	7	4	2	2	1	17	3	4

[1] Size distributions were obtained for each estimated parameter, so that elements in each row generally refer to estimates from different regression equations.

[2] Weighted by reciprocal of regression coefficient estimated variance.

[3] For A regressions only.

[4] For one tail tests, the *a priori* sign selected is justified in detail in the text.

Summary of Estimates for Regression Equations
Cross-Section

Equation (3.10P): $I_t = \alpha_0 + \alpha_1 C + \alpha_2 K_t + \alpha_4 P_t$

Observations in A Regression = 60   Total A Regressions = 17

	Coefficient for Independent Variables			Intercept	Multiple Correlation	Relative Prediction Error	Standard Error of Estimate
	C	K_t	P_t				
A Regression[1]							
Smallest	−172.8	−0.00104	−0.0134	−560	0.4672	0.3700	434
First Quartile	−23.7	0.00818	0.1933	−149	0.5971	0.6794	686
Median	58.9	0.01939	0.3085	94	0.6993	0.7721	947
Third Quartile	106.6	0.03826	0.3732	384	0.7610	0.8741	1330
Largest	175.3	0.07799	0.5469	773	0.9175	1.3680	1480
Weighted Average[2]	60.3	0.01956	0.2791				
B Regression	56.3	0.02815	0.2919	—	0.6827	—	1100
	(41.0)	(0.00283)	(0.0255)				
C Regression	—	0.05470	0.3402	−451	0.8708	0.1844	249
		(0.01933)	(0.1306)	(299)			
D Regression	58.6	0.02896	0.3007	16	0.6957	0.8465	1100
	(40.4)	(0.00272)	(0.0240)	(110)			

Significance Tests[3]

Test Structure[4]

	C		K_t		P_t		Intercept	
	One Tail	Two Tail	One Tail	Two Tail	One Tail	Two Tail	Two Tail	One Tail
Number of Coefficients Significant at:	−	±	−	±	+	±	±	+
10% Level	0	0	0	0	1	4	0	—
5% Level	0	0	0	2	5	2	0	0
1% Level	0	0	0	6	10	9	0	17

[1] Size distributions were obtained for each estimated parameter, so that elements in each row generally refer to estimates from different regression equations.

[2] Weighted by reciprocal of regression coefficient estimated variance.

[3] For A regressions only.

[4] For one tail tests, the *a priori* sign selected is justified in detail in the text.

Summary of Estimates for Regression Equations
Cross-Section

Equation (3.11S): $I_t = \alpha_0 + \alpha_1 C + \alpha_2 K_t + \alpha_3 S_{t-1}$

Observations in A Regression = 60   Total A Regressions = 15

	Coefficient for Independent Variables			Intercept	Multiple Correlation	Relative Prediction Error	Standard Error of Estimate
	C	K_t	S_{t-1}				
A Regression[1]							
Smallest	−348.4	−0.03168	0.00144	−401	0.5064	0.3754	416
First Quartile	−257.6	−0.00803	0.01884	177	0.6267	0.5936	678
Median	−72.9	0.00202	0.02474	464	0.7343	0.8113	1020
Third Quartile	−4.1	0.03169	0.03718	815	0.7649	0.8755	1330
Largest	144.3	0.08657	0.05895	1282	0.9150	1.2670	1540
Weighted Average[2]	−88.2	0.00163	0.02819				
B Regression	−101.2 (51.7)	0.01174 (0.00427)	0.02416 (0.00222)	—	0.6845	—	1130
C Regression	—	0.00719 (0.04564)	0.02622 (0.01545)	264 (536)	0.8454	0.1924	266
D Regression	−103.8 (50.2)	0.01146 (0.00401)	0.02437 (0.00204)	470 (134)	0.6978	0.8460	1120

Significance Tests[3]

	C		K_t		S_{t-1}		Intercept	
Test Structure[4]	One Tail −	Two Tail ±	One Tail −	Two Tail ±	One Tail +	Two Tail ±	Two Tail ±	One Tail +
Number of Coefficients Significant at:								
10% Level	1	0	0	1	1	2	2	—
5% Level	1	1	0	1	3	3	3	0
1% Level	0	0	1	3	10	8	1	15

[1] Size distributions were obtained for each estimated parameter, so that elements in each row generally refer to estimates from different regression equations.

[2] Weighted by reciprocal of regression coefficient estimated variance.

[3] For A regressions only.

[4] For one tail tests, the a priori sign selected is justified in detail in the text.

Summary of Estimates for Regression Equations
Cross-Section

Equation (3.11SP): $I_t = \alpha_0 + \alpha_1 C + \alpha_2 K_t + \alpha_3 S_{t-1} + \alpha_4 P_{t-1}$

Observations in A Regression = 60   Total A Regressions = 15

	Coefficient for Independent Variables				Intercept	Multiple Correlation	Relative Prediction Error	Standard Error of Estimate
	C	K_t	S_{t-1}	P_{t-1}				
A Regression[1]								
Smallest	−350.7	−0.03876	−0.01833	−0.1409	−285	0.5081	0.3707	395
First Quartile	−154.7	−0.00355	0.00842	−0.0135	112	0.6828	0.5987	657
Median	−53.3	0.00734	0.01835	0.1611	426	0.7437	0.7807	1030
Third Quartile	11.9	0.02852	0.02619	0.3387	657	0.7725	0.8477	1340
Largest	75.3	0.07777	0.05267	0.5670	1286	0.9188	1.2420	1530
Weighted Average[2]	−63.1	0.00305	0.02263	0.1114				
B Regression	−95.4 (51.9)	0.01204 (0.00428)	0.01875 (0.00282)	0.1139 (0.0365)	—	0.6890	—	1130
C Regression	—	0.03269 (0.05036)	0.00802 (0.01986)	0.2786 (0.2011)	−134 (591)	0.8701	0.1854	258
D Regression	−98.4 (49.9)	0.01174 (0.00406)	0.01858 (0.00256)	0.1250 (0.0338)	428 (133)	0.7033	0.8401	1110

Significance Tests[3]

Test Structure[4]

	C		K_t		S_{t-1}		P_{t-1}		Intercept		Added Variable	
Number of Coefficients Significant at:	One Tail −	Two Tail ±	One Tail −	Two Tail ±	One Tail +	Two Tail ±	One Tail +	Two Tail ±	Two Tail ±	One Tail +	P added to S	S added to P
10% Level	1	0	0	1	2	0	2	1	1	—	1	0
5% Level	0	0	0	1	1	2	4	5	2	0	5	2
1% Level	0	1	1	3	5	4	2	1	0	15	1	4

[1] Size distributions were obtained for each estimated parameter, so that elements in each row generally refer to estimates from different regression equations.
[2] Weighted by reciprocal of regression coefficient estimated variance.
[3] For A Regression only.
[4] For one tail tests, the *a priori* sign selected is justified in detail in the text.

Summary of Estimates for Regression Equations
Cross-Section

Equation (3.11P): $I_t = \alpha_0 + \alpha_1 C + \alpha_2 K_t + \alpha_4 P_{t-1}$

Observations in A Regression = 60   Total A Regressions = 15

	Coefficient for Independent Variables			Intercept	Multiple Correlation	Relative Prediction Error	Standard Error of Estimate
	C	K_t	P_{t-1}				
A Regression[1]							
Smallest	−159.6	−0.00433	−0.0816	−674	0.4791	0.3896	427
First Quartile	−92.7	0.01359	0.1712	−169	0.6320	0.7151	769
Median	107.4	0.02664	0.2681	77	0.6921	0.7862	1070
Third Quartile	158.7	0.04315	0.4406	363	0.7453	0.8503	1360
Largest	238.9	0.06114	0.6189	738	0.9081	1.3570	1540
Weighted Average[2]	96.6	0.02388	0.2454				
B Regression	79.9	0.03197	0.2630	−	0.6683	−	1150
	(45.5)	(0.00311)	(0.0293)				
C Regression	−	0.05098	0.3323	−331	0.8680	0.1788	248
		(0.02124)	(0.1454)	(323)			
D Regression	79.2	0.03230	0.2747	−15	0.6819	0.8639	1140
	(44.7)	(0.00298)	(0.0275)	(122)			

Significance Tests[3]

Test Structure[4]

	C		K_t		P_{t-1}		Intercept	
	One Tail	Two Tail	One Tail	Two Tail	One Tail	Two Tail	Two Tail	One Tail
	−	±	−	±	+	±	±	+
Number of Coefficients Significant at:								
10% Level	0	3	0	0	1	1	0	−
5% Level	0	0	0	2	2	1	0	0
1% Level	0	0	0	8	8	8	0	15

[1] Size distributions were obtained for each estimated parameter, so that elements in each row generally refer to estimates from different regression equations.
[2] Weighted by reciprocal of regression coefficient estimated variance.
[3] For A regressions only.
[4] For one tail tests, the a priori sign selected is justified in detail in the text.

Summary of Estimates for Regression Equations
Cross-Section

Equation (3.12S): $I_t = \alpha_0 + \alpha_1 C + \alpha_2 K_t + \alpha_3[(S_t + S_{t-1}) \div 2]$

Observations in A Regression = 60   Total A Regressions = 15

	Coefficient for Independent Variables			Intercept	Multiple Correlation	Relative Prediction Error	Standard Error of Estimate
	C	K_t	$(S_t + S_{t-1}) \div 2$				
A Regression[1]							
Smallest	−408.4	−0.02940	0.00430	−281	0.5066	0.3777	395
First Quartile	−258.7	−0.01701	0.02085	244	0.6586	0.6079	688
Median	−125.5	−0.00481	0.02804	609	0.7460	0.7876	1020
Third Quartile	−43.1	0.02775	0.03459	912	0.7578	0.8725	1330
Largest	93.5	0.08050	0.05290	1287	0.9139	1.2816	1500
Weighted Average[2]	−112.6	−0.00130	0.02789				
B Regression	−164.5	0.00473	0.02722	—	0.6982	—	1100
	(51.9)	(0.00434)	(0.00219)				
C Regression	—	−0.05765	0.05038	691	0.9321	0.1304	181
		(0.03348)	(0.01116)	(342)			
D Regression	−183.9	0.00251	0.02854	645	0.7160	0.8245	1090
	(50.1)	(0.00415)	(0.00203)	(132)			

Significance Tests[3]

Test Structure[4]

	C		K_t		$(S_t + S_{t-1}) \div 2$		Intercept	
Number of Coefficients Significant at:	One Tail	Two Tail	One Tail	Two Tail	One Tail	Two Tail	Two Tail	One Tail
	−	±	−	±	+	±	±	+
10% Level	5	0	1	0	0	1	2	—
5% Level	0	0	0	1	2	3	4	0
1% Level	0	0	1	2	12	10	0	15

[1] Size distributions were obtained for each estimated parameter, so that elements in each row generally refer to estimates from different regression equations.
[2] Weighted by reciprocal of regression coefficient estimated variance.
[3] For A regressions only.
[4] For one tail tests, the *a priori* sign selected is justified in detail in the text.

Summary of Estimates for Regression Equations
Cross-Section

Equation (3.12SP): $I_t = \alpha_0 + \alpha_1 C + \alpha_2 K_t + \alpha_3[(S_t + S_{t-1}) \div 2] + \alpha_4[(P_t + P_{t-1}) \div 2]$

Observations in A Regression = 60   Total A Regressions = 15

	Coefficient for Independent Variables				Intercept	Multiple Correlation	Relative Prediction Error	Standard Error of Estimate
	C	K_t	$[(S_t + S_{t-1}) \div 2]$	$[(P_t + P_{t-1}) \div 2]$				
A Regression[1]								
Smallest	−380.3	−0.03819	−0.00794	−0.1923	−202	0.5120	0.3665	375
First Quartile	−213.6	−0.01251	0.00960	0.0555	185	0.6940	0.5917	665
Median	−125.1	−0.00260	0.01509	0.2392	526	0.7579	0.7544	1020
Third Quartile	−234.0	0.02744	0.02372	0.3439	770	0.7744	0.8264	1340
Largest	59.4	0.07390	0.04680	0.5733	1241	0.9206	1.2565	1470
Weighted Average[2]	−86.4	0.00224	0.02078	0.1844				
B Regression	−157.6 (51.8)	0.00517 (0.00434)	0.01886 (0.00295)	0.1789 (0.0423)	—	0.7060	—	1100
C Regression	—	−0.03509 (0.03178)	0.03060 (0.01389)	0.3423 (0.1679)	301 (359)	0.9512	0.1161	161
D Regression	−178.4 (49.5)	0.00288 (0.00410)	0.01990 (0.00269)	0.1896 (0.0393)	584 (131)	0.7246	0.8144	1080

Significance Tests[3]

Test Structure[4]

Number of Coefficients Significance at:	C		K_t		$[(S_t+S_{t-1})\div 2]$		$[(P_t+P_{t-1})\div 2]$		Intercept		Added Variable	
	One Tail −	Two Tail ±	One Tail +	Two Tail ±	One Tail +	Two Tail ±	One Tail +	Two Tail ±	Two Tail ±	One Tail +	P added to S	S added to P
10% Level	1	0	2	0	2	2	2	1	1	—	2	2
5% Level	1	0	2	0	5	0	6	0	0	0	6	0
1% Level	0	3	4	3	3	4	1	1	1	15	1	4

[1] Size distributions were obtained for each estimated parameter, so that elements in each row generally refer to estimates from different regression equations.

[2] Weighted by reciprocal of regression coefficient estimated variance.

[3] For A regressions only.

[4] For one tail tests, the *a priori* sign selected is justified in detail in the text.

Summary of Estimates for Regression Equations
Cross-Section

Equation (3.12P): $I_t = \alpha_0 + \alpha_1 C + \alpha_2 K_t + \alpha_4[(P_t + P_{t-1}) \div 2]$

Observations in A Regression = 60   Total A Regressions = 15

	Coefficient for Independent Variables			Intercept	Multiple Correlation	Relative Prediction Error	Standard Error of Estimate
	C	K_t	$(P_t + P_{t-1}) \div 2$				
A Regression[1]							
Smallest	−237.0	−0.01290	−0.0750	−528	0.4739	0.3760	406
First Quartile	−112.0	0.00456	0.2061	−35	0.6861	0.6770	772
Median	55.7	0.01645	0.3629	98	0.6999	0.7551	1040
Third Quartile	81.2	0.03533	0.4809	551	0.7588	0.8405	1340
Largest	193.0	0.06390	0.6140	848	0.9172	1.3631	1460
Weighted Average[2]	52.3	0.01634	0.3477				
B Regression	5.7	0.02372	0.3605	—	0.6881	—	1120
	(45.8)	(0.00327)	(0.0319)				
C Regression	—	0.02626	0.6009	−344	0.9289	0.1334	185
		(0.01760)	(0.1380)	(239)			
D Regression	−2.5	0.02317	0.3829	134	0.7043	0.8385	1110
	(44.7)	(0.00314)	(0.0302)	(119)			

Significance Tests[3]

Test Structures[4]

	C		K_t		$(P_t + P_{t-1}) \div 2$		Intercept	
	One Tail −	Two Tail ±	One Tail −	Two Tail ±	One Tail +	Two Tail ±	Two Tail ±	One Tail +
Number of Coefficients Significant at:								
10% Level	0	1	0	3	2	1	0	—
5% Level	0	0	0	3	2	1	0	0
1% Level	0	0	0	5	9	9	0	15

[1] Size distributions were obtained for each estimated parameter, so that elements in each row generally refer to estimates from different regression equations.

[2] Weighted by reciprocal of regression coefficient estimated variance.

[3] For A regressions only.

[4] For one tail tests, the *a priori* sign selected is justified in detail in the text.

Summary of Estimates for Regression Equations
Cross-Section

Equation (3.13S): $[(I_t + I_{t-1}) \div 2] = \alpha_0 + \alpha_1 C + \alpha_2 K_t + \alpha_3[(S_t + S_{t-1}) \div 2]$

Observations in A Regression = 60 Total A Regressions = 15

	Coefficient for Independent Variables				Multiple Correlation	Relative Prediction Error	Standard Error of Estimate
	C	K_t	$(S_t + S_{t-1}) \div 2$	Intercept			
A Regression[1]							
Smallest	−394.5	−0.0360	0.00998	76	0.6251	0.5176	409
First Quartile	−233.2	−0.0139	0.01943	356	0.7188	0.5547	553
Median	−129.3	−0.0061	0.03008	555	0.8001	0.5733	880
Third Quartile	−104.3	0.0189	0.03774	780	0.8158	0.7075	996
Largest	−20.9	0.0555	0.04372	1310	0.8515	0.8369	1290
Weighted Average[2]	−133.1	−0.0051	0.02908				
B Regression	−164.1	0.0039	0.02651	−	0.7594	−	887
	(41.4)	(0.0035)	(0.00171)				
C Regression	−	−0.0226	0.03785	369	0.9387	0.1210	163
		(0.0293)	(0.00915)	(307)			
D Regression	−177.8	0.0024	0.02750	638	0.7753	0.6806	878
	(40.0)	(0.0033)	(0.00158)	(106)			

Significance Tests[3]

Test Structure[4]

	C		K_t				$(S_t + S_{t-1}) \div 2$		Intercept	
	One Tail	Two Tail	One Tail	Two Tail	One Tail	Two Tail	One Tail	Two Tail	Two Tail	One Tail
	−	±	−	±	+	±	+	±	±	+
Number of Coefficients Significant at:										
10% Level	2	2	2	2	0	1	13	1	4	−
5% Level	2	0	3	2	1	0	13	0	4	0
1% Level	0	0	0	1	0	1	13	1	1	15

[1] Size distributions were obtained for each estimated parameter, so that elements in each row generally refer to estimates from different regression equations.
[2] Weighted by reciprocal of regression coefficient estimated variance.
[3] For A regressions only.
[4] For one tail tests, the a priori sign selected is justified in detail in the text.

Equation (3.13SP): $[(I_t + I_{t-1}) \div 2] = \alpha_0 + \alpha_1 C + \alpha_2 K_t + \alpha_3 [(S_t + S_{t-1}) \div 2] + \alpha_4 [(P_t + P_{t-1}) \div 2]$

Observations in A Regression = 60

Total A Regressions = 15

Summary of Estimates for Regression Equations
Cross-Section

	Coefficient for Independent Variables				Intercept	Multiple Correlation	Relative Prediction Error	Standard Error of Estimate
	C	K_t	$[(S_t + S_{t-1}) \div 2]$	$[(P_t + P_{t-1}) \div 2]$				
A Regression[1]								
Smallest	−385.8	−0.03329	0.00472	0.03359	121	0.6487	0.4962	404
First Quartile	−231.0	−0.01472	0.00797	0.07560	288	0.7366	0.5291	513
Median	145.2	−0.00200	0.02478	0.11990	504	0.8081	0.5705	887
Third Quartile	−62.4	0.01798	0.03080	0.28340	798	0.8354	0.7049	980
Largest	−39.2	0.05204	0.04453	0.34680	1241	0.8550	0.8285	1300
Weighted Average[2]	−122.6	−0.00681	0.02314	0.15920				
B Regression	−158.8	0.00426	0.02043	0.12970	—	0.7642	—	888
	(41.5)	(0.00348)	(0.00234)	(0.03406)				
C Regression	—	−0.01363	0.03051	0.12830	217	0.9416	0.1234	167
		(0.03232)	(0.01374)	(0.17611)	(376)			
D Regression	−173.8	0.00269	0.02176	0.12560	596	0.7797	0.6750	871
	(39.7)	(0.00329)	(0.00213)	(0.03171)	(105)			

Significance Tests[3]

Test Structure[4]

	C		K_t		$[(S_t + S_{t-1}) \div 2]$		$[(P_t + P_{t-1}) \div 2]$		Intercept	Multiple Correlation	Added Variable	
	One Tail	Two Tail	One Tail	Two Tail	One Tail	Two Tail	One Tail	Two Tail	Two Tail	One Tail	P added to S	S added to P
Number of Coefficients Significant at:	−	±	−	±	+	±	+	±	±	+		
10% Level	1	1	2	4	1	2	2	1	3	—	1	2
5% Level	2	1	3	0	3	3	1	2	2	0	2	3
1% Level	0	0	1	2	7	5	3	1	1	15	1	5

[1] Size distributions were obtained for each estimated parameter, so that elements in each row generally refer to estimates from different regression equations.

[2] Weighted by reciprocal of regression coefficient estimated variance.

[3] For A regressions only.

[4] For one tail tests, the *a priori* sign selected is justified in detail in the text.

Summary of Estimates for Regression Equations
Cross-Section

Equation (3.13P): $[(I_t + I_{t-1}) \div 2] = \alpha_0 + \alpha_1 C + \alpha_2 K_t + \alpha_4[(P_t + P_{t-1}) \div 2]$

Observations in A Regression = 60   Total A Regressions = 15

	Coefficient for Independent Variables			Intercept	Multiple Correlation	Relative Prediction Error	Standard Error of Estimate
	C	K_t	$(P_t + P_{t-1}) \div 2$				
A Regression[1]							
Smallest	−197.7	−0.00750	0.1093	−141	0.5385	0.5139	469
First Quartile	−22.3	0.00386	0.2907	−52	0.6863	0.5693	598
Median	3.5	0.02383	0.3619	201	0.7359	0.6582	937
Third Quartile	50.3	0.03202	0.4101	274	0.8187	0.8174	973
Largest	179.5	0.06274	0.4903	787	0.8387	0.8995	1290
Weighted Average[2]	35.4	0.01630	0.3406				
B Regression	16.1	0.02421	0.3329	−	0.7386	−	919
	(37.6)	(0.00272)	(0.0258)				
C Regression	−	0.04835	0.4153	−456	0.9143	0.1422	192
		(0.01878)	(0.1378)	(257)			
D Regression	15.7	0.02466	0.3452	115	0.7500	0.7128	920
	(37.1)	(0.00263)	(0.0246)	(99)			

Significance Tests[3]

Test Structure[4]

	C		K_t		$(P_t + P_{t-1}) \div 2$		Intercept	
Number of Coefficients Significant at:	One Tail	Two Tail	One Tail	Two Tail	One Tail	Two Tail	Two Tail	One Tail
	−	±	−	±	+	±	±	+
10% Level	0	0	0	1	0	1	1	−
5% Level	0	0	0	2	1	0	0	0
1% Level	0	0	0	6	12	12	0	15

[1] Size distributions were obtained for each estimated parameter, so that elements in each row generally refer to estimates from different regression equations.
[2] Weighted by reciprocal of regression coefficient estimated variance.
[3] For A regression only.
[4] For one tail tests, the a priori sign selected is justified in detail in the text.

Summary of Estimates for Regression Equations
Cross-Section

Equation (3.19): $\Delta \log I_t = \alpha_0 + \alpha_1 \log C + \alpha_2 \Delta \log K_t + \alpha_3 \Delta \log S$

Observation in A Regression = 60   Total A Regressions = 14

	Coefficient for Independent Variables			Intercept	Multiple Correlation	Standard Error of Estimate
	$\Delta \log C$	$\Delta \log K_t$	$\Delta \log S_t$			
A Regression[1]						
Smallest	−0.5561	−4.1318	−0.5160	−0.5710	0.1097	0.5174
First Quartile	−0.1950	−2.3691	0.1252	−0.1845	0.1830	0.5789
Median	−0.0636	−1.0385	0.4243	−0.0813	0.2721	0.6613
Third Quartile	0.2922	−0.3675	0.6409	0.1822	0.4354	0.7756
Largest	0.5392	0.6059	1.5243	0.5029	0.5097	0.9301
B Regression	0.0169	−1.1273	0.4384	—	0.1971	0.7290
	(0.0578)	(0.2634)	(0.1119)			
C Regression	—	−1.9822	1.5046	−0.0208	0.9129	0.1494
		(1.8462)	(0.1965)			
D Regression	0.0270	−1.1168	0.9585	−0.0181	0.3978	0.7420
	(0.0588)	(0.2588)	(0.0773)			

Significance Tests[2]

	Test Structure[3]						
	$\Delta \log C$		$\Delta \log K_t$		$\Delta \log S_t$		One Tail
Number of Coefficients significant at:	One Tail −	Two Tail ±	One Tail −	Two Tail ±	One Tail +	Two Tail ±	+
10% Level	1	2	0	1	2	0	—
5% Level	2	1	3	2	0	1	0
1% Level	0	1	3	3	3	2	7

[1] Size distributions were obtained for each estimated parameter, so that elements in each row generally refer to estimates from different regression equations.

[2] For A regressions only.

[3] For one tail tests, the *a priori* sign selected is justified in detail in the text.

Summary of Estimates for Regression Equations
Cross-Section

Equation (3.20): $\log I = \alpha_0 + \alpha_1 \log C + \alpha_2 \log K_t + \alpha_3 \log S_t$

Observation in A Regression = 60　　　　　　　　　　　　Total A Regressions = 15

	Coefficient for Independent Variables			Intercept	Multiple Correlation	Relative Prediction Error	Standard Error of Estimate
	log C	log K_t	log S_t				
A Regression[1]							
Smallest	−0.7836	−0.4282	0.0104	−4.5670	0.6336	0.0749	0.2776
First Quartile	−0.5346	−0.1964	0.6173	−3.5617	0.7134	0.0908	0.3745
Median	−0.3326	0.0755	0.8796	−2.8521	0.7796	0.1100	0.4995
Third Quartile	0.1502	0.2936	1.1083	−2.2041	0.8213	0.1474	0.8083
Largest	0.6426	1.1406	1.4500	−1.4558	0.8728	0.1818	1.1198
Weighted Average[2]	−0.2301	0.1007	0.8550				
B Regression	−0.1773	0.1434	0.8231	—	0.7469	—	0.6425
C Regression	—	−0.3211	1.1713	−2.1383	0.9407	0.0250	0.0268
D Regression	−0.2803	0.0408	0.9283	−2.9373	0.7721	0.1211	0.6298

Significance Tests[3]

Test Structure[4]

Number of Coefficients Significant at:	log C One Tail	log C Two Tail	log K_t One Tail	log K_t Two Tail	log S_t One Tail	log S_t Two Tail	Intercept Two Tail	Added Variable One Tail
	−	±	+	±	+	±	±	+
10% Level	3	0	0	1	0	1	1	—
5% Level	1	1	1	1	4	6	8	0
1% Level	0	0	0	0	10	7	6	17

[1] Size distributions were obtained for each estimated parameter, so that elements in each row generally refer to estimates from different regression equations.

[2] Weighted by reciprocal of regression coefficient estimated variance.

[3] For A regressions only.

[4] For one tail tests, the *a priori* sign selected is justified in detail in the text.

Cross-Section

Equation (3.21): $\log I = \alpha_0 + \alpha_1 \log C + \alpha_2 \log K_t + \alpha_3 \log S_{t-1}$

Observations in A Regression = 60 Total A Regressions = 15

	Coefficient for Independent Variables			Intercept	Multiple Correlation	Relative Prediction Error	Standard Error of Estimate
	$\log C$	$\log K_t$	$\log S_{t-1}$				
A Regression[1]							
Smallest	−0.6738	−0.0923	−0.2560	−4.46	0.6342	0.0775	0.547
First Quartile	−0.1788	0.2262	0.4400	−3.67	0.6942	0.0924	0.629
Median	0.1299	0.3359	0.5893	−2.83	0.7957	0.1101	0.757
Third Quartile	0.4233	0.5183	0.7395	−2.58	0.8129	0.1428	0.910
Largest	0.8960	1.3909	1.1284	−1.33	0.8444	0.1817	1.100
Weighted Average[2]	0.0721	0.3693	0.5961				
B Regression	0.0528	0.3669	0.6049	—	0.7371	—	0.814
	(0.1168)	(0.1011)	(0.0966)				
C Regression	—	0.5641	0.4777	−3.55	0.7912	0.0423	0.291
		(0.9310)	(0.5188)	(4.34)			
D Regression	0.0766	0.3915	0.5801	−2.99	0.7430	0.1264	0.832
	(0.1068)	(0.0878)	(0.0790)	(0.33)			

Significance Tests[3]

	Test Structure[4]								
	$\log C$		$\log K_t$		$\log S_{t-1}$		Intercept		Added Variable
	One Tail	Two Tail	One Tail	Two Tail	One Tail	Two Tail	Two Tail	One Tail	
Number of Coefficients Significant at:	−	±	−	±	+	±	±	+	
10% Level	1	0	0	1	3	3	2	−	3
5% Level	0	0	0	1	4	1	5	0	1
1% Level	0	0	0	0	2	2	7	15	2

[1] Size distributions were obtained for each estimated parameter, so that elements in each row generally refer to estimates from different regression equations.

[2] Weighted by reciprocal of regression coefficient estimated variance.

[3] For A regressions only.

[4] For one tail tests, the *a priori* sign selected is justified in detail in the text.

Summary of Estimates for Regression Equations
Cross-Section

Equation (3.22): $\log I = \alpha_0 + \alpha_1 \log C + \alpha_2 \log K_t + \alpha_3 \log [(S_t + S_{t-1}) \div 2]$

Observations in A Regression = 60   Total A Regressions = 15

	Coefficient for Independent Variables			Intercept	Multiple Correlation	Standard Error of Estimate
	log C	log K_t	log $(S_t + S_{t-1})/2$			
A Regression[1]						
Smallest	−0.9129	−0.4407	0.0784	−4.3779	0.6336	0.5136
First Quartile	−0.5787	−0.2402	0.7317	−3.8050	0.7409	0.5968
Median	−0.2070	0.1320	0.9667	−2.9520	0.7947	0.6864
Third Quartile	0.1353	0.2691	1.1216	−2.5706	0.8267	0.8502
Largest	0.5429	1.0236	1.5316	−1.4878	0.8728	0.9998
B Regression	−0.2297 (0.1117)	0.1091 (0.0957)	0.8646 (0.0919)	—	0.7613	0.7681
C Regression	—	−0.3532 (0.3052)	1.2084 (0.1866)	−2.2294	0.9520	0.1294
D Regression	−0.3352 (0.0977)	0.0020 (0.0789)	0.9711 (0.0724)	−2.9823	0.7833	0.7613

Significance Tests[2]

Test Structure[3]

	log C		log K_t		log $(S_t + S_{t-1})/2$		One Tail
	One Tail	Two Tail	One Tail	Two Tail	One Tail	Two Tail	
Number of Coefficients significant at:	+	±	−	±	−	±	
10% Level	2	2	1	1	0	0	—
5% Level	3	1	0	1	3	1	0
1% Level	0	0	0	0	9	11	14

[1] Size distributions were obtained for each estimated parameter, so that elements in each row generally refer to estimates from different regression equations.

[2] For A regressions only.

[3] For one tail tests, the a priori sign selected is justified in detail in the text.

Summary of Estimates for Regression Equations
Cross-Section

Equation (3.30A): $\dfrac{I_t}{K_t} = \alpha_0 + \alpha_1 \dfrac{P_t}{K_t} + \alpha_2 \dfrac{S_{t-1}}{C \cdot K_{t-1}}$

Observations in A Regression = 60   Total A Regressions = 15

	Coefficient for Independent Variables		Intercept	Multiple Correlation	Relative Prediction Error	Standard Error of Estimate
	$\dfrac{P_t}{K_t}$	$\dfrac{S_{t-1}}{C \cdot K_{t-1}}$				
A Regression[1]						
Smallest	0.0030	−0.0348	−0.0669	0.0515	0.5535	0.0018
First Quartile	0.1018	0.0047	−0.0307	0.2571	0.6116	0.0022
Median	0.2369	0.0286	0.0217	0.4496	0.7806	0.0027
Third Quartile	0.4191	0.0689	0.0488	0.5501	1.0221	0.0070
Largest	0.7186	0.1177	0.0786	0.7235	1.4480	0.0149
Weighted Average[2]	0.1634	0.0342				
B Regression	0.1850	0.0447	−	0.3251	−	0.0065
C Regression	0.3128	0.0365	0.0111	0.6242	0.1828	0.0002
D Regression	0.1922	0.0393	0.0217	0.3388	0.9645	0.0054

Significance Tests[3]   Test Structure[4]

Number of Coefficients Significant at:	$\dfrac{P_t}{K_t}$		$\dfrac{S_{t-1}}{C \cdot K_{t-1}}$		Intercept		Added Variable
	One Tail +	Two Tail ±	One Tail +	Two Tail ±	Two Tail ±	One Tail +	
10% Level	0	0	0	2	1	−	2
5% Level	1	2	2	1	2	1	1
1% Level	11	10	2	1	0	10	1

[1] Size distributions were obtained for each estimated parameter, so that elements in each row generally refer to estimates from different regression equations.

[2] Weighted by reciprocal of regression coefficient estimated variance.

[3] For A regressions only.

[4] For one tail tests, the *a priori* sign selected is justified in detail in the text.

Summary of Estimates for Regression Equations
Cross-Section

$$\text{Equation (3.30B):} \quad \frac{I_t}{K_t} = \alpha_0 + \alpha_1 \frac{P_t}{K_t} + \alpha_2 \frac{S_{t-1}}{C \cdot K_{t-1}} + \alpha_3 \frac{S_t}{C \cdot K_t}$$

Observations in A Regression = 60   Total A Regressions = 15

	Coefficient for Independent Variables			Intercept	Multiple Correlation	Relative Prediction Error	Standard Error of Estimate
	$\dfrac{P_t}{K_t}$	$\dfrac{S_{t-1}}{C \cdot K_{t-1}}$	$\dfrac{S_t}{C \cdot K_t}$				
A Regression[1]							
Smallest	0.0098	−0.04150	−0.03159	−0.1096	0.0565	0.5577	0.0420
First Quartile	0.1274	−0.00915	−0.01389	−0.0314	0.3367	0.6335	0.0463
Median	0.2216	0.02083	0.02104	−0.0014	0.4865	0.7849	0.0522
Third Quartile	0.4142	0.05160	0.06639	0.0400	0.5759	1.1030	0.0848
Largest	0.6019	0.08926	0.13550	0.0785	0.7264	1.4600	0.1200
Weighted Average[2]	0.1437	0.00525	0.02866				
B Regression	0.1521 (0.0226)	−0.00233 (0.01570)	0.06341 (0.01447)	−	0.3546	−	0.0680
C Regression	0.1479 (0.2539)	0.01010 (0.04352)	0.03484 (0.04719)	0.0193 (0.0270)	0.6242	0.1828	0.0128
D Regression	0.1543 (0.0219)	0.00612 (0.01155)	0.05020 (0.01075)	0.0078 (0.0082)	0.3686	0.9535	0.0679

Significance Tests[3]

	P_t/K_t		$S_{t-1}/C \cdot K_{t-1}$		$S_t/C \cdot K_t$		Test Structure[4]		Added Variable
Number of Coefficients	One Tail	Two Tail	One Tail	Two Tail	One Tail	Two Tail	Two Tail	One Tail	
Significant at:	+	±	+	±	+	±	±	+	+
10% Level	1	0	2	0	2	0	1	−	0
5% Level	4	4	0	0	0	1	1	2	1
1% Level	7	7	0	0	1	0	0	9	0

[1] Size distributions were obtained for each estimated parameter, so that elements in each row generally refer to estimates from different regression equations.

[2] Weighted by reciprocal of regression coefficient estimated variance.

[3] For A regressions only.

Summary of Estimates for Regression Equations
Cross Section

Equation (3.31A): $\dfrac{I_t}{K_t} = \alpha_0 + \alpha_1 \dfrac{[(P_t + P_{t-1}) \div 2]}{K_t} + \alpha_2 \dfrac{S_{t-1}}{C \cdot K_{t-1}}$

Observations in A Regression = 60

Total A Regressions = 15

	Coefficient for Independent Variables			Multiple Correlation	Standard Error of Estimate
	$\dfrac{(P_t + P_{t-1}) \div 2}{K_t}$	$\dfrac{S_{t-1}}{C \cdot K_{t-1}}$	Intercept		
A Regression[1]					
Smallest	0.0038	−0.0562	−0.0383	0.0472	0.0352
First Quartile	0.0934	−0.0032	−0.0158	0.2750	0.0464
Median	0.2858	0.0169	0.0277	0.4535	0.0503
Third Quartile	0.4133	0.0482	0.0521	0.5574	0.0768
Largest	0.7972	0.1029	0.0939	0.7484	0.1351
B Regression	0.2333	0.0330	—	0.3428	0.0726
	(0.0248)	(0.0115)			
C Regression	0.4673	0.0189	0.0085	0.7351	0.0112
	(0.1287)	(0.0202)			
D Regression	0.2487	0.0273	0.0256	0.3603	0.0725
	(0.0238)	(0.0093)			

Significance Tests[2]

Test Structure[3]

Number of Coefficients Significant at:	One Tail +	Two Tail ±	One Tail +	Two Tail ±	Two Tail ±	One Tail +
10% Level	1	2	2	0	—	—
5% Level	2	0	2	3	—	2
1% Level	9	9	1	0	—	9

[1] Size distributions were obtained for each estimated parameter, so that elements in each row generally refer to estimates from different regression equations.

[2] For A regressions only.

[3] For one tail tests, the *a priori* sign selected is justified in detail in the text.

Summary of Estimates for Regression Equations
Cross-Section

Equation (3.31B): $\dfrac{I_t}{K_t} = \alpha_0 + \alpha_1 \dfrac{[(P_t + P_{t-1}) \div 2]}{K_t} + \alpha_2 \dfrac{S_{t-1}}{C \cdot K_{t-1}} + \alpha_3 \dfrac{S_t}{C \cdot K_t}$

Observations in A Regression = 60   Total A Regressions = 15

	Coefficient for Independent Variables			Intercept	Multiple Correlation	Standard Error of Estimate
	$\dfrac{(P_t + P_{t-1}) \div 2}{K_t}$	$\dfrac{S_{t-1}}{C \cdot K_{t-1}}$	$\dfrac{S_t}{C \cdot K_t}$			
A Regression[1]						
Smallest	0.0052	−0.0631	−0.0603	−0.1328	0.0363	0.0352
First Quartile	0.1176	−0.0114	−0.0407	−0.0249	0.3408	0.0450
Median	0.2613	0.0251	−0.0070	0.0049	0.4697	0.0498
Third Quartile	0.3840	0.0772	0.0279	0.0473	0.5755	0.0824
Largest	0.8296	0.2619	0.0846	0.0943	0.7485	0.1249
B Regression	0.2034	−0.0184	0.0700	—	0.3788	0.0722
	(0.0253)	(0.0153)	(0.0138)			
C Regression	0.3980	0.0123	0.0133	0.0095	0.7400	0.0112
	(0.2113)	(0.0260)	(0.0314)			
D Regression	0.2090	−0.0068	0.0539	0.0090	0.3951	−0.0714
	(0.0246)	(0.0122)	(0.0102)			

Significance Tests[2]

Test Structure[3]

	One Tail	Two Tail	One Tail	Two Tail	One Tail	Two Tail	Two Tail	One Tail
	+	±	+	±	+	±	±	+
Number of Coefficients Significant at:								
10% Level	0	1	0	1	2	1	—	
5% Level	1	0	0	0	0	1	0	
1% Level	9	10	3	3	0	0	11	

[1] Size distributions were obtained for each estimated parameter, so that elements in each row generally refer to estimates from different regression equations.

[2] For A regressions only.

[3] For one tail tests, the *a priori* sign selected is justified in detail in the text.

Summary of Estimates for Regression Equations
Time Series

Equation (3.9S): $\Delta I_t = \alpha_0 + \alpha_2 \Delta K_t + \alpha_3 \Delta S_t$

Observations in A Regression = 14

Total A Regressions = 60

	Coefficient for Independent Variables		Intercept	Multiple Correlation	Relative Prediction Error	Standard Error of Estimate
	ΔK_t	ΔS_t				
A Regression[1]						
Smallest	-2.1957	-0.1395	-275	0.0486	-237.10	104
First Quartile	-0.4403	0.0056	-3	0.3839	-5.88	326
Median	-0.1704	0.0279	91	0.5430	5.94	672
Third Quartile	-0.0162	0.0424	344	0.6963	17.86	1340
Largest	1.5616	0.1170	1649	0.9111	1035.65	3540
Weighted Average[2]	-0.0841	0.0232				
B Regression	-0.1638 (0.0276)	0.0246 (0.0037)	—	0.3298	—	1310
C Regression	0.0152 (0.0252)	0.0205 (0.0063)	-8 (20)	0.5375	1.86	110
D Regression	-0.1381 (0.0227)	0.0257 (0.0032)	85 (46)	0.3207	20.87	1220

Significance Tests[3]

Test Structure[4]

Number of Coefficients Significant at:	One Tail −	Two Tail ±	One Tail +	Two Tail ±	Two Tail ±	One Tail +
10% Level	7	7	5	6	3	—
5% Level	10	9	10	7	4	12
1% Level	10	6	7	4	0	6

[1] Size distributions were obtained for each estimated parameter, so that elements in each row generally refer to estimates from different regression equations.

[2] Weighted by reciprocal of regression coefficient estimated variance.

[3] For A regressions only.

[4] For one tail tests, the *a priori* sign selected is justified in detail in the text.

Summary of Estimates for Regression Equations
Time Series

Equation (3.9SP): $\Delta I_t = \alpha_0 + \alpha_2 \Delta K_t + \alpha_3 \Delta S_t + \alpha_4 \Delta P_t$

Observations in A Regression = 14   Total A Regressions = 60

	Coefficient for Independent Variables			Intercept	Multiple Correlation	Relative Prediction Error	Standard Error of Estimate
	ΔK_t	ΔS_t	ΔP_t				
A Regression[1]							
Smallest	−2.1897	−0.0772	−0.8536	−419	0.2061	−244.00	106
First Quartile	−0.4248	−0.0051	−0.3280	−0	0.4881	−5.83	324
Median	−0.1837	0.0347	−0.0470	91	0.6014	5.74	668
Third Quartile	−0.0242	0.0547	0.1281	379	0.7094	18.44	1390
Largest	1.4458	0.1396	0.7430	1647	0.9147	1081.61	3410
Weighted Average[2]	−0.0889	0.0233	0.0064				
B Regression	−0.1638	0.0246	−0.000025	−	0.3298	−	1370
	(0.0290)	(0.0046)	(0.0422)				
C Regression	0.0050	0.0121	0.3206	−17	0.6135	1.76	103
	(0.0241)	(0.0067)	(0.1144)	(19)			
D Regression	−0.1380	0.0255	0.0026	85	0.3207	20.88	1220
	(0.0228)	(0.0038)	(0.0341)	(46)			

Significance Tests[3]

Test Structure[4]

Number of Coefficients Significant at:	ΔK_t		ΔS_t		ΔP_t		Intercept		Added Variable	
	One Tail	Two Tail	One Tail	Two Tail	One Tail	Two Tail	Two Tail	One Tail	P added to S	S added to P
	−		±	+	±	+	±	+		
10% Level	7	4	12	2	5	1	5	−	1	2
5% Level	10	9	4	2	2	1	2	7	1	2
1% Level	6	5	3	4	0	1	0	6	1	3

[1] Size distributions were obtained for each estimated parameter, so that elements in each row generally refer to estimates from different regression equations.

[2] Weighted by reciprocal of regression coefficient estimated variance.

[3] For A regressions only.

[4] For one tail tests, the *a priori* sign selected is justified in detail in the text.

Summary of Estimates for Regression Equations
Time Series

Equation (3.9P): $\Delta I_t = \alpha_0 + \alpha_2 \Delta K_t + \alpha_4 \Delta P_t$

Observations in A Regression = 14 Total A Regressions = 60

	Coefficient for Independent Variables		Intercept	Multiple Correlation	Relative Prediction Error	Standard Error of Estimate
	ΔK_t	ΔP_t				
A Regression[1]						
Smallest	-2.2175	-1.0977	-185	0.0500	-244.78	105
First Quartile	-0.4227	-0.0677	19	0.2981	-5.65	336
Median	-0.1872	0.0995	121	0.4778	6.17	725
Third Quartile	-0.0153	0.2524	378	0.6325	18.82	1410
Largest	1.4276	0.6762	1752	0.9093	1032.65	3260
Weighted Average[2]	-0.0878	0.0489				
B Regression	-0.1610 (0.0283)	0.1148 (0.0332)	—	0.2568	—	1350
C Regression	0.0268 (0.0213)	0.4140 (0.1040)	-11 (20)	0.5832	1.79	105
D Regression	-0.1271 (0.0233)	0.1240 (0.0297)	132 (47)	0.2343	21.42	1260

Significance Tests[3]

	Test Structure[4]					
	One Tail −	Two Tail ±	One Tail +	Two Tail ±	Two Tail ±	One Tail +
Number of Coefficients Significant at:						
10% Level	6	2	6	3	2	—
5% Level	10	10	8	5	4	7
1% Level	6	6	2	2	0	6

[1] Size distributions were obtained for each estimated parameter, so that elements in each row generally refer to estimates from different regression equations.
[2] Weighted by reciprocal of regression coefficient estimated variance.
[3] For A regressions only.
[4] For one tail tests, the *a priori* sign selected is justified in detail in the text.

Summary of Estimates for Regression Equations
Time Series

$$I_t = \alpha_0 + \alpha_2 K_t + \alpha_3 S_t \quad \text{Equation (3.10S)}$$

Observations in A Regression = 17   Total A Regressions = 60

	Coefficient for Independent Variables		Intercept	Multiple Correlation	Relative Prediction Error	Standard Error of Estimate
	K_t	S_t				
A Regression[1]						
Smallest	−0.33540	−0.05863	−3126	0.05869	0.3220	90
First Quartile	−0.06447	0.01526	−273	0.36200	0.4622	338
Median	−0.00187	0.03293	307	0.61240	0.5524	506
Third Quartile	0.04034	0.05538	1046	0.71670	0.6525	1040
Largest	0.48240	0.09885	4431	0.85820	1.5575	2460
Weighted Average[2]	−0.01491	0.02822				
B Regression	−0.00098 (0.00764)	0.02864 (0.00225)	—	0.5152	—	1020
C Regression	0.01685 (0.00566)	0.02037 (0.00307)	218 (88)	0.9085	0.3417	444
D Regression	0.01197 (0.00281)	0.02350 (0.00137)	203 (49)	0.7203	0.8171	1060

Significance Tests[3]

Test Structure[4]

Number of Coefficients Significant at:	K_t One Tail (−)	K_t Two Tail (±)	S_t One Tail (+)	S_t Two Tail (±)	Intercept Two Tail (±)	Intercept One Tail (+)
10% Level	6	3	4	9	4	—
5% Level	6	5	13	13	7	15
1% Level	2	2	20	11	2	17

[1] Size distributions were obtained for each estimated parameter, so that elements in each row generally refer to estimates from different regression equations.

[2] Weighted by reciprocal of regression coefficient estimated variance.

[3] For A regressions only.

[4] For one tail tests, the a priori sign selected is justified in detail in the text.

Summary of Estimates for Regression Equations
Time Series

Equation (3.10SP): $I_t = \alpha_0 + \alpha_2 K_t + \alpha_3 S_t + \alpha_4 P_t$

Observations in A Regression = 17   Total A Regressions = 60

	Coefficient for Independent Variables			Intercept	Multiple Correlation	Relative Prediction Error	Standard Error of Estimate
	K_t	S_t	P_t				
A Regression[1]							
Smallest	−0.32620	−0.04819	−3.7963	−4367	0.0978	0.2837	92
First Quartile	−0.07571	0.01580	−0.2130	−398	0.4600	0.4595	338
Median	−0.00505	0.03202	−0.0577	373	0.6665	0.5311	492
Third Quartile	0.03910	0.06069	0.1732	887	0.7722	0.6415	1020
Largest	0.36310	0.18090	0.8353	7586	0.8978	1.3621	2150
Weighted Average[2]	−0.01500	0.02565	0.0194				
B Regression	0.00179 (0.00810)	0.02549 (0.00304)	0.0587 (0.0362)	—	0.5176	—	1060
C Regression	0.01545 (0.00546)	0.00892 (0.00556)	0.2656 (0.1094)	162 (88)	0.9177	0.3279	425
D Regression	0.01217 (0.00280)	0.01842 (0.00194)	0.1109 (0.0302)	175 (49)	0.7246	0.8121	1050

Significance Tests[3]

Test Structure

	K_t		S_t		P_t		Intercept		Added Variable	
	One Tail −	Two Tail ±	One Tail +	Two Tail ±	One Tail +	Two Tail ±	Two Tail ±	One Tail +	P added to S	S added to P
Number of Coefficients Significant at:	−	±	+	±	+	±	±	+		
10% Level	4	8	6	5	4	5	1	—	4	5
5% Level	7	0	9	7	3	4	7	13	5	7
1% Level	3	3	11	8	2	1	1	19	1	8

[1] Size distributions were obtained for each estimated parameter, so that elements in each row generally refer to estimates from different regression equations.

[2] Weighted by reciprocal of regression coefficient estimated variance.

[3] For A regressions only.

[4] For one tail tests, the *a priori* sign selected is justified in detail in the text.

Summary of Estimates for Regression Equations
Time Series

Equation (3.10P): $I_t = \alpha_0 + \alpha_2 K_t + \alpha_4 P_t$

Observations in A Regression = 17   Total A Regressions = 60

	Coefficient for Independent Variables		Intercept	Multiple Correlation	Relative Prediction Error	Standard Error of Estimate
	K_t	P_t				
A Regression[1]						
Smallest	−0.16000	−2.9609	−3715	0.0264	0.2750	96
First Quartile	0.00241	0.0421	−552	0.3089	0.4906	341
Median	0.03040	0.2465	70	0.5419	0.5726	559
Third Quartile	0.06980	0.4373	836	0.6706	0.7073	1170
Largest	0.36320	0.7444	4598	0.8976	1.3694	2560
Weighted Average[2]	0.02859	0.1305				
B Regression	0.04605 (0.00618)	0.2536 (0.0280)	−	0.4493	−	1070
C Regression	0.01849 (0.00520)	0.4143 (0.0588)	144 (88)	0.9137	0.3324	431
D Regression	0.02713 (0.00241)	0.3146 (0.0221)	156 (51)	0.6950	0.8469	1100

Significance Tests[3]

Test Structure[4]

Number of Coefficients Significant at:	One Tail −	Two Tail ±	One Tail +	Two Tail ±	One Tail +	Two Tail ±	One Tail +
10% Level	1	6	2	6	4	4	−
5% Level	3	4	7	8	6	6	12
1% Level	0	4	13	7	1	1	12

[1] Size distributions were obtained for each estimated parameter, so that elements in each row generally refer to estimates from different regression equations.

[2] Weighted by reciprocal of regression coefficient estimated variance.

[3] For A regressions only.

[4] For one tail tests, the a priori sign selected is justified in detail in the text.

Summary of Estimates for Regression Equations
Time Series

Equation (3.11S): $I_t = \alpha_0 + \alpha_2 K_t + \alpha_3 S_{t-1}$

Observations in A Regression = 15

Total A Regressions = 60

	Coefficient for Independent Variables		Intercept	Multiple Correlation	Relative Prediction Error	Standard Error of Estimate
	K_t	S_{t-1}				
A Regression[1]						
Smallest	-0.3412	-0.08639	-11182	0.1139	0.3145	83.1
First Quartile	-0.0748	-0.00126	-301	0.4118	0.4627	310.0
Median	0.0020	0.02410	226	0.5745	0.5391	545.0
Third Quartile	0.0594	0.05132	1046	0.6985	0.6608	1039.0
Largest	0.5791	0.33080	7988	0.8509	1.3808	2750.0
Weighted Average[2]	-0.0098	0.02070				
B Regression	0.0040	0.02517	–	0.4511	–	1090.0
	(0.0093)	(0.00282)				
C Regression	0.0193	0.02043	215	0.8980	0.3640	483.0
	(0.0061)	(0.00354)	(96)			
D Regression	0.0167	0.02184	218	0.6960	0.8476	1120.0
	(0.0032)	(0.00164)	(55)			

Significance Tests[3]

	Test Structure[4]					
Number of Coefficients Significant at:	One Tail –	Two Tail +	One Tail +	Two Tail +	Two Tail +	One Tail +
10% Level	2	8	5	7	6	–
5% Level	9	5	11	9	2	13
1% Level	1	0	11	7	4	11

[1] Size distributions were obtained for each estimated parameter, so that elements in each row generally refer to estimates from different regression equations.
[2] Weighted by reciprocal of regression coefficient estimated variance.
[3] For A regressions only.
[4] For one tail tests, the *a priori* sign selected is justified in detail in the text.

Summary of Estimates for Regression Equations
Time Series

Equation (3.11SP): $I_t = \alpha_0 + \alpha_2 K_t + \alpha_3 S_{t-1} + \alpha_4 P_{t-1}$

Observations in A Regression = 15   Total A Regressions = 60

	Coefficient for Independent Variables			Intercept	Multiple Correlation	Relative Prediction Error	Standard Error of Estimate
	K_t	S_{t-1}	P_{t-1}				
A Regression[1]							
Smallest	-0.3428	-0.1241	-3.2423	-11019	0.2882	0.2980	87
First Quartile	-0.0784	-0.0173	-0.1156	-371	0.5045	0.4603	305
Median	0.0077	0.0224	0.0993	319	0.6373	0.5369	538
Third Quartile	0.0609	0.0482	0.3186	940	0.7324	0.6652	991
Largest	0.6235	0.5412	1.0193	15281	0.9434	1.3558	2660
Weighted Average[2]	-0.0023	0.0162	0.0285				
B Regression	0.0085 (0.0100)	0.0205 (0.0037)	0.0869 (0.0412)	—	0.4570	—	1140
C Regression	0.0178 (0.0060)	0.0092 (0.0064)	0.2587 (0.1240)	169 (96)	0.9058	0.3537	469
D Regression	0.0168 (0.0032)	0.0161 (0.0022)	0.1269 (0.0339)	189 (55)	0.7017	0.8415	1110

Significance Tests[3]:

Test Structure[4]

	K_t		S_{t-1}		P_{t-1}		Intercept	Multiple Correlation	Added Variable	
	One Tail −	Two Tail ±	One Tail +	Two Tail ±	One Tail +	Two Tail ±	Two Tail ±	One Tail +	P added to S	S added to P
Number of Coefficients Significant at:										
10% Level	1	10	6	6	4	5	10	—	6	6
5% Level	7	5	12	11	4	3	6	14	3	11
1% Level	1	1	4	1	2	1	1	7	1	1

[1] Size distributions were obtained for each estimated parameter, so that elements in each row generally refer to estimates from different regression equations.
[2] Weighted by reciprocal of regression coefficient estimated variance.
[3] For A regressions only.
[4] For one tail tests, the a priori sign selected is justified in detail in the text.

Summary of Estimates for Regression Equations
Time Series

Equation (3.11P): $I_t = \alpha_0 + \alpha_2 K_t + \alpha_4 P_{t-1}$

Observations in A Regression = 15   Total A Regressions = 60

	Coefficient for Independent Variables		Intercept	Multiple Correlation	Relative Prediction Error	Standard Error of Estimate
	K_t	P_{t-1}				
A Regression[1]						
Smallest	−0.2304	−1.2700	−5576	0.08331	0.2966	86.7
First Quartile	−0.0102	−0.0123	−564	0.3978	0.4884	313.0
Median	0.0308	0.2077	29	0.5308	0.5643	581.0
Third Quartile	0.0754	0.4217	749	0.6672	0.6909	1120.0
Largest	0.6137	0.9834	3233	0.9386	1.4734	2730.0
Weighted Average[2]	0.0293	0.0834				
B Regression	0.0470	0.2252	—	0.4147	—	1060.0
	(0.0070)	(0.0321)				
C Regression	0.0208	0.4092	156	0.9021	0.3571	479.0
	(0.0057)	(0.0674)	(96)			
D Regression	0.0299	0.2939	176	0.6805	0.8650	1100.0
	(0.0027)	(0.0253)	(57)			

Significance Tests[3]

	Test Structure[4]					
	K_t		P_{t-1}		Intercept	Multiple Correlation
Number of Coefficients Significant at:	One Tail	Two Tail	One Tail	Two Tail	Two Tail	One Tail
	−	±	+	±	±	+
10% Level	3	8	10	6	5	—
5% Level	1	7	10	5	9	12
1% Level	0	1	6	5	0	6

[1] Size distributions were obtained for each estimated parameter, so that elements in each row generally refer to estimates from different regression equations.

[2] Weighted by reciprocal of regression coefficient estimated variance.

[3] For A regressions only.

[4] For one tail tests, the *a priori* sign selected is justified in detail in the text.

Summary of Estimates for Regression Equations
Time Series

Equation (3.12S): $I_t = \alpha_0 + \alpha_2 K_t + \alpha_3[(S_t + S_{t-1}) \div 2]$

Observations in A Regression = 15   Total A Regressions = 60

	Coefficient for Independent Variables		Intercept	Multiple Correlation	Relative Prediction Error	Standard Error of Estimate
	K_t	$(S_t + S_{t-1}) \div 2$				
A Regression[1]						
Smallest	−0.2806	−0.0471	−5721	0.0548	0.2976	78.4
First Quartile	−0.1056	0.0169	−310	0.4151	0.4336	301.0
Median	−0.0170	0.0378	366	0.6245	0.5227	534.0
Third Quartile	0.0238	0.0777	1176	0.7578	0.6238	986.0
Largest	0.4545	0.1657	7720	0.9097	1.4845	2600.0
Weighted Average[2]	−0.0291	0.0344				
B Regression	−0.0150	0.0337	–	0.5044	–	1060.0
	(0.0093)	(0.0029)				
C Regression	0.0191	0.0197	214	0.8997	0.3611	479.0
	(0.0060)	(0.0033)	(95)			
D Regression	0.0124	0.0239	201	0.7109	0.8302	1100.0
	(0.0032)	(0.0016)	(54)			

Significance Tests[3]

	Test Structure[4]					
Number of Coefficients Significant at:	One Tail −	Two Tail ±	One Tail +	Two Tail ±	Two Tail ±	One Tail +
10% Level	5	4	6	3	3	–
5% Level	6	6	7	9	6	11
1% Level	5	2	19	14	2	19

[1] Size distributions were obtained for each estimated parameter, so that elements in each row generally refer to estimates from different regression equations.

[2] Weighted by reciprocal of regression coefficient estimated variance.

[3] For A regressions only.

[4] For one tail tests, the *a priori* sign selected is justified in detail in the text.

Summary of Estimates for Regression Equations
Time Series

Equation (3.12SP): $I_t = \alpha_0 + \alpha_2 K_t + \alpha_3[(S_t + S_{t-1}) \div 2] + \alpha_4[(P_t + P_{t-1}) \div 2]$

Observations in A Regression = 15   Total A Regressions = 60

	Coefficient for Independent Variables			Intercept	Multiple Correlation	Relative Prediction Error	Standard Error of Estimate
	K_t	$[(S_t + S_{t-1}) \div 2]$	$[(P_t + P_{t-1}) \div 2]$				
A Regression[1]							
Smallest	-0.3839	-0.1154	-5.7848	-8178	0.0636	0.2497	81
First Quartile	-0.1050	-0.0004	-0.2989	-363	0.5678	0.4162	281
Median	-0.0316	0.0240	0.1011	201	0.7156	0.4983	499
Third Quartile	0.0257	0.0713	0.5599	1211	0.7970	0.5850	920
Largest	0.3578	0.3630	1.9235	16467	0.9561	1.3886	2240
Weighted Average[2]	-0.0295	0.0289	0.0600				
B Regression	-0.0081	0.0257	0.1510	—	0.5137	—	1100
	(0.0099)	(0.0041)	(0.0519)				
C Regression	0.0181	0.0095	0.2346	167	0.9068	0.3519	467
	(0.0059)	(0.0060)	(0.1170)	(96)			
D Regression	0.0125	0.0152	0.1929	153	0.7189	0.8199	1090
	(0.0031)	(0.0024)	(0.0395)	(54)			

Significance Tests[3]

Test Structure[4]

Number of Coefficients Significant at:	K_t		$[(S_t+S_{t-1})\div2]$		$[(P_t+P_{t-1})\div2]$		Intercept		Added Variable	
	One Tail −	Two Tail ±	One Tail +	Two Tail ±	One Tail +	Two Tail ±	Two Tail ±	One Tail +	P added to S +	S added to P +
10% Level	5	2	4	3	8	6	5	—	5	2
5% Level	4	6	10	11	5	6	6	15	6	12
1% Level	6	4	11	8	4	4	2	16	4	8

[1] Size distributions were obtained for each estimated parameter, so that elements in each row generally refer to estimates from different regression equations.
[2] Weighted by reciprocal of regression coefficient estimated variance.
[3] For A regressions only.
[4] For one tail tests, the *a priori* sign selected is justified in detail in the text.

Summary of Estimates for Regression Equations
Time Series

Equation (3.12P): $I_t = \alpha_0 + \alpha_2 K_t + \alpha_4[(P_t + P_{t-1}) \div 2]$

Observations in A Regression = 15   Total A Regressions = 60

	Coefficient for Independent Variables		Intercept	Multiple Correlation	Relative Prediction Error	Standard Error of Estimate
	K_t	$(P_t + P_{t-1}) \div 2$				
A Regression[1]						
Smallest	−0.1761	−4.4785	−6415	0.0636	0.2551	86
First Quartile	−0.0214	0.1171	−611	0.4168	0.4706	307
Median	0.0205	0.3724	3	0.5583	0.5388	558
Third Quartile	0.0793	0.6859	709	0.7178	0.6373	1130
Largest	0.3120	1.5175	3214	0.9541	1.3301	2710
Weighted Average[2]	−0.0206	0.2255				
B Regression	0.0353 (0.0070)	0.3710 (0.0379)	−	0.4685	−	1080
C Regression	0.0216 (0.0056)	0.3897 (0.0639)	50 (96)	0.9024	0.3565	476
D Regression	0.0233 (0.0027)	0.3822 (0.0269)	128 (56)	0.7043	0.8380	1110

Significance Tests[3]

	Test Structure[4]					
	One Tail	Two Tail	One Tail	Two Tail	Two Tail	One Tail
Number of Coefficients Significant at:	−	±	+	±	±	+
10% Level	5	7	10	5	6	−
5% Level	1	5	9	7	6	12
1% Level	1	2	11	9	1	12

[1] Size distributions were obtained for each estimated parameter, so that elements in each row generally refer to estimates from different regression equations.

[2] Weighted by reciprocal of regression coefficient estimated variance.

[3] For A regressions only.

[4] For one tail tests, the *a priori* sign selected is justified in detail in the text.

Summary of Estimates for Regression Equations
Time Series

Equation (3.19): $\Delta \log I_t = \alpha_0 + \alpha_1 \Delta \log K_t + \alpha_2 \Delta \log S_t$

Observations in A Regression = 14

Total A Regressions = 60

	Coefficient for Independent Variables		Intercept	Multiple Correlation	Standard Error of Estimate
	$\Delta \log K_t$	$\Delta \log S_t$			
A Regression[1]					
Smallest	−11.1196	−1.7232	−0.3321	0.0670	0.2605
First Quartile	−5.2741	0.3869	−0.0331	0.4330	0.4665
Median	−1.4456	0.9564	0.0588	0.5815	0.6232
Third Quartile	−0.2700	1.4640	0.1870	0.7352	0.7903
Largest	9.0468	2.7526	2.9524	0.9410	1.9306
B Regression	−0.2771	0.8370	—	0.4770	0.8448
	(0.0901)	(0.0688)			
C Regression	0.1998	0.4552	0.0152	0.5631	0.1379
	(0.2891)	(0.2378)			
D Regression	−0.2589	0.8239	−0.0026	0.4790	0.8028
	(0.0837)	(0.0642)			

Significance Tests[2]

	Test Structure[3]				
Number of Coefficients Significant at:	One Tail −	Two Tail ±	One Tail +	Two Tail ±	One Tail +
10% Level	6	7	8	6	—
5% Level	16	16	13	12	7
1% Level	0	0	16	11	19

[1] Size distributions were obtained for each estimated parameter, so that elements in each row generally refer to estimates from different regression equations.

[2] For A regressions only.

[3] For one tail tests, the a priori sign selected is justified in detail in the text.

Summary of Estimates for Regression Equations
Time Series

Equation (3.20): $\log I = \alpha_0 + \alpha_2 \log K_t + \alpha_3 \log S_t$

Observations in A Regression = 17   Total A Regressions = 60

	Coefficients for Independent Variables		Intercept	Multiple Correlation	Relative Prediction Error	Standard Error of Estimate
	$\log K_t$	$\log S_t$				
A Regression[1]						
Smallest	−4.4197	−3.6898	−35.12	0.0538	0.0346	0.0696
First Quartile	−1.0547	0.6089	−8.02	0.5042	0.0599	0.1782
Median	−0.2466	1.2546	−1.09	0.6764	0.0740	0.2568
Third Quartile	0.3307	1.5069	3.78	0.8155	0.1181	0.4709
Largest	8.1609	2.2685	31.67	0.9220	0.4051	3.0261
Weighted Average[2]	−0.3756	1.0704	–	–	–	–
B Regression	−0.1132	0.9452	–	0.5397	–	0.5741
C Regression	0.3276	0.6684	−3.25	0.9100	0.0612	0.1609
D Regression	0.2120	0.7835	−3.31	0.7698	0.1216	0.6348

Significance Tests[3]

Test Structure[4]

Number of Coefficients Significant at:	$\log K_t$		$\log S_t$		Intercept	Multiple Correlation
	One Tail (−)	Two Tail (±)	One Tail (+)	Two Tail (±)	Two Tail (±)	One Tail (+)
10% Level	5	7	3	4	5	–
5% Level	9	7	9	11	5	13
1% Level	5	4	31	26	5	28

[1] Size distributions were obtained for each estimated parameter, so that elements in each row generally refer to estimates from different regression equations.
[2] Weighted by reciprocal of regression coefficient estimated variance.
[3] For A regressions only.
[4] For one tail tests, the *a priori* sign selected is justified in detail in the text.

Summary of Estimates for Regression Equations
Time Series

Equation (3.21): $\log I = \alpha_0 + \alpha_1 \log K_t + \alpha_2 \log S_{t-1}$

Observations in A Regression = 15

Total A Regressions = 60

	Coefficient for Independent Variables		Intercept	Multiple Correlation	Standard Error of Estimate
	$\log K_t$	$\log S_{t-1}$			
A Regression[1]					
Smallest	-5.5634	-0.9734	-45.0699	0.0983	0.2291
First Quartile	-0.9816	0.5421	-8.9918	0.5230	0.4043
Median	-0.1519	1.1998	-1.2408	0.7242	0.4797
Third Quartile	0.5762	1.5848	3.3209	0.8436	0.6322
Largest	5.6275	2.9444	40.0757	0.9712	1.7367
Weighted Average[2]					
B Regression	-0.2086 (0.0752)	0.8415 (0.0604)	–	0.5816	0.7605
C Regression	0.3641 (0.1192)	0.6376 (0.1247)	-3.2880	0.9161	0.3875
D Regression	0.2163 (0.0482)	0.6910 (0.0461)	-2.4163	0.7671	0.8320

	Significance Tests[3]				Test Structure[4]
	$\log K_t$		$\log S_{t-1}$		
Number of Coefficients Significant at:	One Tail +	Two Tail ±	One Tail -	Two Tail ±	One Tail +
10% Level	3	8	3	6	–
5% Level	8	7	12	13	10
1% Level	3	3	27	20	30

[1] Size distributions were obtained for each estimated parameter, so that elements in each row generally refer to estimates from different regression equations.

[2] Weighted by reciprocal of regression coefficient estimated variance.

[3] For A regressions only.

[4] For one tail tests, the *a priori* sign selected is justified in detail in the text.

Summary of Estimates for Regression Equations
Time Series

Equation (3.22): $\log I = \alpha_0 + \alpha_2 \log[(K_t + K_{t-1}) \div 2] + \alpha_3 \log[(S_t + S_{t-1}) \div 2]$

Observations in A Regression = 15　　　　　　　　　　　　　　　　　　　　　Total A Regressions = 60

	Coefficient for Independent Variables		Intercept	Multiple Correlation	Relative Prediction Error	Standard Error of Estimate
	log $[(K_t + K_{t-1}) \div 2]$	log $[(S_t + S_{t-1}) \div 2]$				
A Regression[1]						
Smallest	−5.9380	−1.7962	−52.93	0.0855	0.0332	0.249
First Quartile	−1.7293	0.7349	−5.98	0.4130	0.0582	0.421
Median	−0.6886	1.4006	1.27	0.7218	0.0757	0.511
Third Quartile	0.2016	1.9532	5.51	0.8292	0.1130	0.676
Largest	8.2087	4.0549	46.41	0.9379	0.3136	1.260
Weighted Average[2]	−0.5609	1.2830				
B Regression	−0.2792 (0.1151)	1.0270 (0.0835)	—	0.5056	—	0.756
C Regression	0.3445 (0.1316)	0.6614 (0.1412)	−3.34 (0.65)	0.9004	0.0652	0.434
D Regression	0.2183 (0.5336)	0.7775 (0.0539)	−3.30 (0.28)	0.7615	0.1223	0.805

Significance Tests[3]

	Test Structure[4]					
	One Tail	Two Tail	One Tail	Two Tail	Two Tail	One Tail
	−	±	+	±	±	+
Number of Coefficients Significant at:						
10% Level	5	4	7	4	1	—
5% Level	9	8	9	9	10	12
1% Level	5	4	25	21	2	26

[1] Size distributions were obtained for each estimated parameter, so that elements in each row generally refer to estimates from different regression equations.
[2] Weighted by reciprocal of regression coefficient estimated variance.
[3] For A regressions only.
[4] For one tail tests, the a priori sign selected is justified in detail in the text.

Summary of Estimates for Regression Equations
Time Series

Equation (3.30A): $\dfrac{I_t}{K_t} = \alpha_0 + \alpha_1 \dfrac{P_t}{K_t} + \alpha_2 \dfrac{S_{t-1}}{C \cdot K_{t-1}}$

Observations in A Regression = 15

Total A Regressions = 60

	Coefficient for Independent Variables		Intercept	Multiple Correlation	Relative Prediction Error	Standard Error of Estimate
	P_t/K_t	$S_{t-1}/C \cdot K_{t-1}$				
A Regression[1]						
Smallest	−1.9205	−0.2314	−0.2682	0.0830	0.2354	0.0095
First Quartile	0.1028	0.0068	−0.0410	0.4072	0.4258	0.0229
Median	0.2293	0.0485	−0.0029	0.6123	0.5236	0.0348
Third Quartile	0.4676	0.0943	0.0462	0.7234	0.7145	0.0491
Largest	1.2655	0.3259	0.2368	0.9041	1.8912	0.2160
Weighted Average[2]	0.1229	0.0396				
B Regression	0.1395 (0.0231)	0.0515 (0.0095)	—	0.3004	—	0.0654
C Regression	0.3748 (0.0661)	−0.1143 (0.0572)	0.1299 (0.0484)	0.6248	0.3863	0.0293
D Regression	0.1953 (0.0203)	0.0393 (0.0092)	0.0217 (0.0082)	0.3388	0.9645	0.0687

Significance Tests[3]

					Test Structure[4]	
Number of Coefficients Significant at:	One Tail +	Two Tail ±	One Tail +	Two Tail ±	Two Tail ±	One Tail +
10% Level	4	5	4	4	7	—
5% Level	11	9	11	7	4	17
1% Level	15	12	15	11	3	21

[1] Size distributions were obtained for each estimated parameter, so that elements in each row generally refer to estimates from different regression equations.

[2] Weighted by reciprocal of regression coefficient estimated variance.

[3] For A regressions only.

[4] For one tail tests, the *a priori* sign selected is justified in detail in the text.

Summary of Estimates for Regression Equations
Time Series

$$\text{Equation (3.30B):} \quad \frac{I_t}{K_t} = \alpha_0 + \alpha_1 \frac{P_t}{K_t} + \alpha_2 \frac{S_{t-1}}{C \cdot K_{t-1}} + \alpha_3 \frac{S_t}{C \cdot K_t}$$

Observations in A Regression = 15   Total A Regressions = 60

	Coefficient for Independent Variables			Intercept	Multiple Correlation	Relative Prediction Error	Standard Error of Estimate
	$\frac{P_t}{K_t}$	$\frac{S_{t-1}}{C \cdot K_{t-1}}$	$\frac{S_t}{C \cdot K_t}$				
A Regression[1]							
Smallest	-2.0534	-0.2239	-0.0960	-0.5089	0.2905	0.2451	0.0079
First Quartile	-0.0781	-0.0313	-0.0016	-0.0412	0.5140	0.4158	0.0219
Median	0.0849	0.0230	0.0409	-0.0095	0.6945	0.4931	0.0303
Third Quartile	0.4142	0.0632	0.1209	0.0342	0.7728	0.6411	0.0475
Largest	1.4110	0.3237	0.9002	0.2300	0.9240	1.5586	0.1900
Weighted Average[2]	0.0431	0.0243	0.0339				
B Regression	0.0752 (0.0263)	0.0097 (0.0123)	0.0631 (0.0114)	—	0.3617	—	0.0662
C Regression	0.3835 (0.0705)	-0.0755 (0.1183)	-0.0696 (0.1852)	0.1604 (0.0948)	0.6260	0.3892	0.0295
D Regression	0.1543 (0.0219)	0.0061 (0.0116)	0.0502 (0.0107)	0.0078 (0.0086)	0.3686	0.9535	0.0679

Significance Tests[3]

Test Structure[4]

	$\frac{P_t}{K_t}$		$\frac{S_{t-1}}{C \cdot K_{t-1}}$		$\frac{S_t}{C \cdot K_t}$		Intercept	Added Variable	
	One Tail	Two Tail	One Tail	Two Tail	One Tail	Two Tail	Two Tail	One Tail	Two Tail
	+	±	+	±	+	±	±	+	
Number of Coefficients Significant at:									
10% Level	8	4	2	5	4	6	2	—	4
5% Level	7	6	10	13	15	11	13	20	14
1% Level	4	2	4	1	3	1	1	24	2

[1] Size distributions were obtained for each estimated parameter, so that elements in each row generally refer to estimates from different regression equations.
[2] Weighted by reciprocal of regression coefficient estimated variance.
[3] For A regressions only.
[4] For one tail tests, the a priori sign selected is justified in detail in the text.

Summary of Estimates for Regression Equations
Time Series

Equation (3.30C): $\dfrac{I_t}{K_t} = \alpha_0 + \alpha_2 \dfrac{S_t}{C \cdot K_t}$

Observations in A Regression = 15

Total A Regressions = 60

	Coefficient for Independent Variables $S_t/C \cdot K_t$	Intercept	Multiple Correlation	Standard Error of Estimate
A Regression[1]				
Smallest	−0.1354	−0.4463	0.0720	0.0097
First Quartile	0.0357	−0.0237	0.3036	0.0249
Median	0.0573	0.0025	0.5154	0.0347
Third Quartile	0.1083	0.0342	0.6613	0.0553
Largest	0.6300	0.2746	0.8767	0.1994

Significance Tests[2]

Test Structure[3]

Number of Coefficients Significant at:	One Tail +	Two Tail ±	One Tail +
10% Level	7	5	–
5% Level	12	13	9
1% Level	23	17	10

[1] Size distributions were obtained for each estimated parameter, so that elements in each row generally refer to estimates from different regression equations.

[2] For A regressions only.

[3] For one tail tests, the *a priori* sign selected is justified in detail in the text.

Summary of Estimates for Regression Equations
Time Series

Equation (3.30D): $\dfrac{I_t}{K_t} = \alpha_0 + \alpha_1 \dfrac{S_t}{C \cdot K_t} + \alpha_2 \dfrac{S_{t-1}}{C \cdot K_{t-1}}$

Observations in A Regression = 15

Total A Regressions = 60

	Coefficient for Independent Variables		Intercept	Multiple Correlation	Standard Error of Estimate
	$\dfrac{S_t}{C \cdot K_t}$	$\dfrac{S_{t-1}}{C \cdot K_{t-1}}$			
A Regression[1]					
Smallest	−0.2742	−0.2717	−0.4252	0.2016	0.0078
First Quartile	0.0283	−0.0511	−0.0380	0.3880	0.0243
Median	0.0669	0.0115	−0.0071	0.6127	0.0315
Third Quartile	0.1158	0.0540	0.0337	0.7306	0.0511
Largest	0.6412	0.3242	0.2580	0.9240	0.1960

Significance Tests[2]

	Test Structure[3]				
	$\dfrac{S_t}{C \cdot K_t}$		$\dfrac{S_{t-1}}{C \cdot K_{t-1}}$		
	One Tail	Two Tail	One Tail	Two Tail	One Tail
Number of Coefficients Significant at:	+	±	+	±	+
10% Level	11	7	3	4	−
5% Level	13	7	7	10	14
1% Level	12	11	5	2	14

[1] Size distributions were obtained for each estimated parameter, so that elements in each row generally refer to estimates from different regression equations.

[2] For A regressions only.

[3] For one tail tests, the *a priori* sign selected is justified in detail in the text.

Summary of Estimates for Regression Equations

Time Series

Equation (3.31A): $\dfrac{I_t}{K_t} = \alpha_0 + \alpha_1 \dfrac{(P_t + P_{t-1})}{2K_t} + \alpha_2 \dfrac{S_{t-1}}{C \cdot K_{t-1}}$

Observations in A Regression = 13   Total A Regressions = 60

	Coefficient for Independent Variables		Intercept	Multiple Correlation	Relative Prediction Error	Standard Error of Estimate
	$\dfrac{(P_t + P_{t-1})}{2K_t}$	$\dfrac{S_{t-1}}{C \cdot K_{t-1}}$				
A Regression[1]						
Smallest	−3.4410	−0.3486	−0.3991	0.1529	0.2077	0.0071
First Quartile	0.1990	−0.0374	−0.0420	0.4632	0.4101	0.0233
Median	0.3919	0.0210	0.0021	0.6066	0.5124	0.0326
Third Quartile	0.8044	0.0830	0.0606	0.7680	0.6834	0.0470
Largest	3.5080	0.5178	0.2709	0.9083	2.1410	0.2500
Weighted Average[2]	0.2523	0.0305				
B Regression	0.2000 (0.0355)	0.0422 (0.0126)	—	0.2700	—	0.0681
C Regression	0.3344 (0.0732)	−0.1548 (0.0543)	0.1692 (0.0460)	0.5898	0.4123	0.0312
D Regression	0.2521 (0.0285)	0.0204 (0.0117)	0.0330 (0.0103)	0.3122	1.0079	0.0709

Significance Tests[3]

Test Structure[4]

Number of Coefficients Significant at:	$\dfrac{(P_t + P_{t-1})}{2K_t}$		$\dfrac{S_{t-1}}{C \cdot K_{t-1}}$		Intercept	
	One Tail +	Two Tail ±	Oen Tail +	Two Tail ±	Two Tail ±	One Tail +
10% Level	5	10	4	4	5	—
5% Level	11	6	6	7	5	11
1% Level	18	15	6	5	6	20

[1] Size distributions were obtained for each estimated parameter, so that elements in each row generally refer to estimates from different regression equations.

[2] Weighted by reciprocal of regression coefficient estimated variance.

[3] For A Regressions only.

[4] For one tail tests, the *a priori* sign selected is justified in detail in the text.

Summary of Estimates for Regression Equations
Time Series

Equation (3.31B): $\dfrac{I_t}{K_t} = \alpha_0 + \alpha_1 \dfrac{P_t + P_{t-1}}{2K_t} + \alpha_2 \dfrac{S_{t-1}}{C \cdot K_{t-1}} + \alpha_3 \dfrac{S_t}{C \cdot K_t}$

Observations in A Regression = 13   Total A Regressions = 60

	Coefficient for Independent Variables			Intercept	Multiple Correlation	Relative Prediction Error	Standard Error of Estimate
	$\dfrac{P_t + P_{t-1}}{2K_t}$	$\dfrac{S_{t-1}}{C \cdot K_{t-1}}$	$\dfrac{S_t}{C \cdot K_t}$				
A Regression[1]							
Smallest	−4.1010	−0.3876	−0.2808	−0.5285	0.2301	0.2149	0.0059
First Quartile	−0.0718	−0.1202	−0.0003	−0.0514	0.5608	0.3742	0.0208
Median	0.2570	−0.0258	0.0722	−0.0002	0.7200	0.5312	0.0302
Third Quartile	0.7762	0.0453	0.1857	0.0383	0.8543	0.6088	0.0435
Largest	3.0430	0.5564	1.1750	0.2797	0.9337	1.8940	0.2190
Weighted Average[2]	0.1331	−0.0045	0.0590				
B Regression	0.1096 (0.0402)	−0.0365 (0.0197)	0.1006 (0.0190)	−	0.3445	−	0.0692
C Regression	0.3455 (0.0772)	−0.1002 (0.1260)	−0.0910 (0.1890)	0.2033 (0.0846)	0.5921	0.4151	0.0314
D Regression	0.1940 (0.0301)	−0.0489 (0.0176)	0.0896 (0.0172)	0.0171 (0.0155)	0.3579	0.9913	0.0697

Significance Tests[3] — Test Structure[4]

Number of Coefficients Significant at:	$\dfrac{P_t+P_{t-1}}{2K_t}$ One Tail +	Two Tail ±	$\dfrac{S_{t-1}}{C \cdot K_{t-1}}$ One Tail +	Two Tail ±	$\dfrac{S_t}{C \cdot K_t}$ One Tail +	Two Tail ±	Intercept Two Tail ±	Multiple Correlation One Tail +	Added Variable +
10% Level	7	3	1	5	3	4	1	−	3
5% Level	4	6	2	1	13	11	7	12	11
1% Level	9	6	2	6	6	3	7	24	3

[1] Size distributions were obtained for each estimated parameter, so that elements in each row generally refer to estimates from different regression equations.

[2] Weighted by reciprocal of regression coefficient estimated variance.

[3] For A regressions only.

Summary of Estimates for Regression Equations
Time Series

Equation (3.34A): $I_t = \alpha_0 + \alpha_1(\hat{\beta}S_t - K_t)$

Observations in A Regression = 13

Total A Regressions = 60

	Coefficient for Independent Variable $\hat{\beta}S_t - K_t$	Intercept	Multiple Correlation	Relative Prediction Error	Standard Error of Estimate
A Regression[1]					
Smallest	−0.5798	103.8	0.0170	0.3590	8
First Quartile	0.0280	395.8	0.2417	0.5236	110
Median	0.0877	810.9	0.4294	0.5822	343
Third Quartile	0.1726	1572.2	0.5857	0.7307	1,388
Largest	0.7238	3434.9	0.9147	1.4812	9,712
B Regression	0.0987	—	0.3320	—	1,157
C Regression					
D Regression	0.1527	1078.3	0.4222	1.0695	1,772

Significance Tests[2]

Test Structure[3]

	Coefficient		Intercept	
Number of Coefficients Significant at:	One Tail +	Two Tail ±	Two Tail ±	One Tail +
10% Level	8	4	1	—
5% Level	9	12	5	15
1% Level	10	4	53	5

[1] Size distributions were obtained for each estimated parameter, so that elements in each row generally refer to estimates from different regression equations.

[2] For A regressions only.

[3] For one tail tests, the *a priori* sign selected is justified in detail in the text.

Summary of Estimates for Regression Equations
Time Series

Equation (3.34B): $I_t = \alpha_0 + \alpha_1(\hat{\beta}S_t - K_t) + \alpha_2(\hat{\beta}S_{t-1} - K_{t-1})$

Observations in A Regression = 13   A Regression = 60

	Coefficient for Independent Variables		Intercept	Multiple Correlation	Relative Prediction Error	Standard Error of Estimate
	$\hat{\beta}S_t - K_t$	$\hat{\beta}S_{t-1} - K_{t-1}$				
A Regression[1]						
Smallest	-0.4975	-1.5267	100	0.0755	0.2525	9
First Quartile	0.0225	-0.0867	444	0.3073	0.4656	105
Median	0.0685	0.0383	756	0.4501	0.5735	220
Third Quartile	0.1215	0.1587	1624	0.6602	0.7053	914
Largest	0.9803	1.4321	3423	0.9658	1.5277	7,785
Weighted Average[2]	0.0644	0.0710	-	-	-	-
B Regression	0.0863	0.0717	-	0.3866	-	1,186
C Regression						
D Regression	0.1213	0.0100	1004	0.4744	1.0392	1,673

Significance Tests[3]

Test Structure[4]

Number of Coefficients Significant at:	$\hat{\beta}S_t - K_t$		$\hat{\beta}S_{t-1} - K_{t-1}$		Intercept		Added Variable
	One Tail +	Two Tail ±	One Tail +	Two Tail ±	Two Tail ±	One Tail +	-
10% Level	3	5	5	3	0	-	-
5% Level	8	3	6	7	13	6	-
1% Level	5	5	8	6	103	14	19

[1] Size distributions were obtained for each estimated parameter, so that elements in each row generally refer to estimates from different regression equations.

[2] Weighted by reciprocal of regression coefficient estimated variance.

[3] For A regressions only.

[4] For one tail tests, the a priori sign selected is justified in detail in the text.

Summary of Estimates for Regression Equations
Time Series

Equation (3.35A): $I_t = \alpha_0 + \alpha_1\{[\hat{\beta}(S_t + S_{t-1})] \div 2] - K_t\}$

Observations in A Regression = 13   A Regression = 60

	Coefficient for Independent Variable $[\hat{\beta}(S_t + S_{t-1}) \div 2] - K_t$	Intercept	Multiple Correlation	Standard Error of Estimate
A Regression[1]				
Smallest	−0.6974	120	0.0042	95
First Quartile	0.0193	503	0.1713	329
Median	0.1249	934	0.3160	681
Third Quartile	0.2376	2076	0.4813	1429
Largest	2.6214	4453	0.8350	4148
B Regression	0.1335	—	0.2755	1315
C Regression	0.3489 (0.0770)		0.5178	
D Regression	0.1973	1210	0.3605	1658

Significance Tests[2]

Number of Coefficients Significant at:	One Tail +	Two Tail ±	Test Structure[3] One Tail +
10% Level	3	8	—
5% Level	9	5	4
1% Level	9	5	7

[1] Size distributions were obtained for each estimated parameter, so that elements in each row generally refer to estimates from different regression equations.

[2] For A regressions only.

[3] For one tail tests, the *a priori* sign selected is justified in detail in the text.

Summary of Estimates for Regression Equations
Time Series

Equation (3.35B): $I_t = \alpha_0 + \alpha_1[\hat{\beta}\frac{(S_t + S_{t-1})}{2} - K_t] + \alpha_2[\hat{\beta}\frac{(S_{t-1} + S_{t-2})}{2} - K_{t-1}]$

Observations in A Regression = 13   A Regression = 60

	Coefficient for Independent Variables		Intercept	Multiple Correlation	Standard Error of Estimate
	$[\hat{\beta}\frac{(S_t + S_{t-1})}{2} - K_t]$	$[\hat{\beta}\frac{(S_{t-1}+S_{t-2})}{2} - K_{t-1}]$			
A Regression[1]					
Smallest	−0.8446	−3.8934	116	0.1125	87
First Quartile	−0.0274	−0.2463	521	0.3209	328
Median	0.1146	0.0006	850	0.4415	591
Third Quartile	0.2852	0.1523	2078	0.6355	1362
Largest	2.5434	2.0399	4000	0.8798	3261
Weighted Average[2]					
B Regression	0.1197	0.0328	–	0.2810	1367
C Regression	−0.3222	0.7924	–	0.5592	
	(0.3630)	(0.4193)			
D Regression	0.1526	0.0818	1179	0.3761	1647

Significance Tests[3]

Number of Coefficients Significant at:	Test Structure[4]						Added Variable
	One Tail +	Two Tail ±	One Tail +	Two Tail ±	One Tail +	Two Tail ±	
10% Level	4	4	1	4	–	–	–
5% Level	7	6	7	7	4	–	–
1% Level	7	4	2	1	4	–	19

[1] Size distributions were obtained for each estimated parameter, so that elements in each row generally refer to estimates from different regression equations.

[2] Weigted by reciprocal of regression coefficient estimated variance.

[3] For A regressions only.

[4] For one tail tests, the *a priori* sign selected is justified in detail in the text.

CHAPTER 9

CAPACITY MODEL COEFFICIENTS

9.1 Introduction

Intense interest in the manner in which capacity pressures affect investment demand has been evident in recent economic literature. To advance further understanding on this matter, all the reaction coefficients which have been estimated for a great many different equations are collected in Table 9.1. Distinctions drawn between profit models and accelerator models will be thrust into the background for the purpose of this chapter. Attention is focussed on behavior of individual firms on the assumption that they behave according to the reaction coefficients of capacity-induced investment behavior.

9.2 Some Reaction Magnitudes

A. *Description*

While there is moderate variation in the estimates of Table 9.1 the overwhelming impression emerges that for the *average* firm, the reaction coefficient has an upper limit of 0.15 and more typically, reaction coefficients are in the neighborhood of 0.08. These results are consistent with Koyck's findings described in summary in Chapter 2. They are also approximately consistent with those of Grunfeld, although he used a different model.[1]

Having stated the principal implications of the table, it is now desirable to have a more detailed survey of the large variety of estimates contained in this table. Discussion will be restricted mostly to central tendencies which are either the only estimates, in the case of B and C regressions and the weighted averages (where the weights are recipro-

---

[1] YEHUDA GRUNFELD, "Determinants of Corporate Investment," in ARNOLD C. HARBERGER, Editor, *The Demand for Durable Goods*, 1960.

TABLE 9.1

Time Series Reaction Coefficient Estimates

Equation	Sales Slope			Capital Stock Slope					
				Depreciation Unadjusted			Depreciation Adjusted		
	First Quartile	Central Value	Third Quartile	First Quartile	Central Value	Third Quartile	First Quartile	Central Value	Third Quartile
(3.9S) A regression	—	0.0633	—	0.0162	0.1704	0.4403	—	0.2099	—
Weighted Average of A Slopes	—	0.0523	—	—	0.0841	—	—	0.1236	—
B regression	—	0.0558	—	—	0.1638	—	—	0.2033	—
C regression	—	0.0788	—	—	−0.1031	—	—	−0.0636	—
(3.10S) A regression	0.1123	0.0594	0.0341	−0.0403	0.0019	0.0645	0.0009	0.0576	0.1106
Weighted Average of A Slopes	—	0.0641	—	—	0.0149	—	—	0.0544	—
B regression	—	0.0650	—	—	0.0010	—	—	0.0405	—
C regression	—	0.0979	—	—	0.0057	—	—	0.0401	—
(3.11S) A regression	0.0971	0.0441	0.0006	−0.0594	0.0020	0.0748	−0.0261	0.0441	0.1147
Weighted Average of A Slopes	—	0.0470	—	—	0.0098	—	—	0.0493	—
B regression	—	0.0571	—	—	−0.0040	—	—	0.0355	—
C regression	—	0.0595	—	—	−0.0072	—	—	0.0323	—
(3.12S) A regression	0.1428	0.0806	0.0369	−0.0239	0.0170	0.1057	0.0189	0.0687	0.1481
Weighted Average of A Slopes	—	0.0781	—	—	0.0291	—	—	0.0686	—
B regression	—	0.0765	—	—	−0.0154	—	—	0.0545	—
C regression	—	0.1144	—	—	−0.0577	—	—	0.0972	—

Table 9.1 (*continued*)

Equation		$\dfrac{S_t}{C \cdot K_t}$			$\dfrac{S_{t-1}}{C \cdot K_{t-1}}$		
		First Quartile	Central Value	Third Quartile	First Quartile	Central Value	Third Quartile
(3.30A)	A regression				0.0943	0.0485	0.0068
	Weighted Average					0.0396	
	B regression					0.0515	
	C regression					0.0366	
(3.30B)	A regression	0.1209	0.0409	−0.0016	0.0632	0.0230	−0.0313
	Weighted Average		0.0339			0.0243	
	B regression		0.0631			0.0097	
	C regression		0.0348			0.0101	
(3.30C)	A regression	0.1106	0.0582	0.0358			
(3.30D)	A regression	0.1160	0.0674	0.0314	0.0554	0.0171	−0.0467
(3.31A)	A regression				0.0830	0.0210	−0.0374
	Weighted Average					0.0305	
	B regression					0.0422	
	C regression					−0.1548	
(3.31B)	A regression	0.1857	0.0722	−0.0003	0.0453	−0.0258	−0.1202
	Weighted Average		0.0590			−0.0045	
	B regression		0.1006			−0.0365	
	C regression		−0.0910			−0.1002	

Sum of Coefficients for Equation (3.30D) Estimated from
$S_t/C \cdot K_t$ and $S_{t-1}/C \cdot K_{t-1}$

First Quartile	Central Value	Third Quartile
0.1293	0.0823	0.0362

Equation		$\hat{\beta}S_t - K_t$			$\hat{\beta}S_{t-1} - K_{t-1}$		
		First Quartile	Central Value	Third Quartile	First Quartile	Central Value	Third Quartile
(3.34A)	A regression	0.1726	0.0877	0.028			
	B regression		0.0987				
(3.34B)	A regression	0.1215	0.0685	0.0225	0.1587	0.0383	−0.0867
	B regression		0.0863			0.0717	

Equation		$\hat{\beta}(S_t + S_{t-1})/2 - K_t$			$\hat{\beta}(S_{t-1} + S_{t-2})/2 - K_{t-1}$		
		First Quartile	Central Value	Third Quartile	First Quartile	Central Value	Third Quartile
(3.35A)	A regression	0.2376	0.1249	0.0193			
	B regression		0.1335				
(3.35B)	A regression	0.2852	0.1146	−0.0274	0.1523	0.0006	−0.2463
	B regression		0.1197			0.0328	

cal of parameter variance estimates), or medians in the case of the A or individual firm regressions. Only estimates from time series are tabulated since the findings of Chapters 5 and 6 have inhibited reliance on the cross-section estimates.

The accelerator model can be tested and estimated in a number of different ways. Here are the most relevant alternatives. The capacity-accelerator model can be written in the following way:

$$I_t = b\beta X_t - bK_t. \qquad (9.1)$$

It is clear that the reaction coefficient is not identifiable in the regression parameter estimates of the expected sales variable (which in our case is taken to be either current sales, lagged sales, or the simple average of these two) unless β is known. An extraneous estimate of β, the capital coefficient, however has been used previously in the cross-section estimates as a measure of capital intensity, described in detail in Chapter 3. It is the average capital-output ratio during periods of high level capacity utilization. This estimate has been used in the cross-section regressions as the variable C, the reciprocal of the estimated capital coefficient. The parameter estimate of the reaction coefficient from the capital stock variable however, may be biased because depreciation, proportional to the capital stock, may also be measured by this coefficient. As a variant to equation (9.1) therefore, we write equation (9.1a) below, where d represents effects of "depreciation" to be invested during the current period.

$$I_t = b\beta X_t - (b - d)K_t. \qquad (9.1a)$$

In the case where depreciation is a pertinent variable, it is desirable to estimate the depreciation fraction from the data, which we have done for 1949 and 1950 when straight line depreciation prevailed, unsullied by various forms of more rapid write off, and used this estimate to adjust the regression estimate of the capital stock parameter. The different methods used to estimate the reaction coefficients for Equations (3.9) through (3.12) are indicated by the top column headings. Reaction coefficients estimated for all the remaining equations did not require the rectification procedures associated with the linear regressions.

Equations (3.10) through (3.12) have numerous similarities although the magnitudes differ slightly among the different equations. One of the principal similarities (to be discussed soon in a related context) is that the median depreciation adjusted capital stock coefficient is strikingly similar to that of the sales variable. As usual, this does not hold true for Equation (3.9) with the possible exception of the average data equation. The sales slope estimate of the A regression coefficient, for instance, is one-third of the capital stock estimate. Furthermore, the median capital stock value of 0.21 for the A regressions is the highest one of all. An explanation for the sharp difference between the magnitude of this coefficient and that for the remaining original units equation has been sought without success. It should be noted, however, that when averages are applied, either to the slopes individually in a weighted average or to the data according to the averaged data regression, the estimated magnitude of the reaction coefficient is much smaller. Indeed, perversely enough, it is negative for the average data regression. However, all the central estimates for Equations (3.10), (3.11), and (3.12) possess highly similar magnitudes. This might provide grounds for mistrusting the A regression estimates, which are subject to extremely large dispersion, in part because of the poor fit. While this clear inconsistency is uncomfortable since no highly persusaive explanation for it has been found, the remaining estimates are uniformly consistent. While one can view the first difference estimate of the reaction coefficients as an upper bound, most reliance has been placed upon the others. For a given equation, the sales slope estimates are quite like those for the remaining equations. Since it will be shown that the acceleration hypothesis is consistent with depreciation-adjusted slopes for capital stock for all the other original units equations, greater faith in them is warranted than for Equation (3.9).

The distinct impression emerges from a comparison of the several different sets of reaction coefficients in Table 9.1 for central values in Equations (3.10), (3.11), and (3.12): irrespective of estimation method, the coefficients are closely bunched. This is true when the estimates for a given slope from different equations are compared, and it is also true when comparisons are drawn between the depreciation-adjusted capital stock slope and the sales estimated slope. In nearly all cases the capital stock slope unadjusted for depreciation is smaller than the others. The main observable difference is that the average data estimate from the sales coefficient is larger than the three other estimates. This holds true for the depreciation adjusted capital stock estimate for Equation (3.12), but not for the equivalent coefficients on Equations (3.10) and (3.11). However, concentrating on the minutiae does not serve our purposes well: the fact remains that the median estimates are all of the same order of magnitude, the clear majority of them falling between 0.05 and 0.10. Equation (3.12), for which some preference has been expressed on statistical grounds, has somewhat higher coefficients than the other two, but still falls within the same brackets.

It is also well worth comment that the third quartile value, chosen to represent a "reasonable extreme," varies between about 0.10 and 0.15. Hence there is a fair concentration of the estimate, no widespread dispersion showing up to indicate that a significant fraction of firms have rapid rates of capital stock adjustment. Our results therefore confirm earlier findings, on a much more intensive basis than heretofore, that the rates of reaction to capacity pressures are indeed quite small. Nor are these results altered when alternative estimation procedures are applied.

Equations (3.30A) through (3.30D) and (3.31A) and (3.31B) measure the gross investment divided by fixed assets against capacity utilization. The internal profit rate on capital is also included in the first and last pair of estimating equations. Equations (3.30A) and (3.30B) thus represent behavior in which the capital requirements of the preceding (and/or current) year are conditioned by the current profit rate in determining this period's investment rate. On Equations (3.30A) and (3.31A), reaction coefficients estimated for lagged capacity utilization, depending upon the method of estimation, range from about 0.02 to 0.04. When the current rate of capacity utilization is included in (3.30B) and (3.31B), the picture changes slightly, while the emphasis on low reaction coefficients remains unchanged. The current capacity rate coefficient varies between 0.03 and 0.10, the higher values being associated with (3.31B). If firms are considered to be in a situation of steady growth, it is then appropriate to express the total reaction to capacity pressures by the sum of the two reaction coefficients. In this case, the sum of the coefficients is about 0.06 to 0.07. These are the same magnitudes as those estimated for the single coefficient in the linear models 10 through 12.

Equations (3.30C) and 3.30D) represent pure accelerator versions in which current and lagged capacity pressures are present without any profit variable. In short, this is a pure demand model with no hybrid supply or demand expectation effects from profits. The estimates are consistent with all that has gone on before. The median current reaction coefficient is about 0.07, while the lagged reaction coefficient is about 0.017, indicating a substantially greater weight on current than on prior period capacity pressures. This result is qualitatively consistent with results associated with Equation (3.20) and (3.31) when the profits have been included. The median sum of the coefficients is about 0.08, slightly higher than when profits are included, which, after all, is what one would expect since the profit and capacity utilization variables are positively correlated. Still, the sum of the coefficients in the pure acceleration model for the upper quartile remains a "sensible" magnitude, about 0.129, similar to those found earlier in the linear models.

A final method of viewing reaction coefficients is to make a direct estimate of the capacity requirements by using the estimated capital coefficients multiplied by the current level of sales, and subtracting from this amount, the capital stock at the beginning of the period to create a quantity of "desired" additional capital. Then all that there remains to do is to use statistical methods, i.e., least squares regression to estimate the reaction coefficients directly. These results are shown for Equations (3.34) and (3.35). Equation (3.34A), reflecting only current capacity requirements, has a median value of 0.09, only slightly higher than for most other equations, while the sum of median values of current and lagged capacity requirements of Equation (3.34B) is just slightly more. Equation (3.35) central values are the highest of all, but still cluster around 0.12. The most interesting difference between (3.34B) (but not (3.35B)) and Equations (3.30) and (3.31) is the fairly large weight given to the preceding period capacity requirement. The weighted average and the B regression give equal weights to the current and the preceding period coefficients. Furthermore, the sum of these coefficients is in the neighborhood of 0.15. Because this represents a direct test of the capacity-accelerator hypothesis, and its coefficients turn out to be moderately higher than the transformed equations discussed up until this point, the possibility is raised that the other estimates are subject to moderate downward bias. Still, when all is said and done, the typical reaction coefficient upper limit is about 0.15 (when we sum both the current and lagged capacity requirements, for instance), and the "plausible upper extreme" third quartile measurement is 0.28, also from Equations (3.34B) and (3.35B).

The conclusions reached so far can be simply stated. Using the same body of data in a variety of different ways, estimated reaction coefficients for capital stock requirements are quite low. Since we have used a number of transformations and these yield rather consistent results, there should be few lingering doubts that it was the peculiarity of an arbitrary equation which led to results of a particular sort. By the same token, emphasis upon the similarity of the results, while encouraging, is not altogether surprising, since we have estimated coefficients suggested by one particular theory using the same basic body of data.

B. *Inter-firm Comparisons*

Negative results must be recorded for efforts to explain inter-firm variation in reaction coefficients. The three reaction coefficients estimated for each firm according to Equations (3.10) through (3.12) were correlated with two major characteristics of firm investment behavior over the period, gross rate of investment measured by average investment divided by capital stock and size, represented by average capital stock. These simple correlations are recorded in Table 9.2.

TABLE 9.2

Reaction Coefficient Correlations with Size and Growth

Equation	Size ($\bar{K}_j$)			Growth ($\bar{I}_j/\bar{K}_j$)		
	Sales Slope	Capital Stock Slope	Adjusted Capital Stock Slope	Sales Slope	Capital Stock Slope	Adjusted Capital Stock Slope
(3.10)	−0.0338	0.1381	0.1012	0.1311	−0.1092	−0.0265
(3.11)	0.0061	0.1199	0.0923	0.2480	−0.1216	−0.0610
(3.12)	0.0327	0.1984	0.1684	0.1605	−0.1407	−0.0712

Nearly all of the correlations are small. A scatter diagram, not reproduced here, did not indicate that the low correlation with growth could be attributed to important nonlinearities.

For what it is worth, however, the following characteristics are discernible. First, larger firms have larger reaction coefficients, an observation apparent on the capital stock coefficients but not on the sales coefficients. This particular result may have interesting implications, although they are not related in an obvious way to the theoretical or institutional considerations of Chapter 2. Since the correlations are so close to zero anyhow, further discussion is not warranted. Second, conflicting evidence exists on the influence of growth rates on reaction coefficients. The consistently largest correlation exists between this measure and the sales slope estimate, but the next strongest correlation, with opposite sign unfortunately, is on the unadjusted capital stock estimate. The weakest, but still negative, correlation exists between growth and the adjusted capital stock estimate. Since least faith can be put in the unadjusted estimates, the preponderant evidence, still of the weakest sort, favors the view that the positive sales estimate, growth correlation, most correctly represents the true situation.

Encouragement can be derived from the fact that a positive correlation between the rate of investment and reaction coefficient has been found. This was certainly one of the implications of the theoretical discussions of Chapter 2. However, this set of firms did not behave in ways that would readily identify the theoretical relationship. The reaction coefficient would, one expects, show up on a cross-sectional comparison of firm behavioral parameters where these were fairly substantial variations in the rates of growth. Such is not the case here. The average rate of growth for all firms' fixed assets was 7 per cent. This was associated for all sixty firms again with a standard deviation of 0.03. Hence the average rate of growth was not especially high, and the dispersion around it was fairly tight. Should the relation between growth and rates of reaction be of principal interest, it ought to be studied for a sample of firms with a wide spread in their individual rates of growth, and with a high average rate.

C. Statistical Tests

The t statistic has been used to test for the significance of the sum of two parameters, here two alternative estimates of the same reaction coefficient with opposite sign. The first reaction coefficient estimate comes from the sales parameter adjusted by dividing it with an estimate of the capital coefficient. The second estimate is derived from the capital stock coefficient in two alternative ways. In the first case, it is unadjusted and in the second it is adjusted by subtracting from the estimated regression coefficient an estimate of the depreciation rate in accordance with equation (9.1a). The results in Table 9.3 are tabulated in full detail in order to see whether the entire sample distribution provides a good representation of a t distribution with zero mean. For results which do *not* take account of the depreciation effect, the answer is most emphatically not; the distribution is highly weighted toward the positive values for Equations (3.10), (3.11), and (3.12) with only nine to fifteen of the sixty sample statistics in the negative range. In brief, the median t statistic is about unity for the entire distribution, and the frequency with which the test statistics exceed the theoretical critical values so high that no extended commentary is needed: when no adjustment has been made for depreciation, the accelerator hypothesis has been strongly rejected.

Moderate encouragement, however, is aroused when the capital stock regression coefficient is adjusted for depreciation. The median value for t is always extremely small. Even when the median departs moderately from zero, it is only necessary to shift one or two items away to find an approximately zero t statistic. This outcome might be viewed in two ways. First, it may be taken as joint validation of the depreciation effect in combination with an accelerator, although it must be realized that this is assumed to be the case prior to the execution of the statistical test. It may also be taken for moderately strong support of the accelerator theory, although which of the sales expectation variables is the most relevant does not emerge from comparison of the different equation results, since all of them are in close agreement.

Confirmation, however, is not to be found for the t statistic. It is "too thick" in the tails, particularly the positive tail. That is, the probability of finding t values on the null hypothesis of equality between reaction coefficients estimated from sales and the capital stock indicates that the sales estimated coefficient exceeds the capital stock estimated coefficient with a higher degree of frequency than would occur if the model were completely valid. Critical values at various significance levels have been tabulated at the bottom of the table.

9.3 Autonomous Investment and Variable Reaction Speeds

A. *Cyclical Intercept Patterns*

Charts 9.1 through 9.4 show the cross-section intercept in each year for Equations (3.9) through (3.12). These intercepts contain information that can be interpreted in two ways. They can be viewed as estimates of autonomous investment; after all, intercepts are the mean firm rate of investment after the principal endogenous variables have been taken into account. However, since the intercepts have such large year-to-year variation, they may alternatively be viewed as a variable speed of reaction factor. When the intercept is big, it can be stated that for this particular year the adjustment to a desired stock is especially rapid.

TABLE 9.3

Test for Equality of Reaction Coefficients in Capacity Models *

Test Without Depreciation Adjustment			Test With Depreciation Adjustment		
(3.10S)	(3.11S)	(3.12S)	(3.10S)	(3.11S)	(3.12S)
4.732	4.633	4.496	3.393	3.148	3.616
4.546	4.442	4.485	2.859	2.440	3.100
4.035	4.393	4.279	2.839	2.225	2.859
3.776	3.126	3.993	2.403	2.209	2.776
3.580	2.907	3.508	2.386	1.982	2.552
3.558	2.758	2.445	2.216	1.923	2.148
3.402	2.746	3.389	2.042	1.868	2.026
3.163	2.698	3.179	1.943	1.582	1.850
3.111	2.695	3.014	1.913	1.543	1.836
3.010	2.450	3.009	1.903	1.458	1.691
3.018	2.307	2.626	1.738	1.372	1.657
2.746	2.262	2.619	1.572	1.354	1.366
2.672	2.139	2.445	1.578	1.328	1.310
2.647	2.122	2.425	1.445	1.223	1.202
2.612	2.070	2.154	1.301	1.110	1.207
2.597	2.037	2.036	1.130	1.019	1.116
2.523	2.034	2.015	1.036	0.897	0.925
2.432	1.893	1.955	0.845	0.870	0.775
2.392	1.743	1.890	0.793	0.775	0.767
2.323	1.601	1.754	0.685	0.663	0.714
2.035	1.564	1.734	0.616	0.661	0.694
1.927	1.525	1.597	0.597	0.624	0.684
1.805	1.476	1.495	0.583	0.599	0.565
1.716	1.459	1.278	0.582	0.388	0.478
1.549	1.360	1.260	0.573	0.271	0.426
1.469	1.298	1.268	0.561	0.255	0.379
1.370	1.243	1.247	0.550	0.060	0.369
1.304	1.136	1.234	0.499	0.045	0.270
1.233	1.137	1.207	0.447	0.036	0.269

Median ←———→ Median

1.180	1.086	1.185	0.418	0.021	0.207
1.175	0.912	1.171	0.109	0.001	0.080

* These rank ordered t statistics are based on the usual t test for the sum of two regression coefficients. The coefficients are described in the accompanying text.

The intercepts in Equation (3.10) follow a strongly cyclical pattern, perhaps because reactions are faster, the higher the level of activity, or alternatively, the greater the positive difference between desired and actual capital stock. There is complete sympathy with cyclical magnitudes pre-war except in 1941. Post-war, the large positive intercepts in 1946 and 1947 gave way to virtually zero in 1948 and small negative

Table 9.3 (continued)

Test Without Depreciation Adjustment			Test With Depreciation Adjustment		
(3.10S)	(3.11S)	(3.12S)	(3.10S)	(3.11S)	(3.12S)
1.086	0.878	1.176	0.089	0.001	0.064
1.082	0.793	1.163	0.005	0.000	0.057
1.062	0.755	0.959	−0.030	−0.004	0.048
0.968	0.755	0.853	−0.116	−0.077	−0.041
0.818	0.659	0.821	−0.131	−0.245	−0.148
0.767	0.655	0.819	−0.150	−0.302	−0.235
0.762	0.501	0.817	−0.157	−0.306	−0.342
0.751	0.392	0.731	−0.209	−0.365	−0.344
0.726	0.357	0.466	−0.271	−0.366	−0.346
0.720	0.232	0.369	−0.305	−0.465	−0.364
0.719	0.173	0.330	−0.313	−0.557	−0.385
0.685	0.123	0.316	−0.481	−0.641	−0.421
0.652	0.084	0.312	−0.597	−0.711	−0.608
0.474	0.038	0.236	−0.599	−0.723	−0.924
0.445	0.003	0.162	−0.736	−0.835	−0.941
0.405	0.000	0.043	−0.792	−0.852	−1.020
0.255	−0.041	0.027	−0.904	−0.887	−1.098
0.195	−0.049	−0.189	−0.971	−1.077	−1.126
0.189	−0.093	−0.212	−0.978	−1.272	−1.132
0.033	−0.153	−0.296	−1.124	−1.286	−1.153
−0.046	−0.184	−0.334	−1.145	−1.349	−1.198
−0.132	−0.367	−0.477	−1.140	−1.412	−1.258
−0.183	−0.542	−0.525	−1.170	−1.507	−1.269
−0.344	−0.716	−0.609	−1.235	−1.667	−1.369
−0.667	−1.212	−0.717	−1.317	−1.746	−1.399
−0.677	−1.399	−0.785	−1.440	−1.960	−1.546
−0.702	−1.411	−1.010	−1.475	−2.125	−1.671
−1.128	−1.607	−1.363	−1.519	−2.241	−2.054
−3.122	−2.476	−1.808	−3.605	−2.795	−2.118

Two-tail t Statistic Critical Values

Equation	(3.10)	(3.11)	(3.12)
10% Level	1.761	1.782	1.782
5% Level	2.145	2.179	2.179
1% Level	2.977	3.055	3.055

values in 1949, possibly indicating that the endogenous "speed of response" adequately portrayed entrepreneurial desires. 1950, 1951 and 1952, a period when expectations were strongly influenced by the Korean War, saw very high intercept values. Here we observe a divergence in behavior between the profit intercept and the sales intercept (which is similar to the combined sales, profit intercept). Whereas the autono-

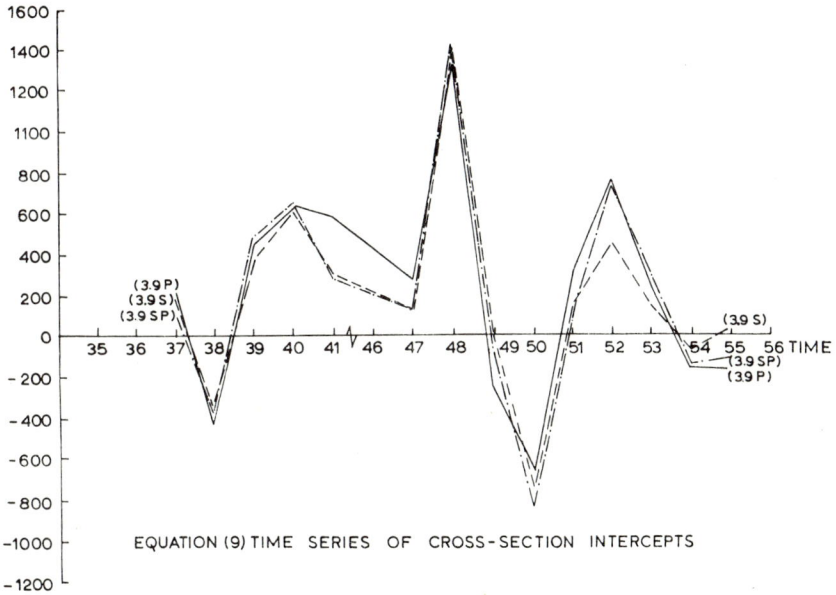

EQUATION (9) TIME SERIES OF CROSS-SECTION INTERCEPTS

Chart 9.1.

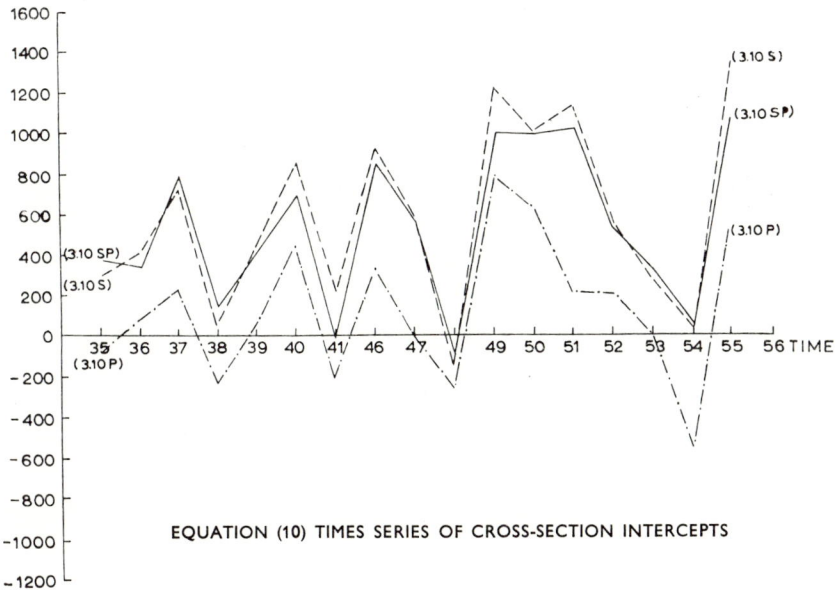

EQUATION (10) TIMES SERIES OF CROSS-SECTION INTERCEPTS

Chart 9.2.

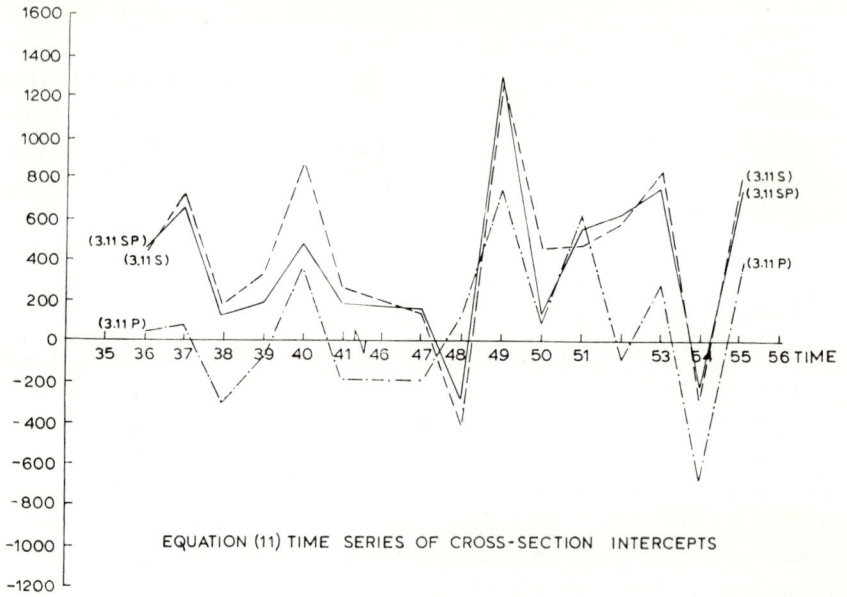

EQUATION (11) TIME SERIES OF CROSS-SECTION INTERCEPTS

Chart 9.3.

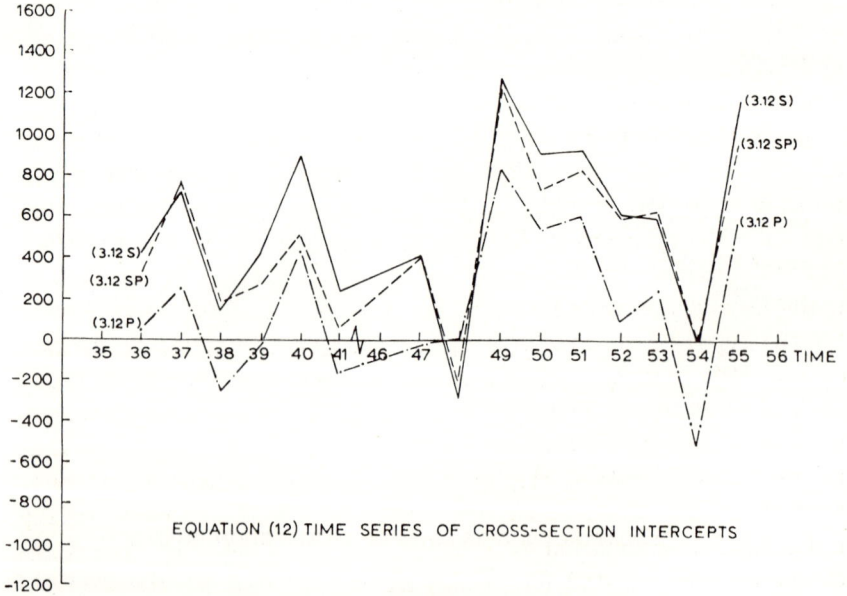

EQUATION (12) TIME SERIES OF CROSS-SECTION INTERCEPTS

Chart 9.4.

mous intercept component with respect to sales remained high in 1950–51, it fell off sharply for the profit intercepts. This may possibly indicate that the endogenous response mechanism was sufficient to the extent that liquidity was heavily generated by the extremely high profit and accelerated amortization provisions of the Korean War period. Anyhow, the intercepts trailed off sharply in 1953 and 1954 as the rate of increase in output slowed sharply from the 1950–1951 period to drop into the 1954 recession, only to increase extremely rapidly, to peak levels, in 1955.

Equation (3.12) follows the same general pattern as Equation (3.10) especially pre-war. Post-war, the pattern was close enough so that no further remarks need be proffered. Equation (3.11) is somewhat different, particularly post-war. Since Equation (3.9) is the rate of change of Equation (3.10), we might expect some conformity in this intercept. But the situation is more complex than that, so that no tight correspondence exists. 1948 for the original unit equations was a year of small intercepts, and ones declining from the prior year, while for Equations (3.9) the largest intercept of all was observed in 1948. A major difference also occurs in 1949 and 1950 when the intercept was sharply negative in Equation (3.9) and for most of the others strongly positive. The rate of change did become negative in 1954, as did the other equations, while the rate of increase out of the trough was negligible on the first difference equation and as commented on above, quite large for the original unit equations.

Concordance is to be observed between cyclical movements in demand and capacity utilization and the cross-section intercepts, a proposition exploited graphically here and submerged in various rank correlation coefficients in Chapter 5, although the rank correlations are seldom large. For material such as this, the forces in common to many firms which vary through time yet are approximately the same for the typical firm, are large and systematically related to cyclical events. It is therefore difficult to use cross-sections in order to study cyclical phenomena. The variation is large relative to average investment for all firms over the entire period of $1,300,000 per year, so that the usefulness of cross-section estimates for cyclical studies is extremely limited except where there are many cross-sections. Substantially more efficient estimation procedures, using the relevant time-series components is essential for most purposes, at least for the study of investment behavior.

9.4 Summary

The principal result of an evaluation of accelerator model reaction coefficients is that reaction coefficients are ordinarily of a quite low order of magnitude, rarely exceeding 0.25, with a value of about 0.10 characterizing our estimates of the median reaction coefficient. These are estimated from a great many different equations in a great variety of ways, with strongly consistent results. This finding has been for a restricted group of firms, although broader findings by others on a variety of different industries lead to the same conclusion.

These findings have implications for both business cycle theory and policy.[2] If firm investment responses are sluggish to the degree indicated by these low reaction coefficients, it is more the violence of the output variations that is responsible for the observed sharp variations in investment than of the firm response mechanism itself. While this solves few problems, it clearly indicates the direction in which policy must move in order to dampen fluctuations in plant and equipment outlays.

[2] See A. W. PHILLIPS "A Simple Model of Employment, Money and Prices in a Growing Economy", *Economica*, November, 1961, pp. 360–70, for a more complete model whose stability depends critically on the existence of low reaction coefficients.

CHAPTER 10

DIVIDEND BEHAVIOR

10.1 Introduction

The relationship of dividend behavior to internal financing and investment policy has been treated theoretically in Chapter 2. This chapter presents estimates of individual firm dividend equations, where the coefficient estimates follow Lintner's formulation. The data problems of the dividend equation estimates differ in a number of respects from those for the investment estimates. These problems are treated in Part 10.5 of this chapter.

10.2 The Dividend Equation

The Lintner dividend equation, to recall, can be written as:

$$D_t = rcP_t + (1 - c)D_{t-1} + a. \tag{10.1}$$

When discussing this equation in Chapter 2, it was observed that the non-homogeneous term represented by the intercept was not compatible with the theoretical model as a whole. It seems, nevertheless, appropriate to test for the importance of the intercept term. One way to answer this question is to estimate the intercept term and see whether or not it is large relative to its standard error. These ordinary significance tests and other parameter estimates collected in Table 10.1 show the relatively infrequent occurrence of significant intercepts.

A second approach to the hypothesis, while straightforward, is slightly more complicated. The Lintner dividend equation can be fitted with and without the intercepts, and from both regressions, estimates of the value of the "desired long-run payout" can be computed. Then one can determine whether theoretical estimates of the long-run

TABLE 10.1

Summary of Coefficients for Homogeneous and Non-Homogeneous Dividend Equations

Homogeneous Equation: $D_t = \alpha_1 P_t + \alpha_2 D_{t-1}$

Non-Homogeneous Equation: $D_t = \alpha_1 P_t + \alpha_2 D_{t-1} + \alpha_0$

Total A Regressions = 72

A Regression[1]

	Coefficient for Independent Variables		Intercept	Multiple Correlation	Relative Prediction Error
	P_t	D_{t-1}			
Homogeneous					
Smallest	-0.0138	-0.0892		0.3315	0.0800
First Quartile	0.1416	0.3065		0.9527	0.1638
Median	0.2214	0.5004		0.9757	0.2544
Third Quartile	0.2877	0.6137		0.9844	0.3908
Largest	0.9800	1.0843		0.9978	3.9209
Non-Homogeneous					
Smallest	-0.0062	-0.5327	-3915.626	0.2662	
First Quartile	0.1316	0.2132	-57.014	0.7665	
Median	0.1952	0.4280	26.052	0.8548	
Third Quartile	0.3079	0.6589	206.118	0.9049	
Largest	2.3839	1.0347	3902.392	0.9842	

Significance Tests

Test Structure[2]

	P_t		D_{t-1}		Intercept	
	One Tail	Two Tail	One Tail	Two Tail	Two Tail	One Tail
Number of Coefficients Significant at:	+	±	+	±	±	+
Homogeneous						
10% Level	2	6	6	3	—	—
5% Level	11	13	11	14	—	0
1% Level	50	42	41	35	—	67
Non-Homogeneous						
10% Level	5	6	6	2	2	—
5% Level	13	14	12	9	6	7
1% Level	39	32	31	28	3	55

[1] Size distributions were obtained for each estimated parameter, so that elements in each row generally refer to estimates from different regression equations.

desired payout from a model fitted *with* the restriction that the intercept equals zero is superior to the estimated long-run desired dividend payout obtained when the intercept is different from zero. The best criterion is not especially obvious. Suppose that over a large number of years businessmen can select behavior parameters so that their desired long-run payout is actually realized on the average. Then one can compare the actual ratio of dividends to profits with the two estimates of the theoretical parameter and see which corresponds most closely to the actual value. The actual average dividend payout has been measured by the ratio of the sum of dividends to profits over the period. It is evident from Charts 10.2 and 10.3 (which present the scatter diagram of the theoretical long-run desired dividend against the ratio of dividends to profits) that the homogeneous equation has a much closer fit than the non-homogeneous equation.

On this basis, the Lintner hypothesis is best supported when the intercept term is restricted to zero. Estimates of the long-run dividend payout are quite different, depending upon whether they are measured from the homogeneous or the non-homogeneous equation, as can be clearly observed in Chart 10.1. Not only are the values in general different, but from the 45° line one can see that the theoretical long-run desired dividend payout is typically larger when the intercept is zero than when it is not. Thus, there is a downward bias to the estimate of the desired payout when the intercept term is not restricted to zero, if it is presumed that the superiority of the homogeneous formulation has been demonstrated. According to Equations (2.53) and (2.54) in Chapter 2, we would expect to find the theoretical exceeding the actual payout, although only by moderate amounts when the rate of growth is small. Actual behavior accords with this prediction according to the tightly fitting scatter of Chart 10.3, but not for the poor fit of Chart 10.2.

Table 10.1 records several values of the frequency distribution for the regression model estimates before the coefficients have been rearranged into long-run desired payout and reaction coefficients according to the Lintner hypothesis. Hence the first slope shows the short-run marginal propensity to pay dividends out of profits and the second slope shows the weight placed on previous dividends. It is evident that the marginal propensity to spend out of profits appears to be similar in both the homogeneous and non-homogeneous models, except for the largest extreme value of 2.3839. The short-run marginal propensity

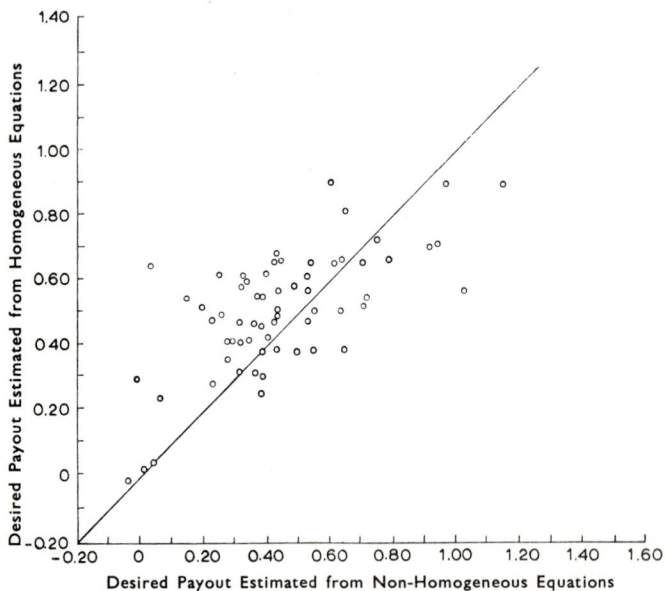

Chart 10.1.

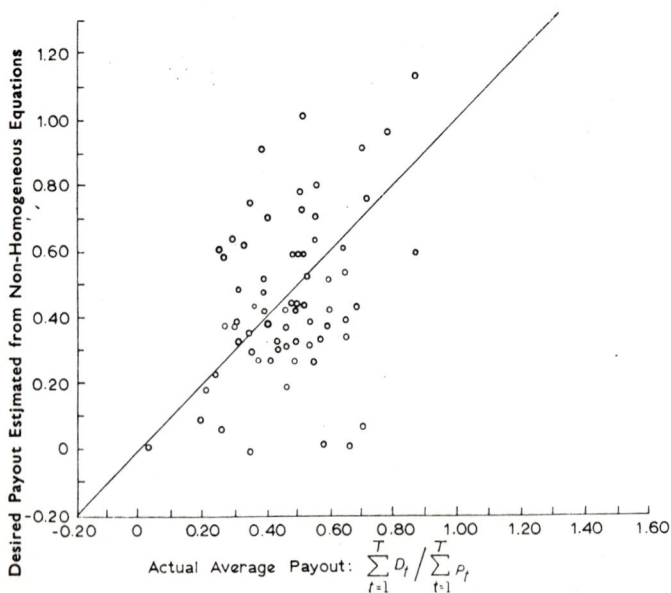

Chart 10.2.

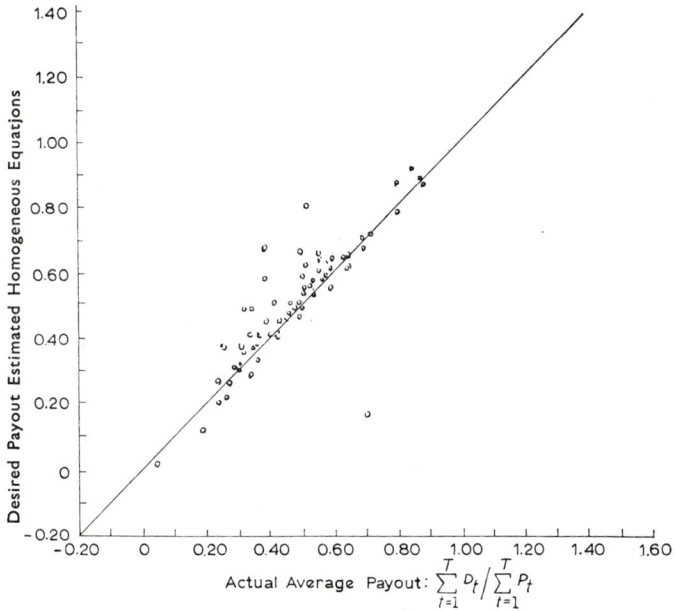

Chart 10.3.

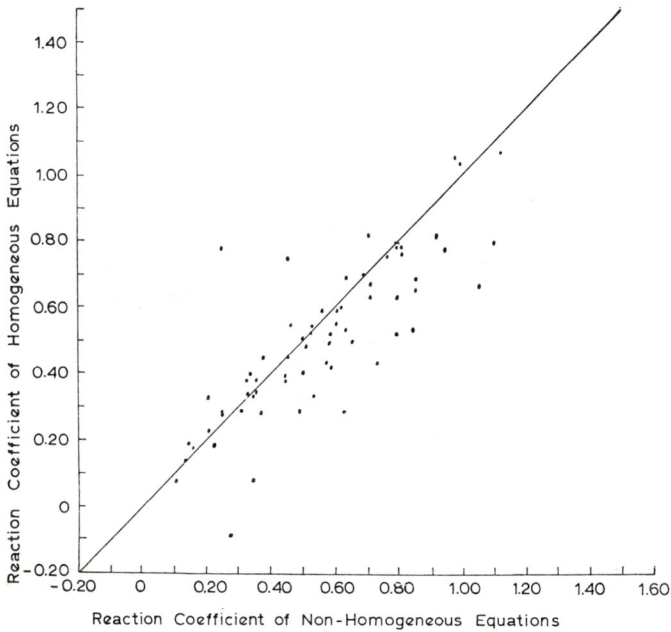

Chart 10.4.

to pay dividends is around 0.20. This is only slightly less than the value Lintner found for all manufacturing, using time series over the 1918–1940 period. The regression coefficient estimates found for lagged dividends is considerably lower; the median is 0.5004 for the homogeneous model. Lintner found the weight placed on previous dividends to be about 0.70 to 0.80 for aggregate manufacturing. Since this is only a small sample of firms in a restricted number of industries, it is pointless to spend much time rationalizing the observed gap. While the diversity in coefficients has been discussed above, it is still interesting to look at the micro-distribution of the marginal propensities to spend out of profits which range from about 0.13 to 0.30. All these annual marginal propensities to pay dividends out of profit are in accordance with the aggregative information that a large faction of (short-run) profit change is retained. The more rapid rates of dividend adjustment implied by the relatively low weight on lagged dividends in comparison with Lintner's results might originate in aggregation or time series bias.

10.3 Reaction Coefficients and Long-Run Desired Dividend Payouts

Table 10.2 contains a frequency distribution of reaction coefficients and long-run desired dividend payouts for dividend estimating equations with and without intercepts. The modal target value for the desired long-run dividend payout falls between 0.41 and 0.60. Some firms have lower desired payouts in the range of 0.21 to 0.40 and about an equal number have higher desired dividend payouts, in the range of 0.61 to 0.80, with a few firms scattered beyond these limits. At this level of generality, it may be said that the results are in accord with what might have been expected from casual observation of the passing financial scene.

Reaction coefficients for both equations have a mode of about 0.50. Since dividends generally change relatively slowly, it is somewhat surprising to find such a high average reaction coefficient. While reaction coefficients in the range of 0.21 to 0.40 are broadly consistent with the general notion of slowly changing dividends, reaction coefficients of 0.50 and higher appear to reflect a more rapid rate of adjustment than is consistent with casual observations of firm behavior. However, these are capital goods producing firms whose income is subject to sharp

TABLE 10.2

Payout and Reaction Coefficients in Dividend Equation

	Long-Run Desired Dividend Payout		Reaction Coefficients	
	Non-Homogeneous Equations	Homogeneous Equations	Non-Homogeneous Equations	Homogeneous Equations
2.45	1			
1.41 to 1.60			1	
1.21 to 1.40				
1.01 to 1.20	2		2	2
0.81 to 1.00	2	4	7	3
0.61 to 0.80	8	14	15	14
0.41 to 0.60	18	23	17	17
0.21 to 0.40	18	12	11	14
0.00 to 0.20	5	2	3	5
−0.19 to 0.00	2	1		1

variations over the business cycle so that these firms might be forced to adjust more sharply downward during periods of adversity than firms with less fluctuating income. In short, the "luxury" of a policy of stable dividends may be restricted to firms expecting comparatively limited fluctuations in their revenues. More serious research on inter-industry dividend behavior is necessary in order to verify or reject this conjecture. The results have been somewhat biased toward high reaction coefficients. Firms with highly stable dividends were excluded from this sample because least squares estimation breaks down in these circumstances. In the limiting case, a firm with perfectly constant dividends would have undefined covariances, and hence indeterminate coefficient estimates. Because firms with very slow changes in dividends have been excluded, the median estimated coefficient for the remainder has an upward bias.

Table 10.3 reveals some of the main inter-relationships between long-run dividend payout and reaction coefficients. While it is identically true that for given estimated coefficients, the higher the estimated reaction coefficient, the lower the dividend payout, the same point does not follow at all when inter-firm comparisons are made, as shown in Table 10.3 This joint distribution does indicate that low dividend payouts are associated with higher reaction coefficients. The relation, however, is not particularly powerful.

A scatter diagram of the reaction coefficient against asset size (not

TABLE 10.3

Joint Distribution of Dividend Payout and Reaction Coefficients
for Dividend Equation

c r	Homogeneous Equations				Non-Homogeneous Equations		
	−0.19 to 0.30	0.31 to 0.50	0.51 to 0.70	0.71 to 1.10	−0.19 to 0.20	0.21 to 0.80	0.81 to 1.53
2.45							1
1.41 to 1.60							
1.21 to 1.40							
1.01 to 1.20						2	
0.81 to 1.00	1		2	1		2	
0.61 to 0.80	5	2	4	3	1	6	1
0.41 to 0.60	3	11	5	4	1	15	2
0.21 to 0.40	2	2	2	6	1	13	4
0.00 to 0.20	1		1			4	1
−0.19 to 0.00		1				1	1

reproduced here) showed such low correlation that no measures of association were computed. In this sample at least, rate of response is only slightly correlated with firm size. One might have hypothesized that smaller firms, more reliant on internal funds than big firms, would respond more quickly and hence preserve their liquidity position through rapid adjustment of dividends. This particular hypothesis was barely discernible for this sample of firms.

10.4 Internal Financing and Dividend, Investment Policy

An outstanding and unexpected characteristic of the estimated reaction coefficients for the dividend model is their large magnitude relative to the reaction coefficients measured in original units for investment Equations (3.10), (3.11), and (3.12) using analogous equations and theoretical forms. It appears, in short, that firms adjust dividends more quickly than their fixed assets. This refutes the speculation of Chapter 2 which sought to link the two decisions; more so, apparently, than the data would indicate is warranted.

In order to suggest possible sources of discrepancies, there exists of course the usual sweeping range of excuses: the data are faulty, or the formulations of the theory inadequate, or the sample period so unfavorable that while in truth the theory holds, the real world perversely hid the truth. The major alternative, I believe, is the omission from the theory of an extremely important element conditioning the reaction coefficient, the fluctuation of inventories and other current assets and liabilities. To the extent that the major fluctuation in asset acquisition arises through variations in inventory levels instead of plant and equipment additions, the dividend decision will be most closely geared to the inventory and other more current assets. The modal value of 0.5 for the dividend reaction coefficient is consistent with a heavy weight on inventories whose reaction coefficients as mentioned in Chapter 2[1] are probably in the neighborhood of 0.5. The next step for empirical investigation will be to evaluate reaction coefficients which take into account the joint plant and equipment, inventory influence on dividend decisions and the interaction of these decisions. Part 2.6 of Chapter 2 sketched out the framework of how such an analysis might be incorporated into a macro-economic model. It appears essential not only to do so at the macro level but to pursue the matter more intensively at the micro, individual firm level, than I have done here.

10.5 Some Particular Data Problems

In this chapter, the dividend equations were estimated initially for 72 firms, 12 more than those appearing in the investment study, since as pointed out in Chapter 3, there were various reasons that made it highly desirable to eliminate these 12 firms from the investment estimating equation which did not apply to the dividend equations. However, there were specal difficulties which exist in the estimation of dividend behavior equations which lead to the exclusion of certain firms. The principal difficulty was that many firms had constant dividends for extended periods of time. Sixteen firms were eliminated on the grounds that either no dividends for too long a period of time were paid or dividends remained stable too long, thereby leading to the possibility of biased estimated coefficients. Even the remaining firms had many regularities and the periods for which their dividends were stable are shown in Table 10.4. While this method of selection biases the results in the direction of observing high reaction coefficients, consideration

---

[1] FRANCO MODIGLIANI and OWEN H. SAUERLENDER, "Economic Expectations and Plans of Firms in Relation to Short-Term Forecasting," in *Short-Term Economic Forecasting*, Studies in Income and Wealth, Vol. 17, by the Conference on Research in Income and Wealth, Princeton, N.J., p. 348, 1955. Also M. LOVELL, "Manufacturing Inventories Sales Expectations and the Acceleration Principle," *Econometrica, op. cit.*

TABLE 10.4

Dividend Regularities

Number of firms with regular dividends for n years

n	2	3	4	5	6	7	8	9	10	11	12	13	14	15
Number of firms non-cumulative	1		2	10	3	2	5	1	3		1	1		1
Cumulative	30	29	29	27	17	14	12	7	6	3	3	2	1	1

must also be given to the bias in the estimation of distributed lags when there are autocorrelated error terms.[2]

It is obvious that the relevant profit figure is net income after taxes instead of the net cash flow which we have been calling profits in the investment study. This indeed has been used here rather than the cash flow concept. All the variables were price corrected with the capital goods price deflator described in Chapter 3, in order to eliminate the pure scale effects of price level change. Since dividend decisions are related in part to investment financing decisions, it seems justifiable to use this particular deflator. The sample spanned the years 1935–55. The war years, 1942–1945, were excluded as were 1937–1938, when a tax on retained earnings distorted the theoretical underlying relation.

10.6 Summary

Lintner dividend equations have been estimated for 55 individual firms, most, but not all of which were among the 60 firms included in the analysis of investment behavior. The choice should be made between the homogeneous Lintner dividend equation and the non-homogeneous one. The empirical tests show that the intercept equation does not reflect behavior as accurately as the homogeneous equation. The typical dividend reaction coefficient of 0.50 was higher than that predictable on the basis of relations between investment and internal financing behavior, theoretically proposed in Chapter 2.

---

[2] Z. GRILICHES, "A Note on Serial Correlation Bias in Estimates of Distributed Lags," *Econometrica, op. cit.* shows that positive serial correlation in the error terms will lead to downward biased estimates of reaction coefficients, in a direct opposite to that of immediate concern.

CHAPTER 11

GROWTH AND EXTERNAL FINANCE

11.1 Introduction

Relationships between rate of growth and external financing were surveyed in Chapter 2. Tests of the hypothesis relating external finance to growth, depreciation rates, profit rates, and dividend retention policy will be presented in this chapter. Information on 22 two-digit industries for the period 1950–1957 provided the basic factual material. The findings, in summary, are these. First, the model has a downward bias since it consistently underestimates the actual resort to external funds. The use of external funds by all manufacturing was 35 per cent and the predicted use was 30 per cent. Second, the absolute errors were correlated with some of the variables entering into the growth formulation, indicating that the greater the growth rate, the smaller the errors in predicting external funds; also, the greater the profit rates, the smaller the actual errors. The relation derived in Chapter 2 is reproduced here for convenience as Equation (11.1).

$$\frac{E_t}{I_t} = 1 - v\left[(1 - r')p + \frac{1}{m}\right], \qquad (11.1)$$

where

E_t = External funds
I_t = Gross investment
v = Present value of an annuity
r' = Actual dividend payout
p = Profit rate on gross fixed assets

$\dfrac{1}{m}$ = Straight-line depreciation rate.

11.2 Data for Growth-External Funds Model

It is most difficult to use individual firm data in order to arrive at the relationship between growth and external funds. Many firms seldom if ever go to the capital markets, while firms which typically use external funds do so irregularly. It seemed best, therefore, to use sub-aggregates which include enough firms so that the probability is high that at least some would use external funds. An alternative approach is to evaluate joint frequency distributions of firms distributed into various categories believed to influence the external funds decision. Because I have a relatively small group of highly specialized firms, this particular approach did not seem worth pursuing here. In a 2,500-firm sample of registered British companies, R. F. Henderson found a close relationship between companies making issues and their rates of growth. This result provides a confirmation of a general relation, but not the specific relation of primary interest.[1] A second study by Prescott Duff investigated how the model of Equation (11.1) fitted the behavior of 15 chemical firms whose rates of growth varied between 5 and 20 per cent per year. He found that the model generally gave valid descriptions.[2]

The basic data came from various issues of *Statistics of Income—All Corporate Income Tax Returns with Balance Sheets*, U. S. Treasury Department, Internal Revenue Service. The time period chosen, 1950 to 1957, was one of high level demand and employment and excluded the major post-World War II adjustment. 1958, a major recession year, was avoided, and for later years no *Statistics of Income* had become available at the time of writing. The hypothesis requires five measures, all shown in Table 11.1: profit rate, growth rate, life of assets, dividend rate, and fraction of external cash funds used. Fraction of external cash funds, the variable whose behavior is to be explained, is computed by taking the ratio of increase in external cash funds—short-term debt, long-term debt and capital stock plus capital surplus—and dividing it by the increment in gross total assets. The total represents the change in total funds, i.e. total investment.

[1] R. F. HENDERSON, "Capital Issues," *Studies in Company Finance*, Edited by BRIAN TEW and R. F. HENDERSON, Economic and Social Studies, Volume 17 of the National Institute of Economic and Social Research, Cambridge, England, 1959, pp. 65–68.

[2] PRESCOTT T. DUFF, "Growth of 15 Selected Chemical Companies, 1929–55," M.S. Thesis in Industrial Management, (unpublished), Dewey Library, M.I.T., 1957.

The profit rate was calculated by dividing gross total assets for each year by net profits of the same year over the period 1950–1957, and then averaging. In similar fashion, the dividend payout was found by averaging the annual dividend to profit ratio for each of the years 1950–1957.

Depreciation expense was computed by taking the average of depreciation plus amortization for 1949 and 1950 and dividing it by the average gross property account for the year. The later figure was obtained by averaging beginning and year-end balance sheet figures for 1949 and 1950. The low retention rate and high depreciation rate for petroleum is related in obvious fashion to the inclusion of depletion allowances in depreciation and their exclusion from reported net profit. This particular period was largely undisturbed by accelerated amortization of World War II and the Korean War and the accelerated depreciation permitted under the 1954 Revenue Act. Finally, the growth rate in gross total assets was found by calculating that annual rate of compound interest which would have increased 1950 assets to the 1957 level of assets.

11.3 Test Outcome

The twenty-two industries with estimated parameters, along with predictions, have been summarized in Table 11.1. The nature of the results can be grasped immediately by an examination of Chart 11.1 which shows a scatter diagram of actual versus predicted external funds. Ideally, of course, the points would be closely scattered about a 45-degree line. Four industries—tobacco, lumber, leather, and non-automotive transportation—account for most of the unexplained variation. The remaining industries are rather well predicted. The first three industries have an extremely high inventory component in their asset structure and, therefore, might not be expected to follow closely a simple model designed to explain fixed asset dominated expansions. Actually, the predicted values ordinarily fall short of the actual results, the error for all manufacturing being 5 per cent in terms of the per cent of external funds used, a 15 to 18 per cent prediction error. Evidently, the variability in the actual resort to external funds is less than that predicted by the model.

The above qualitative assertions are quantitatively summarized in the Theil statistics used earlier in Chapter 8. The Theil inequality coeffi-

TABLE 11.1

Growth Model Predictions of External Fund Requirements

No.	Industry	Proportion External Funds		Errors P − A	Rate of Growth in Gross Total Assets	Profit Rate	Retention Rate	Depreciation Rate	Life of Assets* Years
		Actual	Predicted						
1	Total	0.353	0.305	−0.048	8.50	0.0531	0.4236	0.0542	18.44
2	Beverages	0.330	0.141	−0.189	4.50	0.0394	0.4050	0.0523	19.11
3	Food	0.259	0.164	−0.095	5.00	0.0416	0.3923	0.0508	19.70
4	Tobacco	0.309	0.060	−0.249	3.50	0.0533	0.3253	0.0359	27.89
5	Textiles	0.378	0.171	−0.207	4.00	0.0304	0.4147	0.0418	23.93
6	Apparel	0.264	0.127	−0.137	4.50	0.0246	0.6254	0.0700	14.29
7	Lumber	0.422	0.094	−0.328	7.50	0.0561	0.6120	0.1077	9.28
8	Furniture and Fixtures	0.288	0.185	−0.103	8.00	0.0532	0.6114	0.0524	19.09
9	Paper and Allied Products	0.348	0.313	−0.035	10.00	0.0645	0.5453	0.0413	24.22
10	Printing	0.255	0.117	−0.138	6.00	0.0528	0.5576	0.0397	25.22
11	Chemicals and Allied	0.356	0.304	−0.052	8.50	0.0670	0.3492	0.0501	19.96
12	Petroleum	0.375	0.415	−0.040	9.00	0.0353	0.0344	0.0739	13.53
13	Rubber	0.239	0.223	−0.016	8.50	0.0592	0.5454	0.0483	20.71
14	Leather	0.160	0.037	−0.123	3.50	0.0355	0.4140	0.0526	19.02
15	Stone	0.298	0.324	+0.026	10.50	0.0693	0.4835	0.0464	21.55
16	Primary Metals	0.296	0.363	+0.067	8.50	0.0477	0.4963	0.0378	26.44
17	Fabricated Metals	0.344	0.208	−0.136	8.50	0.0614	0.5621	0.0492	20.31
18	Machinery (except electrical)	0.358	0.280	−0.078	9.50	0.0609	0.4864	0.0554	18.04
19	Electrical Machinery	0.363	0.274	−0.089	9.50	0.0653	0.4356	0.0643	15.56
20	Transportation Equipment (except motor vehicles)	0.271	0.552	+0.281	15.00	0.0498	0.5408	0.0405	24.69
21	Motor Vehicles	0.214	0.256	+0.042	10.00	0.0897	0.4170	0.0500	20.00
22	Scientific Instruments	0.411	0.389	−0.022	14.00	0.0673	0.4907	0.0528	18.94

* Reciprocal of Depreciation Rate.
Source: Described in Text.

cient of 0.59 is large. By comparison, the less ambitious regression forecasts had inequality coefficients of about 0.30 for 1956 and 1957 forecasts. The fraction of the inequality coefficient attributable to correlation is about half of the total fraction of inequality, while bias, arising from differences among the average of prediction and actual outcome, takes up much of the remaining inequality fraction.

Can the observed errors be explained from material at our disposal? Rank correlation coefficients have been computed between the errors and the four series which enter into the growth, finance formulation which are the retention rate, the profit rate, the depreciation rate and the growth rate. These results, shown in Table 11.2, indicate that the rate of growth has a primary influence on the size of error. When the rate of growth is large, the errors are small. Similarly, when profit rates are high, the errors also tend to be small. The first result in particular deserves comment. It was originally stated that the growth, external funds relation would arise under conditions of rapid growth in a "typically" motivated firm. Clearly, from Chapter 2, firms below certain growth rates need have no or slight resort to external funds. For given dividend rates, profit rates and longevity of capital, external funds would have to be sought as an increasing function of the actual rate of growth in capital assets. Hence, if a fairly high proportion of firms within an industry have low growth rates, one might expect that external funds would prove an insubstantial restraint on growth rates actually achieved. Therefore, use of external funds would be governed by other considerations, generally treated as unimportant, at least according to the constructions earlier devised. It is thus somewhat reassuring to find that the most rapidly growing industries can have their external fund requirements most accurately predicted, although it would have been even more pleasant to have found that all industries were predicted with a high degree of precision.

The absolute size of investment or the industry size might also be related to the error. As simple rank correlations show, the errors are significantly correlated at the 5 per cent level with investment over the period 1950–1957, but insignificantly with size, measured by gross total assets. Two other parameters of the external fund growth model, the dividend payout and length of asset life, showed negligible correlations with the errors.

TABLE 11.2

Error Sources: Growth-External Funds Model

A. Theil Inequality Statistics

$U^m = 0.263$	$\bar{P} = 0.241$
$U^s = 0.179$	$\bar{A} = 0.313$
$U^c = 0.557$	$r_{ap} = 0.270$

B. Rank Correlations between Prediction Errors and Related Variables

Kendall Rank Correlation
Between Absolute Error and: τ

Retention Rate	0.065
Profit Rate	-0.325^*
Depreciation Rate	-0.048
Growth Rate	-0.541^{**}
Dollar Investment 1950–1957	0.333^*
Gross Total Assets 1949	0.186

$\sigma_\tau = 0.1535$

* 5% Significance Level.
** 1% Significance Level.

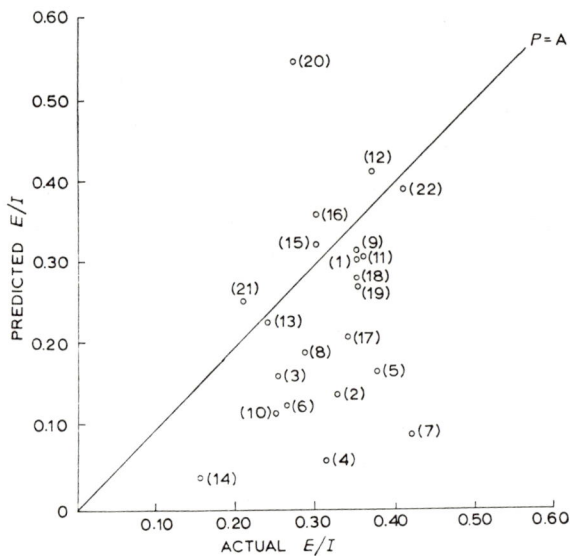

Chart 11.1.

11.4 Summary

Relations between external financing and rate of growth, theoretically derived in Chapter 2, have been tested on twenty-two two-digit industries for the period 1950–1957. The aggregate prediction was moderately accurate in predicting 30 per cent external fund use against an actual 35 per cent. The downward bias in the aggregate was reflected in the twenty-two industries included in the total. The deviations between predicted and actual external fund use showed that the greater the rate of growth, the smaller the errors in predicting external fund requirements and that the absolute errors were smaller when profit rates were large.

CHAPTER 12

A SUMMARY VIEW

12.1 Introduction

The preceding eleven chapters turned out to be exceedingly detailed, so much so that at times even I wondered what was happening. As a traditional and often useful exercise, I therefore propose to present some of the main impressions of the more detailed material. This will be done under three headings, the first on statistical and technical problems, the second on theory, and the third on the economic implications of the empirical results.

12.2 Statistical and Technical Considerations

The sheer volume of computation underlying this study has been enormous. While at times it almost seemed to be getting out of hand, most of the time the calculations were serving one objective of this study, to explore some uses of a new tool, the high-speed digital computer, as an economic research device. While I am far from satisfied that this has been done most efficiently, the possibilities have at least been demonstrated that micro information processed in this general manner can be helpful in one aspect of statistics, the testing of hypotheses.

In short, this was an intensive effort to substitute quantity for ingenuity, hopefully not to the complete exclusion of the latter. The power to discriminate among hypotheses in quite highly aggregative data has proved a most frustrating task. It has been my intention to go to another extreme, the individual firm level, to see if greater discriminatory power exists. The possibility of using micro distributions and comparing the distributions of parameters provides direct access to the economic actor whose behavior we wish to study, instead of an aggregate, as Theil has shown, whose estimated macro parameters are affected by arbitrary weights in ways largely extraneous to the structural behavior of principal interest. While I have been engaged in this study of individual firms, other economists with analogous intent have been using sub-aggregates, such as two-digit industries, for instance, in order to test hypotheses and estimate coefficients more efficiently. Data on such well-defined sub-aggregates allow the investigator to span a wider range of characteristics than I did, which in turn will enable him to explore more fully certain types of behavior. For instance, the included firms were typically small, slow growing, and had similar production and market characteristics. For broader questions of economic policy, it would be essential to study a much greater diversity of industries with divergent growth, size, and market attributes.

Hence, the research strategy pursued here has been expensive, in terms of time, machine resources, and research assistance, while it also suffered opportunity costs in terms of important types of behavior that were not studied, because of the other restraints just mentioned. Furthermore, it would be desirable to have at hand a satisfactory aggregation process so that once the micro exploration had been completed, the results could be suitably combined for aggregative prediction or policy implications. The aggregation chapter touched on only a few of these problems and the results there are exceedingly fragmentary, in part reflecting my own limitations and in part the general state of knowledge. Displeasing though it may be not to have an acceptable aggregation theory, I believe that the gains from using disaggregative data for testing hypotheses have been substantial.

As a practical course of action where alternative hypotheses are difficult to distinguish in aggregative data, tests should be made on micro data or finely divided sub-aggregates. The specification emerging from this intensive micro exploration can then be used to generate equation forms into which aggregative data will be put. Confidence that the final macro equation accurately reflects structural behavior will be much greater (provided of course that certain aggregative, simultaneous equation-type difficulties are also successfully overcome) than for other specifications which have not previously been subject to the micro analysis. As a counsel of perfection, one would estimate on various disaggregative data and then suitably aggregate the information into a macro equation. Short of that, the proposed course of action seems the best available and not altogether an unsatisfactory substitute.

Another technical area of interest was concerned with differences in the information content of cross-sections and time series. It was possible to get fairly complete and valid contrasts in this study because each firm was present in every cross-section, and time series estimates for all the firms could be compared with the cross-section estimates derived from an identical underlying set of information. One fairly obvious, but not trivial, negative conclusion is that cross-sections are likely to be a poor vehicle for testing hypotheses about investment or estimating parameters of investment functions when dynamic disturbances are significant. However, with numerous cross-sections available, variations in the cross-section estimates can be analyzed in order to provide substantive information about the time series specification. For instance, it was found that the parameters in the sales-type regressions had much lower correlation with cyclical indicators than did the parameters estimated from the profit equations, so that it was possible to infer that the sales equation was more adequately specified than the profit equation. Nevertheless, strenuous efforts were not made to use the cross-section estimates for time series purposes, mainly because of the high dispersion in the parameter estimates for cross-sections, as well as important systematic differences between the two sets of parameter estimates.

While the cross-sections indicate considerable parameter heterogeneity according to analysis of covariance criteria, the lag structure had a distinct influence on observable cross-section stability. In particular, the slopes were more similar when lag values were taken into account than when they were not. Similarly, slope homogeneity for cross-sections was much greater when the data were in logarithms instead of original units. However, the fundamentally most disturbing feature about cross-sections, no matter how measured, was the extensive amount of intercept heterogeneity, suggesting that the excluded dynamic characteristics were a major source of the over-all lack of homogeneity.

Another simple, although important, lesson was learned when we discovered that the most homogeneous type of behavior on cross-sections did not prove to be so on time series. This shows once again that qualitative and quantitative differences between errors in cross-sections and errors in time series are large, and therefore, it is dangerous to place reliance on one type of data in order to make inferences about the other. As yet another example illustrating the same point, first differences were quite influential in establishing time series homogeneity, but were actually detrimental in cross-section estimates. Also, logarithmic transformation in time series did not lead to greater inter-firm behavioral homogeneity.

The discovery of so much cross-sectional parameter heterogeneity led to a provisional exploration of the causes, by the simple device of rank correlations between a number of aggregate economic cyclical indicators and the cross-section parameters. Significant correlations suggest significant interaction which could be taken into account in a respecification, should the desire exist for utilizing the cross-sections in time series applications. Observed interactions could also help in the specification of pure time series relations. As remarked upon above, the profit model showed substantially more high correlations with the cyclical indicators than the sales model. Hence, when sales are excluded from an equation, relatively more important factors of a systematic, cyclical sort are not taken into account. This at least suggests the qualitative superiority of the sales, acceleration models.

The error variance properties of cross-sections and time series are exceedingly different. For instance, the error variance in a cross-section is shown to be a substantial over-estimate of the error variance in time series because individual firm effects do not contribute to intertemporal error variations, but are extremely large in many cross-sections. The errors that vary through time but which are constant in a given cross-section, on the other hand, were of small magnitude so that prediction intervals based on cross-section estimates, even in the best of circumstances, must be adjusted to take account of the fundamentally different sources of error. When circumstances are not so good, the inevitable mis-specifications which occur in a particular econometric investigation can lead to biases in cross-sections quite different in character from those in time series. There is nothing in principle to prevent combination of the two types of information, but the warning is clear—differences in the error generating mechanism are often substantial so that it is careless to ignore them and difficult to make allowances explicitly for divergences. This reason is closely related to, and perhaps explains, the observation made earlier that the parameters estimated from the different data sources typically turn out to be different, and consistently so.

This error analysis was of material assistance in helping to choose between profits and sales models, as well as among alternative lag structures. The average time constant error was twice as large for the profit model as for the sales model. The introduction of lags substantially reduced the time constant effects, demonstrating again that the determination of the lag structure, however simplified and crude it has been is this particular study, must be a major influence in the specification of investment functions. While this observation verges on triviality, it does suggest that there are a number of highly relevant criteria often ignored by lag selection procedures which concentrate exclusively on maximizing multiple correlations.

12.3 Theory of Investment

Several aspects of firm decision making were treated in a review of investment behavior. Instead of unified treatment, theoretical statements are various, reflecting indecision or, if you will, a lack of commitment to any unique methodology. Certain simple dynamic models were developed systematically relating the apparent desire of the manufacturing firm for internal finance to their investment behavior. The explicit relations in conjunction with empirically relevant parameters provided stringent upper limits to speeds of reaction to a disequilibrium between desired and actual capital stock, a finding that may partially explain the typically low values ordinarily measured for reaction coefficients.

While certain empirical tests of this specific investment, internal finance link proved unsuccessful, the model developed could be substantially improved if certain important behavior attributes were introduced into the model. First, the typical manufacturing firm has ample liquidity reserves which tend to weaken the simultaneous link between investment and internal financing, a factor ignored in my original formulation. Second, the overall financing problems of the manufacturing concern in the typical business enterprise depend, in the early stage of recovery, primarily upon inventory investment and in later stages on plant and equipment outlays. Inventory and other short-run financing requirements must be counted as sufficiently important complications to merit separate and additional consideration.[1]

In an altogether different perspective, long-term capital acquisition

---

[1] For aggregative manufacturing data, both sets of relations referred to above have been explored by Edwin Kuh and John R. Meyer, *Investment, Liquidity, and Monetary Policy*. The Commission on Money and Credit, 1963.

decisions implied by different financing policies were approached in the context of a growth model. The rate of growth in assets and output can be used to generate a demand for external financing. This model complements the short-term, cyclical, internal finance model. If correct, it suggests that long-term growth considerations will dominate external finance decisions, while dividend-investment policies are concurrently geared to short-run fluctuations in output.

A taxonomic, diagrammatic approach to internal cost of capital functions and their relation to sources of financing was also developed. It is often a sterile exercise to devote strenuous efforts to reconciliation of observed behavior with profit maximization behavior. In the present instance where risk preferences, finance, and investment are related in such a complex way, it appears illuminating to sketch out profit maximization implications of behavior which often, and perhaps needlessly, appear to be only disembodied empirical generalizations.[2]

While it would be a great pleasure to claim that a unified and completely satisfactory explanation of investment has been achieved, to do so would be presumptuous. What can be more reasonably asserted is that some important institutional and behavioral aspects influencing investment decisions have been related to each other. Other branches of capital theory can offer genuine insights using maximization postulates to derive implications for optimal behavior valid for the study of economic growth, for instance. The tough methodological issues in capital theory which have become increasingly clear through the recent efforts of Dorfman, Haavelmo, Koopmans, Solow, Samuelson and several others, as well as the fruitful discussions on economic development investment criteria, are essential to a correct understanding of the capital accumulation process.[3] When the time comes to draw policy implications, it will be essential to understand motivation of the sort studied here, both for prediction and control. The institutional, behavioral branch of capital analysis studied here and also in process of further development by Duesenberry, Lintner, and Meyer, in particular, will ultimately have to be combined with more abstract theoretical analysis in order to have powerful theory that is also relevant.

---

[2] John Lintner has in manuscript a book developing a more formal treatment based upon subjective probability and encompassing similar phenomena.

[3] See especially various articles in *The Theory of Capital*, edited by F. A. LUTZ. The Hague, 1961.

12.4 Economic Implications

The question whether "profits *or* sales" is the only significant explanatory variable of investment, in conjunction with the firm's capital stock, has been attacked by several investigators recently, with similar results. This holds true whether gross or net corporate profits are used, or gross retained earnings as we have done here. In a recent study for the Commission on Money and Credit, Albert Ando, Cary Brown, John Kereken and Robert M. Solow show that profits along with capacity-type explanatory variables carried statistically significant weight in explaining new equipment orders. Using quarterly data for two-digit manufacturing industries, John Meyer has found that gross retained earnings and a relative capacity measure are both important, the gross retained earnings variable having a substantially lower elasticity than the capacity variable. Our results are generally in accord with these findings. The answer then seems to be that both are important but that sales has greater impact.

Turning only to time series results for evidence on this question (since the preceding analysis strongly counsels against using cross-sections for these purposes), it is clear that the independent influence of sales, given the level of capital stock, is substantially greater than the independent influence of profits. It is also true, however, that profits become relatively more important, the greater the lag involved. To the extent that profits do influence investment, they appear to do so with a greater average delay than sales. Since our profit variable is a measure of cash flow, this suggests, provisionally, that the investment planning process is more sensitive to the inflow of, say, a year ago and sales of the current period, than it is to any other timing combination of the variables assessed in this study. While the lag structures used here have been of the most unsophisticated sort, they do suggest a direction in which subsequent investment investigations might push. When the two variables are included in the same regression equation, the most favorable showing is made by profits on the combined lag model, and even then, at the 10 per cent level of significance we find but one significant profit coefficient for every two significant sales coefficients. However measured, the independent statistical weight accorded to the sales variable exceeds that accorded to the profit variable.[4]

[4] One interesting result is that the ratio models show profits to be relative more

The implications of the statistical points enumerated above carry over into the parameters recast as elasticities. Looking at median elasticities evaluated at the means of the independent variables, the profit elasticity is about 0.30 by itself and the sales elasticity is about 1.00 by itself when both variables are unlagged. When the two are combined in the same regression, the sales elasticity remains about unity and the profit elasticity becomes effectively zero. The best show possible for profits occurs when it and sales of the current and prior year are averaged. Then the sales elasticity is slightly greater than unity and the profit elasticity is about 0.50, when each appears along with capital stock only. When the two are combined, there is a 0.92 sales elasticity and a 0.10 profit elasticity. In substance then, where both variables play a role, it would seem that the sales model is substantially more important. The unpublished Meyer study referred to previously reports a profit elasticity for all manufacturing of about 0.26 and a capacity elasticity of about 0.68 for the short-term elasticity of investment with respect to capacity utilization. While these numbers are different, both sets of evidence point strongly towards the substantially greater influence, of sales capacity as compared to profits.[5]

Empirical findings reported in Chapter 8 lend confirmation to the aggregative timing relations that hold for the manufacturing sector. Specifically, it was reported that the strongest influence on investment came from lagged (or the average of lag and current) profit and not from current profit, while the influence of capacity pressure appears strongest in the current rather than in the preceding year. Aggregative data on the provision of prior finance too is in accord with these micro results, both implying a different decision procedure than the one proposed initially. Originally it was thought that internal funds primarily served as a current restraint on investment outlays instead of as a prior source of finance. However, external capital markets as well as substantial average liquid reserve weaken the potency of the fund restraint element. The aggregative data show an average lead of a year to a year and a half for internal fund flows over investment, internal funds reaching a peak or a gentle gradient early in a cyclical recovery while investment is at a

significant than when the variables are measured in original units. Why this is so is not immediately evident.

[5] Unlike my results, Meyer found the gross retained profit variable to have more reliable statistically estimated coefficients than did his relative capacity variable. However, some of my results suggest that aggregation error favors profits relative to sales.

maximum toward the end of a typical recovery.[6] The secondary and revised role assigned to profit seems appropriate and in general accord with both aggregate and these micro data.

By now, most theoretical interest has swung over toward capacity-accelerator models, and with few exceptions the original rigid accelerator has been permanently buried since the bulk of empirical evidence decisively refuted the plausibility of instantaneous adjustment. In recent formulations, the so-called "flexible accelerator" uses the level of sales or output in conjunction with the capital stock, and therefore, interest has concentrated on the speed of reaction to a disequilibrium between desired and actual capital stock. In one of the earliest and most useful efforts, Koyck reported that reaction coefficients were typically small for fixed investment and nearly always less than 0.2 for six industries studied. In this study, I have estimated reaction coefficients from numerous different structural formulations, lags, data transformations, etc. My results are in accord with Koyck's and other individuals' who have investigated this particular magnitude. For my set of firms, a typical reaction coefficient is in the neighborhood of 0.10 to 0.15. Perhaps the principal explanation of this low magnitude in estimated reaction coefficients (and in my case, since these ordinarily are medians, it cannot be attributed to accidents of aggregation) is the pervasive uncertainty of manufacturers about the expected level of capacity utilization. In turn, this will be strongly influenced by the long run expected trend rate of growth. Low reaction coefficients are partly attributable to gestation lags too. Another ingredient, is the extent to which internal finance is generated. If entrepreneurs are reluctant to invest heavily, when to do so would entail external financing, reaction rates will be low. Some relationships between internal finance and investments were theoretically developed in the early part of this study. It was shown there that for the sort of magnitudes one encounters in American manufacturing industry, reliance principally on internal finance will place heavy restrictions on the observed reaction coefficients.

While the theoretical results referred to imply that low values of reaction coefficients are likely to be observed for investment equations, they also suggest that the coefficients of a retained earnings equation too would be small and of the same magnitude. While there were upward biases (discussed in Chapter 10 more fully), nevertheless, the

[6] E. KUH and J. R. MEYER, *Investment, Liquidity and Monetary Policy, op. cit.*

estimates of dividend equation reaction coefficients for my sample of firms were substantially higher than those estimated for the investment equations. This discrepancy casts doubt on the particular formulation I earlier developed to impose financial restrictions upon reaction coefficients. In addition, the dividend reaction coefficients that I estimated on the average exceeded those Lintner found for all manufacturing by a wide margin. The possibility exists that reliance on deflated data and a selection process which removed firms with the slowest rates of reaction led to serious overstatement of the actual rates of dividend reaction.

The previous relation of finance to investment dealt with short-run dynamic responses and concentrated attention upon internal funds generation for purposes of financing investment. Another ingredient of the theoretical developments in the earlier chapter stressed the relation between growth of fixed assets and external finance. The basic model was developed by Domar and modified slightly to meet the particular requirements of this study. Instead of using micro-economic data it was necessary to use aggregate data, in this case two-digit manufacturing industries, because of the discreteness with which external finance is obtained for individual firms. While the growth model did not predict resort to external funds with great accuracy, it proved a moderately reliable predictor. The model systematically understated the actual amount of external funds which were sought.

An outspoken, gimlet-eyed colleague once referred to my sample as "the most over-worked body of data in existence." At this time I am disinclined to dispute the characterization. However, there is one merit in reliance on micro data for statistical exploration. Its ponderosity will substantially reduce "investigator's bias," namely, the standard and understandable propensity of an investigator to invent a hypothesis after looking at the data. In the present instance, there was just too much data to look at in order to pre-judge the outcome, or equivalently invalidate the significance tests, by manipulating the sample prior to conducting tests. The interpretation of test statistics in this particular context is treacherous, but at least one major drawback common to most quantitative investigations has been minimized through principal dependence upon masses of data, no matter how frequently transformed and later examined.

SUBJECT INDEX

AUTHOR INDEX